RENAISSANCE AND REFORMATION

Also by V. H. H. GREEN

THE HANOVERIANS, 1715–1815

Crown 8vo. 512 pages. With Maps, Bibliography
Genealogical Tables and Index.

(Published by Edward Arnold & Co.)

BISHOP REGINALD PECOCK

(Published by the Cambridge University Press.)

RENAISSANCE AND REFORMATION

A Survey of European History between 1450 and 1660

BY

V. H. H. GREEN, M.A., B.D., F.R.Hist.S.

*Formerly Lightfoot Scholar in Ecclesiastical History in the University of Cambridge and
Scholar of Trinity Hall ; Fellow of Lincoln College, Oxford*

LONDON
EDWARD ARNOLD & CO.

PRINTED IN GREAT BRITAIN AT
THE UNIVERSITY PRESS
ABERDEEN

PREFACE

THE period of history under consideration is of such momentous importance and so full of detail that the historian may well be baffled by the difficulty of selecting what is really relevant to his purpose. But I have essayed to write a book which can serve the dual purpose of informing a general reader of what happened in Europe in the sixteenth and early seventeenth centuries and of placing a text at the disposal of the history specialist in a school or the undergraduate at a university. I am only too aware that the difficulties inherent in writing a book of this kind have not always been overcome successfully. Thus the chapter on ' The Renaissance ' can hardly escape being something of a catalogue, so many are the names and ideas that crowd it ; but to have omitted them would have left a false impression, to have considered them at length would have extended the book unduly. A critic might counter that it would have been better to have begun this study at 1494 in the traditional way, but this to my mind has two grave defects— it suggests that the modern age began with a suddenness which is quite untrue to history and it leaves out of account the significant medieval inheritance. But the reader can, if he wishes, omit the first two chapters without losing the thread of the narrative. Nevertheless it is necessary to emphasise the continuity of medieval and modern history. I have tried therefore to cover two hundred years of European history by selecting those topics which are important in historical development as a whole. Since each chapter is complete in itself, this has inevitably meant some repetition. Such conclusions as I have ventured to put forward may well be challenged by the expert. If it is necessary, it is none-the-less difficult to make accurate generalisations about major historical questions. Professor Tout once commented truly enough : ' The more one works at history the less one feels satisfied with any broad statements as to the general character of any age '. To pretend to original research in such a wide field would be an impertinence, nor is there sufficient space to indicate where the printed contemporary documents which bear on the subject can be found. But I have pointed out in the Bibliography some of the works which I have myself found most useful, omitting, with certain exceptions, books written in foreign languages. The Time-chart may help the reader who finds the chronology of the period confusing. If this book serves to throw light on a complicated but fascinating period of history, to inform and to interest its readers it will have fulfilled its purpose.

The pedant may question the spelling of certain of the names and the use of some familiar terms. In general I have followed usage rather than a particular rule. Thus Mainz, Trier and Cologne sound more familiar in my ears than either Mainz, Trier and Köln or Mayence, Trèves and Cologne. Similarly to have described Charles V as Karl V would be unduly pedantic ; on the other hand, to have called Philip II's son, Don Carlos, Prince Charles might well have been misleading. While therefore I have endeavoured to be accurate, I have not tried to apply any particular rule to European names, whether of people or places. Again, some may criticise my use of the words ' Catholic ' and ' Protestant '. The Anglican is entitled, I think, to resent the application of the word ' Catholic ' to members of the Roman Communion alone, but once the historian breaks away from the broad difference of Catholic (or Roman Catholic) and Protestant (or non-Catholic) he enters into a welter of terms which must confuse the reader, especially if he has only a limited knowledge of polemical theology.

An author's most pleasant task is to thank those who have assisted him to complete his work. Space forbids that he stress his own indebtedness to those whose original research has made his own work possible, but it would be discourteous to omit his obligations in this respect. And there are two other obligations which I must mention. No one knows how distressingly fallible an author can be—except his publisher ; he will be constantly finding faults in his work and demanding that they be corrected in his proofs. I would like, therefore, to express my thanks to my publishers and to the printers for their continuous guidance and help, both in respect of *The Hanoverians* and this present book. Finally I find it difficult once again to say how much I owe to the careful vigilance and welcome erudition of my friend, Mr. H. H. Brown, who has saved me from many errors of fact and infelicities of style, and helped me to give the book any of the polish that it possesses ; the imperfections and errors which remain are my own.

V. H. H. GREEN

CONTENTS

7

Contents

8

Contents

A*   9

Contents

MAPS

(With the permission of the University Press, Cambridge, the maps in this book have been based on those appearing in the *Cambridge Modern History Atlas*.)

CHAPTER I

INTRODUCTION

1. *The medieval world-picture*

THE medieval world was not immune from change, but all men's thoughts and activities were formed within a framework of ideas of which the truth seemed absolute. Dante's poem *The Divine Comedy*, written at the start of the fourteenth century, represented the universe as a series of ten translucent and concentric globes or spheres. The Earth was enclosed within the spheres of the Moon, Mercury, Venus, the Sun, Mars, Jupiter and Saturn. The eighth sphere was the sphere of the Fixed Stars; beyond that was the ninth, the sphere of the First Mover (*Primum Mobile*), which imparted motion to all the remainder although it had no star attached to it. Each of these transparent, crystalline globes was moved by Intelligences or Spirits; the ninth which moved more rapidly than the rest, as was indeed fitting for the sphere nearest to Heaven, was impelled by the highest of celestial beings. The Empyrean Heaven constituted the tenth and final sky and, being the home of God and His Saints, was immobile, eternal and infinite. This was the goal of all human effort and divine movement:

> All'alta fantasia, qui mancò possa;
> Ma già volgeva il mio disiro e il velle,
> Sì come rota ch'egualmente è mossa,
> L'Amor che move il sole e l'altre stelle.[1]

In the very centre of this system the unmoving Earth was placed, at the heart of which lay the holy city of Jerusalem. Beneath the Earth Dante visualised the abode of the imperfect spirits, Purgatory, and the home of the damned, Hell.

This detailed cosmology, accepted as certain by all intelligent men in the Middle Ages, in fact owed more to the hypotheses of pagan writers like the Greek philosopher Aristotle and the Alexandrian geographer Ptolemy than to Christian theology. But in the course

---

[1] In Miss Dorothy Sayers' translation:

> Power failed high fantasy here; yet, swift to move
> Even as a wheel moves equal, free from jars,
> Already my heart and will were wheeled by Love,
> The Love that moves the sun and other stars.

of time it had become Christian. Whatever the elements of Aristotelian thought, Roman law and pagan custom in the medieval world-picture, it was based on a Christian philosophy of life which everyone accepted implicitly. The original tension between the claims of reason and faith had itself been resolved in the thirteenth century in the marvellously complete *Summa Theologica* of the Dominican friar, Thomas Aquinas. Here was a philosophy of existence outside which nothing relevant to life could possibly range. Out of His sublime love God, the first Mover unmoved, had created the universe, the world and man. Adam, or rather Eve, tempted by the greatest of the fallen angels, Satan, had fallen into sin which henceforth marred and crusted man's existence. But out of His unlimited love God had sent His Son Christ who through the sacrifice made on Calvary had redeemed mankind. The Church, which He established and endowed with a head in the person of Peter whose authority was transferred from age to age through each successive Pope, was there to guide man, by its teaching and worship, to his eternal home; it was there to help him through the ministration of the sacraments, through the Mass and the Confessional, through the gift of grace, to defeat sin and so to earn God's all-loving reward.

This in brief constituted the foundation of existence which no medieval man was likely to question. He might indeed criticise and condemn the activities of God's appointed representatives, the Pope and the Holy Roman Emperor. He might grumble at the demands which the Church constantly made upon him; but he knew that life on earth was a preliminary to an eternal existence, with Purgatory as a midway house between the abode of bliss, Heaven, and the tortures of the damned in Hell. There was indeed much plain superstition in this. Medieval man imagined witches weaving spells and riding on broomsticks to local covens; he saw pixies and fairies; he knew that comets and shooting stars portended the fate of nations. The reverence which he paid to the saints and to the Blessed Virgin Mary became uncritical worship, sometimes superseding the praise due to God the Father and Christ the Son. Even so his everyday life was saturated by Christian belief. When he was in church he might laugh, chat and occasionally play with his dog, but when the sanctus-bell sounded, indicating that the Mass had reached its climax, in every European church—for in religion Europe was one—he was all attention, for he knew that this was recalling him to the Passion of Christ, and to the making of the Body and Blood. This is when ' the priest ', as one medieval writer put it, ' offereth up the highest sacrifice and the best offering that any heart can devise, that is, Christ, God's Son in Heaven, under the form of bread and wine '.

That Christ's sacrifice had provided man with an avenue of escape from the pains of Hell was the central fact in his long and dreary struggle with the force of evil. The sternest of all realities, the Judgment Day, was frescoed on many a chancel arch, for if medieval man was rarely able to read, he could at least see and understand. 'They', says a contemporary of church pictures, ' be ordained to stir men's minds to think on Christ's Incarnation and on His Passion.' The Church held him, whether he were a Florentine merchant, a French peasant or a Rhineland baron, literally from the cradle to the grave, and as he heard the *Dirige* of the Burial service and listened every Sunday to the reading of the names of the departed on the Bede roll, he could not have helped feeling the nearness of Heaven and Hell, and that he was a member of a great invisible community, the Church Catholic.

The world was indeed a microcosm of the eternal macrocosm of the universe, a reflection of the graded hierarchy of the spheres. Omnipotent and omniscient, incarnation of supreme love, God the Heavenly Father sat enthroned over all; in equal majesty at his right hand there was Christ His Son. And below there were the heavenly spirits or intelligences, seraphs, cherubs and thrones, dominations, virtues and powers, principalities, archangels and angels (which as the lowliest of celestial beings moved the sphere of the Moon, the least perfect of the heavens as the dark spots on the orb indicated). The fifteenth-century Spaniard, Raymond of Sebonde, asserted that ' We must believe that the angels are there in marvellous and inconceivable numbers, because the honour of a king consists in the great crowd of his vassals, while his disgrace or shame consists in their paucity. Thousands of thousands wait on the divine majesty and tenfold hundreds of millions join in his worship.' Marred as was the world by the effects of human sin, there was yet a correspondence between the heavenly hierarchy and the ecclesiastical and civil order on Earth. Emperor and Pope both partook of the nature of divine government. One Pope, Innocent III, could describe his office as ' midway between God and man . . . less than God, but more than man, the judge of all men, judged of none '. And when the Burgundian writer, Jean Molinet, wished to describe one of the less imposing of the medieval Emperors, Frederick III, he compared him with God the Father. The same writer tried to show that the Moon, as the humblest of the heavens, corresponded to the peasantry; Mercury to the merchants; Venus to the bourgeoisie in general; the Sun to the Church; Mars to the aristocracy; Saturn to the old nobility and, in this instance, Jupiter to the Emperor. Medieval society was so patterned and graded from labouring serf to mighty prince that it was thought a disturbance of the divinely appointed order for a man to seek to rise out of that grade of society to which God had been pleased to call him, except through the appointed channel of the Church.

> Triplex ergo Dei domus quae creditur una
> Nunc orant, alii pugnant aliique laborant.

All authority was thus divinely ordered. Ideally the Emperor represented the temporal power and the Pope moral and spiritual power, but from the late eleventh century there was a clash between the two authorities which was in the long run to exhaust the Empire and to lead to the moral degeneration of the Papacy. It is significant that, with very few exceptions, no one questioned that both the Emperor and the Pope owed their power to God. In a similar if inferior fashion the kings and princes of Europe received their commission to rule at their coronation or enthronement. All were committed to serve God's holy Church and to provide good government for His children. Even medieval theorists were forced to recognise that these ideals fell far short of practical realisation. The world was scarred and pitted by the fact of Adam's and Eve's disobedience. There was a constant disturbance of the divine order of the universe, leading to error in the Church and misgovernment in the State. As a sixteenth-century Frenchman, Pierre Boistuau, put it : the world ' is so depraved and broken in all kinds of vices and abominations that it seemeth to be a place that hath received all the filthiness and purgings of all the world and ages'. Some decades later contemporary changes induced the same thought in Shakespeare's mind :

> ' Take but degree away, untune that string,
> And lo ! what discord follows.'

Medieval writers therefore devised expedients to protect the people against the ruthless exercise of the authority which God had conferred on their rulers. They had an inbred horror of all rebellion as a breach of feudal contract and as a disturbance of the divine order ; the heretic and the rebel were equally disobedient, one to the Church and the other to the State. But justice must be served. ' Man ', wrote Aquinas, ' is bound to obey the secular rulers in so far as the order of justice requires. Therefore, if they have not a just title, but a usurped one, or if they command what is unjust, their subjects are not bound to obey them.' It is noteworthy that all such decisions were based on the acceptance of a supernatural order, an ultimate natural law, which found a pale reflection in the world of men and women.

16

Such a view of the world could only exist in a society based on an unchanging economy. Although there was always an enormous gap between theory and practice, the very nature of medieval society helped both to generate and to support this system of ideas. Broadly speaking medieval society was based on the land, whether royal domain, lord's manor, or newly-assarted acres. Although there were exceptions such land usually had a lord served by labourers, varying in status, who were, as the phrase went, *ascriptus glebae*, bound to the soil. This predominantly rural society was never completely static but it afforded a sort of economic stability. Lack of communications forced it to be more or less self-sufficient. Feudal obligations and ancient custom gave the peasant some prescriptive rights and imposed many burdens and services upon him. Although many serfs and villeins moved to the towns, the emigration was never on a scale big enough to upset the existing class structure.

The rise of industry and the development of trade and commerce, especially in the clothing towns of Italy and the Netherlands, threatened to overthrow this stratified society. The Church had indeed long evinced a deep distrust of the business man, more particularly of the usurer. In the early Middle Ages he was condemned without much qualification.[1] ' If covetousness is removed ', wrote one of the early Fathers of the Church, ' there is no reason for gain, and if there is no reason of gain, there is no need of trade.' ' Summe periculosa est venditionis et emptionis negotiatio ' wrote the schoolman, Henry of Ghent. ' Qui facit usuram vadit ad infernum ', noted Benvenuto da Imola, but he added significantly, ' qui non facit vadit ad inopiam '. But who in the Middle Ages would not in theory have preferred temporary poverty to eternal damnation ?

Such was the setting of the medieval world, a small world bounded by unexplored seas and continents, flowing around the Mediterranean. If there were men who travelled to the court of Kublai Khan and told stories of fabled eastern lands, their experiences did not affect the peasant working in his lord's unhedged field. On the whole it was a poor world for him, often reft by famine and plague. Even the towns were little more than large villages, centres

---

[1] It is worthwhile commenting on the qualifications. It was held that where interest was levied on a loan which had to be repaid, it was totally unjustified, but if there was risk of the money being lost interest was justified. Another distinction was made in favour of interest where there was some delay in the repayment of a loan lent for a short time free of interest, or where the lender could have made more profit from his money by engaging it in another venture. Medieval writers described these distinctions as *damnum emergens* or loss arising, and *lucrum cessans* or gain prevented.

17

of a local market or annual fair. Yet some were already magnificent with universities of fine repute, as at Paris, and were splendid with gabled houses and towered cathedrals ; here at least there were the elements of a polite society, and the seeds both of future industry and large-scale finance. It was a partly static and yet a variegated community ; a world of baronial castles and church spires ; of great cathedrals and abbeys where brilliant decoration, coloured glass and gleaming vestments served to impress the worshipper with the substantial superiority of the Church ; a world of basic poverty and great wealth, of gargantuan banquets and grating hunger, of unrestrained passion and unexpected mercy ; a mixed world of barons and princes, bishops, monks and friars, of merchants and cloth weavers, of peasants tilling the soil, of ugliness and yet glittering with a strange beauty, in fine a ' fair felde ful of folke ' living within an ordered universe in which man's final beatitude was asserted to be the ' contemplation of truth '. In a famous passage Hugh of St. Victor summarised the medieval ideal : ' Touch them [men's hearts] with the spark of the fear of God, or divine love, and great clouds of evil passions and rebellious desires roll upwards. Then the soul grows stronger ; the flame of love burns more hotly and brightly ; the smoke of passions dies down ; and the purified spirit rises to the contemplation of Truth. Last of all triumphant contemplation fills the heart with truth ; we have reached the very source of the Sovereign Truth and been enfolded thereby, and neither trouble nor anxiety touch the heart more. It has found peace and rest.'

2. *The waning of the Middle Ages*

There had always been a pronounced gap between the ideas that men and women accepted in the Middle Ages and what they actually did. Even their belief that a misgoverned life might lead them to the long-enduring fires of Hell failed to curb either rank injustice or vicious living. The Pope, as the Vicar of Christ, did not hesitate to use his powers of excommunication to further his family ambitions or to consolidate territorial power. The conflict between the Pope and the Emperor had led to a deterioration in the prestige of both ; where they had failed to keep the world in order, individual princes might do better within the more limited field of the nation-state. Similarly the Church's distrust of trade had not prevented a growing commerce which helped to enrich Italian and Flemish cities, nor was the Church's condemnation of usury taken seriously. Quite early in their history monasteries had not hesitated to borrow funds at interest from wealthy Jews to build their fine abbey churches. In brief two tendencies were at work in the fifteenth century which suggested that the framework of medieval society was about to undergo profound changes.

In the first place the streams of medieval life seemed to be drying up. A kind of wintry pessimism replaced the spiritual optimism of earlier writers. Forms seemed to matter more than their substance. The fantastic gorgeousness of late fifteenth-century costume with its parti-coloured hose suggests that the contemporary noble was seeking to escape from the realities of life into a fanciful world of his own making. Court life, especially that of the court of Burgundy,[1] had never been more colourful, splendid or extravagant. Great tournaments were held, but it was significant that it was now safer to fight in joust than it had once been. Chivalry had been debased by false sentiment and was horribly unreal. Court ceremonial was exceptionally gilded and formal; there was a special official for every function. Precedence and etiquette, decoration and ornament counted for more than the underlying realities of religion and politics. The crusade remained a vision which attracted but never effectively hypnotised its votaries. Symbolism and formalism permeated every activity. When the retainers of Henry of Wurtemberg appeared before Duke Philip of Burgundy dressed in yellow, the Duke knew full well that Henry was his enemy because yellow implied hostility, just as green was amorous and grey and brown were sad, and just as he would have known that when the French court was in mourning everyone dressed in black except the King who wore red. Even in the Church every posture of the priest was instinct with meaning; the stole stood for the ' rope that He [our Lord] was led out to his death; the girdle the bonds that He was bound with to the pillar and to the cross' and the bishop's mitre represented the ' crown of thorns that Christ bare on his head for man's sake. And therefore the mitre hath two sharp horns in token of the sharp thorns.' Formalism and symbolism had overshot the mark, investing society with escapism and frustration. Death often held men's thoughts in train, clearly shown by the popularity of *le danse macabre* in which Death the skeleton and the leveller came to fetch his living subjects, ' Aristocratic life ' was thus ' decorated by ideal forms, gilded by chivalrous romanticism, a world disguised in the fantastic gear of the Round Table '.[2]

The same mark of sterility had touched the political life of Europe. European states were much rent by war; the long struggle between England and France did not end until the middle of the

[1] See *The Court of Burgundy*, Otto Cartellieri (1929).
[2] J. Huizinga, *The Waning of the Middle Ages*, 30.

fifteenth century and its ending was a signal for the beginning of the Wars of the Roses. The eastern frontiers of Europe were challenged by the intruding forces of that magnificent polemical animal, the Turk, who swept the crusading armies and the effete Byzantine emperor before him; long before the last of the Palaeologi, Emperor Constantine XI, died fighting in the breach which the Turks had made in the walls of Constantinople in 1453 the ancient Byzantine empire had sunk to a mere shadow of its former self. The Holy Roman Empire was not in much better stead; in the early years of the century a drunkard was succeeded by an able prince but neither could pay their way. In 1438 the Imperial crown had passed to Albert of Hapsburg in whose family it remained, except for one brief interval, until Napoleon brought the Empire to an end in 1806. Under Albert's successor, the long-reigned Frederick III, the decline in power and prestige became even more marked.

The decline in standing and the growth in disorder were most obvious in the history of an institution which should theoretically have been the very incarnation of the principle of order, the Papacy. The death of the impulsive and ambitious Boniface VIII in 1303 had led to the removal of the papal court to Avignon, the papal enclave in France, two years later; there it remained until 1376 when Pope Gregory XI returned to Rome where he died in 1378. The Romans decided that the prestige and trade of their city had suffered as a result of the absence of the Supreme Pontiff. With shouts of ' lo Romano volemmo ' (we want a Roman) they obliged the terrified conclave of cardinals to elect Urban VI. Preferment turned his head; he became passionate, vindictive and ruthless. In despair the cardinals left Rome, declared that the election was null and void and proceeded to the nomination of one of their number as Clement VII.[1] The next thirty years or so witnessed a pathetic and farcical tragedy, a world divided in allegiance between two men both claiming to be the duly-elected successors of St. Peter. There were two of everything, two sets of cardinals and two papal courts; nations were divided as were cities and religious orders. A futile attempt to heal the breach in 1409 only led to the addition of a third claimant to the papal tiara. At last, to the relief of all good Christians, the Emperor summoned a general council of the Church to meet at the lakeside city of Constance. As a result of its long deliberations unity was restored. The three Popes were deposed or forced to resign and a fourth, Pope Martin V, was soon recognised as the head of the Christian world.

[1] Not to be confused with the Renaissance Pope of the same name and number (1523-34). The earlier Clement VII ranks as an anti-pope.

But the lesson of the undignified tragedy had not been lost. It had in fact sunk much deeper into medieval life than contemporaries realised. In England an Oxford don, John Wyclif, had denounced the Pope as anti-Christ and had questioned a number of accepted religious beliefs; independently of Wyclif but later greatly influenced by him, a Czech, Jan Hus, taught similar conclusions. Aware of heresy, the Council of Constance had taken action leading to Hus's death and condemning Wyclif's teaching; since Wyclif himself had died thirty years earlier it could only trust that his bones should be disinterred and thrown into the river Swift at Lutterworth. But this was not the end. Even if the Lollards, as his followers were called, had a declining influence in England, Hussite teaching in Bohemia and eastern Europe formed a fertile soil for the Reformation of the sixteenth century. If the Council of Constance had a qualified success in dealing with heresy, it was far less successful in fulfilling its other objects. It intended to remove the abuses and current corruptions of Church life but the coming decades saw a swift increase in laxity. Even its attempt to restore the unity of the Church was modified by the Popes' rejection of conciliar authority. The fathers of the Councils of Constance and Basle hoped to return to an earlier conception of papal authority by which the Pope was to enjoy what might to-day be called constitutional government. They were doomed to fail when papal autocracy came to terms with advancing national monarchy. Thus the Councils had not been able to ensure either that the personal characters of the Popes were in keeping with their office nor that the Popes would abandon their policy of trying to build up a temporal state around Rome.

What may be termed frustration in the Church corresponded to sterility in the teaching of the schools.[1] The imposing synthesis of faith and reason which Thomas Aquinas had put forward in his extensive *Summa Theologica* and *Summa contra Gentiles* was soon challenged on intellectual grounds; both Duns Scotus and William of Ockham attacked Aquinas' emphasis on reason and asserted that faith alone gave certitude to religion. Similarly certain criticisms in matters of detail put forward by John Buridan and his colleagues at the University of Paris indicated significant cracks in the Aristotelian or Dantean view of the universe. This destructive criticism was only met by a repetition of the old views. Orthodox scholarship had become appallingly arid and out of touch with contemporary needs. The geometrical precision of scholastic

[1] This does not mean schools in the modern sense but ' schools ' of theology at the universities.

thought was lost through an exaggerated emphasis on the method of logic; in the books which he wrote against the Lollards an English bishop, Reginald Pecock, placed excessive confidence in the syllogism ' If a man will rule himself thus, he shall never be beguiled about matters of reasoning ', he wrote, ' for why there is no conclusion or truth in the world, but that into proof of it may be had a syllogism well ruled'. The creative stream of scholastic thought had come to an end. The issues to which the schoolmen turned their attention were often ridiculously trivial; one concerned the possible fate of the fish in the Lake of Geneva were they excommunicated by the bishop. It was this feeling of frustration which led on the one hand to an approach towards mysticism, to an irrational faith which in its utter simplicity and promised ecstasy contrasted with the interminable complexities of fruitless scholastic discussion. On the other hand, the flight of reason brought about a renewal of interest in black magic and witchcraft; it is not without significance that it was Renaissance Italy which saw witchcraft accepted as a reality by a papal bull, *Summis desiderantes* of Pope Innocent VIII (1484), and the publication of the classical book on witchcraft, Sprenger's *Malleus Maleficarum* (1487).

All this suggests that civilisation in the fifteenth century was suffering from spiritual and political debility. Yet creative developments were taking place simultaneously within the medieval community which were in the course of the next century to give rise to the world of the Renaissance and the Reformation. It is these more novel movements and ideas which were to bring about the new age, firmly embedded as they might appear to be in the medieval world. They form the second major theme of history in the fifteenth century.

The economic framework of society was itself changing at a comparatively rapid rate. The pattern of European society remained rural, but even the countryside was affected by the rising importance of the towns and the creation of local and distant markets for food and raw materials. As early as the twelfth century Florence had compelled the lords of the countryside to reside for part of the year within its city walls and to place their estates under the supervision of the city authorities. Farming was thus harnessed to the needs of the town. In the Low Countries as in the Italian cities the emergence of a rich merchant class brought about changes in land-holding, and the investment of capital in sea walls, dikes, and pumps worked by windmills. Elsewhere society was less urbanised and money was less plentiful. But even in France, in England though here exceptional because of the high degree of liberty that the English peasant enjoyed by the beginning of the sixteenth century, and in South Germany there was a slow and steady change, a decline in actual serfdom, accompanied by a break-up of what was never a wholly static manorial system, and the intrusion of a money economy into rural society. Growing efficiency did not materially help the peasant whose lot remained dismal throughout Europe.

But the change was most marked in the conditions governing commerce. In rich cities like Bruges or Ypres, Florence or Venice, all the embryonic characteristics of modern capitalism could be found by the fifteenth century : here were wealthy merchants and clothiers controlling an industrial proletariat, a complex system of international credit and exchange, and even to some extent a division of labour and some form of specialisation. The prototype of the modern big-business man can be discerned in an Italian like Roberto Strozzi or the Frenchman, Jacques Coeur. Increasing wealth gave rise to investments in land, in shipping and in new industrial projects ; it was to provide the foundation for the development of the first European colonies and to assist in the growth of the national state through loans to needy monarchs. Thus the cash nexus developing steadily throughout the Middle Ages became the binding relationship in urban society and to an increasing extent in the countryside as well.

Such developments could not be overlooked by the less con-servative churchmen. By the end of the fifteenth century something of the former distrust of trade and investment had disappeared. In the past interest had been justified on the ground of loss and risk ; it was denied that money was by itself productive. By the end of the fifteenth century both an Italian archbishop, Antonino of Florence, and a German schoolman, Gabriel Biel, realised that loan capital was related to the productivity of an enterprise and deserved a monetary reward. In any case what the theologians thought about usury and business had less and less relevance to what was actually happening in economic life.

Man's release from the religious sanctions which had hitherto governed his behaviour appeared also in politics where practice and to a less extent ideas were preparing the way for the rise of the national state. The decline in Imperial and Papal prestige provided an opportunity for the national monarch. By the fifteenth century the political bankruptcy of the feudal baronage had become fully apparent. In France where the nobles had taken advantage of the conflict with England to form partisan cliques completely oblivious of the national interest the King had become the symbol of independ-ence and security. In England the Wars of the Roses helped to produce the same result. The natural sequel was the strong orderly government of the Valois Louis XI in France and of the Tudor

Henry VII in England, both relying more and more on a dependent class for their advisers, on artillery and gunpowder for the destruction of their adversaries, and on a full treasury. In Burgundy there were signs of a new and powerful state under Duke Philip the Good, but this same Burgundian court was also the best expression of the decline of the medieval ideal. Moreover the death of Philip's son, Duke Charles, in battle with the Swiss in 1477 brought whatever hopes there might have been of the formation of a strong middle kingdom to destruction; his was indeed one of the most significant demises in European history.[1] In practice then a new and increasingly powerful entity was emerging which in company with the Reformation and the Renaissance was to break the unity of medieval Christendom.

Political theory lagged behind practical politics, but the medieval conception of political obligation had already been challenged, more especially by an Italian physician, Marsilio of Padua, in his book *Defensor Pacis* written in the fourteenth century. Marsilio asserted that law was derived ultimately from the people or rather from the more influential (*valentior*) of them. His criticism of the Papacy and of Canon Law was corrosive. 'There is nothing left of the Thomist idea that the State, however " sovereign ", is subject to an eternal and absolute order of values, expressed in the body of Divine and Natural Law. The State is the source of Law, and its Law has to be obeyed not only because it is the only rule to be endowed with coercive power, but because it is in itself the expression of justice.'[2] Marsilio's cast of mind was still predominantly medieval but the gateway which was to lead via Machiavelli and Hobbes to the apotheosis of the national state and the absolute authority of the monarchy has been pushed open wider.

Finally, the movement which we call the Renaissance[3] was bringing into being a new view of life different in its scale of values from that which had governed medieval man's activities. In brief the Renaissance made man the measure of things and allowed for his full development, not beyond the world as the medieval theologians taught, but within the world. 'The Renaissance', in one modern view, 'regarded human nature and human history as a realm of unmeasured possibilities and felt that medieval religion failed to do justice to human freedom and human destiny.'[4]

[1] Charles' daughter, Mary, married the Emperor Maximilian, thus paving the way for Hapsburg dominance in Europe and for the long Hapsburg (Burgundy)-Valois conflict.
[2] A. P. d'Entrèves, *The Medieval Contribution to Political Thought* (1939), 63.
[3] See Chapter II.
[4] Niebuhr, *The Nature and Destiny of Man*, I, 317.

3. *The making of the modern world*

The foundations of the modern world were laid in the sixteenth and seventeenth centuries. For years the new world was over-shadowed by the ideas, customs and conventions of medieval society, to an extent that historians are only now beginning to realise. Thus our knowledge of medieval thought, of the ideas of Aquinas and Duns Scotus for instance, does not come from medieval manuscripts but from editions of their works printed in the sixteenth century.[1] Rural society was still largely confined to the pattern of the earlier age, both in its superstitions and in its economic life. Yet there was something new about the period of history between 1450 and 1660 ; above all there was a sense of adventure which was to lead to astonishing developments in every phase of human activity, to the discovery and colonisation of new lands, to the invention of printing and with it a new method of reading,[2] to the creation of new forms in art and architecture, to the development of modern science, to the enfranchisement of modern capitalism, to a steady increase in material comfort, in a phrase to the establishment of a society which a medieval man would have found strange and even terrifying.

What were the salient characteristics which dominated the history of the period ? Unquestionably the rise of the nation-state headed in many countries by an absolute monarch was the most obvious. Under its Tudor monarchs England rose in status and significance as a European power. In spite of many vicissitudes France became steadily more important under its Valois and Bourbon kings ; by 1660 the country was on the eve of the most majestic period in its history. At the beginning of the fifteenth century Spain was still a divided land ; in the course of a century it was united under one head, became swollen with new dominions and wealth and began to decline. The United Provinces, a rich rib detached from the Spanish Empire, became economically the pre-eminent state in the

[1] E.g. ' Between 1501 and 1515 a single printer, Wolff of Basle, produced five massive volumes of the *Summae* of medieval Doctors.' (P. S. Allen, *The Age of Erasmus.*)

[2] ' The medieval reader . . . did not read as we do ; he was in the stage of our muttering childhood learner ; each word was for him a separate entity and at times a problem, which he whispered to himself when he had found the solution.' (H. J. Chaytor, *From Script to Print*, 10.) He brought to his reading an auditory, not a visual memory. And this may help to account for the capacious memories of medieval and sixteenth-century scholars. The change-over from medieval to modern methods of reading had great effects on education and literary criticism.

first half of the seventeenth century as well as a power to be reckoned with in the councils of the nations. Unlike most European states the United Provinces was the one state which did not overthrow its semi-democratic form of government, inherited by a series of chances from the Middle Ages, though here, as in contemporary Stuart England, a determined effort was made to reduce the country to autocratic rule. Under its Vasa house Sweden was made into a powerful national state which, in default of still barbaric Muscovy, soon claimed to dominate the Baltic. Except in England and the United Provinces (though neither were immune from contemporary movements) everything tended to centralise government around the King and his councils. That the King is responsible to God alone became the theme of political writers. ' You are the visible and authentic image of God ', wrote Godeau, Bishop of Vence, of the youthful Louis XIV, ' Your Majesty should always remember that you are a Vice-God.' If there were signs of opposition to the widely accepted theory of divine right, in the birth or re-birth of a theory of contract which made the King responsible to the peoples he governed as well as to God, they were of more importance for the future than for the present. Monarchy was perfumed with the incense of adulation. But the greater monarchs of the age, Philip II of Spain and his father the Emperor Charles V, Elizabeth of England, Gustavus Adolphus of Sweden and Henry IV of France, realised their responsibility to their peoples. That they identified their dynastic interests with those of their countries was not apparently disliked by their subjects, among whom national consciousness was slowly developing, even if what patriotism they had, carefully stimulated by the governing classes, was still more often local than national.

The rise of national states implied a decline in the power of the two great international institutions of medieval Europe, the Holy Roman Empire and the Papacy. Various attempts to revive Imperial power proved a lamentable failure ; in any case it was now less a question of reviving Imperial power than of expanding Hapsburg hegemony in Europe. The other national states as well as many German princes fought against this throughout the period ; France, the most conspicuous adversary of Vienna and Madrid (the Hapsburg royal house ruled in Spain), was helped at one time and another by England, Scotland, the United Provinces, Sweden and Denmark as well as by various German and Italian states. If the Emperor remained a powerful European prince even after the tortuous policies of Richelieu and Mazarin had brought their fight against the Empire to a successful conclusion, it was primarily because he was a Hapsburg and the personal ruler of extensive territory in that area of which the Austrian duchy was the centre. At one time it seemed as if the Papacy was declining as rapidly, if not more so, but the Counter-Reformation brought about a renewal of its spiritual mastery, although its territorial power and political influence remained increasingly circumscribed. Although the Pope was asked to share with Venice an arbitral position at the West-phalian negotiations in 1648, his ultimate protests were without avail. The declining importance of Latin, still the language of diplomacy, and the growth of vernacular literature contributed to this development.

Indeed the unity of Christendom had been broken. Where there had been one Church owing one loyalty to the Pope, enjoying similar services and the same doctrine, there were now a number of churches, Roman, Lutheran, Calvinist and Anglican, to mention only the more important. The sixteenth century ushered in a new age of power-politics, of great wars fought with new weapons and paid for by the riches of trade and commerce; the constant conflict between France and the Hapsburg powers overshadowed all else, but there were also new national rivalries arising less out of religious issues or political ambitions than economic needs. The history of Portugal and of the United Provinces, to mention two of the smaller European countries, was prophetic of the coming clash of imperial powers. In this way too European unity had been shattered.

All this suggests what must be regarded as the second primary characteristic of the age, its growing secularism. At first sight the declining hold of religion is in no way obvious. There were few sceptics, not only because scepticism was often dangerous but because it was still an age of faith. The number of religious was still very large; church attendance was probably little less than it had been a century earlier. Never in any age since the Monophysite heresies divided the city mobs of Alexandria and Constantinople had there been such a spate of religious controversy; fierce passions were an indication of profound emotion and unquestioned belief. Everywhere lip-service, often perfectly genuine, was paid to the religious sanctions on which society rested. It was an age of religious wars. Protestant fought Catholic in national battles and internecine strife. Even the worked-out call to crusade against the Turk had a certain following, including Richelieu's adviser, the Capuchin Father Joseph who wrote an epic poem, the *Turciad*, in four thousand six hundred and thirty-seven hexameters to stimulate crusading ardour; but it had a cool reception.

Despite all this there had been a definite shift in man's scale of values in the direction of secularism. Religious wars often cloaked purely material designs. A Catholic King of France found it possible to ally with the Turk against the Emperor, a fellow-Catholic. Culture was slowly freeing itself from the supervision of the Church. ' Strong and continuous as were the theological issues ', wrote H. A. L. Fisher, ' they were now balanced by an exciting body of new knowledge, having no connection with theology, and the fruit of mental processes which theology was unable to turn to account.' In part an effect of the Renaissance, in part an effect of changing economic conditions and in part a sequel to a new view of the universe, this change appeared in a number of small ways. The decline in man's immediate awareness of Heaven and Hell, and his decreasing feeling of responsibility for the sins of the world, which even the emotionalism of the sects and the intellectual rigidity of Calvinism could not counteract, found a corollary in the increase in material comfort, in frank sensuality, in secular representations in art, sculpture and literature, and perhaps above all in the belief that man could accomplish what he wanted in the world without divine assistance. Where in the Middle Ages it had been customary to build cathedrals to the glory of God, men now built palaces to their own praise.

This process is in no way surprising if it is related to economic development. There was the least change in the countryside, for on the land the feudal tradition of service to the lord survived for centuries to come; except in the Netherlands and the France of Henry IV, and to some extent in England, little was done to improve agriculture. There were indeed changes in land-ownership arising out of increasing prices and the creation of a new nobility, but the new property-owners were as relentless, if not more so, in the exaction of their feudal dues as their predecessors. Moreover internal trade in France and Germany was still impeded by a myriad of internal custom duties and various weights and measures as well as by bad communications.

All the same Europe witnessed striking developments in commerce and trade which anticipated the industrial and urbanised society of modern times. The important American and Asiatic trade led to the shift of the money markets from Venice and Genoa to Antwerp and later from Antwerp to Amsterdam. Antwerp was a symbolic bridgehead from the medieval to the modern world. Patronised by the Dukes of Burgundy and helped by the decline of Bruges it had become an exceptionally wealthy city; indeed the new stock exchange had the words ' for the use of the merchants of all nations and tongues' engraved over its portals. All the leading merchants of Europe, Merchant Adventurers from England, members of the German Hanseatic League, bankers from South Germany, Fuggers, Welsers, Meutings, Hochstetters, flocked to the city. Here were to be found all the apparatus of a modern money market. ' Never has there been a market which concentrated to such a degree the trade of all the important commercial nations of the world.' [1] Money formed indeed the foundation of the modern state; it was the ' sinews of the wars ' which were the main objects of policy in this period. The sixteenth and seventeenth centuries thus witnessed what might be called a proto-capitalistic age, in the great amount of money available for investment, in the amazing enlargement of the economic field brought about by the discovery of new continents, and in the extensive release of economic activity from moral sanctions.

Taken all in all what happened between 1450 and 1660 was a broadening of man's horizons. The enclosed Mediterranean world of the Middle Ages was extended to embody vast new territories in America and Asia which were brought within the scope of European civilisation. The spread of man's mind was equally wide; the period which began with the schoolmen ended with the ideas of Descartes. There had been an astonishing change and to some extent an impressive advance in every sphere of human activity. But a problem remained which the modern world has never solved satisfactorily. The Reformation and the Renaissance had between them shattered the medieval synthesis. ' In the dissolution of the synthesis ', writes one modern critic, ' the Renaissance distilled the classic elements out of the synthesis and the Reformation sought to free the Biblical from the Classical.' And he adds that modern history can be interpreted as the story of the tension between the two. Neither religion nor culture provided the new society with a true focal point. National ambitions and economic greed thus injected an individualistic and class-conscious society with the seeds of its own decay.

[1] Ehrenberg, *Capital and Finance in the Age of the Renaissance*, 234. In spite of the intensive development of deposit-banking in the Fifteenth century, late medieval banking lacked many modern characteristics, e.g. negotiable credit instruments.

CHAPTER II

THE RENAISSANCE

1. *The origins and meaning of the Renaissance*

THE movement generally known as the Renaissance was one of the most significant in European history because it effected a change in man's attitude towards the problem of human existence. The word, which was not used to describe the movement until 1835, implies re-birth and renewal. It has been applied to the revival of ancient learning which began in Italy, to the reformation of religion which, starting in Germany, inaugurated a religious revolution, as well as to the reception of Roman Law which also began in Germany and later spread throughout Europe. Yet in a sense the Renaissance was never more than a minority movement of a few scholars and artists, who were patronised by princes and rich merchants, and whose views gradually circulated throughout Europe by means of the recently-invented printing press. But although the term may only strictly apply to the revival of classical learning, the Renaissance came ultimately to mean much more than this, being in fact no less than a new venture in living which helped to shape the modern world.

The roots of the Italian Renaissance, with which we are more especially concerned, lay deep in the soil of the Middle Ages. It has been pointed out [1] that Italian humanism was in existence long before Petrarch and Boccaccio, usually regarded as its founders, were born; it was indeed a natural result of the classical studies followed at the medieval universities. It is beyond all question that the Renaissance did not start with the flight of Greek scholars from Constantinople after the Turks had captured the city in 1453. Nor is there here much point in trying to trace the Renaissance to its earliest source in medieval culture. There is ample evidence to suggest how deeply embedded the movement was in the medieval world, and how it arose naturally from ideas inherent in medieval society of the thirteenth century. Thus Dante, whose thought was in many ways typically medieval, opened a new era in European literature by writing his great poem *The Divine Comedy* in vernacular Italian. The beginnings of naturalistic art may be traced to Giotto, who died in 1337; his paintings at the Chapel of the Arena at Padua are remarkable both for their luminous simplicity and for the artists'

[1] R. Weiss, *The Dawn of Humanism in Italy* (1947), 21.

understanding of tactile values. Similar poetic imagination combined with spiritual depth characterised the painting of Fra Angelico, the Dominican prior of San Marco at Florence, who was patronised both by the Pope and Cosimo de' Medici. Yet, like Giotto, his attitude to life was instinctively medieval; his paintings are the work of a man of whom it was said that he always knelt in prayer before he began to paint. Nevertheless his technique betrays the Renaissance painter. ' He was ', wrote the critic Bernard Berenson, ' the typical painter of the transition from Medieval to Renaissance. The sources of his feelings are in the Middle Ages, but he enjoys his feelings in a way which is almost modern; and almost modern are also his means of expression.' Nor were these indications of what may be called the Renaissance spirit necessarily confined to Italy; similar feeling may be found in the lyrics of the French troubadours.

But the chief impetus to the Renaissance in Italy was provided less by academic or artistic ideas than by the creation of a favourable environment. The Italian city state was the perfect domicile, since it housed a politically and economically mature community ready to patronise art and literature. A clothing town and a financial centre like Florence had its destinies determined by a rich merchant class with whom the old nobility had coalesced, exploiting a comparatively numerous industrial proletariat. It was natural that the Albizzi ruling clique maintained in power by the Florentine merchants and bankers should in turn give way to the shrewdest business man of all, Cosimo de' Medici. This exceptionally quick-witted banker-statesman, whose interests ranged from London to Sicily and Constantinople, served the interests of Florence well because commerce and foreign policy were in practice much the same. Keeping his family in power by means of a selected caucus whom he bribed with office and financial favours, he used finance to defeat his rivals; both Alfonso of Naples and Venice suffered defeat when he refused to lend them money. His grandson, Lorenzo the Magnificent, lost the papal banking and could indeed only balance his accounts by taking money from the public funds of Florence. Both the Medici illustrate well the new notion of a patron. They were concerned with hitching the new intelligentsia to the wagon of their own class; ' the intellectual leading group supports the power position of the ruling class by the provision of an ideology and by guiding public opinion in the requisite direction. The function had been fulfilled in the Middle Ages by the clerical intellectuals; now it devolved upon the humanists.'[1] In other

[1] Alfred von Martin, *Sociology of the Renaissance*, 36.

words art and literature which had once been employed primarily to serve the Church were now used to glorify the prince. Botticelli's picture *Pallas and the Centaur* illustrates this. Lorenzo the Magnificent faced by a political and financial crisis which threatened to ruin him redeemed the situation by a sudden journey to Naples where he gained the goodwill of King Ferrante. Pallas overcoming the rebellious Centaur represents Lorenzo's victory over the forces of disorder. Renaissance art is socially significant because it was consciously devised to portray for posterity the merits of the class which patronised it. It so happened that both Cosimo and Lorenzo were men of taste who had the perception to patronise what was intellectually and artistically in the first class. What they did at Florence was imitated by less important princes all over Italy. The Renaissance in Italy was thus made possible by the rise of a rich urban society far more sophisticated and intelligent than the baronial class it replaced.

If this was the environment in which the Renaissance flourished and from which it sprang, what were its essential characteristics ? Broadly speaking, it represented a change of outlook as a result of which men began to view the old material of literature and art in a new way, thus arriving at new mental concepts in literature, art, religion and science. Technique rather than subject-matter separated Giotto and Fra Angelico from the medieval world. Yet within a comparatively short time the subject-matter of painting has also changed. Fra Angelico died at Rome in 1455. Gozzoli's richly coloured *Procession of the Magi*, painted in 1459, is only religious in name ; it is in fact a Florentine pageant passing through a pleasing landscape. But nothing new had been discovered. The brothers Van Eyck, who certainly popularised, and may have invented, the process of oil-painting which gradually replaced the earlier methods of tempera and fresco, were medieval in the detailed perfection of their style. The pieces in the medieval puzzle have been shaken up and sorted out into a new pattern. Both Dante and Petrarch wrote love poems but whereas Dante's love for Beatrice appears as essentially spiritual, Petrarch's adoration for Laura is more passionate and sensual, if no less exquisitely expressed. And this too represents a change of mind, a transposition of spiritual and mental concepts. This tendency was also to affect religion. The re-interpretation of what had been long in circulation was more important in promoting the Reformation than the discovery of new ideas ; the teaching of the Fathers, especially the works of St. Augustine, and of the Bible in both of which medieval theologians had been saturated, were treated in such a different way that many of the conventionally accepted ideas about the Church were discarded. The same thing occurred in the history of science, for the discoveries were due less to anything that was positively new than to the re-interpretation of ideas already in existence.

But this re-grouping of familiar ideas in a new way was related to a new theory of human history, arising out of a new appreciation of Latin and Greek antiquity. The medieval world seemed bleak and sterile to the fifteenth-century Italian humanist fascinated by the re-discovery of an ancient world. Revelling in the ideas and literature of ancient Greece and Rome, he came to believe that that age had been the finest hour in human history. Yet history, as Machiavelli said, never alters much in its texture; human values and virtues remain much the same. It had so happened that whereas these had been grouped in a distinctly unsatisfactory way in the Middle Ages, in classical Greece and Rome they had been so manifested as to create a splendid civilisation. The Middle Ages formed the valley which separated the new and coming period of history from the high alps of the classical period. It was thus implied that it would be possible to reach and even to surpass what had been done in Greek and Roman times.

Although the revival of classical learning was in part antiquarianism, it was certainly more than a mere love of antiquity. However much the architects of the new age might be influenced by the writings of the ancient Roman, Vitruvius, they were more than servile imitators. Their standard of beauty was neither essentially classical nor medieval; it had its own particular qualities and significance. It is true, as the historian of the Italian Renaissance, Burckhardt, has said, that the Renaissance 'was not the revival of antiquity alone'. It was through 'its intimate alliance with the genius of the Italian people present at its side', that it 'conquered the world of the west'. The Italian Renaissance presented the world not only with the revival of classical learning—which had indeed occurred on earlier occasions in history—but also with a rich culture which had developed within handsome crenellated cities of Italy.

With this new attitude to life there went a sense of optimism unknown in the Middle Ages. It is possible that the optimism of the Renaissance has been overestimated. Erasmus, writing in 1518, opined that ' I am not so greatly attached to life. . . . I see in this life nothing so excellent or agreeable that a man might wish for it, on whom the Christian creed has conferred the hope of a much happier life.' But he added significantly enough : ' Nevertheless, at present, I could almost wish to be rejuvenated for a few years, for this only reason that I believe I see a golden age dawning in the near future.' There was an air of excitement arising from the geographical discoveries which gave additional significance to discoveries in the world of scholarship. At first sight the two worlds may seem far apart, but, in fact, they had something in common. Many of the early explorers were Italians; Columbus was a Genoese and Cabot was a Venetian. The exploration of the mind as of new seas and strange lands demanded an enquiring spirit. Such is the purport of the letter written by the Florentine scholar, Politian, to King John II of Portugal, probably in 1491 : ' What a scene of things hardly credible would be opened up to my view if I were to commemorate voyages to unknown seas; the contemning of the pillars of Hercules; a sundered world restored to itself; and barbarism, which we scarcely knew even by report, brought back to humanity. Then I could tell of new commodities, new profits, new comforts of life; accession to old knowledge, the corroboration of old things once hardly credible, and, with it, the end of our wonder at them. . . You are recoverer as well as discoverer; you have not only discovered other countries, another sea, other worlds and other constellations—you have brought them back from the eternal shades, and from ancient chaos, into the light of day.' [1] This feeling of enthusiasm and of genuine delight at the new discoveries was a characteristic of the Italian Renaissance, and in a sense of the whole movement. ' How brilliant Valla is ! ', wrote a learned canon of Münster to his schoolmaster-friend in 1469, apropos one of the leading Italian humanists, ' he has raised up Latin to glory from the bondage of the barbarians.' ' Man ', said Alberti, ' can make whatever he will of himself.' And another writer, Pontano, stated ' I have made myself '. This emphasis on the possibilities of the human mind appeared continuously, whether in the writings of the educationalist Vittorino da Feltre, in Dr. Faustus' search for knowledge undeterred by moral sanctions, or in the classical text-books of Elizabethan England. So Shakespeare, himself a child of a Renaissance world, could put into the mouth of Miranda in the *Tempest* :

> O wonder !
> How many goodly creatures are there here !
> How beauteous mankind is !   O brave new world,
> That has such people in it !

[1] Quoted in Sir E. Barker, *Traditions of Civility*, 77.

2. *The Renaissance in Italy*

It is hardly surprising that the Renaissance should have had its original home in Italy. The ancient monuments of the past, gleaming amidst the dark cypresses, were a continuous reminder of the grandeur of Rome. It was characteristic of the movement that whereas Roman remains had for long been a quarry for modern Roman houses, a Pope, Pius II, could order their preservation and that one of the great artists of the Renaissance, Raphael, could serve as Superintendent of Roman Antiquities. But it is probable that contemporary Byzantium rather than ancient Rome was the more decisive in awakening Italians to an appreciation of the classical tradition. The Turkish threat induced the Byzantine emperors, much against their peoples' will, to work for union with the Roman Church in the hope that western Europe would come to the aid of the east. There was thus frequent contact between Italy and Constantinople, furthered by Venetian and Genoese trade as well as by theological discussion. Manuel Chrysoloras coming into Italy on a political mission stayed to teach Greek at Florence. Later a Byzantine theologian, Bessarion, illuminated Greek studies in Italy by his work on Plato and might have been elected Pope, had not the College of Cardinals taken alarm at the thought of a bearded Greek pontiff. Before the Turks captured Constantinople many Italians went to study there. Giovanni Aurispa brought back some 238 manuscripts with him to Italy in 1423. Chrysoloras' son-in-law, the Platonist Filfelfo, studied for seven years in the libraries of Constantinople.

One other factor helped to make Italy the first home of the Renaissance. Economic development had created an environment favourable to new studies. The Florentine house of Medici, the petty despots of many a small city-state and the rich bourgeoisie preferred to patronise an intelligentsia to some extent free from religious obligations, and ready to recognise personal achievement independent of rank and birth. In return their patrons provided the humanists with the wealth and comfort necessary for their work and with a higher status in society. Although many of the painters and scholars of the age were extraordinarily versatile, they were treated as ' artists ' rather than as paid craftsmen. Thus although not a mason Giotto was appointed master of the works of Florence Cathedral and architect to the city in 1334 on the grounds that ' in the whole world no one better could be found in this and many other things'. Nearly two centuries later Michelangelo left his work at Rome simply because he felt insulted by some of the papal servants. Cosimo de' Medici commented sympathetically on the artistic temperament of Fra Lippo Lippi: ' one must treat these people of extraordinary genius as if they were celestial spirits, and not like beasts of burden '. And in fact they were often treated with great consideration. All were equal at the meetings of the Platonic Academy which met at the delightful country villa near Careggi which Cosimo gave to Marsilio Ficino. ' The Florentines ', wrote Clive Bell, ' . . . felt that their art was the greatest glory of their state.' [1] He adds less justly: ' In Tuscany the merits of painters and sculptors were canvassed as hotly as in Yorkshire are those of footballers and jockeys.' Such a setting favoured the artistic effulgence of the next two centuries.

In its earliest stages the Italian Renaissance was mainly concerned with the reclamation of Latin and Greek literature, more especially with the study of old texts. Although humanism developed naturally from classical studies in late medieval Italy, Petrarch and Boccaccio did much to infuse their contemporaries with a new appreciation of the contents of the classical manuscripts which had long laid mouldering on the shelves of medieval monasteries. The abusive and licentious Poggio Bracciolini, most elegant of stylists, proved an assiduous collector of ancient manuscripts (ancient less in the sense of age than of content), discovering, for instance, a priceless manuscript of Quintilian, the *Institutio Oratoria*, at the abbey of St. Gall in 1416; from this particular work many of the leading educational ideas of the Renaissance were to spring. Petrarch was significant in another way. In an academic world dominated by the thought of Aristotle and the methodology of scholasticism, he challenged the authority of both, asserting, though he was ignorant of Greek, the superiority of the Greek philosopher Plato. It was thus but a short step from Rome to Athens. Greek manuscripts were brought back to Italy in increasing numbers. Leonardo Bruni made accurate translations of Plato and Aristotle. Gemistus Pletho brought Plato in the original Greek to Italy. Platonic academies were founded at Florence, Naples and Rome. These scholars tried to embody Roman virtues and Greek ideas in their lives. In his book *Illustrious Men* the humanist Vespasiano da Bisticci sees the civic virtues of ancient Rome represented in the patriotism of modern Florence. It was idyllic, artificial and to some extent profoundly conservative.

At first this may appear a sterile and antiquarian approach to classical learning. To some extent it subordinated the creative impulse to a fastidious emphasis on style which did much to make

[1] Clive Bell, *Civilization*, 68.

Latin into a dead language. Sophisticated clergy found the barbarous Latin of the Breviary a leading reason for its revision. Cardinal Bembo, most Ciceronean of letter-writers, warned Sadoleto against studying St. Paul's Epistles in the original Greek lest they might spoil his style. Sannazaro's poem *Arcadia* is so classical in its theme and treatment that his shepherds have never wandered over Italian hills. Yet there was a positive side to this rediscovery of ancient Greece and Rome. There was a steady assimilation of the vernacular into Renaissance literature. No one now reads the tedious Latin of Petrarch and Boccaccio but the Italian sonnets of the former remain as fresh, melodious and sensitive as when they were first written in the fourteenth century; while in the folk-tales which the Florentine lords and ladies tell each other in limpid Italian prose to pass the time in the rural retreat they have made for themselves from the plague, Boccaccio created a new literary form, that of the short story. So nearly a century later Politian could delight the court of Lorenzo de' Medici with charming songs, classical in taste but written in his native Italian. Perfect classical technique married to the vernacular reached its apogee in Ariosto's great poem, *Orlando Furioso*, first published in 1516.

The return to the classics gave these Italians something more, a new view of history which stimulated them with the desire to emulate the past virtues of Athens and Rome, and a new sense of liberty characterised by a passionate desire for knowledge and a willingness to experiment. The attempt to establish a natural emotional relationship between the persons whom they were seeking to portray implied a break with the stylized and rigid paintings of the earlier Middle Ages. Where Giotto led the way, other painters followed. Thus Uccello worked out new principles of perspective. Pollaiuolo was passionately interested in depicting the naked male realistically; the muscles of his figures writhe with life. This scientific spirit may be said to reach its climax in the work of Leonardo da Vinci, the universal genius of the age; no one had ever before grasped the significance of anatomical accuracy or applied colour as he did. Unfortunately his zeal for experiment has robbed the world of his full achievement, for the pigments he used have faded. As a result none of his surviving paintings give a fair impression either of his marvellous versatility or depth. 'Curiosity and the desire of beauty', wrote the nineteenth-century critic Walter Pater, 'these are the two elementary forces in Leonardo's genius: curiosity often in conflict with the desire of beauty, but generating, in union with it, a type of subtle and curious grace.'

The zest for knowledge combined with the will to experiment

were characteristic of the Florentine Renaissance. For if Florence witnessed the early Spring of the Renaissance, Rome saw its high Summer and Venice its late Autumn. Moreover art and literature blossomed here long before the Medici established their despotic state. Brunelleschi designed and Luca della Robbia ornamented the new Foundlings' Hospital at the cost of the civic authorities. It was the consuls of the Arte della Calimala, the famous woollen merchant gild, who commissioned Ghiberti in 1424 to work on the eastern door of the Baptistry. Thus it was in a society in which some attempt at least was made to put the civic patriotism of ancient Rome and Greece into practice in modern Florentine politics that art came to maturity. ' Wherever men are given the hope of attaining honour in the state, their minds aspire and rise to a higher plane ', wrote Leonardo Bruni, ' wherever they are deprived of this hope, they grew idle and their strength fails.' It was the dangerous situation in which Florence found itself as the result of the rise of an aggressive despotic government at Milan which led to the rise of Cosimo de' Medici. Whether Florentine humanism developed under the patronage of the Commune or the Medici dukes, its richness and versatility are not in dispute.

A list of the great Florentines of the period is like a running commentary on the history of the early Renaissance. Architecture was dignified by Brunelleschi, designer of the dome of the cathedral and the famous church of San Spirito, and by the incredibly versatile Leon Alberti who planned the Palazzo Rucellai for a rich merchant for whom he had already adorned the façade of the church of Santa Maria Novella. He summarised his feat in the phrase ' the harmony and concord of all the parts (was) achieved in such a manner that nothing could be added or taken away or altered except for the worse '. Donatello, most gifted of sculptors, was a Florentine. Luca della Robbia won fame through a different medium ; starting with marble, he turned his attention to terracotta which he invented. The blues and whites of his reliefs are remarkably vital and fresh, reflecting the aesthetic richness of his environment. Another aspect of contemporary life is represented in Andrea Verrocchio's splendid equestrian statue of the *condottiere* Bartolommeo Colleoni ; the vigorous and overwhelmingly virile personality of the hard military leader who for so long brought disorder to contemporary Italian politics lives on in stone. But Verrocchio was completely overshadowed by his pupil, Leonardo da Vinci, equally master of classical composition (as in his *Last Supper*) and of romantic (as in his *Gioconda* and *Virgin of the Rocks*). From Giotto onwards the Florentine painters form one continuous line, each contributing a particular quality to a rapidly developing art; Fra Angelico, spiritual serenity; Masaccio, dramatic sense; Sandro Botticelli, a fusion of simplicity with sophistication, as instanced by the *Birth of Venus* and *Primavera* painted for the Medici villa; da Vinci, intellectual achievement; Michelangelo, dynamic energy; and Raphael, serene balance. The brilliance of Florentine artistic life is epitomised in Bisticci's portrait of the scholar, Niccolo de' Niccoli: ' First of all he was of a most fair presence, lively, for a smile was ever on his lips, and very pleasant in his talk. . . . To see him at table, a perfect model of the men of old, was in truth a charming sight. He always willed that the napkin set before him should be of the whitest, as well as all the linen. . . . Niccoli having friends everywhere, anyone who wished to do him a pleasure would send him marble statues, or antique vases, carvings, inscriptions, pictures from the hands of distinguished masters, and mosaic tablets. . . . Florence could not show a house more full of ornaments than his, or one that had in it a greater number of graceful objects, so that all who went there found innumerable things of worth to please varieties of taste.'

By the opening years of the sixteenth century pre-eminence had passed from Florence to Rome. This was in part a result of the disorder into which the French invasions and the fall of the Medici House had plunged Florence, but it also represented the continuous interest which the Popes had taken in literature and art. Nicholas V founded the Vatican library, and his successor Aeneas Sylvius Piccolomini of Siena, a scholar in his own right, as Pius II proved the most munificent of patrons. Such papal enthusiasm helped to preserve the monuments of imperial Rome from complete destruction and to enrich the city with noble churches and fine palaces, but it also obliged the Church to come to terms with secular taste and so greatly weakened it in its coming struggle with the Protestant reformers. Lorenzo Valla, who advocated what may be euphemistically called an Epicurean way of life and who had proved the falsity of the Donation of Constantine[1] on which medieval Popes had based their claims to temporal power in a brilliant piece of criticism, was a Papal Librarian. This too was the office which Pope Sixtus IV conferred on Platina for writing an avowedly mendacious history of the Popes. Machiavelli's political tract, *The Prince*, was printed by the Pope's printer. The College of Cardinals seemed indeed to place a higher value on a classical style and witty

[1] The Donation of Constantine was a document forged in the eighth century which purported to prove that the Roman Emperor Constantine had given Pope Sylvester a great part of the western world. Its authenticity had been challenged by the English bishop, Reginald Pecock, independently of Valla, and by Cardinal Nicholas of Cusa.

conversation than on a moral life. Such sophistication at Rome could only do a grave disservice to the spiritual life of the Church. 'The main fact in the Italian Renaissance', wrote the nineteenth-century historian, Lord Acton, himself a Roman Catholic, 'is that an open conflict [between the Popes and the secular-minded critics of religion] was averted at the cost of admitting into the hierarchy something of the profane spirit of the new men, who were innovators but not reformers.'[1] It was the warrior Pope, Julius II, on whose tomb Michelangelo worked for forty years, who planned to rebuild St. Peter's Cathedral. Characteristically, Donato Bramante, to whom he gave the commission to rebuild in 1506, designed it as a centralised building, for Renaissance churches were central rather than longitudinal buildings as they had been in the Middle Ages. 'The prime function of the medieval church', writes Professor Pevsner, 'was to lead the faithful to the altar. In a completely centralised building no such movement is possible. . . . The building has its full effect only when it is looked at from the one focal point. . . . The religious meaning of the church is replaced by a human one. Man is in the church no longer pressing forward to reach a transcendental goal, but enjoying the beauty that surrounds him and the glorious sensation of being the centre of this beauty.' It remained to the septuagenarian Michelangelo, whom Paul III appointed architect of St. Peter's, to design the magnificent dome which was eventually to crown the cathedral. It was symbolic that both Raphael and Michelangelo, Florentines by origin, should have ended as Romans. Highly esteemed and justly so by contemporaries Raphael's paintings have never lost their original dignity and grace; perhaps his paintings, especially his many Madonnas, are the most purely beautiful works of the High Renaissance period. But his work has less depth than that of Michelangelo; it is charming to the eye, exquisitely coloured but intellectually far less satisfying. The contrast between the two men's portraits tell the same story. Raphael's clear features have an almost feminine beauty; Michelangelo's are lined, with broken nose and determined jaw, an impressive, even a terrifying head. Indeed he was probably the greatest sheer creative artist of the Renaissance; as fine a writer of poetry as a chiseller in stone and marble. All his work is massive, grandiose, flawless in conception as in execution, sublimely impressive; he denied that he was a painter but the fresco of *The Last Judgment* which he painted for the Sistine chapel is as masterly a work as any that the Renaissance produced. His work has such spiritual depth that the secular humanism of the High Renaissance

[1] *Lectures on Modern History*, 79-80.

was obviously beginning to fade into the Catholic piety of the Counter-Reformation. As architect of St. Peter's he refused to take a salary and he offered to give his services to the new Society of Jesus (founded in 1540) free of charge.

Summer was fading as autumn drew near. The commercial city of Venice, so closely associated with eastern trade, formed an ideal centre for an artistic life, vivid in its expression, brilliant in its colouring, but aristocratic and even superficial in its conceptions. Titian, who represented the period perfectly, died almost a centenarian in 1576. His experience of life was therefore a commentary on the whole of the Renaissance. After studying under Bellini and Giorgione, the two founders of the Venetian school, he succeeded the former in 1516 as official painter to the Republic. His early paintings are full of bright blues and reds, but the subjects are primarily secular. His later paintings are more serious and sombre in colour, if no less rich in tone and perfect in technique. Indeed by this time in Italy, as elsewhere, in painting as well as in literature ('Tasso's fine poem, *Jerusalem*, is more a work of the Counter-Reformation than of the Renaissance), the Catholic revival which we know as the Counter-Reformation had made its impact on the Renaissance. The magnificent pageantry of Venice was henceforth to be put to religious use. Thus Tintoretto (the little dyer, a reference to his father's trade), the most prolific of great painters, turned his attention more and more to religious subjects. The atmosphere of his *Marriage Feast at Cana* is not only radiant but has been created by the painter's genuine faith in the miracle which he was trying to depict. On the other hand when his fellow-Venetian, Paolo Veronese, painted the same subject the masterly treatment cannot disguise its purely secular nature; the portraits of the guests at the feast are in fact held to be those of well-known contemporary men and women. Veronese was instructed by the Dominican friars of the church of San Zanipolo to paint a *Feast in the House of Simon*. The finished picture was as sumptuous in its colouring as it was magnificent in its execution; but it had one grave defect, it lacked the central figure of Mary Magdalene, so necessary to the story. The Inquisitors ordered the painter to appear before the tribunal and charged him with irreverence. They were, however, satisfied by the removal of a couple of the offending figures and a change of title to *The Feast in the House of Levi*. It was an insignificant incident but it showed that the full flush of joyous living, so typical of the High Renaissance, was at an end and that art was once more to be chained to the moral force of religious faith.

Nevertheless the Italian Renaissance had proved an effective agent in generating both a new culture and a new attitude to life. In the long run the new scholarship was bound to penetrate to the schools and the universities. The study of classical Latin meant significant changes in the curriculum in the shape of new text books and new methods of teaching. The pioneer in all this was Vittorino da Feltre who started a school at Mantua in 1425 with the object of providing an all-round education. He not only taught a knowledge of the best classical authors of Greece and Rome, but manners and physical training. It was through the schools that the teaching of the Renaissance, which in its early stages has the appearance of an aristocratic movement, spread through all the literate classes. The universities long remained the strongholds of the old ideas but steadily the new learning penetrated there too; this is clearly illustrated by the way in which Greek studies were taught at the Universities of Oxford and Cambridge. The formation of a new reading-public was perhaps the most significant effect of the Renaissance; it was to lead in its turn to the creation of an informed public opinion. Thus while the Renaissance may appear to be hypnotised into apparent dormancy by the teaching of the Reformation and the Counter-Reformation many of its leading ideas had penetrated deep into the intellectual life of Europe.

3. *Erasmus and the Renaissance in Northern Europe*

Italy was the home of the Renaissance but the movement was not confined to one land. The clothing cities of the Netherlands housed wealthy burghers aware of the new trends in society and willing to patronise art and culture, as is indeed illustrated by Jan van Eyck's amazing picture of the merchant Jan Arnolfini and his wife. The free city of Nuremberg, another important trading centre, was a home of humanism in the last half of the fifteenth century; it was here that the engraver and painter Albert Dürer, and the bronze-founder Peter Vischer, did their work. Moreover much of the Netherlands was part of the duchy of Burgundy whose dukes liked to patronise art and learning; Charles the Bold's intense interest in ancient heroes, in Hannibal, Alexander the Great and Julius Caesar, was certainly in accord with the Renaissance view of history. But a close examination of the paintings of Claus Sluter and the brothers Van Eyck suggests that their work was still governed primarily by medieval standards, as is instanced by their command of detail and by their desire to give concrete expression to every idea. It is true that there were some outstanding figures in the literary world of northern Europe in the fifteenth century. As early as 1409 a Parisian, Jean de Montreuil, an admirer of Petrarch, defended Cicero and Virgil. Cardinal Nicholas of Cusa, like the Dutchman, Rudolph Agricola, was as versatile as any Italian scholar; a philosopher, a mystic, a supporter of the Conciliar movement, a churchman and a scholar, he was esteemed by his contemporaries for his library and for discovering twelve rather salacious plays of the Roman, Plautus. Another sign of the future was the emphasis which the Brethren of the Common Life placed on the study of the Latin classics in the schools which they founded at Deventer and Gouda. But this was no more than a false presage of Spring, long delayed by the cold, grey skies of the north.

Yet in one direction, that of the printing-press, the Germans contributed more to the Renaissance than any other people. Printing on movable type made workable by John Gutenberg of Mainz about 1450 brought about a more extensive diffusion of culture and crystallised the learning of the humanists in books that were easy to handle, exquisitely printed and relatively cheap to buy. Two Germans, Sweynheym and Pannartz, were the first to set up a printing-press in Italy, at the monastery of Subiaco. Three other Germans established a press in the Sorbonne at Paris five years later (1470). Printing from movable type was carried to London in 1477 and to Madrid in 1499. ' As the apostles of Christ formerly went through the world announcing the good news', wrote the patriotic German educationalist, Jakob Wimpheling of Schlettstadt, ' so in our days the disciples of the new art [of printing] spread themselves through all countries, and their books are as the heralds of the Gospel and the preachers of truth and of science.'

The Northern Renaissance had one outstanding figure, Erasmus, of whom his most recent biographer goes so far as to say ' If one were to regard the Renaissance simply as the impact of classical literature on the modern world, one might be tempted to say that for a time Erasmus *was* the Renaissance '.[1] He was the illegitimate son of a priest born between 1466 and 1469. Leaving the school of the Brethren of the Common Life with little money and no close relations, Erasmus and his brother were thrown into a hard world with a dark future in front of them. It was uncertainty and loneliness rather than a true vocation to the monastic life which led Erasmus to enter the Augustinian monastery of Steyn. He was physically, mentally and spiritually unfitted for the discipline, the discomfort and the intellectual inelasticity of monastic life. Joyfully he accepted an invitation from Henry of Bergen, Bishop of

[1] M. M. Phillips, *Erasmus and the Northern Renaissance*, 225.

Cambrai, to become his Latin secretary. Given leave by his Superiors he was never to return. Indeed the fear of being recalled dogged his footsteps, and it was a great relief when as a scholar of international reputation he received the necessary papal dispensation from his monastic vows. Bishop Henry sent him to study at the dreary Collège Montaigu in Paris. At first he was disappointed at the old-fashioned mode of instruction. ' You would not know me ', he wrote, ' if you could see me sitting under old Dunderhead, my brows knit and looking thoroughly puzzled.' But his enthusiasm for classical literature, as distinct from the scholastic stock-in-trade, grew in proportion to his knowledge. As a result he published his first book, a little volume of proverbs which was to grow in time into one of his most famous works, the *Adagiorum Chiliades*, published by the Aldine Press in 1506.

Erasmus made his début at Paris. Henceforth his life was cosmopolitan. Visiting England in 1499, whence he came in the train of his patron young Lord Mountjoy, he soon made friends with Colet and Sir Thomas More. He was charmed by his experience ; ' If you are wise ', he wrote, ' you will fly over here . . . there is a fashion which cannot be commended enough. Wherever you go, you are received on all hands with kisses. . . . Oh Faustus, if you had once tasted how sweet and fragrant these kisses are, you would indeed wish to be a traveller, not for ten years, like Solon, but for your whole life in England.' But a later visit in 1511 was less fortunate. He did not appreciate the academic society of Cambridge which had appointed him Lady Margaret Professor— ' Cyprian bulls and dung-eaters ', he rather crudely calls its members —and he found both the beer and the climate intolerable. Early in 1514 he went to Basle which with some interruptions became his home for the remainder of his life. This cosmopolitan city, enhanced by a long tradition of liberty and the home of a university distinguished for scholarship, probably provided Erasmus with the happiest days in his life. But the violent activity of the Protestants in the city disturbed and disgusted him. ' The Council ', he wrote, ' has kept the riot in check by allowing the smiths and carpenters to take whatever they liked out of the churches . . . all the frescoes have been whitewashed over. Everything which would burn has been set on fire, everything else hacked into little pieces. Neither value nor artistry prevailed to save anything.' Much as Erasmus had criticised image-worship and its attendant evils, violence always saddened him, especially when it was associated with intolerance. Disconsolately he left for the Austrian Catholic town of Freiburg in Breisgau, only returning to Basle to die. And there in the red sandstone Minster, high above the Rhine, overlooking Germany and the Black Forest, a memorial tablet commemorates the greatest of Basle's adopted children.

What did Erasmus contribute to the story of the Renaissance during his long life ? He was no artist and seems to have been largely indifferent to the revival of art which was taking place in Italy at the time. He wanted to visit Italy because it was here that he could consult the recently discovered Greek manuscripts. He was not always an accurate or penetrating scholar, but his enthusiasm for classical learning knew no limits. He realised that the invention of printing could be used to popularise the classics and bring them within the reach of the literate man ; his editions of the classics, whether Greek or Latin, would establish his fame, had he written nothing more. But he was no dry-as-dust scholar, painfully weighing up the significance of minor emendations with vast erudition. He found new and wonderful vistas in classical learning unknown to the Middle Ages. He was perhaps above all concerned with the creation of a pure style ; in the choice of a right word, in the elegance of a phrase, in his effusive love of words, he found the same joy as the painters had experienced when experimenting with new pigments and new forms.

But Erasmus was not merely a classical scholar. He never made the classical virtues into a religion. He believed that the thoughts and ideas of the great writers of classical antiquity were in perfect conformity with the teachings of the Gospel ; he perceived an inner sympathy between the philosophy of Plato and the doctrines of Christ. He criticised much in the contemporary Church because it obscured Christ's teaching. He never forgot the sight of Pope Julius II clothed in all the rich habiliments of a warrior and he found in this as in the luxury and corrupt manners of the papal court a damning contrast, as John Wyclif had done before him, with the primitive simplicity of Christ and His apostles. Although he strenuously denied it, there is little doubt that Erasmus was the author of the satirical *Julius Exclusus* which described the Pope's surprise at the poor reception which he receives from St. Peter at the heavenly gates. The worship of relics, the exploitation of piety by pilgrimages to sacred shrines, the mumbo-jumbo and skullduggery of many contemporary religious practitioners only raised a bitter, satirical laugh from Erasmus. His own experience at Steyn made him, possibly unjustly, view monastic life with a deep loathing. In all this he was doing much to supply Luther and other critics of the Church with an inexhaustible store of ammunition. No one has perhaps summarised Erasmus' achievement better than the eighteenth-century poet Alexander Pope who, in his *Essay on Criticism*, declared :

> ' At length Erasmus, that great injur'd name,
> (The glory of the priesthood, and the shame !)
> Stemm'd the wild torrent of a barb'rous age,
> And drove those holy Vandals off the stage.'

But he was neither a Lutheran nor a sceptic. He wanted the Church to reform its abuses and to adopt a bold, renovatory policy which would bring it into tune with the new humanism. These ideas lay behind the most significant of all his works, an edition of the Greek New Testament, somewhat hastily prepared and ready for publication in 1516.[1] Imperfect as was Erasmus' critical scholarship, his work did much to bring the real words of the Gospels, which had to some extent been overlain and obscured by the medieval commentators, before a wider public. ' If there is any fresh Greek to be had, I had rather pawn my coat than not get it, especially if it is something Christian, as the Psalms in Greek or the Gospels.' It is no wonder that some of his more obscurantist opponents cackled furiously in spite of the fact that the new edition of the New Testament was dedicated to Pope Leo X.

By thus helping to recover the authentic texts of the Bible and of the ancient Fathers of the Church, Erasmus was obviously preparing the way for the Protestant reformers, all of whom owed him an incalculable debt. During a stay at Sir Thomas More's house at Bucklersbury in 1509 he wrote a light-hearted satire called *The Praise of Folly*. Erasmus, it was his worst fault, had let his pen run away with him, for what started as a piece of good-humoured banter contained a bitter attack on the schoolmen with their sterile and hair-splitting logic and on the wasteful fussiness of monastic life. He draws a picture of the Last Judgment where the monks seek to enter Heaven by detailing their daily life on earth. ' One shows a trough full of fish, another so many bushels of prayers, another brags of not having touched a penny for sixty years without at least two pairs of gloves on, another that he has lived for fifty-five years like a sponge, always fixed to the same place. But Christ answers them : " There is only one law which is truly mine, and of that I hear nothing." ' The delightfully written *Colloquies* was equally outspoken. Some stigmatise the belief that celibacy is superior to marriage : others condemn the practice of sending young boys to

[1] It is improbable that Erasmus wanted to get his work published before the Greek text of Cardinal Ximenez' *Complutensian Polygot*, prepared by scholars of Alcala University, which, though printed in 1514, was not actually published (and then outside Spain) until 1522.

monasteries. One of the most famous describes a pilgrimage which Erasmus and a friend made to the two shrines of Our Lady at Walsingham in Norfolk and of St. Thomas at Canterbury. Erasmus was disgusted by the fraudulent relics—the milk of Our Lady in abundance and the familiar wood of the true Cross (enough in Europe, as he commented, to build a ship)—and the wealth piled up at the shrines which could have been put to better purpose.

Although Erasmus may thus be termed the foster-father of the Reformation, the superficial amity which had first seemed to mark his relations with Luther soon turned to bitter hostility. There was a great contrast between the cultured and tolerant scholar and the emotional German with his passionate conviction of his own and the world's sin; even their experience of monastic life had been very different. Yet their views seemed similar until 1517. There was much in Luther's denunciation of indulgences which pleased Erasmus but, frightened by the prospect of a disunited Christendom, the latter advised caution. ' Luther's freedom of action is loved by the best in the land '; he wrote to Prior Lang at Erfurt, ' I have no doubt that his prudence will take care lest the affair should turn towards faction or rupture'. With dismay, he watched the growing breach between Luther and the Pope. ' I am deeply disturbed about the wretched Luther ', he wrote when he heard of the papal bull of excommunication, ' If they [i.e. his opponents] pull this off, no one will be able to bear their insolence '. But his sympathies were changing ; when he heard of Luther's marriage he commented : ' this stupid and pernicious tragedy, perhaps one should call it a comedy, since it ends with wedding bells '. Luther hoped that Erasmus would sympathise with his stand ; the Pope expected Erasmus to refute the reformer's ideas. When at last he broke into print with his *Essay on Free Will* he annoyed the papalists as well as Luther by his studied moderation. The German reformer did not spare his opponent in his reply *De Servo Arbitrio ;* Erasmus was dismissed as ' a babbler, a sceptic ' or ' some other hog from the Epicurean sty ' and his work was compared incidentally to glue, dirt and garbage. The critic and the reformer had parted, not unnaturally, since while Erasmus epitomised the Renaissance, Luther represented the reaction against it.

Yet even when he was most depressed Erasmus had never ceased to be an optimist. He never lost his belief in the final victory of education and knowledge over ignorance and stupidity. Erasmus may well seem in advance of his age in his hatred of intolerance, in his denunciation of war and violence and in his advocacy of hygiene but his confidence in the future typifies the Renaissance. He was brushing away the cobwebs, rejoicing in a glorious, as yet unfulfilled, inheritance. But he never allowed his Christian faith to be subordinated to Platonic philosophy. In his brilliant *Enchiridion Militantis* Erasmus summarises the guiding principles of his devotion, knowledge and prayer, and he shows that throughout life faith must take precedence of reason. In this too Erasmus acted as the schoolmaster of the Renaissance in northern Europe. Broadly speaking whereas the movement in Italy was more concerned with classical and secular learning and ideas, in the north of Europe it was much more closely related to the rehabilitation of Christian literature and to the return to more accurate texts and a purer life within the Church. Thus Luther's friend, the classical scholar Melanchthon was more concerned with the Greek text of the New Testament than with the works of Plato. The German scholar Reuchlin learned Greek at Basle and spent much time in Italy but he placed the writings of the Greek Christian Gregory Nazianzen above those of Homer. He studied Hebrew in order that he might be better equipped to interpret the Old Testament. As a result he was involved in a controversy which aptly sums up the difference between contemporary conservatism and Renaissance learning. A converted Jew called Pfefferkorn charged Reuchlin with heterodoxy as a result of his Hebrew studies. After being originally acquitted, Reuchlin was ultimately condemned; in the meantime his case had been taken up enthusiastically by humanists all over Europe. His condemnation proved ineffective in a world already fraught with greater issues, but the case in itself deserves notice, as showing the way in which the new studies were regarded by leading scholars. The study of Greek, like that of Hebrew but more so, was the foundation of the more intellectual aspect of the Reformation. However deeply the Renaissance may have been rooted in the medieval soil, it was everywhere uprooting accepted ideas. Even if the occasional anticlericalism of a Valla or the hedonist philosophy of a Masuccio can be discounted, the new attention paid to the study of the Bible and the emergence of new ideas about the universe were bound to challenge the Church, forcing it either to repudiate the new ideas or in some measure to assimilate them.

4. *The scientific revolution*

Like the Renaissance and the Reformation the scientific revolution formed one aspect of the general movement which transformed the medieval into the modern world. It was characterised by the same looking back over the plain of the medieval world to the intellectual ranges of classical antiquity and by the same transposition of mind which enabled men to visualise the old ideas in a fresh light. With a few exceptions among whom Roger Bacon was the most notable, medieval scholars had been much more interested in philosophical and logical systems than in the exact description of natural objects or in practical experiments. Completely indifferent to statistics, they fell back on scientific generalisations that were worse than useless; they maintained that the ideas of Galen and Aristotle were still true even when the actual evidence of the eyesight plainly contradicted them. Thus whereas there was no final reason why the highly developed mind of the medieval scholar should not have anticipated modern scientific ideas, the actual cast of his thought prevented him from making such an approach, quite apart from the fact that his background was unfavourable to anything like scientific research. Yet even so great an admirer of Erasmus as P. S. Allen admitted that ' Under its great masters, Albert the Great, Thomas Aquinas, Duns Scotus, scholasticism had been rounded into an instrument capable of comprehending all knowledge and of expressing every refinement of thought; and, . . . the acute minds that created it, if only they had extended their enquiries into natural science, might easily have anticipated by centuries the discoveries of modern days '.[1]

Some progress had been made in mathematical studies, partly as a result of the constant pressure which Islamic civilisation exerted on the medieval world and partly because the science of number had a theological, even a mystical, appeal about it. William of Ockham had played with it in the fourteenth century. Nicholas of Cusa wrote about it in the fifteenth century. Other practical developments, especially in accountancy (a by-product of growing trade), ballistics and architecture, helped to create an increasing interest in mathematics. The first algebraic treatise, that of Luca Pagioli de Burgo, appeared in 1494; the first Latin translation of Euclid

---

[1] *The Age of Erasmus*, 255. Nor were all medieval scholars lacking in scientific aptitude. Albertus Magnus, for instance, based his description of the ostrich on a bird which he had seen at Cologne where he was lecturing on theology in the thirteenth century. He added : ' It is said of this bird that it swallows and digests iron; but I have not found this myself, because several ostriches refused to eat the iron which I threw them. However, they eagerly devoured large bones cut into small pieces as well as gravel.' Observation and experiment were therefore not entirely lacking in the Middle Ages. The Franciscan friar, Roger Bacon, was a true experimentalist. Even Geoffrey Chaucer had a curiously modern view of sound :

' Soun ys noght but eyr ybroken,
And every speche that ys spoken,
Lowd or pryvee, foul or fair,
In his substaunce ys but air . . .'

was made at Venice in 1505. John Widman of Eger invented the plus and minus signs. More noteworthy was the work done in algebra and geometry by Cardan, whose *Ars Magna*, published in 1545, first discussed cubic and biquadratic equations, and by Viète and Stevin to whom are attributed the first use of decimal points. Unimportant as these developments may appear in themselves, they formed the working tools by means of which the scientific revolution got under way.

By the fifteenth century the impact of new ideas, in part freed by the literary discoveries of Renaissance Italy, encouraged a more questioning spirit. The mathematicians of the University of Paris found the Aristotelian theory of impetus intellectually defective and put forward a reassessment of evidence of vital significance for the future. Cardinal Nicholas of Cusa revived the ancient Greek theory that the universe is infinite, and that the Earth must have motion, an idea out of harmony with the accepted Aristotelian and Ptolemaic views of the universe. It was because Copernicus was dissatisfied with the accepted views of his own age and because he believed that there was a growing gap between theory and recorded observations that he wrote *De Revolutionibus Orbium Coelestium*, published shortly before he died of apoplexy in 1543. The author was a remarkably versatile Polish cleric, who had studied Canon Law at Bologna, and medicine at Padua; his ten years stay in Italy vitally affected his intellectual development since it enabled him to read Greek and to come into contact with the movement which ' aimed at reviving the Pythagorean ideal of the exhaustive mathematical analysis of natural phenomena '. Returning to Ermland he carried out his duties as a Canon of Frauenburg with great assiduity, but he found time to make a primitive observatory for himself in one of the turrets in the wall around the Cathedral precincts. What he saw in the sky made him more and more convinced that the two existing planetary systems, those of Aristotle and Ptolemy, were unsatisfactory, and he hoped to put forward a hypothesis which would resolve these difficulties. ' I, therefore, deemed that it would readily be granted to me also to try whether, by assuming the Earth to have a certain motion, representations more valid than those of others could be found for the revolution of the heavenly spheres.' His solution was more important for the stimulus it was to give to the astronomical studies of his successors than for the views which he himself formulated. He had interchanged the wheels of the celestial machinery so that, within a similar set of spheres, the Earth now moved round the Sun. Few at the time, least of all Copernicus, perceived the significant implications of a theory which made the Sun rather than the Earth the centre of the universe, but the reorganisation of the traditional stock-in-trade made possible the work of Brahe, Kepler and Galileo.

It was left to these three men to carry Copernicus' work forward to more far-reaching conclusions, if conclusions there can be in the science of astronomy. In this they were helped by two tendencies, the insatiable desire for knowledge so typical of the Renaissance scholar and the increase in the actual observation of the sky. On the other hand they were retarded by the growing suspicion with which both Protestant and Catholic Churches viewed the new ideas that threatened to overturn the traditional conceptions of the universe. From the start the Protestants criticised the Copernican hypothesis as being opposed to the teaching of the Bible; the Protestant astronomer, Kepler, found refuge with the Jesuits when he was turned out by the Protestant professors of Tübingen in 1596. The Catholics had been at first less concerned with these developments; Copernicus' book had been dedicated to Pope Paul III. It was nevertheless placed on the Index in 1616, and its views were condemned as heterodox.

Meanwhile significant developments had taken place. The Danish astronomer Tycho Brahe proved a poor philosopher but an unrivalled observer. It was he who in 1572 asserted that a bright ' new star ' was further away from the Earth than the Moon, thus challenging the Aristotelian doctrine that this kind of change was impossible. Five years later he noted the appearance of a new comet, so striking at the old Ptolemaic and Aristotelian view of the universe because the comet's path went straight through what had hitherto been regarded as the impenetratable but transparent crystal spheres. He spent his time in his observatory on the little island of Hveen cataloguing the stars; his *Progymnasinata* contains an accurate plotting of 777 fixed stars. The ' chaos ' of observations which he left behind him formed an excellent foundation for the work of his young colleague, John Kepler. Primarily a mathematician, Kepler failed in his attempt to find some mathematical formulae which would explain the multifarious phenomena of nature, but he formulated three planetary laws of exceptional importance.[1] He taught that the centre about which a body turns must be a *body*, not a mere point in space, and he was far more emphatic than

---

[1] (1) Planets travel in ellipses with the Sun in one focus. (2) The area swept out in any orbit by the straight line joining the centres of the Sun and a planet is proportional to the time. (3) Squares of the periodic lines which different planets take to describe their orbits are proportional to the cubes of their mean distances from the Sun.

Copernicus in asserting the heliocentric theory, thus reducing once again the significance of the Earth *qua* Sun.

Galileo's appearance in the same field was a fortunate accident, for no man was better fitted to make use of the newly acquired knowledge. When he was thirty-five (1609), hearing of Lippershey's invention of the telescope in Holland, he made one for himself with which he discovered three of Jupiter's moons. His observations did much to upset the old Aristotelian-Ptolemaic ideas. They showed, among other things, that far from the Moon being the only imperfect body, many of the other perfect and unchangeable spheres were spotted and scarred. The Aristotelians, strong at Galileo's own University of Padua, were alarmed by these new discoveries. 'Ye Galileans, why stand ye gazing up into heaven?' was the apposite text chosen by a hostile preacher at Florence in December, 1614. In 1616 the Inquisition condemned the Copernican hypothesis as unworthy of credence. Undeterred as yet, Galileo decided to make a thorough investigation of the planetary systems. The result was his greatest theoretical work, a series of dialogues entitled *The Two Principal World-Systems* which showed beyond shadow of doubt that the Copernican hypothesis was intellectually the superior of the Aristotelian. The Inquisition could not overlook a book which had had to some extent the semi-official approval of the Church. Its author was hailed before it—and silenced. He decided to submit and was allowed to live under surveillance at Florence, concentrating on the study of physics in which he made a number of important discoveries. But in fact the Inquisition was flogging a dead horse; everywhere intelligent men were accepting the heliocentric theory of the universe.

While this revolution in man's understanding of the universe, with all its infinite social, political and theological implications, was proceeding, other significant developments had been taking place in the realm of anatomy. Nothing better indicates the unscientific view of the medieval world than medieval artists' and doctors' dependence on ancient classical writings for their knowledge of human and animal anatomy. Da Vinci's anatomical studies are thus almost as important as his paintings as an indication of the new developments that were taking place in the sixteenth-century world. The real pioneer was Vesalius, whose book *De Fabrica*, published like *De Revolutionibus* (and the first translation of Archimedes' works) in 1543, was the first work to treat the structure of the human body in a really scientific way. Vesalius realised that the accepted Galenical view of what we should call to-day the circulation of the blood was probably inaccurate but he did not offer a satisfactory solution. In the half-century that followed his death, certain advances were made. The heretic Servetus first discovered the pulmonary circulation of the blood. Vesalius' successor at Padua, Colombo, described what is known as the ' smaller circulation ', but it was not until the Englishman, William Harvey, himself a student at Padua, published his *De Motu Cordium* in 1628 that the full theory was formulated. He discovered that the heart threw out more blood than could be accounted for by anything it received. Unless the blood was streaming through the body the whole time it was impossible to say where the blood came from or where it went.

The discovery of the circulation of the blood was interesting for the close attention to detail which it represented and for Harvey's reliance on observation and experiment. This emphasis on precision was to create the frame of mind which later made the inventions of the Industrial Revolution possible. The attempted classification of plants and the new work in botany, exemplified by the studies of the English Protestant Dean Turner of Wells (who taught his dog to seize the caps of recalcitrant papists) and the papal physician Andrea Cesalpino among others, and the new interest in clocks and clock-making [1] all point in the same direction.[2] The microscope, the thermometer, the pendulum clock and the telescope all sprang into existence in the seventeenth century. Practical experiments replaced authority as the deciding factor in scientific truth. Thus both Galileo's rejection of the Aristotelian planetary system and Harvey's discovery of the circulation of the blood represented the refutation of ideas which had governed men's attitude to life for centuries, and so showed new and startling avenues in astronomy and physiology.

Moreover this interest in science was slowly becoming fashionable. It was always difficult to know what was science and what was sheer quackery. Magicians like Cornelius Agrippa and Dr. Dee, who claimed to raise spirits, and men who sought the philosopher's stone or the elixir of life, received as much credence as the true scientist, if such there was, for between the scientist and the quack there was frequently a distinction of small difference. All the same men felt more and more fascinated by mechanical ingenuity and scientific speculation. The Emperor Charles V liked clockwork

[1] The new awareness of the passing of Time is another of the significant characteristics of the Renaissance. In the Middle Ages decades would be spent in the building of a Cathedral. Now pressure of business and politics gave a new value to Time. It was only after the fourteenth century that Italian city clocks struck every hour.
[2] The discoveries of the New World, both in plants and races of men, tended to arouse a similar scientific interest.

toys. Queen Christina of Sweden wrote letters to famous mathematicians and physicists and, it is alleged, helped to kill the French
philosopher Descartes by bringing him to wintry Stockholm where
he caught a chill and died. Grand Duke Ferdinand of Tuscany
and Prince Rupert of the Rhine both enjoyed experimenting in
science. Thus a new public was being created, more interested in
the mechanical and scientific workings of the world than in abstruse
theology.[1]

This changed attitude was bound to affect man's attitude to life.
The decline of Aristotelian ideas and of scholastic thought could
only be met partially by an increased reliance on faith for such was
the answer that the Protestant reformers Luther and Calvin put
forward. Puzzled and frustrated, yet confident and even com-
placent, intelligent men began to speculate with new ideas. The
belief in progress, which was to be inseminated into the human
mind in the eighteenth century, was just beginning to take shape.
The much-persecuted and tortured Dominican friar, Campanella,[2]
whom the Spaniards kept in prison for twenty-seven years, could
yet exclaim in his strange socialistic Utopia, *The City of the Sun* :
' Our century has more history in its hundred years than had the
whole world in the previous four thousand years ; more books have
been published in the last century than in the five thousand years
before ; for it has profited by the recent invention of typography,
cannon and the mariner's compass.' Such optimism was an essential
characteristic of the Renaissance.

5. *The significance of the Renaissance*

The modern world is largely the creation of the Renaissance
scholar and the shrewd capitalist, whereas the medieval world was in
the main the bequest of Roman imperialism and the Christian religion.
This may seem to imply that the Renaissance was anti-religious.
In its early days it certainly provided an impetus to anti-Catholic
teaching ; the bitter criticism of contemporary monasticism which

[1] But it is important to emphasise the fact that however much the up-
holders of the old scholastic method might dislike the intrusion of the new
ideas, the innovators were in no way stimulated by a desire to criticise or
question the Christian faith. ' Rather ', says Canon C. E. Raven, ' they
claimed to take up the age-old task of the Church by interpreting afresh the
meaning of God's creation . . . the new studies based upon observation
and experiment would supplement the old ; since new and old alike were
devoted to a fuller understanding of God, there could be no serious clash
between them.' (*Science, Religion and the Future* (1943), 24.)

[2] 1568-1639. He was imprisoned for taking part in a futile rebellion
against Spanish rule in Naples.

flowed from the pens of practising Catholics like Erasmus and Rabelais must be coupled with the purely agnostic teaching of the Renaissance philosopher, Pomponazzi. But on the whole the anti-religious trend of the Renaissance did not endure long. It had to seek accommodation with one of its major patrons, the Catholic Church; many of its leading representatives were genuinely devout men. Thus the Renaissance was never divested of an underlying spirituality, revealing itself in its classical churches, in its religious pictures and in the Greek and Latin texts of the Bible and of the Church Fathers. Again the Renaissance never escaped completely from its medieval setting. Moreover it was soon brought face to face with Protestantism and the Counter-Reformation, both forces hostile to its underlying ideas. It was in time compelled to come to terms with both. Just as Tasso's great poem *Jerusalem* represented the marriage of the Counter-Reformation piety and Renaissance skill, so Milton's *Paradise Lost* expressed the compromise reached between the Protestant churches and the Renaissance.

All the same a tension existed henceforth between the religious and secular trends in society, as a result of which the secular tendency ousted the religious more and more, thus shattering the unified conception of life accepted during the Middle Ages. There was an increasing faith in the possibilities of the human will; man's will to achieve what he set out to do lays behind the great geo-graphical discoveries as well as the splendid literary achievements of the sixteenth and seventeenth centuries.[1] 'The Renaissance con-cept of individuality, rooted in the idea of the greatness and unique-ness of man, naturally implies his liberty.' It was thus that the French *curé* of Meudon, Rabelais, could fasten the legend 'Faites ce que voudras' above the abbey of Thelema in his astonishing *Gargantua and Pantagruel*. No book better represented this secular optimism, in its gross naturalism, in the fecundity and sonority of its words, in its abundant humour and overwhelming erudition, in its dislike of pedantry and asceticism. Rabelais' *rire immense* re-sounds as an illustration of the new and disturbing joy with which men viewed their lives, freed from the shackles of medieval tradition.

Yet the old order of things had been broken and nothing sys-tematic had been put in its place. The *Essays* of another French-man, Montaigne, are pervaded by a gentle scepticism. He has

---

[1] If the contemporary controversy over free-will and predestination is taken into account, this emphasis on the powers of free-will is the more striking; Valla's *De libero arbitrio*, Pomponazzi's *De fato, libero arbitrio et praedestinatione* and Erasmus' *De libero arbitrio* all show the scholar's concern with this problem.

neither faith in human reason nor in religious doctrine. He was a practising but not a believing Catholic. It was left to a third Frenchman, René Descartes, who had a clear mathematical mind and a pleasing style, to present the world with a new philosophical formula in his short *Discourse on Method* (1637). The author had served with the Bavarian army during the Thirty Years War, and he tells us that during the cold winter of 1619-20 he got into one of the large farmhouse stoves and stayed there practically the whole day engaged in speculation. Such was the strange birth of what is called Cartesian philosophy. Beginning with the idea that nothing can exist except the consciousness that I who do the doubting must exist, he constructed a beautifully logical system of thought. ' I think, therefore I am ' formed the basis for a philosophy of life which took into account the intellectual achievements of the last century and a half. Cartesianism was a Christian philosophy but it regarded man as the starting-point of things, thus reversing the medieval order.

The Renaissance also helped to create the philosophy of power-politics which governed the formation of nation-states. Although Machiavelli was not a Renaissance scholar by temperament and was writing for a particular purpose, limited in scope and operation, he was yet helping to bring into the open the amoral foundation on which the princes of the Renaissance world based their policies.[1] His significance arises less from what he actually said than from the way in which he omitted certain fundamentals, from which medieval theorists had never departed. They had believed that religion formed the basis on which all political behaviour should be founded whereas Machiavelli held that religion was no more than a useful social convention. ' As the observance of divine worship is the cause of the greatness of a state ', he wrote, ' so the contempt of it is the cause of its ruin ', but he added that there is no need for the prince to believe in religion since it is at worst rank superstition and at best merely a guide to civic virtue.

Machiavelli's famous book *The Prince* was not intended as a philosophy of politics. The author had served the republican government of Florence as Secretary to the Chancellery until the return of the Medici in 1512 shattered his career. He was imprisoned, tortured and eventually banished to his country estate where he died in 1527. *The Prince* was intended to convince the

---

[1] This statement should be further qualified. Machiavelli was only recognising what had been long practised. ' Machiavelli's concept of power corresponds to an actuality which has been present in all historical states and in their relations with each other.'

government which had removed him from office that he was indispensable. His recommendations were intended as a particular programme for a particular situation. Prevailing disorder has brought political life to so low a level that only radical and ruthless measures can bring about the return of *virtu* in Italy. The word *virtu* is practically untranslatable. Machiavelli might have called it 'public spirit' which he asserted time and time again in his *Discourses* was the chief ingredient in the creation of a truly happy state, but it was a 'public spirit' more pervaded by Italian *bravura* than by an English sense of duty.

All the same *The Prince* and *The Discourses* formed a landmark in the history of political theory. By looking back to the days of the Roman Republic, as did so many Renaissance scholars, Machiavelli looked forward to secular totalitarianism. He was mainly concerned with what was expedient for the Italy of his time, but he undoubtedly came to identify expediency with right conduct. *The Prince* is chiefly concerned with the way to acquire and hold a state. Success is the redeeming virtue of princes. If the prince feels endangered by the popularity or unpopularity of a faithful adviser, he should sacrifice him ruthlessly in his own interests. He instances the case of Ramiro d'Orco who restored order in Caesar Borgia's principality of the Romagna by sternness and so drew upon himself (as upon his master) a measure of unpopularity. When he had completed his task, Caesar Borgia 'one morning caused him to be executed and left on the Piazza at Cesaria, with the block and a bloody knife at his side. The barbarity of this spectacle caused the people to be at once satisfied and dismayed.' It may suit the Prince to keep his word and to be just, but he need not do so unless it serves his interests. Particularly is this so in war. 'For when the entire safety of our country is at stake, no consideration of what is just or unjust, merciful or cruel, praiseworthy or shameful must intervene.' His own experience of the shady field of Italian politics had given him a low opinion of human nature. 'Because it is to be asserted in general of men that they are ungrateful, fickle, false, cowards, covetous and as long as you succeed they are yours entirely; they will offer you their blood, property, life and children, as is said above, when the need is far distant, but when it approaches they turn against you.' Machiavelli is therefore mainly interesting as the secularist who recognises no higher law than that of the State. Reviled by his contemporaries so that his name become a synonym for cunning treachery, cherished by a few including Thomas Cromwell and Benito Mussolini, rarely read in his entirety, he was an isolated yet symbolic figure.

The Renaissance

Machiavelli's admiration for classical history, his view of the historical process and his persistent appeal to secular motives and ends reflect some of the dominant trends in the Renaissance. The Renaissance presented the world with a vastly enriched view of human life but greatly weakened spiritual ties. The Protestant Reformation and the Catholic Counter-Reformation to some extent stemmed its more markedly secularist trends; the study of the Christian scriptures provided a partial means of reconciling the critical humanist scholar and the Christian teacher. Yet the Renaissance quickened the impulses which were leading to the creation of a purely secular society.

CHAPTER III

THE UNIFICATION OF SPAIN UNDER FERDINAND AND ISABELLA, 1479-1516

1. *The creation of a united Spain*

THE beginning of modern Spanish history had this in common with that of Tudor England and Valois France that it witnessed the creation of a national state in which the authority of the King was extended at the cost of local liberties and feudal privileges. But Spanish history had certain characteristics all its own. Many indigenous differences remained within the country, arising out of the fact that medieval Christian Spain had consisted of five separate kingdoms; Ferdinand and Isabella were never able to do more than impose a precarious unity on states deeply permeated by strong local feelings and sturdily entrenched local rights. The unification of Spain was centred on the pre-eminent Christian state, Castile. Another characteristic was also a bequest from the past, the presence of a large Moorish population in the south, restricted at the end of the fifteenth century to the emirate of Granada. In the early Middle Ages Moorish civilisation in Spain had produced a brilliant culture and scholarship, but internal divisions and crusading valour had slowly forced back the Moors into a small slice of territory in southern Spain. Even so their presence provided the Catholic Kings[1] and their Hapsburg successors with a major problem which they solved in a senseless and cruel way. Yet after the problem had vanished, its influence remained. The Moorish contribution to Spanish life has been incalculable.

Apart from these problems, the issues facing Ferdinand and his wife Isabella were broadly speaking similar to those with which Henry VII of England had to deal. Isabella succeeded her feckless brother Henry IV as Queen of Castile in 1474 to find her country plunged into chaos, and faced with a disputed succession and a Portuguese invasion. 'For no justice was left in the land', wrote the chronicler and parish priest, Andrés Bernáldez, 'the common people were exterminated, the crown property alienated, the royal revenues reduced to such slight value that it causes me shame to

[1] A title conferred on Ferdinand and Isabella by Pope Alexander VI in 1494.

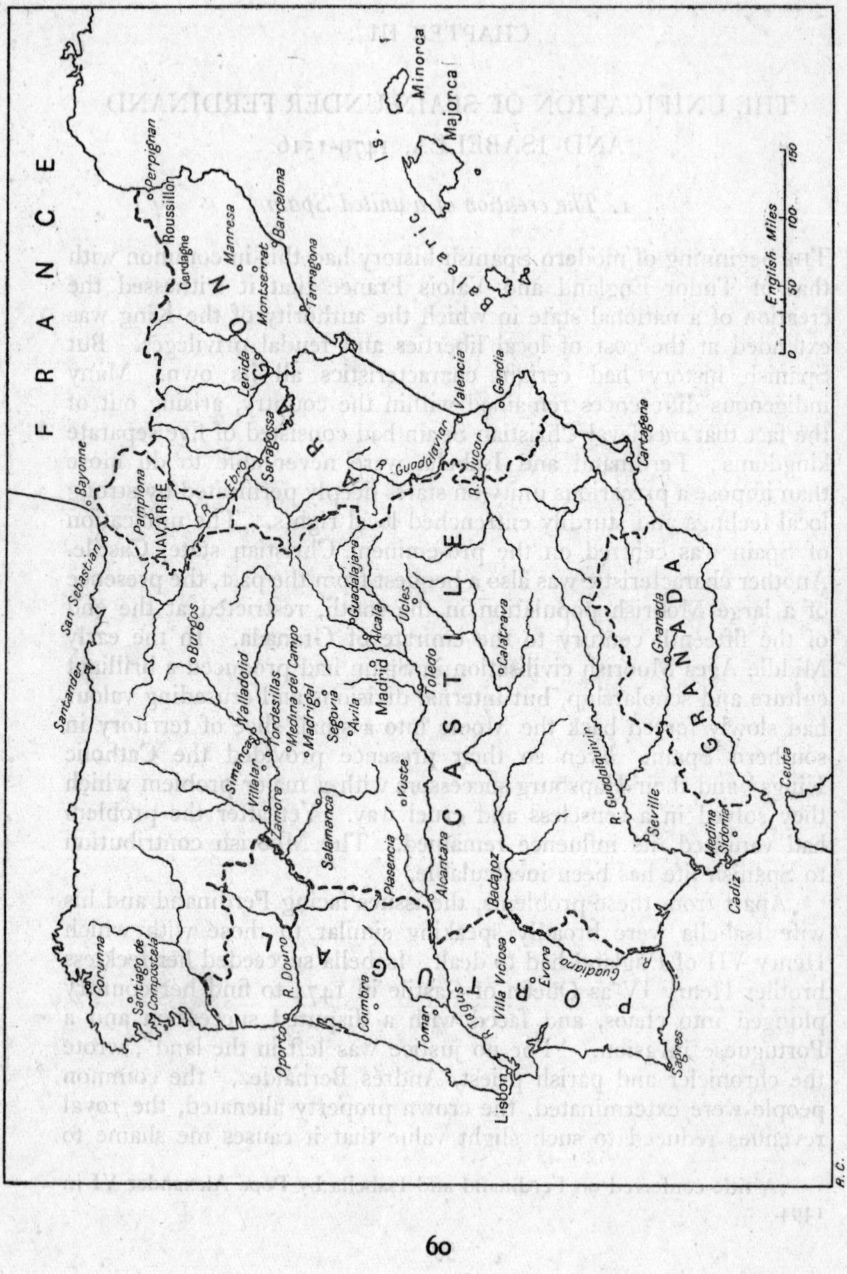

FRANCE

Perpignan
Roussillon
Cerdagne
Bayonne
San Sebastian
Pamplona
NAVARRE
Ebro
Manresa
Montserrat
Barcelona
Tarragona
Lerida
Saragossa
Minorca
Majorca
Balearic Is.
R. Guadalaviar
Valencia
Gandia
R. Jucar
Cartagena

Santander
Burgos
Valladolid
Simancas
Tordesillas
Medina del Campo
Madrigal
Segovia
Avila
Madrid
Alcala
Ucles
Toledo
Guadalajara
Calatrava
Granada
GRANADA
Ceuta

Corunna
Santiago de Compostela
R. Douro
Oporto
Zamora
Villalar
Salamanca
Yuste
Plasencia
Alcantara
Coimbra
Tomar
Tagus
Villa Viciosa
Lisbon
Evora
Badajoz
Guadiana
R. Guadalquivir
Seville
Medina Sidonia
Cadiz
Sagres

PORTUGAL
CASTILE

English Miles
0   50   100   150

R.C.

Map I.—The Spanish Peninsula at the beginning of the sixteenth century.

speak of it; whence it resulted that men were robbed not only in the open fields but in the cities and towns, that the regular clergy could not live in safety, and that the seculars were treated with no respect, that sanctuaries were violated, women raped, and all men had full liberty to sin as they pleased.' But the young Queen of twenty-three was a woman of great piety, bravery and determination, married to a husband as able as herself. Her husband, Ferdinand, who succeeded to the compact and orderly kingdom of Aragon on his father's death in 1479, was a perfect illustration of the Machiavellian prince at work. ' Cautious, calculating, and persistent; parsimonious . . . he never acted impulsively, never struck unless he was well able to follow up the blow.' Informed that Louis XII of France had complained that he had been deceived twice, the Spanish King satirically remarked : ' He lies, it is the tenth time.' Statecraft counted with him, as it had done with his father, above affection, and, more to the purpose, he had the necessary ability for putting his deeply-laid plans into practice.

As in Lancastrian England the authority of the Crown could only be restored by the re-imposition of law and order, by the reduction of baronial power and by an increase in the wealth of the king. In suppressing disorder in Castile Isabella placed great reliance on the militia of the fortified towns known as the *Hermanedad*, a well-established institution brought under royal control and made to serve a new purpose. Each member-city possessed squadrons of archers who ran down criminals in the districts under its control; for long the supreme penalty was to be shot to death with arrows. Thus under royal guidance the *Hermanedad* proved a remarkably efficient instrument for restoring justice and for checking the nobility whose licentious behaviour was one of the principal reasons for persistent anarchy.

The subjection of the baronage formed then the biggest single task in Spanish policy. During the past fifty years the feeble and divided rule of Henry of Castile had provided the nobles with a grand opportunity for feathering their own nests. Backed by the Castilian Cortes, Ferdinand and Isabella issued writs for the destruction of many fortified castles and further reduced baronial power by removing the greater nobles from the responsible positions they had held in the royal councils and royal household. Their claws were cut at every stage. Thus the Cortes of Toledo passed an act in 1480 ordering them to restore all land alienated from the Crown in the previous reign. Another way in which the nobles had dominated the land was through their control of the grandmasterships of the three chivalric orders, Santiago, Alcantara and

Calatrava, which placed a considerable armed force at their disposal, for use, if necessary, against the Crown. When Isabella learned of the death of the Grand Master of Santiago in 1476, she rode hard for three days, the latter part in torrents of rain, from Valladolid to Ucles to ensure that the magnates should elect her husband as their new Grand Master. It was typical of Ferdinand that having been offered the grand-mastership, he was content to allow the original nominee to stand. And, indeed, before he actually became Grand Master of Santiago (in 1499), he had already been elected to the grand-masterships of the two other orders, a process completed when the Pope ordered the incorporation of all three orders in the Crown of Castile in 1523. The Catholic Kings were concerned with preventing the nobles from challenging the royal authority, not with eliminating them as a class. The grandees retained many of their privileges, such as that of standing ' covered ' in the presence of the sovereign, and were often granted honorary office. But, for the moment, they only retained the vestiges of power; the reality had passed to the trained lawyers, the *letrados* [1] who made up the majority of the royal counsellors.

The reorganisation of royal government, of which this was a part, was probably the most important as well as the most lasting of all the reforms undertaken by Ferdinand and Isabella. During the Middle Ages, each Spanish state had had its own Cortes, roughly equivalent to the English Parliament, [2] of which the Cortes of Castile was the most important. Like the Tudors the Catholic Kings used the Cortes to overcome baronial insolence and to reduce noble power. Once this was done, no further use was made of the Cortes except for the necessary purpose of confirming the succession to the Castilian throne and for granting money to carry on the Italian wars. [3] Thus although the Cortes continued to have the

[1] Described by Diego de Mendoza as ' men of middle condition, between great and small, carrying neither offence to the one or the other, and whose profession is to study the law '.

[2] The Cortes consisted of three Orders, the clergy, the nobility, and the commons (only representing the cities and the territory under their control). Each Order sat separately and had considerable, if undefined, powers in financial matters and in legislation; the Cortes of Aragon (consisting of four Orders; the nobility were divided into greater and lesser nobles) was in an even stronger position than the Cortes of Castile to defy the King.

[3] Mariéjol concludes that there was a close correlation between the calling of the Cortes and the ups and downs of Ferdinand's foreign policy. In the short period, 1474-83, when Isabella was restoring order in Castille, two very important sessions of the Cortes were held at Madrigal (1476) and Toledo (1480). In the next fourteen years (1483-97) there was no meeting.

right to petition the sovereign, its authority had been steadily whittled away; nor was there any likelihood of the members' political experience enabling them to resume and to increase their power.

This was in part a result of the great development of the conciliar system of government, which formed the basis of Spanish administration in the next few centuries. Once again old institutions were remoulded to serve a new purpose. The reorganised Council of Castile possessed a tremendous reserve of administrative, judicial and legislative power, in the disposal of which the professional middle class had the main say. The aristocracy was in fact virtually excluded from the councils which it had so long dominated. However hard the counsellors worked—the Council sat every day except Sundays and festivals—they could not deal with the vast and growing amount of business. Thus as early as the reign of Ferdinand and Isabella there was the development of a feature typical of all conciliar government, the proliferation of the main council into a series of committees which were in time to rank in authority little below the original conciliar body. It was through the Councils, all of which, including the *Suprema* or Council of the Inquisition, were totally subject to the King's control, that Ferdinand and Isabella ruled Spain. Owing to the decay of municipal liberties and feudal privileges, except possibly in Aragon, they were able to exert direct control over every aspect of government. They made particular use of an official called the *corregidor*, a direct representative of the central government with wide powers of administration and supervision whom Merriman has called the ' omnicompetent servant of an absolute king '.[1] The *corregidor* could thus act as an agent of the royal council, both in checking baronial power and in stemming separatist feeling by focusing everything around the authority of the King.

The Spanish Church formed another instrument for forging Spanish unity and creating a strong monarchy. Here circumstances undoubtedly helped the Catholic Kings. Firstly there was the known piety and Christian enthusiasm of Queen Isabella. Secondly, the

The Cortes met twelve times in the last nineteen years of Ferdinand's reign, but mainly to grant money to the King for the conduct of his foreign policy.

[1] Merriman thus describes his work : ' Inspection and regulation of the relations of Moors and Christians, oversight of gambling houses and prevention of forbidden games, superintendence of local customs dues, general police and executive authority, and above all the securing of the impartial administration of justice to all men, both in civil and criminal affairs.' (*Rise of the Spanish Empire*, ii, 149.)

secular ambitions of the contemporary Popes made them willing to bargain spiritual authority in return for political assistance. Thus Sixtus IV gave the Spanish monarchs full powers over episcopal appointments in 1482, so bringing to an end the unwarrantable use which earlier Popes had made of provision to Spanish sees. Another Pope, the Spaniard Alexander VI, not only settled the dispute over the newly-founded colonies in Spain's favour but gave Ferdinand and Isabella full control over all clerical appointments as well as the disposal of tithes in the American dominions. They were assisted in their work by a churchman of great integrity, singular piety and inflexible intolerance, Cardinal Ximenez, Archbishop of Toledo. Fully sympathising with the aims of the Catholic Kings, he eliminated abuses and indiscipline from the Spanish Church, inspiring his inferiors with such enthusiasm that it may be said that Ximenez was one of the reasons why Spain avoided a Protestant Reformation. Intolerant as he may have been in his dislike of Jews and Moors, he showed himself a patron of scholarship as well as of religion, founding the University of Alcala. The Spanish Inquisition was yet another of the tools placed in the hands of Ferdinand and Isabella. Originally established by Pope Sixtus IV in 1478 at the request of Isabella for coping with so-called Christian Jews or *Conversos* for use in Castile, it was not long before its peculiar ' combination of the mysterious authority of the Church with the secular powers of the Crown ' was fully revealed. All appointments from that of the Inquisitor-General downwards were vested in the Spanish Crown. It controlled its policy and established its council the *Suprema*. Even the revenues confiscated by its orders went into the pocket of the Crown. Thus while the main purpose of the Inquisition was the suppression of heresy, it was in the last resort the most powerful weapon in the hands of the Crown for dealing with the heterodox in the Church or in the State.

Ferdinand and Isabella had two other main objects : the creation of a well-trained military force under the direct control of the Crown, and the formation of a prosperous and united state that would produce rich revenues for the King. The reorganisation of the Spanish army under a series of brilliant and reliable officers headed by Gonzalvo de Cordova and Gonzalvo de Ayora ensured that the first of these needs was met.

To fill the Treasury was more difficult but it was a problem with which the calculating and mean-minded Ferdinand, like Henry VII of England, was well-fitted by character and training to deal. First of all, a more efficient collection of the taxes was instituted, the number of those who claimed exemption was reduced, and the coinage was reformed and standardised. As a result the annual revenue of Castile rose from 885,000 reals at the time of Isabella's accession to over 26 million at the time of her death thirty years later. It reflects the underlying conservatism of the Catholic Kings that only two additional sources of revenue were tapped during the reign; the first treasure which arrived from the Indies and a tax called the *Cruzada*.

Ferdinand realised that the revenues of the state depended ultimately on the prosperity of the country. Under his rule there was a greater correspondence between the actual prosperity of Spain and the fiscal demands of the government than there had been ever before or was indeed to be again. This was a result of the economic revival which took place everywhere except in Catalonia and Majorca. Through the system of regulation and restriction, which later helped to stifle industrial enterprise, the woollen industries of Toledo and Seville flourished, as did the silk industry of Andalusia. Ferdinand and Isabella abolished the internal customs barriers which had been set up in Castile in the last reign and greatly improved the roads. Furthermore in their desire to increase foreign trade and so enrich the realm by attracting bullion to it, as well as from a natural wish to exploit their newly-won American territory, they did what they could to promote Spanish shipping. They even did something to improve the lot of the peasant, bringing about the end of serfdom as a legal status in Castile. But, like their successors, they paid too much attention to the great corporation of Castilian sheep-farmers known as the Mesta, which was brought more and more under the direct control of the Crown only to have its privileges and powers greatly enhanced. The ordinary Spanish farmer never really had a chance against this highly organised political and economical machine. The age-long problem of Spanish agriculture remained. All the same Spain was in a flourishing economic state when Ferdinand died in 1516.

The unification of Spain was still incomplete in 1490. But it was clear from the early days of Isabella's reign that the Moorish emirate of Granada was in no fit state to defy for very long the crusading enthusiasm of the Spanish armies. When Isabella demanded tribute from the King of Granada in 1476, he made his defiance clear by stating that his mints 'no longer coined gold, but steel'. Six years later Ferdinand and Isabella were strong enough to take the offensive, while the Moorish state had been greatly weakened by a disputed succession and even treachery. The Spanish campaign was one of a cautious but steady advance, leading to the surrender of Granada early in 1492. It had been endowed with all the characteristics of a crusade; the King and Queen paid a pilgrimage to the national shrine of Santiago de Compostella; a giant silver cross, a gift from the Pope, formed the gathering point of the army. The terms which Ferdinand granted the vanquished seemed at first sight chivalric and magnanimous, but the sequel was not. Despite all promises to the contrary the Moors were faced with the alternative of accepting Christianity or being expelled from Castile (in which kingdom Granada had been absorbed). The edict of 1502 ordered that all unconverted Moors should leave Leon and Castile before the end of the coming April. As the edict was only issued on the previous February 12th its conditions could not be fulfilled. The unfortunate Moors were therefore faced with extreme hardship and possibly death or mass and meaningless baptism to the Christian faith. The responsibility for this policy, as for the expulsion of the Jews, ordered on March 30th, 1492, rested more with the pious Isabella and her high-principled adviser Ximenez than with the wily Ferdinand.[1]

Thus by the opening years of the sixteenth century the Catholic Kings had created a rich and powerful state in which there existed a high degree of centralised power, and the prestige of which in Europe had grown steadily more and more during the last twenty years. In R. B. Merriman's words: ' At the most critical stage of its existence the realm was transformed from a turbulent oligarchy, whose lawlessness was partially redeemed by a somewhat undisciplined passion for freedom, into a monarchy so omnipotent that nothing, save the national tendency towards separatism, could hold out against it.'[2]

2. *The foreign policy of Ferdinand and Isabella*

Ferdinand's policy towards foreign affairs was formulated to further the objectives which governed all his activities, the extension of Spanish power and the increase of his own prestige. As King of Aragon (which included the Mediterranean islands of Majorca, Minorca and Sicily) he was vitally interested in the balance of power in Italy. As King-Consort of Castile he inherited the long-drawn out struggle with Portugal which was now to be extended to the New World through the discoveries of Columbus and the other great sailors of the age. Two other leading issues affected every

---

[1] The expulsion of the Moors from Aragon did not take place until the reign of Ferdinand's grandson, Charles I (Emperor Charles V).

[2] R. B. Merriman, *The Rise of the Spanish Empire*, ii, 127.

decision which Ferdinand had to make in foreign policy, the succession to the thrones of Aragon and Castile, and Ferdinand's wish to annex the kingdom of Navarre in northern Spain. While Ferdinand's achievements in the realm of foreign affairs were considerable, he laid the foundations of the fatal Valois-Hapsburg rivalry which was to dog European history for the next two centuries.

He was probably most concerned with the problem of passing on a strong and undivided empire at his death. In one sense this constituted his, and Spain's, greatest failure. However carefully he arranged things, every move was haunted by disaster, for he could neither control birth nor death, and it was these two forces which played a magisterial part in determining the future of the Spanish empire. Ferdinand and Isabella had five children, a son, John, and four daughters, Isabella, Joanna, Maria and Catherine. As John was the heir it was vitally necessary to find him a wife who would enhance Spanish prestige and serve Ferdinand's dynastic interests. After prolonged negotiation, he was married to the Princess Margaret, the daughter of the Hapsburg Emperor Maximilian, a marriage which bound the Castilian house to the most important family in Europe. John's sister, Joanna, was married to the Archduke Philip, Maximilian's son. With John safely wedded, Ferdinand decided to allow the marriage of his eldest daughter, Isabella, to King Manuel of Portugal. Negotiations were also reopened for the marriage of his other daughter, Catherine, to Arthur of England, son and heir of Henry VII. It appeared as if Ferdinand was arranging for the succession to the Spanish dominions and was putting into practice a deeply-laid plot for the encirclement of France.[1]

These dynastic marriages did not fall out as he had hoped. John the heir died in 1497 ; the child of his sensible and attractive widow was still-born, thus divesting the Spanish royal house of direct heirs in the male line. To Ferdinand's chagrin the succession passed to Isabella and her children, but she died giving birth to a son in 1498 who also died two years later. The tantalising prospect of adding the Spanish dominions to the Portuguese empire continued to fascinate King Manuel. Subsequently he married his dead wife's sister, Maria, and when she died in 1517 he married the elder sister of Charles V, the Princess Eleanor. Meanwhile the Spanish succession passed to the eldest remaining daughter, Joanna, the wife of the Archduke Philip, a handsome but selfish and foolish youth. Ferdinand and Isabella were undoubtedly alarmed by the thought that their dominions might in time pass to the foreign issue of this

[1] See the genealogical table, p. 411.

couple, who might have the additional and primary burden of Imperial rule in Germany. If this were to happen, it would threaten all that the Catholic Kings had tried to do and nullify the unity and independence of Spain. Ferdinand's irritation grew deeper still after the visit which Philip and Joanna made to Spain in 1502 in company with a train of Flemish advisers whose arrogance offended the native Spaniards. Nor could any reliance be placed on Joanna. Her husband's unfaithfulness aroused her to an hysteria not far short of madness. She was still sane but she was morbid and passionate. Meanwhile Isabella willed that Joanna should succeed her in Castile as ' queen proprietress ' with her husband as ' king-consort '. A clause of some significance also provided that Ferdinand should act as regent until her son should come of age if Joanna ' should prove unwilling or unable to govern '.

Isabella's death in 1504 proved Ferdinand's first severe test. He played his cards so well that he was declared regent for his daughter and managed to outwit his son-in-law who died at Burgos in September, 1506. The death of Philip I, as he appears in the list of Castilian kings, removed Ferdinand's most serious rival, and enabled him to administer Castile on behalf of his daughter, who was soon to be immured in the gloomy castle of Tordesillas where what at first sight appeared to be moody hysteria settled into final insanity.[1] But this did not solve the problem of the succession. Joanna's heir, Charles, was being educated as a Fleming in the distant Netherlands which he had inherited from his father. If Ferdinand could have overridden the well-established rules of succession, he would have settled the throne on his namesake, Charles' younger brother, Ferdinand, who was being brought up a Spaniard, but he did not feel that the time was yet ripe for that. There remained one other possibility. He might marry and so secure a direct heir. With typical foxiness he married into the Navarrese royal family in the hope that his new wife, Germaine de Foix, might bring him Navarre as well as a son. The son, born in 1509, died. And Ferdinand was forced to realise that his vast inheritance must pass to his grandson, the Flemish prince Charles.

The other aspect of Ferdinand's diplomacy, that which was intended to win him land and prestige at the expense of France, brought him better rewards, even if they were in the long run to prove a disastrous drain on Spain's resources. The creation of a strong and united country and the formation of an efficient army

---

[1] Although Joanna was eventually mad, it is not improbable that at first Ferdinand deliberately circulated accounts of her insanity to prevent her from governing Castile.

precluded any direct intervention in foreign affairs for the first ten years of his reign. Indeed it was part of his policy to use force only when diplomacy had failed. He was always eager to conserve his resources and to let others fight on his behalf if he could persuade them to do so.

His first major entry into foreign affairs was typically tortuous and a good illustration of the methods which earned him Machiavelli's admiration. Taking advantage of the fact that the French King, Charles VIII, was involved in a struggle in Brittany, he came to terms with Henry VII of England, hoping that the English King would intervene in Brittany in order that Spain might regain the provinces of Cerdagne and Roussillon. The shallow and feather-pated French King, on fire to win military glory in Italy, proved ready to pay off both Henry VII (by the Treaty of Etaples) and Ferdinand V (by the Treaty of Barcelona in 1493 by which Spain gained Cerdagne and Roussillon). Ferdinand had thus won back important territory at no cost to himself.

For the next ten years his attention was fastened on Italy,[1] where he had a three-fold objective; so to settle the balance of power in Italy that Spanish rather than French interests were uppermost; to check papal pretensions; and if possible to win the kingdom of Naples for the Spanish crown. He manipulated the situation in a masterly if unscrupulous fashion, turning French victories into virtual defeats and at length he gained control over what had once threatened to be a precarious and even dangerous situation. By the Treaty of Blois signed in 1504 Louis XII of France recognised Ferdinand's claim to the Neapolitan crown.

The remaining years of his life were largely concerned with the acquisition of the frontier-kingdom of Navarre, a leading object of his father's policy. Realising that the complex succession question, arising from Isabella's death, in Spain made French friendship necessary, he signed a second Treaty of Blois with Louis XII in October, 1505. By this treaty Ferdinand agreed to marry Louis' niece, Germaine de Foix, of the royal house of Navarre, to whom Louis in his turn resigned all his claims on Naples, declaring, however, that if Germaine died without children, he would demand the territories which Ferdinand had agreed to give him by the Treaty of Granada in 1500 and of which the Catholic King had since deprived him. Within a few years the death of the Archduke Philip and Germaine's failure to bear him a son made Ferdinand no longer interested in maintaining the French alliance. When, therefore, Pope Julius II formed the Holy League against the

[1] See Chapter VI on 'The Italian Wars'.

French, Ferdinand joined it in the hope that the mountain kingdom of the Pyrenees would be his reward. Navarre was ruled by the D'Albrets, but the younger line of the House of Foix refused to accept the D'Albret claim to the throne; [1] on the death of Gaston de Foix in battle in 1512 his pretensions passed to his sister Queen Germaine. With tortuous diplomacy Ferdinand pursued his ends, using deceit until he felt safe to use force, with the result that Spanish Navarre was vested in the kingdom of Castile with all due solemnity in 1515. [2]

This was the great King's last act, for he died at Madrigalejo on January 23rd, 1516. He had created an empire out of a relatively disunited group of states, capable, though he hardly knew it, of almost unlimited expansion and rumoured rightly to hold incredible riches. His dominions, which included outposts in North Africa like Oran, the Canary Islands in the Atlantic, as well as Sardinia, the Balearic Islands, Naples and Sicily in the Mediterranean and the new territory in America, were relatively well-governed and efficiently administered. There were indeed weaknesses inherent in the structure which time was to reveal but he had raised a mighty state. ' Certainly ', says Merriman as he closes the second volume of his great history, ' it was the bitterest irony of fate that at the very moment when Spain's national unity had been attained, her national independence should have been lost. Ferdinand and Isabella had earned the everlasting gratitude of their country by giving her the one, and by increasing, beyond the most ambitious dreams of their contemporaries, the wealth and extent of her dominions overseas. Yet their reign had also resulted in depriving her of the other, and in bequeathing her the almost insoluble problem of reconciling the national interests with the dynastic ambitions of a race of alien kings.' [3]

---

[1] See genealogical table, p. 410.

[2] The D'Albrets continued to rule over French Navarre until their descendant Henry of Navarre became King Henry IV of France in 1589.

[3] R. B. Merriman, *Rise of the Spanish Empire*, ii, 349.

CHAPTER IV

THE RISE AND DECLINE
OF THE PORTUGUESE EMPIRE

THE rise and decline of the Portuguese empire is one of the most remarkable and significant of stories. The small state of Portugal had first emerged as an independent kingdom in the early twelfth century as a result of a victorious crusade against the Moors. Enriched by a fertile soil and a moist climate, it had expanded as Moorish power steadily declined. Favoured by an Atlantic seaboard, its fishermen became the most experienced deep-sea sailors in Europe. During the fifteenth and early sixteenth centuries the country was ruled by a succession of princes of the House of Avis, many of them extremely able : John I (1383-1433), Duarte (1433-38), Alfonso V (1438-81), John II (1481-95), Manuel I (1495-1521) and John III (1521-57). These Kings were as ambitious as their contemporaries of France and Spain ; [1] indeed at one time Manuel had hoped to bring about the union of the Peninsula under the Portuguese royal house by a series of marriages with the Castilian royal family. Ironically the converse of Manuel's hopes occurred ; the death of the Cardinal-King Henry in 1580 was followed by the incorporation of the Portuguese empire in that of Spain for sixty years.

Moreover, like many another monarch of the time, these Portuguese Kings tried to strengthen their own authority by reducing the power of the nobles, though less successfully than their contemporaries in Spain. The Portuguese Cortes was called less and less frequently.[2] The Portuguese Church was subjected to royal authority ; the Inquisition was made permanent in 1536. But Portugal's geographical position made the country into an Atlantic rather than a Mediterranean power. The part which Portugal played in European politics was therefore limited by the implications

[1] Spain was used to describe the whole Peninsula. Hence the indignation of Manuel I when Pope Alexander VI granted Ferdinand of Aragon the right to call himself King of Spain.

[2] ' John I, who had based his power on the support of the commoners called twenty-five cortes in his long reign ; King Duarte four in his brief reign of six years ; Alfonso V, twenty-two ; John II, four ; and Manuel four in a reign of twenty-six years. His successor John III held three cortes in thirty-one years.' (H. V. Livermore, *History of Portugal*, 223).

of its colonial policy. The Portuguese were thus much more concerned with increasing their influence outside Europe than with the course of European conflicts.

This was why the ventures associated with Prince Henry the Navigator were so significant. His father, John I, sent him in 1415 when he was twenty-one years old to attack the Moorish fort of Ceuta and thus to win his spurs as a true knight by striking a blow in the continuous crusade against the Saracens. The decision to hold Ceuta after it had fallen to the attackers initiated the story of Portuguese territorial expansion. Moved as he undoubtedly was by the hope of discovering a new way of attacking the Turks, possibly in conjunction with the mythical prince, Prester John, Prince Henry seems to have had something of the scientific curiosity later typical of the Renaissance. Appointed governor of the Algarves, he established a remarkable little court at Sagres where men of all races, navigators like da Nola of Genoa and Cadamosto of Venice, cartographers like Jaime de Mayorca, put their sea-faring and geographical knowledge at his disposal. Although he never travelled farther than Ceuta and Tangier, he sent a number of expeditions to investigate the west coast of Africa before he died in 1460.

Progress was relatively slow. Sailors did not wish to sail beyond Cape Bojador as rumour asserted that their ships might then reach the dread, mythical green sea of darkness, but gradually an advance was made. In 1442 Gonçalves brought back gold dust and negro slaves, a sure indication of the economic possibilities of the region and a beginning of that trade in negro slaves which was so greatly to influence the rivalry of the great powers. Six years later a Portuguese fortress and factory was established on Arguim island. After Prince Henry's death a relatively quiet period followed, partly as a result of the disturbed conditions in Portugal, but the country gained an incidental advantage by the Treaty of Alcaçovas which ended the dispute with Castile in 1479. By this treaty Castile recognised the Portuguese claims to monopolise the west African coast and to govern all the Atlantic islands except the Canaries (i.e. the Azores, Cape Verde islands, Madeira where Prince Henry had introduced the sugar cane from Sicily, so halving the price of sugar in Europe, as well as the Malvoisie grape from Crete, the source of Madeira wine).

The accession of John II in 1481 opened a new era in the history of the monarchy. Determined and ruthless, he greatly strengthened the royal authority. As soon as he became King he called the Cortes to Evora imposing a more severe form of vassalage on his subjects.

He enhanced the power of his own agents, the judges or *ouvidores* and the *corregedores*, with the object of repressing the turbulent nobility, the chief of whom, the Duke of Braganza, was executed in the public square of Evora on a summer day in 1484. As shrewd as he was emotional, he gave refuge to the Jews expelled from Spain by the devout Isabella in order that he might extract money from them to finance war against the Moors in Africa. He determined to preserve and to extend the Portuguese monopoly over the African trade; he decreed that all foreign ships interloping on the Guinea coast should be sunk or seized and their officers and men consigned to the sharks. In 1482 another fortress and a trading centre was established by Diogo de Azambuja at Elmina on the Bight of Benin. Five years later Bartholomew Dias accidentally rounded the Cape of Good Hope and reached Mossel Bay on the Indian Ocean. Thus the way lay open to the trade of India, dazzling in its variety; but a decade passed before Vasco da Gama made his epochal voyage, ending at the great spice port of Calicut in the early summer of 1498.

Da Gama, who sailed under the patronage of the industrious and musically-minded Manuel the Fortunate,[1] heralded imperial dominion. But the Portuguese were not yet interested in annexing new territory. What they wanted was the control of the profitable trade in spices, in the pepper, cinnamon, nutmeg, mace and cloves which made food palatable in the sixteenth century. By 1500 this was almost wholly in the hands of Arab traders who transported it in their dhows to the ports of the Red Sea and Persian Gulf; thence it was carried overland to the Mediterranean where the Venetians took charge and sold it for large profits to an eager Europe. The Portuguese could only secure a monopoly of this trade by wresting it from the Arabs by force. 'Devil take you, what are you doing here?' had been the highly relevant question to the first of da Gama's landing parties. The masterly acumen of Albuquerque proved equal to this gigantic task. He became governor of the little Portuguese settlement in India in 1509 in succession to Francisco de Almeida who had shown the calibre of the Portuguese galleons by defeating a combined Egyptian and Gujerati fleet off Diu in 1509, thus helping to ensure Portuguese supremacy in the Indian Ocean.

---

[1] ' He was very musical, so that usually at his office, and always for the siesta and after he had got into bed, it was to music, and both for his chapel he had excellent singers and players that came to him from all parts of Europe. . . . Every Sunday and saint's day he dined and supped with music of pipes, sackbuts, horns, harps, tambourines, fiddles and on special festivals with drums and trumpets that all played each one after its kind while he ate.' (Contemporary chronicle quoted in Livermore, *History of Portugal*, 222.)

Next year Albuquerque made a start in his plan for consolidating Portuguese control by the capture of the island of Goa which could serve both as a trading centre and as a naval base. The seizure of the islands of Socotra and Ormuz enabled the Portuguese to control the two main extremities of the Arab trade routes. In 1511, at some risk to his hold on Goa, he turned east and captured Malacca which helped the Portuguese to establish control over the Arab routes across the Bay of Bengal. Two years later a Portuguese ship entered the Chinese port of Canton, thus initiating the lucrative trade with China which was soon to be based on the Portuguese settlement at Macao. To complete the picture the Portuguese arrived off the Spice Islands, the Moluccas, which brought the source of the most lucrative of all trades under their control.

This remarkable story, through which Albuquerque's unerring judgment, capacity and foresight shone until his death in 1515, gave the Portuguese a practical monopoly of an exceptionally rich trade and the beginnings of a colonial empire within a few decades. It was soon apparent that the desire to capture some part or all of this was one of the motives which was to shape future European History. From the very start the Spaniards had been jealous of Portuguese success; Columbus' voyage to the West Indies had in part received Spanish support because it was supposed that he might find a way of reaching India without coming into conflict with the dominant Portuguese. Yet it was essential that some *modus vivendi* should be reached in this scramble for trade between two neighbouring nations. Although John II believed that Columbus' description of his discoveries was probably dishonest, if not inaccurate, as a matter of form he claimed the newly-discovered land on the ground that it was part of the Azores, the Portuguese right to which had been recognised by Spain some years earlier. In reply Ferdinand and Isabella appealed to the Pope, the highest international authority and fortunately a Spaniard by birth. Pope Alexander VI confirmed the Spanish possession of Columbus' discoveries and by the bull *Inter Caetera* gave Spain authority over all territory more than a hundred leagues west or south of the Portuguese Cape Verde islands or Azores. John II refused to take this pro-Spanish decision without protest and wheedled out of the Spanish sovereigns a modification of the papal proposals. Still believing that Columbus had in fact opened the way to the riches of India, Ferdinand agreed to the Treaty of Tordesillas by which the boundary-line was moved two hundred and seventy leagues further west. Vague as this was, it later proved important to Portugal because it enabled that country to claim the whole of Brazil.

The Treaty of Tordesillas, signed in 1494, was too indefinite to settle the dispute between the two nations. The Portuguese had secured a bargain of which they were not slow to take advantage. Both Popes Julius II and Leo X, the latter fascinated by the performing elephant which the diplomatic Albuquerque had thoughtfully sent to Rome, sided with the Portuguese against Spanish attempts to re-interpret the Treaty of Tordesillas. But this state of affairs so favourable to Portugal was upset by Magellan's circumnavigation of the globe.[1] He was a Portuguese who had sailed in the service of Charles V (as King of Spain) in spite of the fact that the Portuguese had used every possible means, even considering the possibility of assassination, to prevent his expedition from sailing. His arrival in the Spice Islands challenged Portuguese control. But the Spaniards knew that they could not easily expel the Portuguese; this belief, combined with the impoverished state of the royal finances and the necessity for carrying on the war against France, convinced Charles V that it was an opportune moment to come to terms with Portugal. By the Treaty of Saragossa, signed in 1529, he pledged all his rights in the Moluccas to Portugal in return for a money payment of 350,000 cruzados.

This was really another Portuguese victory. While Spain was thus recognising their monopoly of the spice trade, the Portuguese were busily engaged in consolidating their position in India. When they first reached there, the part of the country which concerned them was ruled by Moslem sultans and the Hindu King of what was then the powerful state of Vijayanagar. Had they understood Indian politics better they would have seen that it was to their interest to support the Hindus against the Moslems, but their Indian policy was so vacillating and indecisive that they alienated both Moslem and Hindu. In any case the arrival of a new set of invaders led by the relentless Babar was soon to upset the balance of power in India through the establishment of the Mogul Empire. The Portuguese seem to have displayed no political insight, with the result that although they increased their settlements, these were not securely founded on good relations with the reigning native potentates; a solitary mission to the great Mogul Emperor, Akbar, could not make amends for this. As the English were later to understand full well, immediate strength in India depended on native goodwill. Nor was the Portuguese position any stronger in the East Indies. Thus so far as the East was concerned the Portuguese

[1] Since Magellan was killed before the voyage ended, the actual distinction of circumnavigating the globe belongs to his associate del Cano.

in fact failed to avail themselves of the opportunities which the Treaty of Saragossa would seemingly have given them. Even in the West their empire developed slowly. It was not until 1560 that the Brazilian sugar production reached Madeira's average.[1] The slave-trade of which they had once had the monopoly was beginning to fall into other hands.

At home there were also signs of incipient decay. The tremendous profits which had resulted from their early trading ventures soon led to a slump and a reduction in the prices of such important products as pepper and sugar. It was discovered that many ships fell into the hands of French and other pirates, and that the cost of running the newly-founded settlements outstripped the revenue which came from them. Moreover this wealth was so unevenly distributed that a rich mercantile class lived side by side with a peasantry depressed and exploited by a feudal aristocracy. In any case, instead of the money remaining in Portugal, more and more of it went abroad to pay for food and manufactures which the country would, or could, not produce itself. The introduction of slave labour was another discouragement to native industry. On all sides there were signs of a moral and political decline, as well as of a rising state debt, which the policy of the rather mediocre John III did nothing to avert. The humanist, Nicholas Cleynarts, commenting on the situation, concluded in 1535 : ' If agriculture was ever despised, it is certainly in the parts where I reside. What is everywhere regarded as the main sinew of nations is here regarded as insignificant and useless. Should anyone assert that the Portuguese do not live slumbering body and soul in indolence, I could assure them that in that case there is no people that deserves the accusation of inertia.'

Thus, rich and extensive as the Portuguese colonial empire might appear to be in 1580, its weakness was already visible when Philip II of Spain became its King. On the whole the union with Spain accentuated its deterioration. The death of John III in 1557 had brought the line of able Portuguese kings to an end ; his successor, a child of three, Sebastian, grew up as a kind of throwback to the old crusading ideals of an earlier Portugal. All his energies were concentrated on a campaign against the Moors of

---

[1] Tobacco was imported into Portugal about 1550. The French envoy, Jean Nicot, sent some leaves to the French Queen, Catherine de' Medici, in the belief that it had medicinal properties. Hence the word ' nicotine '. The nature of the Brazilian civilisation established by Portugal is analysed at length in Gilberto Freyre's *The Masters and the Slaves*, trans. Samuel Putnam, 1946.

Morocco. He would have mortgaged, and very nearly did, his whole empire to win a single battle. In spite of the disapproval of his uncle, Philip of Spain, he led his army across Morocco and perished at the battle of Alcazar-Kebir in August, 1578. His successor, his great-uncle, Cardinal Henry, thought of securing a dispensation from his ecclesiastical vows in order that he might marry and sire an heir to Portugal, but he only lived two years. As soon as he was dead, the Spanish ambassador, Don Cristobal de Moura, took control, and with the help of the Spanish army under Alva's command overcame all resistance; the other claimant to the throne, Don Antonio, Prior of Crato, was defeated and fled from the country. Philip ruled his new dominions with understanding, agreeing at the Cortes of Tomar to appoint only Portuguese officials to posts in the Portuguese empire and to respect the rights and liberties of the country. And while the Spanish Hapsburgs kept their promises they had little of which to complain in the loyalty of their new subjects.

Whether this union was in effect as advantageous to Spain as might at first appear must be doubted. Spanish possessions in the Philippines might do much to strengthen the Portuguese control over the Spice islands. But if Spain had absorbed a profitable trade and an extensive empire, it had also to take on the responsibilities of protecting it against its enemies, for the union of Portugal with Spain made the fast Portuguese caravels as well as the lumbering Spanish galleons fair game for Drake and his fellow raiders.

Furthermore this imperial dominion was already in an advanced state of decay. The weaknesses of the Portuguese empire resulted from the comparatively small population of the mother country and the unimaginative policy that it had pursued in the colonies. Lack of white women led to intermarriage; colonial administration as well as the manning of ships suffered from the way in which the country was forced to depend on the half-caste race which intermarriage caused to come into being. ' Decline in manning efficiency ', writes one historian, ' was accompanied by growing carelessness in buoyage and pilotage ', and he added that between 1498 and 1580 ' 620 ships left Portugal for India. Of these, 256 remained in the East. 325 returned safely to Portugal and 39 were lost. In the next forty odd years—from 1580 to 1612—186 ships sailed, 29 remained in the East, 100 returned safely, 57 were lost. In the first period, therefore, 93 per cent. of the ships which sailed from Portugal reached their destination safely; in the second period only 69 per cent. found harbour. This decline in the efficiency of the fleets struck at the very root of Portuguese power in the East—

the command of the sea lane from Asia to Europe.'[1]   Nor was this in any way counteracted by friendly relations with the native rulers. Those whom they had not made into enemies by their political and economic policy, the Portuguese alienated by the rigidity of their ecclesiastical policy, so much so that they would not even recognise the ancient Nestorian Christian Church of India. This bigoted and short-sighted policy became the more marked after Philip II ascended the Portuguese throne.

Towards the end of the sixteenth century and the early seventeenth century the Portuguese empire, already weakened internally, was threatened by the pressure of European foes to such an extent that it might have disappeared from the map. The English defeated the Portuguese fleets off the Indian coast, at Swally Roads. The Dutch fastened like a clam on the ' spicerie ', pushed the Portuguese from the East Indies, then from Malacca (1641) and finally from Ceylon (1658), and took over the monopoly of the spice and the carrying trade. Elsewhere foreign competition shattered Portuguese prosperity. They had been first in the African slave trade, but had soon been challenged by both Spaniards and Englishmen. In this respect union with Spain favoured the Portuguese as it enabled them in part to regain their control over the trade. For the Spanish government put forward the idea of an *Asiento*[2] in 1595 which was in this and subsequent years granted to Portuguese contractors. Even here, however, the Dutch challenge became increasingly dangerous. Their interloping activities led to the conquest of Elmina, the Portuguese slave-trading centre on the west African coast, in 1637. Nor was the Dutch interest confined to slaves. In 1624 the Dutch West India Company attacked Portuguese Brazil and for the next thirty years it controlled the sugar-producing region along the coast from Bahia to the Amazon ; hence the demand for slaves to work in the sugar-plantations. But the Portuguese of Brazil were more resilient than some of their fellow-colonists. The country was gradually brought back under Portuguese control, though the lead in the world sugar-market had been lost to the English and French West Indies.

The story of the Portuguese empire is thus a sorry one, but the heart of a nation which had produced in 1572 one of the greatest of epic poems,[3] Camões' *Os Lusiadas*, remained patriotic. Camões

[1] J. H. Parry, *Europe and a Wider World* (1949), 95.
[2] The *Asiento* was an agreement to let out the slave trade or the greater part of it to a contractor.
[3] The subject is excellently treated by C. M. Bowra in Chapter III of *From Virgil to Milton* (1945), 86-139.

embodied all the glories of Portuguese achievement in his age, together with an indomitable faith in his country's destiny, modified, perhaps, by his own feeling that things were not quite as they should be.   He was a humanist who had imbibed classical learning at the University of Coimbra and a soldier who had lost an eye fighting the Moors.   He had served in India and had sailed to Macao. He had been shipwrecked off Siam and had been imprisoned at Goa.   Clothed as is much of his verse in the conventional mythology of his time, there is an element of refreshing realism in it.   Here is the King of Melinde splendid in gold, velvet and jewels ; there the pavilions of the Samudri of Calicut.   There are the Javanese with their poisoned darts, the elephants of Hydal-Khan, volcanoes and sandal-trees, all the glow of a vigorous and vital people.   For the poem is the national story of Portugal.   It was his original intention to write a poem which should rival and indeed surpass the *Aeneid* of Virgil.   While Virgil sang of pagan Rome, Camões would praise Christian Portugal, the symbol of Christian civilisation and the world's defence against the Moors.   Ironically enough the poem closes with an appeal to the young Sebastian to take up arms against the Moors :

> Making Mount Atlas tremble at your sight
> More than at that of dire Medusa's head,
> Or putting in Amplusian fields to flight
> The Moors in Fez and black Morocco bred.

Yet it is an imperial as well as a crusading poem :

> We are the Portuguese from the West,
> We go to seek the countries of the East.

Vasco da Gama is the Aeneas of the poem, the hero around whom the epic truly centres :

> Th'illustrious Gama in the rear I name,
> Who robs the wandering Trojan of his fame.

This rich heroic story epitomises the better side of Portuguese colonial achievement, a splendid monument to contemporary patriotism.   Camões would have bitterly disliked the accession of a Spanish King to the throne had he lived to see it, but he would not have lost faith in his country's future.   With a population of little more than a million, Portugal had taken on commitments which it could not meet.   Its union with Spain brought it face to face with that country's enemies whom it could not defeat.   The increasing failure of the Spanish Kings and their ministers to honour the Constitutions of Tomar caused growing discontent with Spanish rule.   Burdensome taxation, unsuccessful war, irritation with the appointment of Spanish officials, the unrequited ambitions of the nobility, the work of foreign agents [1] coupled with genuine patriotism led to a full-scale revolt in 1640 and the proclamation of John, Duke of Braganza, as King John IV. Spain was too much involved in its war with France to pay much attention to Portugal. Although the war went on for over a quarter of a century, the Portuguese victories, the greatest at Villa Viciosa in 1665, made the country's independence of Spain certain.

But the imperial brightness had faded. Portugal was henceforth to play a relatively small part in European history. Only in the fortresses and churches which it had scattered over the globe, from Abyssinia to China, in the century and a half of its greatness, may a fitting memorial be found.

[1] Trouble at Evora in 1637 may in part be traced to the intrigues of the Portuguese Jews and of Richelieu, whose representative, Saint-Pé, continued to work for a rebellion.

CHAPTER V

THE MAKING OF MODERN FRANCE, 1461–1559

1. *The creation of a strong monarchy*

THE foundations of French greatness in the seventeenth century were laid in the late fifteenth and early sixteenth centuries. There was a period towards the end of the sixteenth century when something approaching political chaos and economic disruption was caused by the civil conflicts known to the historian as the French Wars of Religion. But if at times these struggles seemed to threaten the very existence of all that had been so far achieved, in fact the setback was only temporary. What had already been accomplished in strengthening and centralising the French monarchy formed the foundation on which Henry IV, Richelieu, Mazarin and Louis XIV were to build. To the exclusion of all else, the increase in the power of the Crown, challenged from time to time by great noble families, was the thread which ran through the French history of the period. It came less from the personality of the monarch than from the belief of his advisers, backed to an increasing extent by the influential middle-class, that only a strong King could ensure the maintenance of law and order necessary for French prosperity and for the expansion of French power. Only Louis XI was really outstanding among the later Valois line [1] of kings. His son, the malformed Charles VIII, was a futile, hot-headed enthusiast with no conception of a realistic policy. Charles' successor, Louis XII, was a conscientious prince but was as mesmerised by the ill-fated Italian policy as his predecessor. The genuineness of his care for his people is well revealed in an ordinance of 1513 : ' On no account will we lay further burdens on our poor people, knowing the hardships of their life and heavy burdens, whether in the shape of *tailles* or otherwise, which they have hitherto borne and still bear, to our great regret and grief.' That he is said to have died as a result of the exhausting fêtes and gaiety with which he indulged his third wife, young Mary of England, is a testimony to the warmth of his affection, if not to his good sense. His successor, Francis I, was superficially attractive, witty, handsome (except that his legs were rather spindly), courageous, a patron of Renaissance literature and art, a fit counterpart to Henry VIII at the Field of the Cloth of

---

[1] See pp. 403, 406.

Gold. ' He was magnanimous and generous and a lover of good literature which, through his means, lit up the shades of ignorance which had reigned up to his time ', wrote Martin du Bellay, ' He loved all men of learning and founded at Paris colleges for Latin, Greek, and Hebrew studies.' But this splendid prince was also abominably vain, thoroughly selfish, inconsistent and without real skill either as a statesman or as a soldier. Nor were the qualities of his son, Henry II, in any way remarkable; like all the members of his house, a passionate follower of the chase, he was built on a smaller model than his father but pursued the same policy. His wife, the Italian-born Catherine de' Medici, who had to suffer the ignominy of being over-shadowed by her husband's mistress, the sumptuous beauty, Diane de Poitiers, was a really able woman through whose efforts in some sense France may be said to have been kept together during the reigns of her inauspicious brood.

Louis XI was thus the most significant of his line and left a personal impress upon his kingdom. Pitted by skin-disease, he was a thoroughly odious man, devoid of scruple and mercy. He was a neuropath, mistrusting even those in close attendance upon him, and exhausting himself and his entourage in feverish journeys through his kingdom. Amoral in all his actions, he was yet a prey to constant superstition. He would never again wear a costume nor ride a horse if he were wearing the dress or riding the horse when bad news was announced. In his political behaviour he was a Machiavellian before *The Prince* was written; he did not know what it was to keep troth. But he had a sense of duty and he knew that what France wanted was a strong monarchy, flourishing trade, law and order, and repute abroad. In spite of many setbacks, especially at the start of his reign, this was what within certain limits he was able to give the country. His less capable Valois successors owed him a debt for what he achieved, even though some return to orderly government had been accomplished by the father whom Louis hated, King Charles VII.

The situation before Louis became King in 1461 was gloomy. Not only had France suffered from repeated English invasions, damaging the crops and disrupting the life of the nation, but it had also endured a long period of political anarchy while the throne was occupied by a mad King, Charles VI, cuckolded by his wife, Isabeau of Bavaria, mistress of a dissolute court which loathed and despised him. His son, Charles VII, had watched the country split by rival factions, but his reign also witnessed a slow recovery. Twenty years after Joan of Arc had been burned at Rouen—the ninth year of Charles' reign (1431)—the English vacated all France, save

Calais. By the end of the century agriculture and commerce had largely returned to normal. But the Crown was still faced with the major problem of asserting its authority. This was the issue with which Charles VII's son, Louis XI, and his successors had to deal.

The problem was a legacy from the Middle Ages. The medieval French monarchy had been firmly embedded in a feudal setting, from which leading kings of the houses of Capet and of Valois had tried to free themselves, first by assuming the primacy among the feudal barons and latterly by increasing the extent of the royal domain, by centralising authority round the Crown and by reducing the power of intermediary bodies. In this struggle for supremacy the Crown had been opposed by two institutions, the Church and the Nobility. Not only were the greater prelates of the Church feudal vassals, they were also the representatives of an international institution often in conflict with French Kings who resented papal interference in appointments to French bishoprics and the export of French gold to the papal court at Rome. In one such conflict in the early fourteenth century the French had actually laid sacrilegious hands on the papal person; and it was a symbol of the declining force of the Papacy in the Middle Ages that two years later when a Frenchman [1] was elected Pope, he could move the Papacy to Avignon, a papal enclave within French territory. This, however, had provided no real solution to the ultimate question of what was the amount of authority which the French King could hope to enjoy over the French Church. In 1438 Charles VII had agreed to the Pragmatic Sanction of Bourges. This document was anti-papal in character and represented the feeling of those churchmen who resented the attempts which the Popes were making to overthrow the authority of a General Council, like that recently held at Constance. After asserting that the authority of a General Council was superior to that of the Pope, it forbade all appeals from France to Rome, and made the financial payments which had hitherto been obligatory into voluntary gifts. Appointments to bishoprics and abbacies were placed in the hands of cathedral and abbey chapters, not into those of the King. In practice the Pragmatic Sanction displeased the Pope, without greatly increasing royal power over the Church. Thus both Pope and King soon favoured a revision of this agreement. With his reputation enhanced by a recent victory at Marignano in 1515, Francis I met Pope Leo X at Bologna and concluded a Concordat, which proved of the utmost

---

[1] Bertrand de Got, Archbishop of Bordeaux, who became Clement V in 1305, was actually a Gascon and a subject of Edward I of England, but he had come to terms with Philip IV of France.

significance for the future history of the French monarchy and Church. The French King was granted the right to nominate to vacant French bishoprics and abbacies; in return the Pope secured the right to receive annates from the newly-appointed prelates (that is the first year's income after appointment). Although the Pope had always to confirm the King's nominations, the Concordat virtually conceded to the King full political authority over the French Church. From the point of view of the Church it was disastrous, for it made the best offices in the Church the reserve of those men of high rank and infrequent vocation whom the King wished to reward. Tied to the apron-strings of the monarchy, the Church, as the first Estate of the realm, was to be forced down with the King when the Revolution broke out in 1789. But the Crown had not only secured a reservoir of power—the long list of cardinals who held the post of first minister is a proof of this—it had won an ally and eliminated a possible enemy. With so much gained there was no reason why the French King, unlike the English and Swedish monarchs, should ally with the reformers against the Church. Crown and Church had made a somewhat one-sided marriage.

But the nobility presented a different and greater problem. If the long-continued conflicts with England had helped to wipe out some noble families, as did the Wars of the Roses in England, they had also helped to create a feudal reaction to which royal weakness had greatly contributed. The greatest lords of all, such as Anjou, Bourbon, Orléans and Brittany, still wished to dominate the royal council in their own interests. Even the nobles of middling rank endangered political and economic stability. Their economic and political privileges were excessive. They were exempt from all the direct taxes of the state, from the *taille*, the leading property-tax and from the exceptionally unpopular *gabelle* or salt-tax. Moreover as local *seigneurs* they were empowered to exact a large number of feudal dues and services which hindered the development of French agriculture and were an oppressive burden on the French peasant. They possessed considerable judicial authority. Entrenched in strongly fortified stone castles, served by a peasantry who could be little other than faithful, they were sometimes able to defy the King especially when, as was the case during the religious wars at the end of the century, they were led by one or other of the great noble families.

Like their contemporaries, the Kings of England and Spain, the Valois monarchs placed increasing reliance on the royal Council, which they tried to free from noble domination, and sought to strengthen their own power by whittling away the privileges of the

French nobility. Thus Louis XI no longer allowed the nobles to raise taxes without his permission and often interfered with seigneurial justice. He and his successors did what they could to reduce the power of the intermediate authorities through which the nobles had been able to defy the King. The States-General was perhaps the most obvious of these. Superficially it might appear a semi-democratic institution, consisting as it did of representatives of the three Estates of the realm, the Church, the Nobility and the Commons or *Tiers État*. It certainly put forward claims which would have seriously reduced the power of the Crown, but such claims represented the initiative of the nobility, not a genuinely democratic movement among the people. For as all the three orders voted *par ordre* rather than as individuals, *par tête*,[1] the two first Estates could always outvote the Commons. Relying more and more upon the Council, the French Kings called the States-General less and less. They were able to do this with impunity because as early as 1439 the States-General had given the King (not in theory, though in practice, permanently) the right to maintain a standing army and to levy the *taille* (to pay for the army). Thus whereas the English Parliament was in a position more and more to overawe the Crown through its control of the purse, in France the King had no such need to consult the States-General.

There was another French institution which had no counterpart in English history, the Parlement. There were in fact a number of parlements, at Toulouse, Bordeaux, Grenoble, Dijon, Rouen, Aix and Rennes, but they all took their lead from the Parlement of Paris. The latter was the supreme judicial court of France, and as such had helped to strengthen the King's hand by withdrawing legal cases from noble and ecclesiastical supervision. Unlike the Parlements of the eighteenth century, the sixteenth-century Parlements were favourable to the royal interests and were one of the means by which the King increased his power. The Parlement's chief function was to register royal edicts, that is to make them binding on all Frenchmen. Although the King could enforce registration and overcome opposition by holding what was called a *lit de justice*, it was obvious that this afforded a possible cause of future conflict with the King.

Noble authority remained strong in the provinces but here also the Crown gradually extended its control, both by diminishing the

[1] Since final decisions depended on a majority out of the three orders (i.e. Church and Nobles could easily outvote the Commons), voting *par ordre* did not benefit the Commons. Hence the demand in 1789 for voting *par tête* which would enable the Commons, if of sufficient number, to stand a better chance of gaining their objects. *Par tête* means individual voting, a decision reached by a majority.

power of the provincial Estates (which were overawed by the nobility) and by the creation of royal officers who would uphold the power of the central government. In addition to the *baillis* or *senéchaux* there were also lieutenants-general from the reign of Francis I, but, far from strengthening the Crown, these officials tended to weaken it as their offices fell into the hands of the great noble families. The outbreak of the long Italian Wars carried off some of the more turbulent of the provincial nobility; it is well to remember that the French Wars of Religion in which many of the greater and lesser nobles played a prominent part did not begin until the era of the Italian Wars had ended.

Finally, economic factors to some extent helped the King as the rise in prices was to the detriment of the nobles who relied on fixed rent-charges for their income. But the sale and division of noble estates, much of which occurred in the first part of the sixteenth century, only produced a new nobility eager to exact feudal rights down to the last sou. What therefore the Valois kings had achieved in the first half of the century was an incomplete subordination of the nobility to the Crown; the nobles were still powerfully entrenched and able to resist a weak king. It was left for Richelieu to assure the final victory of the monarchy in the first half of the seventeenth century, though curiously enough the nobility had its revenge in 1788 by initiating the Revolution, a movement which was eventually to bring both to the dust.

It was taken for granted by all European kings who were engaged in creating strong national states that a full treasury and a prosperous kingdom were necessary for security at home and successful war abroad. Although France had no pre-eminent minister—Louis XII's Cardinal d'Amboise was the most able—and despite the fact that its kings were not on the whole of the calibre of Ferdinand of Spain nor of the Tudors of England, the country grew steadily richer with subsequent benefit to the treasury. Since the nobility and to some extent the Church were practically exempt from taxation, the vast and inequitable burden fell mainly on the middle classes and on the peasantry. The former were greatly benefiting from the return of law and order and from the general expansion of trade throughout Europe. To reduce imports and so keep as much gold as possible in the country both Louis XI and his son encouraged a number of new industries. The attempt to establish a silk industry at Lyons was the most interesting of these. The merchants at Lyons did not at first take kindly to the royal policy and continued to import Italian silks. But through the heavy duties imposed on imported pieces and the encouragement given to foreign workers to settle in France, a flourishing silk industry was established at Lyons, Tours and Nîmes by the middle of the century. Similarly Louis XI encouraged the great fair at Lyons, held four times a year, with a view to ruining the fair of Geneva; the barter to which this fair gave rise attracted Italian and German bankers. For a time it seemed as if Lyons might rival Antwerp as a European money-mart, but the impecuniosity of the Crown caused a terrifying credit crisis in 1557-59 from which the Lyons money market never recovered. All the same French trade had made significant strides. Louis XI tried to break the monopoly of the Italian merchantmen and to develop the harbour facilities of Marseilles, La Rochelle and Bordeaux, but with only limited success. Francis I made a treaty with the Sultan of Turkey which allowed the French merchants to have their own consuls in Ottoman territory, symbolic of the vast expansion of French trade in the eastern Mediterranean. French sailors were also beginning to follow in the wake of their Spanish and Portuguese confrères; in 1534 Jacques Cartier sailed up the St. Lawrence river. Next year the merchants of Rouen established a company to trade with India. There were therefore many signs of growing prosperity in the towns of early sixteenth-century France.

At a first glance France seemed in 1559 a vital, rich country. The magnificent Palace of the Louvre, the façade of which was designed by Pierre Lescot in 1546, housed a splendid court, delighting in the rich joyousness of Renaissance literature and art. The poems of the last and greatest of the poets of medieval France, François Villon, rake, wit and cynic, ' produce ', wrote Lytton Strachey, ' the impression of some bleak desolate landscape of snow-covered roofs and frozen streets, shut in by mists, and with menacing shiver in the air. It is

> " sur la morte saison,
> Que les loups se vivent de vent,
> Et qu'on se tient en sa maison,
> Pour les frimas, prés du tison ".' [1]

But now all was changed. Refined artistry, sincere, smooth and gay, was the hall-mark of the work of Clément Marot, the herald to the group of writers known as the *Pléiade*, of whom Ronsard was the most distinguished. Ronsard's shorter poems are delicate, exquisite and joyous, full of blue skies, roses and skylarks, emblematic of the optimism of the age. The enchanting châteaux of the Loire, those of Blois and Chenonceaux above all the rest, were another reflection of the elegant taste of a cultured noble class.

[1] Lytton Strachey, *Landmarks in French Literature*, 26.

The towns too were greatly improved; society was happier, more sure of itself, than it had ever been before.

But it is easy now to see the cracks in this outwardly secure structure. Fundamentally France was an agricultural state; its peasants were oppressed by feudal dues and services. Little or nothing had been done to improve either the lot of the peasant or the land itself. Internal trade was hindered by innumerable customs and *octrois*, and by the absence of uniform coinage and weights and measures. Industry, which played only a minor part in economic life, was creating something like an industrial proletariat at Lyons to which Protestant teaching was to make an instant appeal. For the ideas of Erasmus and the sermons of Luther were already making an impact on the educated classes, on men like Bishop Briçonnet or the scholar Lefèvre of Etaples and even on the French King's sister, the Princess Margaret; the ' slumberous ' state of the French Church provided good opportunities for the teaching of the reformers. Before it was too late the King tried to take action to stem the teaching, as dangerous to the Crown as to the Church, by edicts against heresy and by setting up special judicial tribunals to try and burn heretics; but not before the new learning had attracted and captured the Reformation's greatest champion, the Picard from Noyon, John Calvin. Equally serious for the future was the fact that the Crown had overcome but not effectively vanquished the great nobles; their struggle to retain privileges and political powers was just about to begin. The promise of the dawn proved premature. Even so the monarchy was to prove strong enough to stand the shocks of the ' religious ' wars which were to disturb France during the last half of the sixteenth century.

2. *French foreign policy*

The attitude which the French Kings took towards external problems was fundamentally an extension of their domestic policy, part and parcel of the attempt to create a strong national state. But this policy had two sides, a personal side and a national side. The French monarch of the period was still partly a feudal knight, eager for reputation regardless of national interest. This may help to explain the fatal fascination which Italy had for the imaginative mind of Charles VIII and, to a lesser extent, for his successors. Here was a land, divided by internal feuds and rich with all the commerce of the Mediterranean and the artistic treasures of the Renaissance, where French Kings could win personal renown as courageous and successful generals and at the same time gain titles for themselves and territory for their country. But the medieval desire to win personal distinction on the field of battle which drew the French Kings so frequently to Italian battlefields was being replaced by scientific calculation of what was possible for and what was profitable to France. Louis XI, at least, was unlikely to lose himself in the quixotic irrationalism of chivalry. Since the early Middle Ages each successive French King had tried to extend his royal domain and to subordinate his vassals to his own authority. Roughly speaking the growth of the French monarchy was the story of the steady absorption or annexation of territory adjoining the Crown lands. On the circumference of the monarchy itself there were important states, either nominally vassals of France or claimed as vassals by the French King. In the fifteenth century both Burgundy and Brittany constituted such states, the former at one time appearing potentially so strong that it might have taken its place among the great states of Europe, as Duke Philip the Good aimed that it should.

This policy of outward expansion brought the French King into contact with his neighbours, most of them as mistrustful of his policy as he was of their ambitions. Until 1558 he continued to be exercised by the bogy of Calais and after that date by the continued use of the title King of France by the Tudor monarchs, and by the claims which Ferdinand of Aragon made to the kingdom of Navarre. Treaties of friendship alternated with war, but the pattern behind this changing activity can be perceived. In time French policy was to find a focal point in the long conflict with the Hapsburg rulers of Madrid and Vienna to which the policy now under review formed a prologue.

Louis XI proved a calculating and effective diplomat. Although he made many costly mistakes, the 'universal spider', as he was called, could justly state at the end of his reign that ' he had defended and governed, augmented and increased all parts of his realm '. Supported by the lesser nobility and the townsmen, he was at last able to turn the tide of fortune in his favour. By the Treaty of Pecquigny in 1475 he neutralised the possible danger from England by agreeing to pay an annual subsidy to the English King, Edward IV. Thus he could now turn his attention to his chief enemy, Duke Charles of Burgundy, who had inherited his father's ambitious policy only to find that he stirred up a hornets' nest as soon as he tried to put it into practice. Spurred on by Louis XI, the Dukes of Lorraine and Austria, the Rhineland towns and the Swiss formed a league against him. It was the Swiss who triumphed, first at Grandson and Morat in 1476 and then the next year at Nancy where Duke

Charles perished in battle, leaving his dominions to his daughter, Mary. It was Louis' great opportunity. Ignoring his goddaughter's pleas, he seized Picardy and Artois, the duchy of Burgundy and the Franche Comté. This in its turn caused a reaction among the Flemings who resented French overlordship. Mary's husband, the Archduke Maximilian, later Emperor, came to her assistance and defeated the French at Guinegâte in 1479. Nevertheless Louis had the satisfaction of knowing that the Burgundian state had been cut up and that the French dominions had been greatly extended when he signed the Treaty of Arras with Maximilian (whose wife had just died) in 1482. The King gained the duchy of Burgundy and recovered Picardy and the Somme towns; Franche Comté and Artois were ceded to France as part of the dowry of Maximilian's daughter Margaret, who was to marry the Dauphin.[1] Meanwhile the extinction of the noble Angevin house enabled Louis to absorb Anjou and Maine together with the imperial county of Provence including Marseilles and Toulon into the royal domain. The little county of Roussillon was another addition won from Aragon. Louis' work was unfinished but at least it provided his successors with some useful signposts.

The gauche youth, Charles VIII, who succeeded him, made two significant moves. He repudiated the arrangements which had been made for his marriage to the young Archduchess Margaret and instead married Anne, Duchess of Brittany in her own right, who had previously been betrothed to the Emperor. At the cost of making an enemy of Maximilian, Charles had thus absorbed the semi-independent duchy into France. According to the terms of the marriage agreement when Charles died, his successor, Louis XII, married his widow—after repudiating his own wife.[2] This guaranteed a continued hold on Brittany. Duchess Anne regretted that her matrimonial ventures threatened to deprive the sturdy Bretons of their independence, but all her efforts to avoid this failed. In 1506 the States-General held that Brittany as well as Burgundy were inalienable from France, and the marriage of Anne's eldest daughter, Claude, to Louis' successor to the French throne, Francis I, clinched the issue.

Meanwhile all these last three Kings had been involved in war in Italy. Charles VIII was drawn originally to Italy by a desire for military glory which in a sense has dogged and doomed French history, and by an imaginative if wild-cat scheme for using Italy

---

[1] She eventually married Ferdinand of Aragon's heir, John. See p. 67.
[2] The reasons were somewhat thin; they included the charge that she was excessively ugly. Queen Jeanne has been recently canonised (1950).

as a jumping-off ground for regaining the Holy Land from the Turks.[1] To gain security for this venture he gave up much that Louis had won; Ferdinand recovered Roussillon and Maximilian justly regained Artois and the Franche Comté. The neutrality of England was purchased by the Treaty of Etaples. Louis XII, more practical than his predecessor, was soon entangled in a series of similar schemes (bereft, however, of their imaginative quality), which in his turn he bequeathed to Francis I. By this time, indeed, the situation had somewhat changed since what was now at issue was no longer mere military success in Italy but the necessity for bringing Imperial and Spanish pretensions in Italy to nothing. Although Italy was the main theatre of what was now the Hapsburg-Valois conflict, the Netherlands frontiers, the Rhineland and the Pyrenees were also involved. Such campaigns proved costly and mainly futile but in the long run helped to bring the Hapsburg hegemony in Europe to an end.

Thus French foreign policy depended ultimately on power-politics, on the need for extending and safeguarding the royal authority and for preventing any one power or group of powers from dominating Europe.

[1] It should also be mentioned that Ludovico Sforza of Milan, urged on by the French barons, had invited Charles VIII to Italy to save his (and their) own interests.

Italics labels on the map (upper):

English Miles
0 20 50 100 150

10   9

14   8   9
13   7   6
12
15   11

Lucca   5
Florence
Pisa   4
Siena
3   2
Spoleto
Orvieto
Viterbo   Chieti

CORSICA
(to Genoa)

Rome

Cerignola   Apulia

R. Gorigliano   Naples   1
La Cava

SARDINIA
(Spanish)

Palermo   Seminara

SICILY
(Spanish)

Romagna
Sinigaglia
Dalmatia

Labels on the map (lower):

Chiavenna
R. Adda   Tyrol
Valtellina   Trent

M   Feltre   E
I   R. Piave
L   V   E   N   Treviso
A   Brescia   I   C
PIEDMONT   Novara   N   Vicenza   E
Mt. Cenis   Milan   Verona   Padua   Venice
Turin   Marignano   R. Adige
Mt.   Pinerolo   Landriano   Agnadello
Genèvre   Pavia   Cremona
Casale   R. Po   Mantua
Asti   Piacenza
Saluzzo   MONTFERRAT   M   A   N
Saluzzo   Fornovo   Parma   Mirandola   R
Col d'   Reggio   F   A
Argentière   GENOA   E   R
Nice   Savona   Genoa   R   Ravenna
Villafranca   Bologna   A   Faenza
Nice   Lucca   PAPAL   Rimini
English Miles   Florence   STATES
0 10 20 40 60 80   Pisa   Sinigaglia

R.C.

MAP II.—Italy in the sixteenth century.

CHAPTER VI

THE ITALIAN WARS, 1494-1516

1. *The origin of the Wars*

THE tedious story of the Italian Wars is important because nothing
else so well represents the power-politics which governed the history
of the first half of the sixteenth century. To seek for clues in this
tangled haystack proves most unrewarding, but certain basic factors
are worthy of record. The condition of Italy at the end of the fifteenth century invited war. The country was merely what Metter-
nich called it three centuries later ' a geographical expression '. In
the south there were the two kingdoms of Naples and Sicily. Once
the scene of an interesting mixed culture, Sicily had been ruled by
the Aragonese royal family since the beginning of the fifteenth
century. On the other hand, Naples had been governed since
1458 by an illegitimate branch of the same royal house whose claims
were bitterly disliked by the legitimate line. The Papacy, the focal-
point of all Italian politics, had tended to become more and more
one Italian state among many, desirous above all of territorial expansion; the head of an international institution, enriched by many
contacts with the non-Italian world, spent the greater part of his
time in petty and disastrous quarrels and in fulfilling worldly ambitions. It may be pointed out in extenuation of the militant secular
policy pursued by the Renaissance popes, that they could only
bring order and security to a city often disturbed by feudal elements
by a policy that was both forthright and severe. The power of the
old Roman nobility steadily waned as the bourgeois families, Branca,
Altieri and Tedallini, took a more active part in the administration
of Rome. The Borgia Pope, Alexander VI, and his successors were
striving to create a strong temporal power; judged by this objective

---

Key to Map Opposite

1. Kingdom of Naples.
2. Papal States.
3. Republic of Siena.
4. Republic of Florence.
5. Republic of Lucca.
6. Duchy of Ferrara.
7. Principality of Mirandola.
8. Marquisate of Mantua.
9. Republic of Venice.
10. Duchy of Milan.
11. Republic of Genoa.
12. Marquisate of Montferrat.
13. County of Asti.
14. Duchy of Savoy.
15. Marquisate of Saluzzo.

their activities appear explicable and to some extent remarkably successful. North of the extensive papal states there were a number of duchies and republics, none of them politically stable. Florence, ruled by the Medici, the home of banking and the woollen industry, had long been riddled by political strife; opposition to the reigning duke, Piero, was stimulated by the virulent preaching of the Dominican prior of San Marco, Girolamo Savonarola. Pisa, now under the rule of Florence but once proudly independent, only wanted an opportunity to free itself from the control of the inland city on the Arno. The duchy of Milan was equally disturbed. It was ruled by the Sforzas, originally established in power in 1450 by a *condottiere*, Francesco, who displaced the Visconti family which had previously governed the city. At a later date Louis XII of France claimed the duchy on the grounds that he was the grandson of Valentina, the sister of the last Visconti duke. West of Milan were the rich naval republic of Genoa and the influential but as yet unimportant duchy of Savoy whose domains touched the Swiss cantons and France. Last but second only in importance to the Papacy, there was Venice, the great maritime republic ruled by the Doge and the Council of Ten, enriched by trade, beautified by art and extended in territory through conquest, a city of which the remaining Italian states were acutely jealous. Such a country invited invasion, for there was no sign of unity or true patriotism throughout its whole length and breadth. Occasional writers like Machiavelli might yearn for a strong Italian prince to drive away the ' barbarous dominion ' but there were few who took such things seriously and fewer still who thought that they were practical.

Political disunity was not the only precondition of war. The Italians, a civilised people, sensibly disliked the barbarities of war and preferred to employ professional mercenaries to fight for them, but it was one thing for mercenaries to fight each other, and quite another for them to engage a strongly-armed foreign invader. Foreign invaders found themselves opposed less by native Italians than by other semi-alien armies like the Spaniards or by the redoubtable Swiss mercenaries. Italy was therefore a comparatively defenceless land.

Besides this, the country was one of the richest in Europe, one of the most rewarding to loot as well as one of the easiest on which to park an army. Furthermore, it was the geographical crossroads of the conflicting powers. Aragon and Europe were linked by Sardinia and the north Italian passes. The historic valley of the Valtelline formed a passage leading from northern to southern Europe. The French found it much easier to approach the Alps from the west than the Savoyards did to approach France from the east. The passes of the Mont Cenis, Mont Genèvre and Col d'Argentière were practicable. The valleys of the Durance and the Isère offered no real barrier to an invading army. Similarly the Brenner pass gave the Imperial armies an easy, low-altitude approach from the Danube by the valleys of the Inn and the Adige.

But these were the conditions of war rather than its causes. The real causes of the wars, incidentally finding their outward expression in various claims not worth the manuscript on which they were made, are to be found in the materialistic and dynastic ambitions of the great powers. Charles VIII of France inherited a claim to the kingdom of Naples from the last Angevin claimant, René of Anjou, the possessor of many crowns and no kingdoms. He intended that Naples should be the starting-point for a crusade which would eventually rescue the Holy Land from the Turks; the words ' Voluntas Dei ; missus a Deo ' appeared strangely on his banners. But the French motives soon become more explicable. The French wished to prevent the Hapsburgs from so acquiring power and influence in Italy that the balance of power in Europe might turn in their favour. On every occasion when Hapsburg power reached a summit, especially after the Treaties of Madrid in 1526 and of Cambrai in 1529, the French renewed the war. While it is certain that they were also interested in winning new territory—and the claims on Milan and Naples were at least useful bargaining points—the French were mainly concerned with extending their sphere of influence in Italy. They regarded Italy as the most vulnerable part of Hapsburg power, more especially after 1519 as it formed the connective link between the Empire and Spain. For their part the Hapsburgs not only inherited the age-old claims of past Holy Roman Emperors, such as that of suzerainty over Milan, but also the effective power which the Spanish King, Ferdinand of Aragon, had created for himself in the south. Italy was in fact a part of the Holy Roman Empire, the possession of which was vital, or seemed so, to hegemony in Europe. Furthermore Italy contained the Papacy. In an age when the Pope's views on doctrine and politics could sway a nation's life, whoever had power in or near Rome came near to possessing the keys of the kingdom. The French, the Imperialists, the Spaniards, each in turn, tried to acquire control over what may not improperly be called the heart of the matter. This flourishing, civilised, if, as Machiavelli rightly insisted, politically corrupt people thus became the prey of foreign armies and mercenaries who fought out a battle irrespective of Italian interests.

2. *The course of the Wars, 1494-1516*

The Italian poet Ariosto came near to summarising the whole topic when he wrote in *Orlando Furioso :* ' All who hold the sceptre of France shall see their armies destroyed either by the sword or by famine or by pestilence. They will bring back from Italy short-lived rejoicing and enduring grief, small profit and infinite loss, for the lilies may not strike root in that soil.' [1] Every victory proved illusory and was followed by a change of fortune worthy of a Greek tragedian. The Italian Wars are in fact only historically significant because the fight for the balance of power in Europe can be discerned beneath the intricate formation of alliance and counter-alliance.

Charles VIII, whom the Florentine historian Guicciardini described as ' more like a monster than a man ', crossed into Italy in 1494 by the pass of Mont Genèvre and occupied both Pisa and Florence. His arrival coincided with the expulsion of the Medici duke, Piero, and it provided that ardent Puritanical friar, Savonarola, with a text which he ceaselessly impressed on his listeners with burning eloquence. The French, like the Assyrians of old, were the sword of the Lord, the divinely-imposed punishment of the city ; there followed a series of political experiments designed to create a Florentine theocracy, not a very propitious object as Savonarola later found out.[2] Meanwhile the French army, headed by the Swiss mercenaries marching to the sound of their wind instruments, entered Rome by torchlight and forced the worried Borgia, Alexander VI, to comply with its demands. The victorious campaign closed with the occupation of Naples in February, 1495. It is here that, as a prototype for all the other Italian wars, Charles began to lose grip and to become immersed in the fatal maelstrom of Italian politics. His victories, as well as the licentiousness and rapine of his troops, provoked a reaction as a result of which most of the Italian states, excepting Florence, aided by the Emperor and King Ferdinand both of whom wished to check French power, and blessed by the Pope, formed the League of Venice to drive the French from Italy. With long communications, Charles was bound to retreat and was only saved from disaster by a swift victory (the battle lasted only a quarter of an hour) over the Venetians at Fornovo in July, 1495. The French garrison left behind in Naples under

[1] Canto xxxiii, 10.
[2] Excommunicated by the Pope, he was eventually seized by his enemies and hanged (May, 1498). Previous to his seizure, he had agreed that the issue should be decided by ordeal of fire, but a bad thunderstorm prevented this.

D'Aubigny continued to hold out and even imposed a defeat on the Spanish general, de Cordova, at Seminara ; but without support from France and with disease undermining its health and morale, further resistance was useless. Thus the French had been defeated without being crushed ; they had witnessed ' the glory and helplessness of Italy ' and by coming within an ace of winning were encouraged to try again.

Charles' successor, Louis XII, once more decided to invade Italy to assert his claim to Milan, a demand indignantly repudiated by the subtle, usurping Sforza duke, Ludovico il Moro, and by the Emperor who held that Milan, as an Imperial fief, should have reverted to him. Meanwhile the weakly-constructed League of Venice collapsed under the pressure of the mutual rivalries, dislikes and deceits of the member states. Pope Alexander VI, wanting to create a duchy out of the Romagna for his son, Caesar Borgia, and to avenge himself against the King of Naples (who had refused to allow Caesar to marry his daughter), welcomed an understanding with Louis XII. The Venetians, angered by the way in which Ludovico Sforza had double-crossed them in 1495, also came to terms with the French at the price of Milanese territory in the form of Cremona and Chiara d'Adda. To make himself doubly secure Louis bought off the Emperor by restoring some towns in Artois to his son and heir, the Archduke Philip. It appeared as if nothing could save Ludovico from disaster. The French entered Milan in triumph on October 6th, 1499, but helped by Swiss mercenaries from the Grisons and the Valais, Ludovico was back in possession of his duchy by the following February. Such a reversal of fortune could not last. The Common League of the Swiss Cantons, which had never approved the employment of Swiss soldiers by Ludovico, agreed to help the French who won an astonishingly decisive victory at Novara in April, 1500.[1] Ludovico was caught as he tried to escape disguised as a Swiss mercenary and spent the remainder of his life at the French castle of Loches where a sundial incised by him on the wall of his prison-chamber measured the slow passage of his days till his death in 1508. His claims to Milan passed to the Imperial house and his territories fell into the hands of his enemies.

Encouraged by the relative ease with which he had regained Milan Louis decided to follow the example of his cousin, Charles, and establish his claim to Naples. He had a wily if as yet a secret antagonist in Ferdinand who wished to add Naples to his Sicilian

[1] Both Ludovico and Louis had an almost equal number of Swiss mercenaries, but Ludovico's Swiss refused to fight against Louis' Swiss, thus leading to the French victory.

kingdom. In November 1500 the two would-be aggressors, temporarily united by greed, decided, by the Treaty of Granada, to divide the Neapolitan kingdom between themselves, justifying their immoral bargain on the specious grounds that Federigo, the King of Naples, was intriguing with the Turks. By the end of March 1502, all resistance was at an end but the terms of the Treaty were so deliberately vague that Ferdinand easily provoked a quarrel, leading to the French defeat on the river Garigliano, and their withdrawal.[1]

Before many years had passed a new combination of predatory powers was formed. The League of Cambrai, arranged in 1508, had its motive force in Pope Julius II's hatred of Venice; his main objective was to 'constrain Venice to make the concessions he demanded, yet to prevent the predominance of any single foreign power by uniting all in a common action'. With singular skill, Julius II guided the Emperor, the Kings of Spain, France and Hungary, together with some of the Italian princes, to form this treacherous league, confirmed with due religious ceremonial in the cathedral of Cambrai in mid-winter, 1508. The Pope could argue that whatever happened, the temporal interests of the Papacy would suffer no harm. If the Venetians were defeated, he would be able to round off the Romagna through the acquisition of Ravenna, Rimini and Faenza. If the allies fell out among themselves, this too would strengthen the papal power in Italy. The Venetians were decisively defeated at Agnadello on May 14th, 1509, but the backwash of the victory was not quite what the Pope had expected. It swept the French back into power again at Milan (Julius had hoped that he could play off the French against Ferdinand in Naples) and this disturbance of the balance of power in Italy in France's favour so affected the Pope that he concluded a treaty with the Venetians and absolved them from the penalties of excommunication.

This was the first step in the formation of a new anti-French league. An attempt to defeat Louis' ally, the Duke of Ferrara, and

[1] The Treaties of Blois, signed in 1504 and 1505, provide a postscript to this miserable story. The Emperor Maximilian, supported by his son Philip, wanted to curb Spanish power by arranging a marriage between Louis' daughter, Claude (aged five) and Philip's son Charles (aged four), with Milan, Genoa, Brittany and Blois as Claude's dowry. (1st Treaty of Blois). But circumstances changed. The death of Isabella in November, 1504, made Philip king-consort of Castile. Ferdinand had therefore to win Louis from his understanding with the Hapsburg. The second Treaty of Blois (1505) provided Louis with a substantial money payment in return for the cession of his claims to Naples.

to drive the French from Milan having failed, Julius realised that more allies were needed if his plans were to materialise successfully. In October, 1511, he formed the ironically entitled Holy League between Venice and Ferdinand of Spain, later joined by Henry VIII of England and the Emperor Maximilian. Meanwhile, in 1510, on the advice of the bitterly anti-French Bishop Schinner of Sion, now much in attendance upon Pope Julius, a five years alliance had been signed with the Swiss, by which they agreed to protect the Pope and to lend him a force of 6000 men in return for the payment of an annual subsidy. At last it appeared as if the disgraceful compacts of Granada and Cambrai were to be brought home to one of the signatories. Although the French general, Gaston de Foix, won a magnificent victory over the forces of the League at Ravenna on April 11th, 1512, his death in battle and the reappearance of the Swiss mercenaries on the scene brought about a French withdrawal from everywhere, except the fortress of Milan. Raphael's fresco depicting the expulsion of the heathen commander Heliodorus from the Temple at Jerusalem symbolised the papal achievement, for Julius II is there witnessing the miracle by which the angelic hosts drive the heathen king, no less than Louis XII, from the sacred precincts of the Temple. The victorious powers then proceeded to a distribution of the spoils. To the Emperor's obvious disgust Milan was restored to a scion of the Sforza house, Maximilian Sforza, who rewarded the Swiss with important concessions which gave them a firmer control over the strategic Alpine passes. At the same time the Spanish army brought back the Medici to Florence.

Julius II, the creator of the Holy League, was probably the most able of the worldly Renaissance popes. Had he applied his talents to purely spiritual matters, he might have been a second Hildebrand. But, to adapt Dante's words, it was he ' che fece il gran rifiuto ' by making the expansion of his temporal power his principal objective. Some would see in him an elementary Italian patriotism, but his dislike of foreign intervention was purely selfish. In some ways he was splendidly successful, for he had driven the French out of Milan, persuaded the Emperor to accept his plans for Florence and Milan, had consolidated papal control over the Romagna, had subordinated the Venetians and had remained friendly with the Spaniards. Rome he helped to glorify, culture he patronised but the teaching of Christ he disregarded. The face which peers at us from Raphael's masterly portrait lacks fire but is calculating, shrewd and determined.

At his death the tedious tale of the Hapsburg-Valois struggle began again. Allied to Venice Louis XII invaded Italy in the hope that he might recover Milan before his enemies, Henry VIII, the Emperor, the new Pope Leo X and Ferdinand of Spain (bound together by the Treaty of Mechlin) could effectually carry out their plan for the invasion and dismemberment of France. Within three weeks La Trémouille and Trivulzio swept through Milan and Genoa but disaster stood in the wings. The Swiss mercenaries imposed a shattering defeat on the French outside Novara in the early summer of 1513. ' Never ', says Guicciardini, ' did the Swiss nation make a finer and bolder resolve ; a few against many, without horsemen or field-pieces to attack an army so admirably provided with both of these. . . . The conquerors returned to Novara in triumph, having acquired such renown throughout the whole world that many have ventured, considering the courage of the advance guard, the visible contempt of death, the boldness of the struggle and the luck, to reckon this deed of arms more highly than most of the memorable actions recorded of the Greeks and the Romans.' It might well have been supposed that this calamity, followed by English and Imperial invasions of France itself, would suffice to bring Louis XII to his knees.

But the nature of the victory proved the French King's greatest strength. Inevitably the victors disagreed among themselves, thus enabling Louis to negotiate separate treaties of peace. On Louis' death in 1515, his successor, Francis I, young, ambitious and eager for knighthood, reasserted the French claim to Milan. Crossing the Alps by a hitherto untried route, from Embrun over the Col d'Argentière, his army pushed aside the Milanese at Villafranca on August 15th, 1515, and less than a month later (September 13th) decisively defeated the Swiss, under the lead of Schinner, resplendent in his red cardinal's robes, in a fierce and bloody two-day battle at Marignano. The news of the victory resounded throughout Europe. It enabled Francis to negotiate the exceptionally favourable Concordat of Bologna with the Pope.[1] The Swiss agreed not to support the enemies of France in return for a money payment by the ' Perpetual Peace ' signed at Fribourg in the following November. Henceforward the Swiss played a relatively small part in the Italian Wars. The French victory was followed by an inevitable reaction which led to a regrouping of the powers hostile to France. In spite of this the Treaty of Noyon in 1516 reflected Francis' achievement. The new King of Spain, Charles, with whom the treaty was negotiated, agreed to recognise the French rule in Milan. The French King's infant daughter, Louise, was betrothed to Charles, with a promised dowry in the shape of Naples (already, of course, in

[1] See pp. 83-4.

Spanish hands). It might seem as if the dynastic rivalries which had been splitting Europe for thirty years were about to end. But these efforts to bury the hatchet proved fruitless. What might have seemed the fortunate closing scene was really only another act in the long and tedious drama of the Italian Wars.

The next forty years witnessed continuous intrigue and sporadic fighting, which served no Italian interests. The detail of the later Hapsburg-Valois fight appears elsewhere; [1] the scheme, the decisive victory, the automatic reaction, the formation of a new league to defeat the victor, the renewal of the war, the grim realism of the political ambitions and the unrealistic nature of the policy which prompted them remained much the same. As far as the Italians were concerned these wars helped to preserve their disunity without crippling either their trade or their culture; the armies were too small to do much more than lay waste selected localities. If Italian wealth declined, this was a result of the changing economy of Europe, the shifting of the trade routes from the Mediterranean area, not an effect of war. It is possible that the coming and going of campaigning armies may have helped to carry the Renaissance beyond the Alps but far more was done by the printing-press and by ordinary travellers. It was only in the actual art of warfare that the Italian Wars were socially or intellectually significant. Thus in winning the battle on the Garigliano the Spanish general, Gonzalvo de Cordova, showed the superiority of arquebus fire to the use of cavalry and pikemen. Again Marignano proved that the Swiss infantry were powerless against an intelligent combination of infantry, cavalry and artillery. Apart from this, the wars mainly served to make Italy the graveyard of Imperial ambitions and the leech of French manhood.

[1] See p. 151 sqq.

CHAPTER VII

THE EMPEROR MAXIMILIAN AND IMPERIAL REFORM,
1493-1519

1. *Imperial reform*

THE Holy Roman Empire and the Papacy were the two supreme institutions of the Middle Ages. In an age of change like the sixteenth century their continuance mainly depended on their ability to adjust themselves to the needs and ideas of the new period of history. At one time it had seemed as if the very worldliness of the Papacy, its concern with temporal power, might prove its undoing, but by the end of the century it had been able to adapt itself to the needs of the new world, mainly through the movement which we call the Counter-Reformation. In any case the Papacy had two immense advantages that the Empire lacked ; a permanent secretariat and a world-wide organisation which carried on in spite of a weak or secular-minded Pope, in addition to its claim on the devotion and loyalty of millions of Christians which went back to the days of the Roman Empire.

The position of the Holy Roman Empire was very different. Although the Emperor claimed to be the heir of Caesar (hence the title Roman), the Empire was in fact a younger and weaker institution than the Papacy.[1] Enfeebled by its long struggle with the Popes, its hold over its lieges, being feudal rather than spiritual, had always been less than that of its rival. Moreover the Empire itself was an astonishing mosaic, consisting of no less than three hundred semi-autonomous states, free cities, prince-bishoprics, countships and an increasing number of really powerful princes such as the Elector of Brandenburg, the Duke of Bavaria, the Elector of Saxony and the Elector Palatine. Even when there was a strong Emperor it was virtually impossible to exert an effective control over this strange conglomeration of differing authorities. The Hapsburg Emperor, Frederick III, who was the nominal head of this institution for fifty-three years, in any case preferred alchemy and astrology to the more realistic task of government.

Furthermore the actual constitution of the Empire was hopelessly inefficient. The Imperial Diet or Reichstag, which was the

[1] It is in practice impossible to speak of a continuous Holy Roman Empire from the days of Charlemagne (*d.* 814). The Holy Roman Empire from the fifteenth century onwards was essentially a Hapsburg creation.

official council of the empire, was a cumbrous and costly body, about whose exact procedure there was much uncertainty. Technically the Diet consisted only of the Emperor's tenants-in-chief but as there seemed no effective method of putting any resolutions that it might pass into practice, the Emperor relied more and more on combinations of groups within it. The Diet was supposed to consist of three Estates, the first including the seven Electors, the second the princes, and the third (after 1489) the Imperial Cities. Of these the first Estate was obviously the most important, since the Electors under the Golden Bull of 1356 were responsible for electing each successive Emperor. The Electoral College or *Kurfursstentag* consisted of the three Elector-Archbishops of Mainz, Trier and Cologne, each a secular as well as a spiritual potentate; the Count-Palatine of the Rhine; the Duke of Saxony; and the Elector of Brandenburg, together with the King of Bohemia who as a foreigner took no part in its ordinary proceedings.[1] It was among the greater German princes rather than in the Empire itself that the idea of creating for themselves strong absolute states, so much to the fore in England, France and Spain, took root. Apart from the Diet, which proved quite unable to supply the Emperor with a sufficient revenue or an effective executive force, there were a number of leagues of cities, towns, knights and princes, none more important than the Swabian League founded in 1488. Thus the general picture was singularly confused; even at the end of the fifteenth century the Empire, in spite of its great prestige, seemed an archaic institution unlikely to be able to adjust itself to the new age of national monarchies.

Indeed Germany was in a transitional state. The feudal lord had not yet become a modern prince; many a court was barbarous and crude. The absence of ordered government hindered trade and travel; sporadic attempts to enforce the Public Peace, no longer an Imperial responsibility, proved worse than useless. Yet there were signs of change. There was a current of rather artificial national feeling among the Renaissance scholars whom the Imperial dreamer, Maximilian, liked to patronise. Moreover there were signs of significant economic expansion, arising in part from the development of the south German mines and from the commercial and financial prosperity of many German towns. Here at least at

[1] After the death of Louis II of Hungary and Bohemia fighting the Turks at Mohacs in 1526, the elective crown of both states fell to the Emperor's brother, Ferdinand (who had married Anne, the daughter of King Ladislas of Hungary and Bohemia (*d.* 1516) whose successor, Louis II, married Maximilian's granddaughter, Mary). Thus Bohemia became a Hapsburg possession.

Augsburg and Frankfort among other cities there were already men amassing fortunes, which were to prove the mainstay of Imperial power in the coming century.

It may even be true that this economic revolution was the most important event taking place in Germany at this time. Expressed by a rise in prices, which had already started before silver and gold entered Europe from the New World, this economic change caused social trouble both in the towns and in the countryside where the feudal exactions increased rather than diminished in the first half of the sixteenth century. Such social agitation rather than religious trouble helped to cause the Peasants' Revolt in 1525 as well as the Anabaptist Rising at Münster ten years later.[1] At the same time, rising prices, the process being accelerated by the disturbing effects of the import of American treasure, caused a reduction in both Imperial and princely incomes. But where the princes were able to meet the situation by imposing fresh fiscal burdens on their subjects, the Emperor was never to find a solution.

The poverty and impotence of the Emperor in part explain why the more intelligent Germans supported a movement for the reform of the out-moded Imperial Constitution. Its leader was one of the ecclesiastical electors, Berthold of Henneberg, Elector Archbishop of Mainz since 1484. How far Berthold was the patriotic idealist that some historians have made him out to be may be doubted, but he was a singularly skilful and far-sighted statesman who believed that to be good, government must also be efficient and effective. His advice proved so persuasive that of all the leading princes only the Duke of Bavaria failed to support him. His demands, first formulated before the Diet of Frankfort in 1485, included the institution of a single system of currency for all Germany, the imposition of a *Landfriede* or Public Peace and the establishment of a Supreme Court of Justice to try offenders who were too powerful to be dealt with in the ordinary courts. Although Frederick III made some promises in return for a money-grant to carry on war against the Turks, they were never fulfilled. Berthold and the Estates must needs try again.

The accession of Maximilian [2] altered the situation. Whether that volatile prince, whose face peers at us so familiarly from Dürer's

---

[1] See pp. 141-3.

[2] 'The most delightfully unprincipled hero of the age of transition, always in every feast and every fray, always wanting money and selling himself for promises, and never getting the money and never keeping his engagements ; a good deal of the rake and a good deal of the knight-errant.' (Bishop Stubbs, *Lectures on European History*, 337.)

drawings, ever took the project of reform seriously may be questioned, but his financial requirements, more especially for his improvident military ventures, at least made him appear more willing than his father had been. Soon after his accession Berthold's party took heart. The Emperor was not indeed the man to give way without hard bargaining. If Berthold wanted to set up a Council of Regency (*Reichsregiment*) which should formulate Imperial policy, thus checking the Emperor's power, and see that the Public Peace was enforced, then the Emperor could at least demand military reforms which would lead to the formation of a large permanent army, and fiscal changes which would free him from the grinding poverty which haunted him in spite of his great estates. The reformers naturally feared that if Maximilian gained his ends, he would be strong enough to disregard the other provisions, which was almost certainly what he intended to do. They were therefore particularly desirous that the army and the treasury should be kept under their control.

The Diet of Worms, which met in 1495, went some way to meet the demands of both parties. The reformers wanted results; Maximilian, involved in Italy, wanted money. A Supreme Court of Justice (*Reichskammergericht*) was instituted. Perpetual Peace was decreed; all private armies were to be disbanded. Even the Emperor's most cherished hope seemed about to materialise when the Diet accepted the idea of a universal tax for the whole Empire, the Common Penny. But when all seemed to be going well, the Emperor hedged. He would not accept the proposals for the Council of Regency which, he rightly argued, was bound to limit his power, for the Emperor was only to nominate three of its twenty intended members. Seeing that the Emperor was adamant, the reformers contented themselves with his acceptance of a plan entailing the calling of an annual Diet, without whose consent the Emperor promised to make no important decision.

The decisions of the Diet of Worms proved too much of a compromise to afford any chance of real success, but this was not the real reason for their failure. The idea of the Common Penny proved universally unpopular; the clergy, with whom the collection rested, found the very greatest difficulty in collecting even a minimum of the assessed amount. Nor was there yet any effective administrative machinery for seeing that the decisions either of the Diet or of the Supreme Court were put into practice. As for Maximilian he merely stood aside and watched the reforms evaporate; he had not got his money nor the means of collecting it. He had no enthusiasm for any of the other reforms. Furthermore, the attempt to impose the Common Penny was greeted with fury by the Swiss who saw in it a threat to their much-cherished autonomy. As a Swiss historian has phrased it : ' So far as the relation of Switzerland to the Empire was concerned, their effect [of the decisions taken at Worms] was similar to that of the Stamp Act and the Boston Harbour Bill upon the relation of the North American colonies to the motherland.' [1] ' They want to give us a master ', was the cry of every canton, ' the Swiss must have a master, the bull of Uri must bow his neck beneath the yoke, the bears of Berne are to be hunted.' Burgher and peasant took up arms ; victory after victory attended their efforts, at Triesen and Hard, at Brüderholz and Triboldingen, at Frastenz and Dorneck. Maximilian bowed to the inevitable and in practice recognised the independence of Switzerland by the Treaty of Basle on September 22nd, 1499.[2] Meanwhile the Emperor's continued pressing need of money and more especially his anger at the French conquest of Milan made him turn again to the Estates. Only three years ago he had sworn : ' I have been betrayed by the Lombards. I have been abandoned by the Germans. But I will not again suffer myself to be bound hand and foot as at Worms ', but circumstances obliged him to reconsider his policy.

The Diet which met at Augsburg in 1500 hammered out what might have seemed another effective compromise. Instead of the detestable Common Penny the Estates agreed to supply the Emperor with a paid Imperial army 34,000 strong. Instead of the unwieldy annual Diet he consented to Berthold's pet remedy, the Council of Regency. This was to consist of twenty members, with the Emperor as President, representing all the leading Estates of the Empire. For administrative convenience the Empire, excepting the important Hapsburg territories, was to be divided into six circles, responsible for appointing six of the Council of Regency, for the Public Peace and for putting the decrees of the Supreme Court into practice.

Had the decisions of Augsburg come into effect, they would have sabotaged Imperial power and have turned the Empire into an oligarchy. The Council began its work by trying to settle the difficulties with France where Maximilian had so far failed to achieve a settlement. But fundamentally the conditions for constitutional experiments of this kind were unfavourable. With the death of Archbishop Berthold in 1504, no one of ability was left to head the reforming party ; the irresolute electors were quite unable to cope with the broken promises and subtle manœuvrings of the Emperor. Deprived of popular and princely support the Council of Regency

---

[1] William Oechsli, *History of Switzerland*, 8.

[2] Theoretical independence was not recognised until the Treaty of Westphalia in 1648.

collapsed and with it the Reform movement as a whole. New proposals made by Maximilian in 1505 proved fruitless. In 1507 Germany was divided into ten circles for administrative purposes but this only encouraged the individualism of the princes. What had once seemed so fair had degenerated into the selfish tactics of individuals or groups of princes seeking to extend their own power, irrespective of national or popular interests.

The Emperor Maximilian had killed the reform movement. Yet his reign had not been without its positive side. Dilettante as he was, Maximilian was perhaps more shrewd than historians have supposed. He placed his main reliance on strengthening the Hapsburg dominions and was so successful in this that, in the view of one historian, ' he established the administrative organisation which up to 1918 held together the various regions and races of which the Hapsburg monarchy was composed '.

Abroad he was far less successful, although his Burgundian inheritance and the dynastic marriages he arranged were to have the very greatest influence over future European history. His marriage to Mary, the daughter of the last Burgundian duke, led to the important addition of the sixteen provinces, including future Holland and Belgium, to his empire. From the Burgundians he inherited a mistrust of France which, together with a divergence of interests elsewhere, prepared the way for the long rivalry of Hapsburg and Valois. When he was Archduke he tried to circumvent the plans of the young French king, Charles VIII, by marrying Anne of Brittany as his second wife but in vain. The search for allies and a wife continued, leading in 1493 to Maximilian's marriage with Bianca Sforza, a union which gave him a powerful handle when Charles entered Italy in 1494. In 1495 and later in 1513 it was Maximilian who headed the league of princes against France. But even in foreign policy he was rarely consistent; between 1504 and 1512 he found it to his interests to recognise French power in Italy.

If the Hapsburg-Valois conflict originated in Maximilian's reign, so in a sense did the future extent and greatness of the Hapsburg family. His son and heir, the cherished but selfish Philip the Fair, was married to the daughter of Ferdinand and Isabella, Joanna. From this unfortunate union the Hapsburgs of Austria and Spain both sprang, and for that matter so did much of future history.

What had Maximilian achieved? Superficially, it might seem little. Even in Italy he had been obliged at the last (1516) to admit that the French were victors in Milan as in French Burgundy. He had been forced to recognise the independence of the Swiss and the virtual exemption of the members of the Swabian League from Imperial taxation. His son predeceased him by thirteen years, and it was to his Flemish grandson Charles that he must leave his Hapsburg estates. Yet he had done much to shape the future destiny of the Empire. He had established the close connection between the personal estates of the Hapsburg family and Imperial power which formed the basis of Imperial history until the Empire ended in 1806. Finally it was in part a result of his policy that the Empire failed to come to terms with the new age and was to remain for ever a medieval ghost in modern guise. What his grandson, Charles V, hoped to do, his grandfather, the Emperor Maximilian I had already made impossible before death claimed him in 1519.

2. *The imperial election of* 1519

The election of the Emperor in 1519 raised wide interest. The past three Emperors had been members of the Hapsburg family but the hereditary principle was not so firmly established that the Electors might not break it. Maximilian had himself supposed that they would chose his grandson, Charles, and had tried to ensure this by the judicious distribution of bribes. But the Emperor's death in January, 1519, pushed everything back to its starting-point.

There were three candidates for the Imperial throne, the nine-teen-year old Charles, already Duke of Burgundy and King of Spain, the young and highly-reputed Francis I, King of France, and the young King of England, Henry VIII. No one in Germany knew very much about Charles, except that he had a rich and scattered inheritance. Both his riches and his weakness proved to be in his favour. Supported by the great Fugger banking-house of Augsburg, who refused to cash French bills of exchange, he could outbid his competitors; in all nearly a million gold gulden was spent,[1] the greater part in bribes to the electors and their satellites. In return the Fuggers received lands and privileges in Hapsburg territory, in Swabia, and the Tyrol. The Electors were also attracted by Charles' apparent weakness. If his revenues might suffice to support his Imperial claims, his non-German dominions would tend to free the German princes from Imperial interference. The last king of a Spanish house to sit on the Imperial throne,[2] had they remembered

[1] Ehrenburg reckoned : ' the total loan now rose to over 850,000 florins, of which the Fugger lent 543,000 florins, the Welser 143,000 florins, the Genoese and the Florentines together 165,000 florins. The merchants' acceptances were handed over by Charles' representative piecemeal in re-turn for the votes.' (*Capital and Finance in the Age of the Renaissance,* 77.)

[2] King Alfonso X of Castile, 1257-72.

it, had in practice been obliged to let the Empire go its own way. As for Francis, he was equally willing to disburse money to the Electors, but he could not call on loans as freely as Charles. It is also probable that his own boasting did him a disservice. In practice he would have found it essential to focus all his attention on his compact kingdom of France had he been elected, but at the time of the election he spoke glowingly of the wars which he would fight to defend the Empire against the Turk, of the roads which he would build, and of the law and order which he would bring to a country still notable for its lawlessness. But the German princes did not want roads or law and order; they wanted the maximum amount of freedom to go their own way. Little need be said of the third candidate, Henry VIII, whose claims were not taken seriously, although both the other candidates were keenly interested in the support which he was likely to give to either of them. Eventually he let it be known that he would prefer the election of Charles whereas the Pope, Leo X, unwisely gambled on Francis, a blunder which in itself weakened Francis' candidature as the German princes were wholly opposed to pressure from Rome.

The seven Electors were by no means hidebound in their views; they were quite shameless in their acceptance of money from both parties. Richard von Greiffenklau zu Vollraths, Archbishop of Trier, was too near the Hapsburg dominions in the Netherlands to be anything but pro-French. His colleague of Cologne, Hermann von Wied, could not make up his mind. The two Hohenzollerns, Albert, Archbishop of Mainz, and his brother, Joachim, the Elector of Brandenburg, at first favoured Francis. The Elector-Palatine, Ludwig, and the Elector of Saxony, Frederick, had both suffered from the Imperial policy of Maximilian and seemed unlikely to support his grandson's candidature. The King of Bohemia was a child of thirteen. With all these points in his favour, Francis mismanaged the situation, partly because he could not distribute bribes as freely as Charles. Both the Pope and the French King tried to bring pressure to bear on the one comparatively honest man among the Electors, Frederick the Wise of Saxony; the papal agent von Miltitz suggested that if the election of the French King was impossible, Frederick should stand for the Imperial throne himself. Refusing to do this, he stood steadfast for Charles, a decision in which all the other Electors concurred, only Elector Joachim of Brandenburg later declaring that he had voted ' out of very fear and not out of very knowledge '. The election took place on June 28th, 1519, at Frankfort; the twenty-two trumpets of the Elector-Palatine and the Elector of Brandenburg announced to the world that the Holy Roman Empire had a head. The coronation took place over a year later, on October 23rd, in the cathedral of Aix-la-Chapelle. Charles took the oath, was acclaimed by the people, ' anointed, clothed in the tunic of Charlemagne, girt with the great Emperor's sword, crowned with his golden crown, and then with ring on finger, and ball and sceptre in hand, he was led to the stone seat of Empire '.[1] ' Sire ', wrote his Chancellor Gattinara three weeks after the election, ' God has been very merciful to you : he has raised you above all the kings and princes of Christendom to a power such as no sovereign has enjoyed since your ancestor Charles the Great. He has set you on the way towards a world monarchy, towards the uniting of all Christendom under a single shepherd.'

[1] Edward Armstrong, *Charles V*, I, 67. Charlemagne or Charles the Great had been the first of the Holy Roman Emperors, crowned at Rome on Christmas Day, 800.

CHAPTER VIII

THE REFORMATION AND MARTIN LUTHER

1. *The origins of the Reformation*

THE Reformation occurred in the second and third decades of the sixteenth century because a certain set of circumstances created a situation which made its outbreak both possible and probable. Many of the factors which gave rise to the Reformation were not new nor was there any one cause which brought it into being. It was the particular correlation of events which produced a situation in which the teaching of the reformers met with an active response. But the reformers did not cause the Reformation; they were the instruments through which it was expressed. They were interpreting an obscurely-felt need in convincing popular terms. If there had been no necessity for their teaching, they would certainly have elicited a much less striking response. But the impact of men like Luther, Calvin and Zwingli cannot be properly measured; their particular cast of mind, profound emotions and established ideas all helped the Reformation as a movement to take the path it did, and to shatter the unity of Christendom. At the same time the reformers were responding to a widespread discontent with contemporary religion.

This dissatisfaction with the existing state of the Church had two aspects, firstly discontent with the Church as an institution and secondly a desire to return to a more satisfying personal religion, based more closely on the Gospel story than was that of the contemporary Church. Throughout the Middle Ages good churchmen had ventilated complaints about abuses and corruption. No one criticised the Church of his day more fiercely than did Erasmus but he died a Catholic. Dissatisfaction was in time to evoke the religious revival within the Roman Church which we call the Counter-Reformation. Similarly the desire to return to a simpler form of religion, in which there was less dependence on the mediatory powers of the priest and greater emphasis on the personal religion of the individual, had been a constant factor throughout Church history.[1] If, however, these two underlying issues had been present in the Middle Ages, the situation at the end of the fifteenth and the

---

[1] Such is the theme of the two splendid volumes of Ernst Troeltsch, *The Social Teaching of the Christian Church.*

beginning of the sixteenth century was definitely propitious for a religious revolution.

What in fact made the situation in 1500 so different, say, from what it had been in 1400 and 1200 ? It is impossible to escape the conclusion that the Church was more corrupt, especially in respect of its higher officials, at that time than at any period of history since the tenth century (when circumstances being different there was no question of a Protestant Reformation, though there was Hildebrandine reform). It may be true that neither the nepotist Sixtus IV, the libertine Alexander VI, nor the soldier Julius II, were quite as bad as they have been made out to be by certain historians, but no one can deny that Sixtus IV showered benefices and offices on his family, [1] that Alexander VI had a mistress, Rosa Vanozza, and children whose careers he forwarded unscrupulously, or that Julius II was more interested in the expansion of the papal dominions than in the reform of the Church or that Leo X was at heart a charming, cultured but secular-minded gentleman. And none of these things should have characterised the *servus servorum*, the successor of St. Peter. The Pope had made himself into an Italian prince, much more concerned with the expansion of the temporal power of the Papacy than with the interests of the universal Church. ' Papal history ', wrote the American historian H. C. Lea, ' after the Holy See had vindicated its supremacy over General Councils, becomes purely a political history of diplomatic intrigues, of alliances made and broken, of military enterprises. . . . No one could conclude that the Papacy represented interests higher than those of any other petty Italian Prince, save when—in a papal letter—an unctuous expression is used to shroud some peculiarly objectionable design.' To the fulfilment of such a policy as this the Popes devoted great ability— for these men were often intelligent and shrewd—and much money which they had amassed from the faithful throughout Europe. The pilgrim visiting Rome could not fail to be dismayed by the lack of spirituality, impressed as he might be by the magnificence of the papal court.

This rot had spread throughout the Church. Impartial evidence, much of it culled from episcopal visitations, is appallingly plentiful, as to simony, nepotism, plurality,[2] non-residence, immorality and

---

[1] Thus Sixtus was almost certainly aware of the plot engineered by his nephew Girolamo Riario in 1478 which resulted in the murder of Guiliano de' Medici and the wounding of his brother while at Mass. The Pope's support of the whole iniquitous business reveals the depth to which such nepotism could sink.

[2] There are innumerable illustrations, but note the following account (*Cambridge Modern History*, I, 659): ' Rodrigo Borgia (subsequently

neglect of duty. Although council after council had attacked these faults they were widespread throughout the fifteenth-century Church. The Conclave of the Sacred College of Cardinals which elected the Pope was as open to bribes as the Electoral College of the Empire. Moreover the unwillingness of the authorities to do anything to arrest the decay was another indication of how low the Curia had fallen. With the exception of some Spanish and English bishops, the European episcopate was gravely at fault. One small country provides an illustration the like of which could be found throughout Europe. There were six dioceses in Switzerland : Sion, Lausanne, Geneva, Constance, Chur and Basle. Cardinal Matthias Schinner, Bishop of Sion, an extremely able man who was nearly elected pope in 1521, was a statesman and warrior who delighted to lead the Swiss mercenaries into battle ; political feuds had, however, made it impossible for him to live in his diocese in the Valais.[1] The Bishop of Geneva, John of Savoy, was a bastard of the ducal house placed in the see to serve his family's interests. The Bishop of Lausanne, Aymo of Montfaucon, was a servile tool of the French. Paul Ziegler, Bishop of Chur, 'chose his mistresses from the nunneries of his diocese' while his colleague of Constance, Hugo of Hohenlandenberg, 'derived a rich income from the concubinage practised by his priests, raising the penalty payable for every priest's child from four gulden to five'. Alone among the Swiss bishops, Christopher von Uttenheim, the Bishop of Basle, was genuinely trying to repair the abuses which rent church life in his diocese.[2]

Cardinal) in his youth . . . accumulated benefices to the aggregate of 70,000 ducats a year. Guiliano della Rovere (Julius II) likewise owed his cardinalate to his uncle, Sixtus IV, who bestowed on him also the archbishopric of Avignon and the bishoprics of Bologna, Lausanne, Coutances, Viviers, Mende, Ostia, and Velletri, with the abbeys of Nonantola and Grottaferrate.' Cf. Jean of Lorraine who became coadjutor-bishop of Metz at the age of three (1501), was later Bishop of Toul (1517), of Terouanne (1518), Cardinal, of Valence and Die (1521), Verdun (1523), Archbishop of Narbonne (1524), Rheims (1533) and Lyons (1537), Bishop of Albi, Macon (1536), Agen (1541) and of Nantes (1542). This much-mitred prelate, who lived in such great state that he was always poor, also enjoyed the revenues of no less than nine abbeys.

[1] 'He was as cunning and as obstinate as a peasant', commented Gonzague de Reynold, 'Often he forgot those who had helped and served him ; but he drove every slight into his memory, as one drives a rivet into steel plate. . . . He never let himself be beaten. He was ever for renown, and for profit ; coming of a poor race, he knew the value of gold, and he was sustained until the day of his death by that one great thought.'

[2] Some idea of what he was trying to do may be gauged from the following warning to his clergy ' not to curl their hair with curling-tongs, nor to carry on trade in the churches, or to raise a disturbance there, not to keep drinking-booths or engage in horse-dealing, and not to buy stolen property '.

And this account may be regarded as a sample of the state of the Church throughout Europe. Such secularisation had also penetrated deeply into the lives of the lower clergy.

But perhaps these ranker and more dramatic vices were less dangerous to the Church than the apathy and indifference which characterised the lives of so many priests, both secular and religious. That a canon of Notre Dame should have turned his house into a gambling den was doubtless highly reprehensible, but that hundreds of men were being ordained or entering monasteries, which, like Erasmus, they often loathed, without any vocation, was a much more significant fact. The evidence certainly suggests that the number of monks was—proportionate to the population—less than it had once been. With certain exceptions, among them the Austrian abbey of Melk,[1] monasteries were too often affected by what medieval moralists called *acedia*, a boredom with religious duty ; there were also a neglect of masses, an unauthorised use of private property, in fine an attitude to life which found expression in harmless (and not always so harmless) secular activity.

Had there been a deterioration in the religious life of the laity as well as that of the clergy ? This question is difficult to answer, simply because the quality of religious life in the Middle Ages was so different from that of the twentieth century. Certainly church-building showed little sign of diminution ; England at least is rich with churches dating from the end of the fifteenth century. But there are a number of points which suggest cumulatively that religious life was lacking in balance. Adoration of the saints and of the Blessed Virgin had greatly increased. Masses, later abolished by the Church, had been instituted in honour of every detail of the Blessed Virgin's life, of her piety, of her seven sorrows, of her sisters and so on. The Mass had become for many a superstitious ceremony, a miracle without moral significance. In general, superstition increased rather than declined in the fifteenth century. Although the incomes of the great shrines, like those of St. Thomas of Canterbury and St. James of Compostella [2] grew less, relic-worship continued unabated. Louis XI, whose callous and cruel

[1] It is perhaps important to point out that some monasteries had been reformed in the fifteenth century. Thus the Bursfeld Union or Congregation, so-called because it was initiated by Abbot Dederoth of Bursfeld near Gottingen, had led to a higher standard of life in the many monasteries which made up the Congregation, often in spite of opposition. The Windesheim Congregation did similar work in the Low Countries, and its example was followed by a number of French Benedictine houses.

[2] At Santiago in Spain, elevated by Pope Sixtus IV to the same rank as the Holy Places of Palestine.

nature cannot be denied, was peculiarly superstitious. Frightened by the idea of dying, he had the world searched for the relics of saints who might yet save his life. ' He also ', says the chronicler, ' sent for a great number of male and female bigots and devout people like hermits and saintly creatures, to pray God incessantly to allow that he should not die and that He might let him live longer '. Venice, careless of papal interdicts, was willing to offer ten thousand ducats for the so-called seamless coat of Christ in 1455 but the bid was insufficient. Cardinal Pierre d'Ailly criticised the increasing number of saints' days and the prolixity of church services. Pilgrimages continued but had more and more the appearance of a ' bank-holiday ' outing; people went on them for ' folle plaisance '. The Burgundian, Chastellain, writing in the fifteenth century, describes to what depths the once solemn procession, carrying the relics of St. Lievin from St. Bavon-le-Gand to the village of Houthem and back, had sunk. Where once there had been ' great and deep solemnity and reverence ' there was now (in 1466) ' a mob of roughs, and boys of bad character ', shouting and bawling ' and all are drunk '. Nearly eighty years later Charles V suppressed this pilgrimage which an anti-Lutheran cleric described as ' almost a mahometry and idolatry '. ' It was a pilgrimage ', he wrote, ' rather of malediction than of devotion, wherein ten thousand mortal sins were yearly wrought, what with drunkenness and quarrels, homicides and lechery, blasphemies, execrable oaths, and other great and enormous sins and wickedness.' In some instances the sacraments of the Church could be bought for money. There was a growing interest in black magic, often a sign of a diseased society.[1]

In general, religion seems to have become more mechanistic and materialistic than it had once been. There was what may be called a ' penny-in-the-slot ' attitude towards the Mass. Anecdotes and wills show clearly enough that many laymen believed that they could make their Eucharistic prayers more efficacious simply by multiplying them. To multiply candles or prayers was another way of increasing the soul's chance of salvation. Thus a layman was entitled to join a Cologne society by an annual subscription of 11,000 *Paternosters* and *Ave Marias*. The popularity of indulgences was yet another indication of the people's attitude towards religion. The indulgence system had originated at the time of the Crusades as a means by which a man could compensate for his inability to

[1] The extraordinary outbreak at Arras in 1460 is graphically described in Dr. Cartellieri's chapter ' La Vauderie d' Arras ' in his *Court of Burgundy*, 194 ff.

go on Crusade and yet gain the promised pardon for sin by a money payment to the Church. Theologically this rested, as the papal bull, *Unigenitus*, published in 1343, showed, on the belief that the merit represented by Christ's sacrifice exceeded what was needed for the redemption of the whole human race; as a result this super-fluous merit [1] constituted a treasure placed in the hands of the Church. 'Now this treasure is not hidden in a napkin . . . but he entrusted it to be healthfully dispensed—through blessed Peter, bearer of heaven's keys, and his successors as vicars on earth—to the faithful, for fitting and reasonable causes, now for total, now for partial remission of punishment due for temporal sins, as well generally as specially (as they should understand it to be expedient with God), and to be applied in mercy to them that are truly penitent and have confessed.' Less and less emphasis was placed on the penitence involved in an indulgence and more and more on the mechanical pardon which the payment of money secured. Religion was thus pervaded by material and mechanical forms. There were, for instance, statuettes of the Virgin Mary which opened and dis-closed the Trinity seated within.

All this represented a coarsening, often accompanied by anti-clericalism and profanation of religious things. People never seemed to weary of hearing attacks on dissolute monks and guzzling friars; the famous *Narrenschiff* (Ship of Fools) written by Sebastian Brandt was only one of many similar attacks on the monastic order. Resentment against the sacramental and jurisdictional powers of the clergy, exerted through a whole series of Church courts and unpopular officers as well as through the Mass and the Confessional, was very general throughout Europe. The Church had gained its mastery over the masses but seemed to have lost its mastery over its own soul. Some of these things, as many faithful Catholics recog-nised, could be, and later were, righted without a Reformation, but, and the point is significant, there was not much sign of this at the beginning of the sixteenth century.

This feeling had already led to some sort of return to a simpler and more personal religion. The popularity of the mystical writings of Tauler and Denis Ruysbroeck or of a simple devotional work like the *Imitation of Christ* reflected current dissatisfaction with the more formal side of religion and the desire to push behind the ceremonial façade to spiritual reality. Not every one could achieve, let alone pierce, the Dark Night of the Soul, but a more devotional teaching

---

[1] To which had been added ' the merits of the blessed Mother of God and of all the elect, from the first just man to the last . . . and no diminution or washing away of this treasure is in any way to be feared '.

conveyed a more personal and simpler view of religion. But so far there was nothing to suggest that this might lead to a revolution in the actual teaching of the Church. That was why Luther's reaction was to be so epochal. He not only found the spiritual life of the Church inadequate but bull-like he blundered into the conclusion that the doctrine on which it was based was partly untrue.

Yet if the Reformation was primarily religious—and the contention is certainly controversial—it was assisted, indeed largely made possible, by secular developments. The rise of strong national monarchies made it certain that the State would do what it could to lessen the amount of papal interference in its internal affairs, to reduce papal control over church appointments, to break the Church's monopoly of education and to cut off the payment of money which was draining the country of its gold according to contemporary economic opinion. In particular the Papacy's intelligent exploitation of every possible source of revenue—annates, tithes, sales of dispensations and offices, indulgences, absolutions—aroused the jealous wrath of the national monarch. The Pope maintained his power in foreign countries by means of nuncios and legates who upheld his interests; he possessed a considerable appellate jurisdiction as well as immense patronage. A clash between the universal power of the Pope and the national authority of the monarch was clearly inevitable. For the past two centuries there had been a growing challenge to the Church's interpretation of her claim to universal dominion; as early as the fourteenth century the Roman lawyer, Bartolo of Sassoferrato, had remarked ' Rex in regno suo est imperator regni sui '. But whereas the Kings of France and Spain found that they could make arrangements with the Pope to suit their own interests, the Kings of Sweden and England found that a denial of papal authority was almost a corollary of the maintenance and extension of their regal power. In this step they were largely supported everywhere by a middle class, gaining in influence and confidence, individualistic enough to dislike the mediatory authority of the priest and avid of church property.

Finally the Renaissance had led to changes which favoured a Reformation. In Northern Europe it had a specifically Christian character. Through the detailed study of the Greek text of the New Testament, and the increasing availability of Bibles, brought about by the invention of printing, thoughtful men found that much that was typical of the contemporary Church had little support in the Gospels; there was, as one man put it, ' little about the Pope but much about Christ '. The study of the Greek text led to a more pronounced emphasis on the literal text of the Bible, as opposed to the allegorical and other methods of interpretation popular in the Middle Ages. Moreover the new translations of the Bible into the vernacular sometimes made significant alterations in the sense of the text; it is difficult to over-stress the importance of a translation which, for instance, replaced bishop (Gk. *episkopos*) and priest (Gk. *presbuteros*) by superintendent and elder, or church (Gk. *ekklesia* or Lat. *ecclesia*) by congregation, or to do penance (Gk. *metanoein* or Lat. *facere poenitentiam*) by to change one's attitude. Nor can the destructive criticism of Valla and Erasmus have passed unnoticed. The acid sarcasm which permeates Ulrich von Hutten's attack on the schoolmen, the *Epistolae Obscurorum Virorum* (1514), was a sign of the bitterness with which some of the humanists regarded the Church and its teaching. Although Luther was not himself a humanist, some of his followers, including the Greek scholar Melanchthon, were. Both Zwingli and Calvin owed much initially to the classical teaching of the Renaissance.

But the Reformation was as much a reaction from as a result of the Renaissance. In the reformers' philosophy of life, St. Paul and St. Augustine counted for more than Aristotle and Plato. The Puritan streak in medieval catholicism, which was so characteristic of Savonarola's bonfire of vanities,[1] reappeared more strongly than before in the teaching of the reformers, in their emphasis on sobriety and decency, on the strict observance of Sunday, in their attacks on Church finery and ceremonial. To some at least the Renaissance in Italy must have seemed paganism in disguise. In some ways the conservatism rather than the radicalism of the reformers' teaching is the more significant.

These factors taken together brought a religious and political revolution which shattered the unity of medieval Europe and helped to create the modern state and the modern Church. But there had to be a leader to act as the outward and visible expression of an inward and spiritual discontent. And the hour had such a man in Martin Luther.

---

[1] Many works of art and other treasures were piled on to this flaming pyre (last day of the Carnival at Florence, 1497). See Burckhardt, *Civilization of the Renaissance*, 252. Cf. Savonarola's opinion : ' An old woman knows more about the Faith than Plato.'

2. *Martin Luther*

It is a tribute to the force of Luther's personality that neither John Calvin nor Ignatius Loyola has provoked such excessive veneration and intense dislike.[1] Nor is his personality by any means capable of simple analysis. Its curious and unexpected twists darken rather than clarify it. A neurotic and a would-be ascetic, guided by the single light of the love of God, affectionate and kind, rejoicing in music and prayer, courageous and prophetic, there can be no question that he was a religious genius. Yet there were times when he was tormented by depression and the possibility of failure, and haunted by obsessions and fantasies. Self-confident and proudly assertive, he was as pontifical as the Pope in his decisions and, in his own eyes, far more infallible. His language was sometimes profoundly abusive, vigorous and obscene, though no more so than that of his contemporaries. Vulgarities occur most frequently in his polemical writings and certainly reflect his disgust with what appeared to him to be wholly blasphemous ; it is possible that he used words designedly to arouse repulsion in his readers. But he also wrote German prose as noble as any that has been penned ; his theological works indicate the richness and intellectual and spiritual depth of his mind. Indeed ideas poured out in such profusion that he was never very successful at distinguishing the wood from the trees.

Luther was perhaps governed more by his emotions than by his intellect ; music, he was an expert lutanist, always moved him ; he could weep over a violet hidden by the snow. Contemptuous of reason which he described time and time again as the 'devil's whore' on occasions he allowed his feelings to dominate his decisions to an unwarrantable extent. Like all sensitive people, easily bruised, he repaid his opponents in their own coin. Subject to sudden fits of melancholy, he would move as rapidly to a feeling of superb exaltation. Fascinated and agonised by the problem of sin, he

---

[1] His character had been debated endlessly. The Roman Catholic historians, Hartmann Grisar, S.J., and Denifle, in practice conclude that he was so psychologically perverted as to be regarded as a spiritual degenerate. The distinguished Catholic philosopher, Jacques Maritain subtitles his essay ' Luther or the Advent of the Self', and states 'What first impresses us in Luther's character is egocentrism '. (*Three Reformers*, 14) ' He is ', he says, 'a man wholly and systematically ruled by his affective and appetitive faculties ' (28). P. F. Wiener has tried to lay German Nazism to his credit (*Martin Luther, Hitler's Spiritual Ancestor*, 1945), drawing a trenchant and convincing reply in E. G. Rupp's *Martin Luther, Hitler's Cause or Cure ?* (1945). For modern views of Luther consult R. Bainton, *Martin Luther* and E. G. Rupp, *Luther Until 1521* (1951).

resolved it by a total reliance on faith and the predestinating grace of God. Eleven days before he died (February 18th, 1546) he wrote to his wife a characteristic letter : ' Dear Kate, You ought to read Saint John and what the catechism says about the trust we should have in God. You really worry too much, as if God were not all-powerful and could not produce new Doctor Martins by the dozen if the old one happened to get drowned in the Salle or perished in some other way. There is One who looks after us better than the angels and you yourself could possibly do; He is seated on the right hand of God the Father Almighty. So calm yourself.' But there was only one ' Doctor Martin ', a truly gigantic figure in the history of his times.[1]

His background was in no way exceptional. His father, Hans, was a Saxon miner living at Eisleben in Thuringia where Martin was born on November 11th, 1483. When he was eighteen he entered the University of Erfurt, for his father, who had risen to be a foreman of the mine and was now a magistrate of the town of Mansfeld, intended that his son should become a lawyer. Luther was, however, more interested in philosophy than in law. ' At Erfurt ', wrote his friend Melanchthon, ' Luther became immersed in an intricate and hair-splitting dialectical method '; but the spell did not last. With equal enthusiasm he embraced the writings of the medieval mystics. After graduation, he studied theology with the intention of being ordained. On July 17th, 1505, he presented himself at the house of the Augustinian Eremites at Erfurt, was ordained priest, probably on April 3rd, 1507, and a year later was transferred to the Augustinian house at Wittenberg, so that he might act as the professor of philosophy at the University recently founded there by Elector Frederick of Saxony. Apart from a visit to Rome in 1511, a city which depressed him, nothing significant occurred until the critical year, 1517.

Yet this does not allow for the all-important development of Luther's mind. He read widely in contemporary scholastic theology but made the study of the Bible, and of St. Paul's Epistles, more and more the centre of his attention. He learned Greek in order that he might be able to read the New Testament in the original. Nor was his life wholly academic. Writing to his friend Lang on October 26th, 1516, he says : ' I ought to have two secretaries. I am engaged nearly all day long writing letters. In addition I have

---

[1] Cf. Professor Butterfield : ' even if Christianity disappeared so that he survived only as a maker of myths he would still be a colossal figure— almost the greatest of the giants in modern times ' (*Cambridge Review*, May 24th, 1947).

to preach in the convent and the refectory, and I am also asked to preach every day in the parish church. I am District Visitor, that is to say, Prior eleven times over. I am responsible for the fish pond at Leitzkau ; I have to attend the trial of the Herzberg Brethren at Torgau ; I am lecturing on St. Paul, making notes on the Psalms and spend my whole day writing.[1] I rarely have as much time as I should for my canonical hours and reading my Mass, and needless to say I am beset by all the temptations of the world, the flesh and the Devil. You see what an idle fellow I am !' The humorous, bantering tone of the letter conceals the bitter inner struggle which was rending Luther's mind and soul at this time. He was overwhelmingly convinced of the tremendous reality and power of sin, and alarmed to find that nothing that he could do would free him from temptation. Scholastic writings availed him nothing. Austerity of life served him no better. He read the sermons of the Dominican writer, John Tauler, and a little fourteenth-century work *Theologica Germanica* (which he attributed to Tauler) in which, as he put it, ' all the science of our time is mere common clay by comparison '. Partly on the advice of the Augustinian vicar-General, Staupitz, he was making an intensive study of St. Paul's Epistle to the Romans in which he found something of that unqualified faith in God and utter reliance on His grace which, he was soon convinced, could alone give him the peace of mind and soul for which he longed.

It may be imagined that the indulgence system, with its mechanical view of sin and repentance, aroused Luther's indignation. Albert of Brandenburg, Archbishop of Mainz, a cultured humanist of extravagant habits, owed thirty thousand florins to the banking house of Fugger, a debt he had incurred as a result of the heavy sums he had to pay the Pope for his appointment to Mainz and for a papal dispensation to hold two other bishoprics together with that of Mainz. He hoped to recoup himself by acting as papal agent for the sale of indulgences for the re-building of St. Peter's Cathedral at Rome, and for a crusade against the Turks. The prospectus which he drew up explained that anyone desirous of obtaining the remission of sins—' a free gift of grace and grace is beyond price '— must have a contrite heart and have confessed before the indulgence is given. A table of rates laid down the price, reckoned according

[1] An examination of the course of lectures he gave at Wittenberg where he had succeeded Staupitz as Professor of Biblical Theology—on the Psalms in 1514, on Romans in 1515-16, on Galatians in 1516-17, on Hebrews in 1517-18—shows that much of his theology had been worked out before the break with Rome.

to the rank of the recipient; the poor were not excluded, 'for the kingdom of God should be open to the poor as much as the rich' and could pay for the indulgence by prayer and fasting. In return for the money-payment the buyer was promised full and complete absolution of all sins and plenary indulgence for the souls of dead relatives who would straightway be released from the pains of Purgatory. The Archbishop's representative, the Dominican friar, John Tetzel, used every means at his disposal to attract attention: 'When the papal commissioner was ushered into the town', says a contemporary, Myconius, of Tetzel's visit to Annaberg, 'he was preceded by the Bull of the Sovereign Pontiff carried on a piece of scarlet and gold velvet. The people, priests and monks, the town council, the schoolmasters and scholars, men and women, went out in a procession to meet him, with lighted candles, standards unfurled and flags fluttering in the breeze while all the bells in the town rang out full peal. In the church, in the middle of the nave, a huge red cross was raised upon which the pontifical banner was fixed; in short, one may think they were receiving God himself.'

Tetzel's arrival at Jüterbog, a town a few miles away from Wittenberg, disturbed Luther intensely. The Elector Frederick of Saxony had banned Tetzel from his dominions. Luther was therefore all the more angry when he learned that the indulgence-seller was visiting the two towns of Zerbst and Jüterbog, both so close to Wittenberg that its inhabitants could buy indulgences without transgressing the Elector's ban. On All Saints' Eve, 1517,[1] he fastened to the door of the Castle Chapel at Wittenberg the famous ninety-five theses declaring that the sale of indulgences led to such abuses that they ought to be condemned. 'Those who assert that a soul straightway flies out (of Purgatory) as coin tinkles in the collection-box are preaching an invention of man.' Although some of the theses directly criticised the Pope, Luther's action was in no way extraordinary. It was a normal thing to post such matter for discussion, nor did Luther intend to treat what he had put forward as necessarily true. The theses formed tentative objections to which he wished to call the attention of the Church. In general

[1] The choice of All Saints' Eve was significant, for everyone in the town and many strangers went to the Church on the following day, All Saints' Day (November 1st) which was the anniversary of the consecration of the building. Moreover in spite of his ban on Tetzel the Elector had secured an indulgence for all who came to the services on that day and inspected his collection of holy relics (5005 in number according to a list of 1509; 17,443 in 1518, including 204 portions and one whole corpse of the Holy Innocents. To them was attached an indulgence of 127,799 years and 116 days).

he had concluded that although an indulgence may remit an ecclesiastical penalty imposed by the Church, it cannot delete guilt or affect divine punishment for sin or bring about the release of souls from Purgatory. But there was yet no reason why, with careful handling, Luther could not still be kept within the bosom of the Roman Church.

Nevertheless 1517 is rightly regarded as the official starting-date of the Reformation, even though the immediate aftermath was not particularly exciting. At first it appeared as if the squabble over indulgences might degenerate into a controversy between two monastic orders, the Dominicans and the Augustinian Friars, but with the delation of the matter to Rome the question was taken a stage further. The Pope, Leo X, summoned Luther to Rome. For his part he agreed to appear before the papal legate, Cardinal Cajetan, at Augsburg where the Imperial Diet was meeting. Troubled as he was by illness, Luther was superbly confident of the outcome; indeed opposition was more likely to make him take an extreme position than to overawe him; but the meeting at Augsburg proved fruitless.

Unless Luther agreed to withdraw, his excommunication could not be long delayed. He had been outspoken already about papal authority; 'the Pope', he wrote a month after the Augsburg meeting (November 28th, 1518), 'is fallible. . . . His authority cannot prevail over the Holy Scriptures.' A fortnight later he was writing to a fellow friar : ' You may rest assured that I am right in suspecting the court of Rome of being governed by the real Antichrist of whom St. Paul spoke.' The authorities acted cautiously at first. They knew that Luther had the support of many of his fellow Germans including the Elector of Saxony, Frederick the Wise, and the leader of the German Knights, Franz von Sickingen. The new papal agent, Karl von Miltitz, himself a Saxon, was instructed to try to win over both the Elector and Luther. But Luther was not in a mood to be coaxed into submission; he was already aware of the significant meaning of the doctrine of justification by faith; the revelation came to him in a situation unusual for the reception of such matter. 'And I was consoled and fortified, having acquired the certainty that God's justice is not that which inflicts severe punishment, but that which makes the repentant sinner just, and secures him eternal bliss. All of a sudden my heart was at peace. . . . It was an illumination wherewith I was filled by the Holy Spirit itself.'

Thus equipped Luther made his way to Leipzig to meet the Catholic theologian, Eck, in public debate. With great brilliance, Eck put forward arguments supported by a catena of authorities, decretals, councils, patristic writings and papal bulls, so forcing Luther back to his final resource, the Word of God, the Scriptures. Both adversaries left Leipzig full of indignation with each other. ' At Leipzig ', Luther wrote later, ' we have just bungled the whole business because we did not know we should have to deal with wolves.'

Meanwhile the ' the Wittenberg Nightingale ', as Hans Sachs christened him in 1523, was trying to clarify his position and gain support for his cause by writing. In his *Discourse on the Most Holy Sacrament* he questioned the Roman doctrine of transubstantiation. *The Address to the German Nobility*, published at the end of August, 1520, was an aggressively-worded document in which Luther appealed to the Emperor and condemned the Pope and the papal court in the most severe terms. The Romanists have tried to escape condemnation by asserting that the temporal power has no jurisdiction over them, by saying that no one may interpret the Scriptures except the Pope, and by declaring that no one may call a general council but the Pope. ' Rome is the greatest thief and robber that has ever appeared on earth, or ever will. . . . Poor Germans that we are—we have been deceived ! We were born to be masters and we have been compelled to bow the head beneath the yoke of our tyrants. . . . It is time the glorious Teutonic people should cease to be the puppet of the Roman pontiff.' Another pamphlet, entitled *On the Babylonian Captivity of the Church*, written in Latin, appeared at the end of October. It was a trenchant attack on the Pope, on the traffic in indulgences and indeed on much of the medieval sacramental system. Although Luther himself probably did not understand the full significance of the stand he was making, he was gratified when Froben, the famous printer of Basle, told him that his writings were being read as far away as Paris. The rapidity with which his pamphlets reached the confines of Germany was in itself an indication of the great interest that his ideas had already aroused.

After some delay Leo X had issued the bull of excommunication, *Exsurge, Domine et judica causam tuam*, dated June 2nd, 1520, and penned, it was said, appropriately enough at his castle of Magliana where he was engaged in boar-hunting. ' Arise, O Lord, plead thine own case ; remember how the foolish man reproacheth Thee daily ; the foxes are wasting Thy vineyard, which Thou hast given to Thy vicar Peter ; the boar out of the wood doth waste it, and the wild beast of the field doth devour it.' Even now sixty days grace was granted to Luther to withdraw the forty-one propositions condemned by the bull. The would-be heretic was in no way willing to do this. ' I accuse you ', he replied, ' and declare to your faces that if this Bull is of your doing I myself with all the authority of a child of God . . . do advise you to reflect, to cease your blasphemies.' When the period of grace expired, the Wittenbergers celebrated it with a great bonfire into which Doctor Martin flung the papal bull while the university students sang a *Te Deum*. On January 3rd, 1521, a further bull *Decet Romanum Pontificem*, excommunicating Luther, was sealed. Battle was joined.

Much now depended on the attitude taken by the secular authorities. Without their co-operation the bull would be completely ineffective. Luther was supported by the Elector of Saxony but how the young Emperor Charles V would view the situation remained to be seen. He had summoned an Imperial Diet to Worms to consider, among other things, the Lutheran problem. On Ash Wednesday, 1521, the Papal Legate, Girolamo Aleander, read out the bull of excommunication and informed the Imperial Diet in a speech two hours long that Luther was another John Hus. The Diet did not wish to be overawed by a papal agent and signified its intention of giving Luther a hearing. Although Luther himself feared that his journey to Worms might lead to his death in spite of the Imperial safe-conduct accorded him, his entry into the city was like a triumphal procession. Anti-papal feeling ran high both within the Diet and the city itself. Aleander himself supplies plentiful evidence of this in the letters he sent to Rome. He complained that ' every stone and every tree cried out " Luther ",' that he was the victim of rude caricaturists and was forced to live in a stoveless attic.

The historic meeting which occurred on April 17th-18th, 1521, was the only occasion on which the Emperor and the reformer faced each other. A natural anxiety and perhaps a rather unaccustomed feeling of inferiority made Luther less impressive than usual when he first spoke on the afternoon of the 17th ; but he was much more confident at the session on the following day, Thursday, April 18th. After justifying his writings, he refused to recant and appealed to the Emperor : ' If His Imperial Majesty desires a plain answer I will give it to him, *neque cornutum neque dentatum*, and it is this : It is impossible for me to recant unless I am proved to be in the wrong by the testimony of Scripture or by evident reasoning ; I cannot trust either the decisions of Councils or of Popes, for it is plain that they have not only erred, but have contradicted each other. My conscience is bound to the word of God, and it is neither safe nor honest to act against one's conscience. God help me ! Amen ! ' After the Emperor had left the room some Spaniards pressed towards Luther booing him, but he was protected by his fellow-Germans. As he passed from the hall he raised his hand high above his head like a victorious German *landsknecht* who had unhorsed his adversary, a significant and symbolic gesture.

' Our Father, Doctor Martin ', commented the Elector of Saxony, ' spoke extremely well before the Emperor ', but the Emperor was unimpressed. ' This man ', young Charles is reported to have said, ' will never make me a Lutheran '. On April 26th Luther left Worms ' after toasting slices of bread for the day's consumption and fortifying himself with several glasses of Malmsey wine '. On May 26th the Imperial Edict placed him under the ban of the Empire ; he was to be arrested as a heretic and handed over to the Imperial authorities. The die had been cast.

3. *Luther's ideas*

The movement which Luther had started, gathering impetus under the pressure of secular ambition and religious devotion, started a world-revolution. Both Calvin and Zwingli to a greater or lesser extent depended on what Luther had already achieved. The unity of the Church had been broken. It was clear that the only possible historical stimulus to the reunion of Christendom must come from a threatening third force. There was nothing like this in the sixteenth century, for the western sovereigns only took the Turkish threat to the integrity of Europe seriously at moments of crisis. Protestantism was in itself a dividing force. Almost in spite of itself it fostered both political and economic individualism ; it allowed greater freedom of interpretation of the faith and, perhaps because of this, it helped the slow drift from religious to secular individualism.

Luther's ideas formed a foundation for this. Yet three qualifications must be made if his position is to be properly understood. In the first place, he was not a consistent thinker. Secondly, Luther's theology was deeply interpenetrated by medieval scholastic thought. However contemptuously he may speak of Aristotle and the schoolmen, he owed an immense debt to medieval ideas.[1] Thus he never clearly visualised the separation of the Church and the State because they were for him two parts of a single whole, teaching which was in full accord with the medieval point of view. His political and

---

[1] The university of Erfurt had been a stronghold of Nominalist teaching ; Luther was therefore widely read in the teaching of the Occamists (the followers of the English Nominalist of the fourteenth century, William of Occam), which he was later to attack but by which he was certainly influenced.

economic ideas were grounded in medieval sociology. He looked on the German princes and nobles as the natural guardians of the Church. Genuinely frightened by the democratic interpretation which some of the more extreme among his followers gave to his teaching, he emphasised the sinful nature of rebellion. ' He was teaching the duty of obedience to constituted authorities as clearly and emphatically before the disaster of the Peasants' revolt as he was after it.'[1] His conservatism in economic matters is revealed by his ideas on trade and his dislike of interest. Thus many of his ideas were medieval, and to think of him as a modern German is to falsify history. A third point must be noted, his reading and appreciation of German mystical theology. ' Neither in Latin nor in German ', he wrote of Tauler's work in 1516, ' have I found sounder or more wholesome doctrine, nor any that so fully accords with the Gospel.' His faith was undoubtedly coloured by mystical ideas which he found difficult to express coherently. He denounced transubstantiation without abandoning the real presence in the Eucharist; Christ is actually present ' just as fire is introduced into a bar of red-hot iron '.

For Luther the Word of God was the start and the finish of his faith. He attacked the scholastic writers because they had replaced the Word of God (*Gotteswort*) by man's teaching (*Menschenlehre*). Similarly he opposed papal authority because it conflicted with the Word of God. Yet it is not always clear what he actually means by this expression. Until 1520 he almost certainly identified it with the divinely-inspired Scriptures. ' The Gospel ', he wrote in his *Commentary on Romans*, ' is not just what Matthew, Mark, Luke and John have written. It is the Word of the Son of God, who became flesh, suffered and was glorified.' But after 1520 he came to the conclusion that not all the Scriptures had equal validity. Only those which preached the Gospel and Christ could be regarded as the True Word. In his preface to the translation of the New Testament into German he declares that the Gospel of St. John, St. Paul's Epistles, especially those to the Romans, Galatians and Ephesians, I John and I Peter are the ' noblest ' of the books because they lead the Christian to salvation.

But who is to be the interpreter of the Word of God ? Luther answered that the true Christian would recognise what it meant;

[1] J. W. Allen, *History of Political Thought*. Cf. ' Rebellion cannot be right, however just the cause : more injury than benefit is ever the result of it. I take and always will take his part who suffers from rebellion, however unjust his cause may be : and will set myself against him who rebels, let his cause be ever so just, because rebellion cannot take place without injury and shedding of blood ' (*Admonition* of 1522).

' It is written down, once and for all, in the pages of the Bible, and all can read it there. The meaning of the Word of God is perfectly plain throughout, and is agreed on by all whose minds are not corrupted by the Papacy's heresy and ambition.' Yet history soon showed the limitations of this argument. While Luther himself had no doubt that he was interpreting the Word of God correctly, he vehemently denounced those among his own followers who cavilled at his teaching. His reliance on the Word of God was bound to confuse the whole problem of authority and to encourage political as well as religious individualism.

This is at once apparent in his teaching on the nature of the Church. Influenced by reading the works of the fifth-century Church Father, Augustine, he held that the true Church is invisible and known only to God. Its membership is determined by the ' eternal decree of God's predestinating grace ', and ' by the activity of the Word of God in this world '. What was the relationship between the ' invisible ' and the ' visible ' Church ? In one of his writings, dated 1523, he distinctly states that there is a *christliche Gemeinde* or ' Christ-like congregation ' wherever the Word of God is preached. In practice this meant wherever there was a Lutheran congregation. It would appear that Luther originally accepted the ' priesthood of all believers ' and the governance of the church by the congregation ; writing to the people of Prague he urges that every Christian is entitled to preach and administer the Sacraments, but for the sake of order one or more should be ' chosen or accepted to exercise this right in the name and place of all, who nevertheless have the same right '. But circumstances forced him to abandon this ideal and in effect to place the church under the control of the local prince. For, he argued, the civil ruler as the chief member of the church, *praecipuum membrum* is bound to use his authority in its service.

Luther had no systematic theory of the State. He simply took over the medieval conception and adapted it to his teaching on the Word of God. The prince's authority was divinely given and in a sense as spiritual in essentials as that of the priest. He was the natural guardian of the Church and the defender of Christian doctrine. Rebellion could only be justified if he deliberately broke his obligations as a Christian ruler. But this created a major problem which the Lutheran Church never satisfactorily solved. Admitting that the prince is, as Romans xiii, 1-3, which Luther never tired of quoting, implies, a god-given authority, is there any real limit to his powers of interference in Church matters ? While there is no doubt that Luther would have urged ideally the primary rights of the congregation, the closer the alignment between the princes desire to be free of Imperial control, the more in practice the Lutheran Church fell under the domination of the civil ruler. As a result there was to be a continuous struggle between those who upheld the decisions reached by the Treaty of Augsburg in 1555, granting the prince the right to decide whether the religion of the state should be Roman Catholic or Lutheran, and those who wished to recover the free direction of the Church by the congregation which Luther had once envisaged.

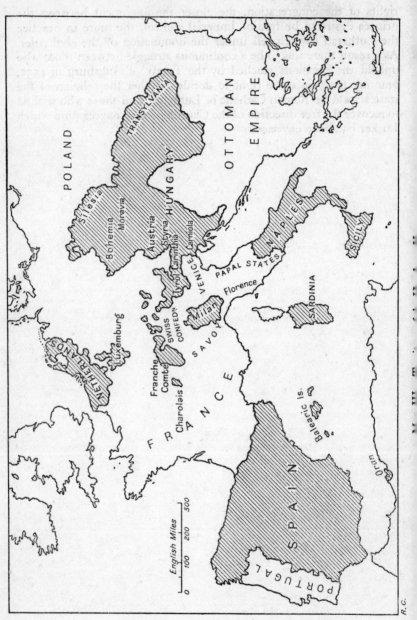

CHAPTER IX

THE EMPEROR CHARLES V, 1519–58

1. *The Emperor and his task*

FOR thirty years all European history centred around the Emperor Charles V. His personality did not necessarily dominate the scene but it affected every single major issue. In part this arose from the unusual number of territories over which he ruled. His grandiose list of titles read in 1519 : ' King of the Romans ; Emperor-elect ; semper Augustus ; King of Spain, Sicily, Jerusalem, the Balearic Islands, the Canary Islands, the Indies and the mainland on the far side of the Atlantic ; Archduke of Austria ; Duke of Burgundy, Brabant, Styria, Carinthia, Carniola, Luxemburg, Limburg, Athens and Patras ; Count of Hapsburg, Flanders and Tyrol ; Count Palatine of Burgundy, Hainault, Pfirt, Roussillon ; Landgrave of Alsace ; Count of Swabia ; Lord of Asia and Africa.' No man in European history had yet governed such a conglomeration of territory, and whether any man, however able, could cope with all the manifold problems which were connected with it was extraordinarily doubtful, more especially as his honours were conferred upon him in quick succession while he was still young and inexperienced. The way in which this imposing list of titles is grouped at once reveals a major weakness. What counts is not the association of lands or races but the order of precedence. This reflects the medieval nature of the Empire to the headship of which Charles had been elected in 1519.

The Imperial dignity was an authority more suitable to the medieval than the modern world, theoretically comprising an overlordship in secular matters parallel to the Pope's spiritual authority. Charles was never to possess the means for making it effective. German unity was an impossibility in the face of the growing desire of the princes to be free of the Emperor and the disturbances caused by the rise of Lutheranism. Imperial reform became more and more a remote dream. Quite apart from the fact that the Emperor had often to be absent in other parts of his dominions, he lacked an efficient executive, a permanent army, a full treasury and a loyal people. Nor was he able to feel that he had the support of the Pope, even during the brief period when his old tutor, Adrian VI, was Head of the Church. Charles' first title ' King of the Romans ' was little more than nominal; he was soon to pass it on together with the care of the hereditary Hapsburg estates in Austria to his younger brother, Ferdinand. Yet it was as King of the Romans that he marched into Italy, and as Archduke of Austria that he defended the eastern frontiers of the Empire against the ever-present threat of the Turk.

The title ' King of Spain ' also showed how illogical and difficult was his position. He succeeded his grandfather, Ferdinand, as King of Aragon in 1516, and ruled, nominally as Co-Sovereign with his mad mother, Joanna, as King of Castile. His reign began with risings but ended in quiet if melancholy glory for Spain. Spain became the home to which he retired when he laid down his dignities, but if he eventually won the Spaniards' affectionate loyalty, he never overcame their unwillingness to be used as a milch-cow for his Imperial conflicts. If he had been King of Spain alone, the history of that unfortunate country might have taken a very different course, but destiny called him to other crowns, and Spain's treasure was poured out in wars only remotely connected with its real interests.

Two other titles illustrate a similar point. Charles had succeeded his father as Duke of Burgundy in 1506, but the Netherlands were strongly permeated by feudal privilege and separatist feeling. There were problems enough here to provide him with a life's work. In addition to this there was his fanciful claim to the Kingdom of Jerusalem, now many years under Turkish rule. ' Wherefore ', as the Turkish Grand Vizier wrote in 1533, ' does he presume to style himself to my lord as King of Jerusalem ? Is he ignorant of the fact that my mighty Emperor and not himself, Charles, is Lord of Jerusalem ? . . . In the same way he calls himself Duke of Athens, which is now Sethine, a small town, and belongs to me.' The Turkish peril which threatened the borders of the Empire in the Mediterranean and in Hungary and Austria was very far from fanciful. It represented, as Charles rightly saw, a threat to the very integrity of western Christian civilisation but so many were the demands upon him that he could never pay this major problem the attention it deserved.

And what of this man, Charles, called at six to be Duke of Burgundy, at sixteen King of Spain and at nineteen Holy Roman Emperor; and then at fifty-six laying down his crowns with a sigh of relief so that he might spend his remaining years amidst the serenity and the sunshine, the good food and the clockwork toys of the Imperial villa beside the Hieronymite monastery at Yuste in Spain. Hereditarily he was as cosmopolitan a prince as could be found in Europe. His mother and maternal grandmother were Spaniards. His father was a Burgundian as was his paternal grandmother. His grandfather was a German, the son of a Portuguese princess and an Austrian prince.[1]

Charles developed slowly. This tongue-tied youth, delighting in horsemanship and jousting, seemed intellectually ill-equipped for his immense task. He was not a good linguist. His native tongue was French but even in this he was not fluent. He did not begin to learn Flemish until he was thirteen. Neither his Latin nor his German were good. He knew next to nothing of Spanish two years after he had become King of Spain. He had only a rudimentary knowledge of Theology. He began to study Mathematics when he was over thirty because he believed it would help him to master the art of war. He liked History, a taste no way surprising in that splendid traditionalist Burgundian court where epic stories received daily representation in pageantry.

Although as a youth Charles bore himself gracefully, he appeared at first sight a colourless personality in whose eyes alone strength of character and natural intelligence could be discerned. Yet, as his surviving portraits show, this rather callow adolescent grew into an experienced and confident man. Bernart van Orley, painting him in half-profile in 1522, suggests that there was a measure of arrogant determination and self-confidence in the prognathous Hapsburg chin. It reveals that three years of Imperial rule have turned the boy into the man. Ten years later, Christopher Amberger painted another portrait of the Emperor; in this there is pride coupled with simplicity but no arrogance. If experience had not yet brought disillusionment, it had at least bestowed a measure of maturity. Sixteen years later Charles' favourite painter, Titian, depicted his master sitting on a chair before brocaded tapestry. If this portrait, or its fellow painted a year later, is compared with that of Amberger's, the contrast affords a commentary on what has happened to the man in years of toil and turmoil. He looks far more than forty-eight years old. 'Here is the Emperor, the master of all the world; yet he sits before us in all simplicity, close to us, human, plainly dressed, simple, unposed. He is alone and sunk in thought. The face, the lips, the hands; whose action never alters in all his pictures, betray some narrowness, some indefinable rigidity of outlook. Yet everything about him bears witness to the

[1] In his excellent life of the Emperor, Karl Brandi mentions that ' This child, who was to carry the Hapsburg dynasty to the height of its power, was hardly yet a Hapsburg. Among all his thirty-two ancestors, one line alone was derived from German stock—that of his grandfather Maximilian and his forefathers ' (p. 42).

self-possession, the inner intensity of his being. Years and cares have left their mark.'[1]

What were the guiding principles upon which Charles built his life? His devotion to the Catholic faith was undeniable. His reply to Luther at Worms betrays the depth of his feelings: ' Ye know that I am born of the most Christian Emperors of the whole German nation, of the Catholic Kings of Spain, the Archdukes of Austria, the Dukes of Burgundy, who were all to the death true sons of the Roman Church, defenders of the Catholic faith . . . who have bequeathed all this to me as my heritage, and according to whose example I have hitherto lived. . . . It is certain that a single monk must err if he stands against the opinion of all Christendom. . . . Therefore I am determined to set my kingdoms, my friends, my body, my blood, my life, my soul upon it.' Although religion was to him a matter of fact rather than of emotion, his devotion to it overrode and affected all the disquieting issues which faced him. He took his Imperial duties as God's vicegerent seriously. No less indeed than his son, Philip II, he identified the will of God with the policy of the Hapsburgs. But his loyalty to the Church was perfectly sincere. Nothing probably gave him so much grief and irritation as the constant refusal of individual Popes to co-operate wholeheartedly with him. He never questioned either their office or their authority. Now and again, a hurt and angry man, he abruptly stemmed the unctuous pleading of a papal nuncio, but all that he could say was ' God knows why the Pope acted thus '. His faith gave him strength to face repeated disaster calmly. ' We must thank God ', he wrote to his brother, Ferdinand, after the failure of the Algerian expedition in 1541, ' and hope that after this disaster He will grant us of His great goodness, some great good fortune.' ' Great good fortune ' was pitifully lacking but seven years later he could tell his son ' seeing that human affairs are beset with doubt, I can give you no general rules save to trust in Almighty God. You will show this best by defending the faith.'

Charles' religion, deep as it was, was conventional and traditional; so too with the dynastic interest which lay at the base of all that he did. The Dynasty and the Church gave his Empire its unity. His brother, Ferdinand, by right of inheritance, became King of Hungary. Of his sisters, one was married to the unpleasing Christian II of Denmark who, unlike Henry VIII of England, rid himself of his wife with comparative ease, another to John III of Portugal, while an

---

[1] K. Brandi, *Charles V*, 586.

elder sister, his beloved Eleanor, already widow of Manuel of Portugal, was married to Francis I of France. A fourth sister, Mary, formerly Queen of Hungary, acted as Regent of the Netherlands. Although ordinarily the most moral of contemporary princes, there had been occasions when 'he had sported with Amaryllis in the shade', and he also cherished ambitions for his illegitimate children. 'For him', as his biographer suggests, 'the dynastic principle did not merely mean the theory of hereditary kingship for the permanent security of the state; it was also a profound moral, almost a religious duty.'

Given these two guiding principles it is difficult to add much more to Charles' action. He possessed comparatively little imagination and perhaps no more than average ability; it was his sense of duty which led him to unexpected triumphs. He had no large-scale plans, as his Chancellor Gattinara regretted, for dealing with his host of problems. Endowed by God with Imperial power, he must do his best for the weal of Christendom. He would seek to eliminate heresy as displeasing to God, to fight Francis I of France as a foe of world peace which it was his duty as Emperor to maintain, and to attack the Turk. He would try to give peace and order to his numerous dominions. But he inherited too many problems at too young an age ever to combat them successfully. Although he would have liked to centralise everything round his authority, no institution was ever so decentralised. There could be no doubt as to his ultimate failure. In the closing words of Armstrong's admirable biography: 'He was not quite a great man, nor quite a good man, but, all deductions made, an honourable Christian gentleman, striving, in spite of physical defects, moral temptations and political impossibilities, to do his duty in that state of life to which an unkind Providence had called him.'[1]

2. The revolt of the 'Comuneros'

Although Spain later became the most cherished of all Charles' possessions, it was a foreign and troubled land which he inherited from his grandfather in 1516. The removal of King Ferdinand's strong personality from a country insufficiently welded into a unity, and full of conflicting currents, provided an opportunity for discord, which the Regent, the aged Cardinal Ximenez, was in no position to control. The towns resisted his attempt to revive the old militia; the nobles' natural turbulence found expression in a movement to

[1] Edward Armstrong, *Charles V*, ii, 387.

place Charles' younger brother, Ferdinand, who had been brought up in Spain, on the throne. Everything made it imperative that Charles should leave the Netherlands for his new kingdoms as soon as possible.

But it was only on September 8th, 1517, after long delays, that the royal ship, with its beautifully decorated sails, left Flushing on its momentous voyage. Landing on the remote Asturian coast, Charles and his Flemish courtiers picnicked for the first few weeks. But on October 30th the King made contact with the Constable of Castile. After visiting his mother, Queen Joanna, at gloomy Tordesillas, he progressed slowly towards Valladolid where the Cortes was to meet and which he entered with colourful ceremonial on November 18th, drawing the admiration of the Castilian on-lookers by his splendid horsemanship.

The remaining months of his first visit were marked by the growing chorus of complaints and the visible signs of approaching trouble. Ximenez had died at Toledo before Charles could meet him,[1] and with incredible folly this rich see, which carried with it the primacy of Castile, was bestowed on the nephew of Charles' Flemish adviser Chièvres, the sixteen-year-old William of Croy. The Cortes of Castile opened on February 2nd, 1518; Charles swore to observe the customs and privileges of the country and to give office only to its natives—but his answer on the latter score was irritatingly ambiguous. He was, however, recognised as joint Sovereign with his mother and was granted a subsidy for three years. But opinion was growing increasingly hostile. ' He says little, is not of much ability, and is entirely ruled by his Flemish advisers' was one contemporary comment. It was apparent that Charles' attempts to gain subsidies from the various Cortes of his dominions would lead to trouble. Even his efforts to introduce orderly government roused the jealous indignation of a nobility, freed by Ferdinand's death, to start afresh its profession of disorder and injustice. ' Every hour', wrote the Bishop of Armagh to Cardinal Wolsey, ' was murder and robbery without punishment . . . many of the lords being possessed of all their lands by robbery, so that there is likely to be no end of these Cortes unless justice be set apart.'

The necessity for the granting of such subsidies was made greater by the news of the Emperor Maximilian's death. Charles was naturally eager to leave Spain as soon as possible to take over

---

[1] It has been said that Charles contributed to his end by his last letter, recommending his resignation, but the Cardinal was dead before it reached him. His resignation was in any case suggested on the score of age and growing infirmity.

the Imperial throne to which he was about to be elected. But the news only provoked greater irritation among the Castilians, a proud people, unwilling that their land should be treated as a mere annex to the Empire. His eagerness to depart, his failure to make a progress through Castile, his appointment of a Fleming, Adrian of Utrecht, as virtual Regent [1] his demand for a further subsidy, and the summons of the Castilian Cortes to the remote and relatively unimportant city of Santiago in Galicia, completed the country's disillusionment with its new King.

Unquestionably Charles was leaving Spain on the brink of revolt. At Valladolid, the mob, supported by the arrogant Andalusian noble, Pedro de Giron, would have prevented the King's departure by force if it had been able to do so. The proceedings of the Cortes were stormy, and the subsidy was only voted after much wrangling; more impressive still was the conspicuous absence of the delegates from Salamanca and Toledo. For Toledo was already in armed revolt and Valencia was immersed in chaos before Charles set sail from Corunna, leaving his disturbed state to the nerveless hands of the unpopular mediocrity, the Flemish churchman, Adrian of Utrecht.

The revolt of the *Comuneros* of Castile represented the union of the two most powerful social forces in the state against the Crown; the towns, led by Juan de Padilla and Pedro Laso in Toledo, and the nobility headed by Pedro de Giron. In many places the Church also supported this movement of national resistance against a foreign and unconstitutional sovereign; it too had a leader, the most dramatically belligerent of all, a wild and splenetic republican, Antonio de Acuña, Bishop of Zamora. The rebels carried all before them and in August 1520 formed a government, the *Santa Junta*, which declared that the Regent and his council had been displaced, and that it was the only legally constituted authority. At the end of August the rebels reached Tordesillas where they asserted that Joanna was free and sane. Although the Queen showed signs of unusual animation, she soon relapsed into her usual state of indifferent gloom, nor would she sign the document which the rebels presented to her. Had Joanna signed it, she would have given the revolt the backing of the royal house, and so might have changed the future fortunes of Spain.

The *Junta's* demands were a curious mixture of past grievances and newly-formulated constitutional requests. Thus the old

[1] This counteracted the relief felt at the death of the Chancellor Chièvres and the appointment of an innocuous and extremely capable Piedmontese, Mercurio Gattinara, as his successor.

jealousy of foreigners,[1] both of officials and of merchants, reappeared as did the normal complaints about the exodus of precious metals from Spain, and rising prices. It was perhaps an indication of a new spirit abroad that the towns—though limited in number to eighteen—demanded a thorough reform of the Cortes which would have increased their own power and have diminished that of the Crown had the reforms been put into effect. ' It was provided that the Cortes should meet every two or three years, without royal summons, should debate in private, and appoint the notaries who attended, and who had hitherto been the King's officials.' One further demand may be mentioned. Possibly as a result of democratic pressure from some sections, an attack on noble privileges showed signs of developing, both in respect of the employment of the nobles by the Crown and their exemption from taxation.

This division in the rebel ranks was to prove the Crown's salvation. Hitherto Charles had maintained a stubborn silence in the face of the Regent's pitiful tale of woe: ' I am astonished ', wrote the Co-Regent, the Constable, in November, 1520, ' to see the little attention which your Highness vouchsafes to the interests of our kingdoms and their pacification, for neither in the shape of money, men or artillery has your Majesty sent me any aid—no, not even in paper and ink '. But at last the King showed interest, and with it a conciliatory spirit, especially towards the nobles. And rightly so, for it was through the nobility that the Crown eventually regained control over the situation. The civil war in Castile was centred around Valladolid and Toledo where Bishop Acuña was proclaimed Archbishop by the people (but not by the Chapter of the Cathedral whom the militant cleric tried to starve into submission). The revolt in the north was led by Padilla whose forces were defeated in a skirmish at Villalar, leading to the surrender of Valladolid. Toledo held out until October 1520; the Bishop was captured on the Navarrese frontier and after murdering the deputy governor of Simancas with a leather breviary case in which he had inserted a stone,[2] he was executed by the secular authorities, being hanged from a turret of the castle. With the fall of these two places the revolt in Castile had ended.

[1] There seems to have been a profound antipathy between Spaniards and Flemings, displayed on the occasion of Philip the Fair's visit in 1505, again during the first few years of Charles' rule, and also during the reign of his son, Philip II. This may represent the contrast between the soldier, contemptuous of the business man, and the man of the counting-board averse to war.

[2] He finished the murder with a knife. The governor's son would have suffered a similar fate had he not fled.

The trouble in Valencia had yet to be overcome. From the start it had been a social war in which the people fought the nobles, both disregarding the Crown's attempts to restore order. The Valencians made no contact with the Castilian rebels, but in Valencia as in Castile it was eventually the nobles who won the day.

Thus when Charles returned to Spain accompanied by German soldiers and seventy-four noble guns (their names survive: The Great Dragon, The Great Devil, The Young She-Ass, The Saint James, The Wait-For-Me-I'm-Coming Here), he found a state very nearly pacified. He could well afford to be generous. The odium of suppressing the rebellion had not fallen on him. Although there were some three hundred exceptions from the amnesty he promised, his general policy was merciful. The failure of the *Comuneros* meant the end of 'parliamentary' government and the victory of royal absolutism. In Gomara's words: ' The Communes of Castile began their revolt, but after a good start had a bad ending, and exalted, beyond what it had previously been, the power of the King whom they desired to abase.' Although the Cortes did not disappear, either in Castile or in Aragon, the royal authority in future overcame all possible opposition, whether from the nobility or the towns or the Church. Moreover, Charles' championship of the Church against the Lutherans ministered to the religiosity of Spain and the acquisition of the Imperial title to their pride. The Spanish revenues, both from the old and the new world, were hitched to Charles' Imperial wagon. Henceforth his position in Spain was to be unchallenged, even though he took some care not to offend the Castilians and did much to earn their affection by the policy of Hispanicisation which he adopted throughout his Spanish dominions.

3. *The German problem*

Charles V was really much more interested in the Empire, representing the dynasty and his hereditary estates, than in Germany, which he regarded only as one among his many dominions. None of Charles' leading advisers at home or abroad was a German by birth. The Emperor himself spoke French rather than German. Nothing occurred during Charles' reign that was in any way constitutionally important so far as Germany was concerned. The various Imperial institutions continued to function in their normal, haphazard and inefficient way. The Council of Regency or *Reichsregiment*, the only reform instituted by the Diet of Worms in 1521, met for the last time at the Diet of Nuremberg three years later. The only important addition to the Imperial constitution was a new legal code, *Constitutio Criminalis Carolina,* put into operation in 1532. Apart from these comparatively minor matters Charles' government left no positive impress upon Germany. It is even possible that his own interest in the German problem lapsed, for after 1531 he left the day-to-day business in the hands of his brother Ferdinand who was more concerned with extending his hereditary estates than with maintaining the Imperial dignity.

Yet Charles' reign was of the utmost significance in German history. Whatever hopes there might have been of making Germany into a strong national monarchy like France or Spain were brought to nothing through the particularism of the princes and the number and the nature of the problems facing the Emperor. His policy towards Germany was Imperial rather than German. As Emperor he had duties towards the vassal princes in return for which they owed him certain services. The restoration of Imperial authority was thus one of the first of his tasks, even if it was to prove impossible of achievement. In general terms he saw himself as the champion of peace and justice, whether against the rebellious peasants, unruly knights or disobedient princes. Finally he was the divinely appointed guardian and defender of the true faith against the German Protestants. Expediency might oblige him to compromise but the unity of the faith was, he believed, the foundation of the unity of the Empire. All these problems would have been more than enough for one man had he not had to deal also with the Turks, the Spaniards, the Netherlands and Francis I.

When Charles went to the first of his Imperial Diets, that of Worms, in 1521, he was confronted by three major questions, all of which were closely interrelated and which were ultimately to bring to nothing his plan for restoring Imperial power. First there was the question, which had faced his grandfather, Maximilian, of making the Imperial constitution more workable. It was once again suggested that Imperial policy should be determined by a Council of Regency (*Reichsregiment*), but Charles was opposed to the creation of an instrument which would place all power in the hands of the princes. The Council which was then set up had thus only a limited authority and could only act independently during the Emperor's absence abroad. Its life was therefore uncertain and short. ' The government which was formed was too weak to weld Germany into a political whole, able to withstand the disintegrating influence of its own particularism and of the Hapsburg dynastic interest ; and Charles was left free to pursue throughout his reign the old Imperial maxim, *divide et impera*.'[1] The slow break-down of Imperial authority placed more and more power in the hands of the individual German princes with whom the final responsibility for maintaining stable government was eventually to rest.

The second problem was closely linked with the preservation of internal peace, seriously challenged in the next four years by two separate outbreaks of violence. The first concerned the Imperial Knights (*Ritterschaft*), a feudal class directly responsible to the Emperor, the incomes of which had suffered from rising prices. The Knights' liberty had been further restricted by the increase in the power of the princes, the replacement of feudal custom by Roman Law and by the prohibition of private war and brigandage which had for long been their main occupation. Under the lead of Franz von Sickingen, the Rhineland knights rejected the authority of the Supreme Court of Justice (*Reichskammergericht*), which had been re-established by the Diet of Worms, and shortly afterwards attacked the city of Trier. In a vain effort to gain public opinion to their side, and enrich themselves, they took advantage of the religious troubles to attack Church property. Sickingen and his colleague, the fierce, critically-destructive Franconian humanist and knight, Ulrich von Hutten, were both genuinely attracted by Luther's teaching. But the Knights had no place in, and little support from, the modern world. Sickingen perished at the siege of his own castle of Landstuhl in May, 1523. The able but obstreperous Hutten fled to Switzerland where he found a refuge on the little islet of Ufenau at the eastern end of the Lake of Zürich and there died in 1523, leaving, as Zwingli put it, ' nothing but his pen '. But it was the princes rather than the Emperor who put down the Imperial Knights, a suggestive signpost to future history increasingly dominated by the princes.

It was the princes rather than Truchsess' Imperial soldiers who suppressed a new set of disorders arising out of the Peasants' War. The peasants rebelled for a number of reasons ; because of age-old grievances connected with tithes, game laws and exploitation by their landlords ; because of the stricter interpretation which some of the new lords were trying to give the peasants' fulfilment of their feudal services, which the imposition of a uniform Roman Law undoubtedly assisted ; because of rising prices. Their demands, expressed in the Twelve Articles issued in March, 1525, were similar to those which the peasants had put forward in earlier risings. They asked that their customs and laws should be respected, and complained of the way in which landlords appropriated

[1] *Cambridge Modern History*, ii, 149.

their woodlands and forced them to undertake services for which there were no precedents. The movement, which was directed in the main against the princes, was thus conservative rather than radical. It was in no way an effect of Luther's teaching, but the new religious ideas, with their implied emphasis on human brotherhood and their attacks on Church property, fitted in with the economic and political aspirations of the peasants. It was a former follower of Luther, Thomas Münzer of Zwickau who preached rebellion in Thuringia and tried to establish a semi-communistic settlement at Mühlhausen in Saxony. ' Arise! Fight the battle of the Lord!', ran one of his proclamations, ' On! On! On! . . . Rouse up the towns and the villages; above all, rouse the miners. . . . On! On! On! while the fire is burning let not the blood cool on your swords! . . . God is with you.' Starting in the Black Forest, on the estate of the Count von Lupfen whose wife, it was asserted, had ordered the peasants to collect on a public holiday snail-shells which she wanted for her embroidery silks, the rising spread rapidly through south-west Germany and towards Austria and Saxony. It was a violent spontaneous movement, without much plan or programme, directed against monasteries, baronial castles and fortified towns in some of which the workers rose in revolt against ecclesiastical and feudal control. But the princes, supported by Catholic and Lutheran alike, were not backward in using force to suppress the crude peasant armies. Luther, who had an almost medieval veneration for order, hounded on the princes to crush the peasants in his bitter pamphlet *Against the murdering, thieving hordes of Peasants*. Philip of Hesse and the Elector John of Saxony defeated Münzer's peasant bands at Frankenhausen in May, 1525, and the rising soon after collapsed. It was another victory for the princes and the territorial landlords rather than for the Emperor. Peace and order had been restored at the cost of a continuance of social and economic injustice.

Elements of social and religious disorder remained but were stifled and pushed underground. Yet one other outbreak deserves mention. It was caused by a group of men known as the Anabaptists whose teaching on religion, economics and politics was exceptionally revolutionary. Apart from their emphasis on adult baptism, which they regarded as a fundamental of their religion, they believed that the congregation should elect its pastors, and held semi-communistic and pacifist views. In 1535 certain Dutch Anabaptists, headed by Jan Matthys, a baker of Haarlem, and Jan of Leyden, invited to Münster to strengthen the Protestant cause there by its left-wing leader Rothmann, overthrew the existing order and tried to turn the city into a New Jerusalem. Success clearly went to the head of their leader, Jan of Leyden.[1] Dismissing the ' Twelve Apostles ', he announced through his prophet Dusenschur that God willed that he should become king of the world and initiate the Fifth Monarchy of the Apocalypse. The Bishop of Münster, helped by other German princes, eventually recaptured his rebellious city, and executed the Anabaptist leaders whose mutilated bodies (they had been tortured with red-hot pincers), contained in iron cages, hung long from one of the church towers of Münster to emphasise the sin of disobedience to lawful authority. The Anabaptist rising revealed the discontent seething under the surface of society ; but society, represented by the princes and the merchant classes, had again triumphed.

However, the principal German problem facing Charles V throughout his reign was that of Lutheranism which was to foster the particularism of the princes and so to diminish the Imperial authority as well as to shatter the unity of the Empire. Although Charles could never have become a Lutheran, he wanted the Church to mend its ways. He believed that this could be best achieved by calling a general council, for if the abuses which the Lutherans attacked were abolished, then the way would be open for a renewal of German loyalty to the Holy See. But Charles could only carry out this policy if the Pope helped him. Moreover what at the Diet of Worms might have appeared as a universal German revolt against the Papacy was rapidly crystallising into an organised and separate religion with a definite territorial and political sphere of influence. Lutheranism had become closely allied to the political particularism of the German princes. Whether the prince was genuinely converted to the truth of Lutheran ideas or not, he enjoyed worldly gains through the confiscation of Church property to his own use, increased control over Church affairs, and a greater degree of independence of the Catholic Emperor. Thus Charles was not only faced by a spreading Lutheran Church, organised along lines very different from that of Rome, but was opposed by a political and religious organisation supported by a number of the German princes, John Frederick of Saxony and Philip of Hesse in particular, as well as by some of the Imperial cities.

In any case Charles had a very restricted opportunity to enforce the decree of the Diet of Worms against Luther. The many other

[1] He believed in communism of property and wives—he had sixteen—though some authorities believe that polygamy was encouraged by Jan's love for Matthys' widow, Divara, whom he could not obtain in a legitimate manner.

problems which claimed his attention, especially the wars which he had to wage against Francis I in Italy and against the Turks, could only be conducted successfully if peace was assured in Germany. This in its turn could only be obtained by granting concessions to the Protestant princes. Thus the innumerable diets which punctuate the story of Charles' dealings with the Lutherans record his strength or weakness at the particular moments of their meeting. If his position abroad was weak, then his decisions would inevitably favour the German Protestants. If it seemed strong, then the outlook for them was more grim. But on the few occasions when he seemed strong enough to crush the Lutheran princes and enforce the edict of the Diet of Worms, he was nearly always hampered by the arrival of new problems before he could finish the task.

Luther's condemnation at Worms had in fact been followed by a rapid expansion of Lutheranism. The reformer himself had been ' kidnapped ' for his own safety by his supporter, the Elector Frederick, and was letting his tonsure grow and living as ' Junker Georg ' at the Saxon castle of Wartburg. But his presence was no longer vital to the revolt. He had provided it with an impetus which nothing could now stop. Much the greater part of popular literature printed in Germany between 1518 and 1525 was inspired by his teaching and was a popularisation of it. One of the best-known Lutheran propagandists, John Eberlin of Günsburg, purposely addressed his works chiefly to the ' ordinary ' man. He rubbed in the fact that the Roman Curia had been systematically robbing Germany, to the tune of 300,000 gulden a year so he reckoned. As a former Franciscan friar, he was inevitably hard on the monks and friars of whom he could not say a good word. Among his many pamphlets, *Of the forty days fast before Easter and others which pitifully oppress Christian Folk ; How very dangerous it is that priests have not wives ; Why there is no money in the country ; Against the false clergy and bare-footed monks*, may be taken as typical titles. In town after town the people, often led by one or other of the local clergy and inspired by Luther's views, took matters into their own hands, attacked the monasteries and began to break the images in the churches, to destroy the vestments and otherwise challenge the old order. At Wittenberg the left-wing Carlstadt swept away the Mass, instituted communion in both kinds,[1] wore lay clothes and dispensed the Lord's Supper in ' evangelical fashion ', that is to say, he left everything out which suggested that the Mass

[1] The Medieval Church had only provided the laity with the Communion in one kind, i.e. with the bread. The Protestants demanded Communion in both kinds, i.e. bread and wine.

was a Sacrifice. In disorderly and rather chaotic fashion similar things happened all over Germany. The Reformation began at Magdeburg with a poor weaver singing two of Luther's hymns [1] in the market-place; when the Burgomaster ordered his arrest the people came to his rescue (May 6th, 1524). Luther himself was seriously perturbed by the radical nature of some of the changes, more especially by the activities of a body of extremists known as the Zwickau prophets [2] and by what Carlstadt and Zwilling were doing in his own town at Wittenberg. Still dressed as 'Junker Georg' he reappeared there and arranged the reformation according to his own ideas. 'To marry, to do away with images, to become monks or nuns, or for monks and nuns to leave their convents, to eat meat on Friday or not to eat it, and other like things—all these are open questions, and should not be forbidden by any man', he told his people, 'If I employ force, what do I gain . . . what we want is the heart and to win that we must preach the Gospel.' Meanwhile he continued to work at his translation of the Bible into German; the New Testament was published in 1522 and the Old Testament in 1534. Thus, in spite of various setbacks which included Luther's own marriage to an ex-nun, Catherine Bora, in 1525, and his implied support of the bigamous marriage of Philip of Hesse in 1540, Lutheranism throve in many parts of northern and eastern Germany. [3]

But what chance had Charles, often away from Germany, often faced with other problems, of striking a mortal blow at this dynamic

[1] Hymn singing played an important part in the spread of Lutheranism (as it did of Methodism). The German poet Heine called *Ein' Feste Burg ist unser Gott* (A safe stronghold our God is still) the *Marseillaise* of the Reformation.

[2] Zwickau was a little weaving town sixty-four miles south of Wittenberg. The three men who had carried out the reformation there, Nicolaus Storch, Thomas Münzer and Marcus Stübner, came to Wittenberg in 1521. Partly through their influence a thorough Reformation along extremist lines took place at Wittenberg, expressed in the ordinance of January 1522 which reformed public worship and also initiated significant social reforms.

[3] Although one of the leading Protestant princes, Philip of Hesse did not live a moral private life. He was married to a Saxon princess, Christina, but now wished to marry, in addition to his own wife, Margaret von der Saal. He consulted Bucer, Melanchthon and Luther who replied that although bigamy should be denounced, it was not expressly forbidden by the New Testament. 'The pastorate, in individual cases of direct need, and to prevent worse, may sanction bigamy in a purely exceptional way.' They urged, however, that such a marriage should be kept secret. When, as was inevitable, the news of the marriage leaked out, it caused a first-class scandal and did much damage to the reformers' reputations. While Luther's action cannot be justified, it should be added that he had been misled by Philip of Hesse.

force? It was supported by many of the princes as well as by merchants and by working people. It was the Elector John of Saxony, not the bishops, who organised the Church throughout his territory in 1528-29, who instituted the Lutheran pastors, abandoned the daily Mass and otherwise introduced reform. Everything now pointed to a division of Germany into those who supported the Emperor and those who would fight on Luther's behalf. When the papal nuncio addressed the Diet at Nuremberg in January 1523, even a vehement reminder of the fates meted out to Dathan and Abiram, Ananias and Sapphira, Jerome and Hus only drew from the assembled members a demand for a general council and for the Pope to surrender German annates. The next year's Diet proved as un-cooperative and urged that a German national council should be summoned at Speyer as a preliminary to a general council, a project utterly repugnant both to the Emperor and to the Pope. What was happening was also revealed by a meeting of Catholic princes arranged by the papal legate at Ratisbon in June, 1524, and another meeting at Dessau some months later, to which Philip of Hesse and the other Lutheran princes replied with a Lutheran league.

Meanwhile Charles' great victory at Pavia in 1525 had so enhanced his prestige that when the Diet met at Speyer in 1526, he instructed his brother, the Archduke Ferdinand, to veto all innovations in religion and order that the Edict of Worms should at last be put into force. This was a vain hope. Quite apart from the fact that the Turkish victory over the Hungarians at Mohacs,[1] which coincided with the Diet's meeting, made German unity imperative, the Lutherans were in too strong a position to be overawed. The Imperial cities again demanded that a German national council should be called. The princes declared that in all religious matters each prince ' should so conduct himself as he could answer for his behaviour to God and to the Emperor ', thus asserting the principle which was for so long to govern German religious history. Thus the Diet of Speyer revealed the clear division of parties and the growing power of Lutheranism.

Yet by the end of 1529, the date of the meeting of another Diet at Speyer, the situation had again turned in Charles' favour. The Turks had been turned away from the gates of Vienna. The Treaty of Cambrai had brought peace with France and the Treaty of Barcelona was soon to guarantee, if but for a while, papal subservience to Imperial diplomacy. The new Diet, meeting before the

[1] See p. 384.

Turkish peril had passed, was predominantly Catholic and after a short show of independence complied with Charles' demands. At its start he had affirmed that the important clause which he accepted in 1526 ' on which the Lutherans relied when they founded their territorial churches ' had been ' of (so) much ill counsel and misunderstanding ' that it was abolished by his ' imperial and absolute authority '. The Diet then went on to agree that while the Catholics should be fully tolerated in Lutheran states, Lutherans would not be accepted in Catholic territory, nor could Zwinglians and Anabaptists be tolerated. The Protestant minority, consisting of six princes and fourteen cities, then issued the famous Protest (from which the word Protestant is taken) refusing to agree to the new orders. To strengthen the Protestant cause and overcome the internal divisions which were impeding its progress, Philip of Hesse tried to arrange a reconciliation between Luther and Zwingli at his castle of Marburg, but without success.[1]

The Lutheran princes' defiance might well suggest that armed conflict was about to begin, but neither side was really eager to use force. Successful as the Emperor had been recently, he could not face the heavy expenditure of a long war, or the effects of German disunity with equanimity. The reformers, themselves disunited, had not yet given up a final hope of reconciliation with the Catholics on agreed terms. Fresh from his triumphs in Italy, Charles crossed over the Brenner Pass and reached Augsburg where he hoped that he might resolve the religious differences. The Lutheran princes, invited by the Emperor to state their position, asked Melanchthon to prepare the necessary memorandum. The Confession of Augsburg, as this was called, was a moderate document designed to emphasise Lutheran respect for traditional Catholic forms and ideas, but there was no real possibility of compromise. The German Protestant princes, realising their impotence, withdrew, leaving the Diet to decide to carry out the Edict of Worms ; six months grace was given to the Lutherans to enable them to return to the bosom of the Church. In the face of this new peril the Protestant princes, under the lead of the Elector John of Saxony and

---

[1] The conference was held between October 30th and November 5th, 1529. The critical point concerned the relationship of the body of Christ to the elements of Bread and Wine in the Lord's Supper. Luther characteristically chalked on the table ' Hoc est Corpus Meum ', saying ' I take these words literally ; if anyone does not, I shall not argue but contradict '. Zwingli denied the Real Presence, holding that the Supper is not a repetition of the Sacrifice of the Cross, but a commemoration of it, and that the elements are merely the signs, *Signa*, of this. Yet something was achieved. Luther and Zwingli agreed on fourteen out of the fifteen Articles of Marburg.

Philip of Hesse, formed a defensive league at a meeting held at the little Saxon town of Schmalkalden in December, 1530.

It was now in 1530-31 that Charles should have made a really determined effort to root out heresy and to suppress his opponents. As yet weak and divided, they might have been easily defeated by the experienced Imperial soldiery. But it was Charles' destiny never to have a completely free hand. If the Protestants were still divided,[1] the Catholic front was very far from solid. The Imperial finances were as chaotic as ever. Once again the threat of a Turkish invasion forced the Emperor to compromise with the princes. In July, 1532, he promised the Diet of Nuremberg that he would suspend all action against the heretics until a General Council of the Church met, a decision which he actually implemented at the ensuing Diet of Ratisbon by promising to call an Imperial Council within six months if the Pope refused to call a Council. By the time the Turkish trouble faded away the Emperor was again involved in Italy; Germany did not see him for nine years. So the dismal series of events had come full circle again.

Another stage in the history of the Valois-Hapsburg struggle ended in 1544 with the signing of the Treaty of Crépy. This victory, coinciding with the Pope's promise to call a General Council, seemed to suggest that fortune had once more favoured Charles. But fortune, as the Emperor had good reason to know, is a fickle jade. Helped by divisions within the Schmalkaldic League, the Emperor had won over Duke Maurice of the junior Albertine line of Saxon princes by the promise of his cousin's electoral estates. Thus by the time that the Diet of Ratisbon met in July, 1546— Luther had died the previous February—Charles once more decided that the time had come to impose the Edict of Worms. ' If the Emperor ', the Venetian ambassador reported, 'does not succeed in bringing the Protestants to reason, it will be necessary for him to remain in Germany or in the Netherlands ; for in case he withdraws, the common opinion is that novelties prejudicial to him may be introduced into these last-named territories which are already to a great extent infected with Lutheranism.'

The die cast, the Imperial victory proved both rapid and effective, but the gain was too qualified to be a true triumph. With the Protestant princes captured on the field of Mühlberg (April 24th, 1547), Charles appeared to have gained the initiative. But having won the war, he mismanaged the peace. Many Germans, especially

---

[1] Zwingli's death in battle in October, 1531, was followed by a *rapprochement* between the Lutheran princes and the South German cities, who had followed Zwingli's lead ; many of them now joined the Schmalkaldic League.

among the princes, thought this treatment of Philip of Hesse and John Frederick of Saxony [1] arbitrary and unkind. They were even more perturbed by his new attempt to reconcile the contending parties. As always he acted with the best of intentions. The insincerity and hostility of Pope Paul III, who was on the point of adjourning, if not abandoning, the recently convoked General Council of the Church now assembled at Trent, tempted Charles to think once more of a *via media* which would satisfy Catholic and Lutheran. Faithful Catholic as he was, he knew that the imposition of religious uniformity by force throughout the Empire would be an insuperable task. In the hope of satisfying all parties, he approved the Interim of Augsburg which admitted 'the universality and indivisibility of the Church, the seven sacraments and doctrine of transubstantiation, but allowed the legality of clerical marriages and, to some extent, the doctrine of Justification by Faith'. The Interim was drawn up by a committee of three moderates, Michael Helding, Julius von Pflug and Agricola, and was accepted by some of the princes and free cities. But in general it was intensely disliked by the Catholics and by the Lutherans who described it 'as a strait waistcoat'. Charles unwisely decided to use force in the shape of Italian and Spanish soldiery, thus alienating many of his well-wishers. Among those whose support he lost at this juncture was the ambitious Maurice, who feared Imperial absolutism and thought that there might be more to gain out of rebellion than obedience. And behind the German storm clouds, there was the energetic and belligerent King of France, Henry II, with whom the Schmalkaldic League of Protestant princes made a compact at Chambord in 1552.

The next three years revealed the extent of Charles' failure. Military defeats forced him to agree to the Convention of Passau, a truce by which he promised to release the two Protestant leaders and to permit the free exercise of the Lutheran faith in order that yet another Diet might be summoned to solve the religious problem. But conflict with France continued. The treacherous Maurice was killed in battle in a private war at Sievershausen but, in truth, the Emperor was completely worn out. In 1553 the English envoy wrote: 'He is so weak and pale as to seem a very unlike man to continue. He covets to sit up and walk, and is sometimes led between two, with a staff also in his hand, but like as he desires to be thus afoot, so immediately after he has been a little up, he must be

---

[1] To be differentiated from his uncle the Elector Frederick the Wise (1486-1525), Luther's original patron, and his father the Elector John (1525-32).

laid down again, and feels himself so cold, as by no means he can attain any heat.' He recovered his health and there were still military successes to report. But for how long could this continue ? Slowly but surely he realised how he had failed in his one supreme task, the restoration of religious unity. One by one he shed his dignities, leaving the Imperial diadem to the last, knowing that his brother Ferdinand, always more moderate in religious matters than he had been, would cope with the Lutheran question.

The Religious Peace of Augsburg of 1555 may not therefore be regarded as Charles' work. By its terms each prince was to decide for himself whether he would adopt Lutheranism or Catholicism ; confiscated Church lands were to be retained by their present owners, but there were to be no further confiscations. At best this could only be a temporary solution. By 1555 Calvinism was firmly established in many parts of Europe and had penetrated into Germany, but no notice was taken of it. The Lutherans were alone recognised. By the ' Ecclesiastical Reservation ' clause of the Treaty any spiritual prince who became a Lutheran lost his property and his dignities ; here was fertile soil for future trouble.[1] But this was not the real weakness of the Peace. The sixteenth century was an intolerant age ; only a few men believed that toleration could be a fundamental of an ordered society. Nor did the Peace of Augsburg uphold toleration. It allowed the existence of two religions, each the choice not of the people or of the Church but of the ruling secular prince, a compromise which invited challenge sooner or later. Expediency might dictate that the Emperor might have to accept this solution for the time being but it was thoroughly imperfect. As the Counter-Reformation spurred on a Catholic revival, so the Catholic princes, backed by the Church, dreamed of regaining their lost territory. On the other side neither the people nor the princes were content with all the clauses of the Peace. Thus within its pages may be disclosed the marks of future war. Yet it must be conceded that there was no real alternative at the time. If its final failure was inevitable, it at least provided Germany with long years of relative but much-needed peace and was a pointer in the direction of religious liberty. But Charles only saw that Augsburg sealed his own failure. In Edward Armstrong's words : ' The Emperor's attitude towards the Peace of Augsburg proved the strength of his religious convictions and the weakness of his political insight.'

[1] This clause, allowing no further secularisation of Church property after 1552, was accepted by the Emperor but was not part of the Treaty accepted by the Diet.

4. *Hapsburg-Valois rivalry*

The complex story of the Italian Wars merged into the wider story of Hapsburg-Valois rivalry with the election of the King of Spain as Holy Roman Emperor in 1519. Francis I of France inherited his cousin's claims to Naples (now in the hands of Charles) and to Milan which was under French control. He realised that Imperial rule in Spain and the Netherlands as well as in Germany and parts of Italy threatened France with encirclement; henceforth French policy was dominated by the desire to demolish Hapsburg hegemony in Europe. Nor had Francis forgotten that the Electors had preferred Charles as Emperor.

Charles' policy was founded on his respect for traditional rights and his conception of his own duty as a peacemaker. He inherited the long if intermittent feud between the Burgundian and the French ruling families. Often advised by men of Burgundian stock and steeped in the traditions of his duchy, he could not forget that the ancient duchy of Burgundy was not originally a part of France. The same respect for feudal rights made him question the French control over Milan, which bestrode the communications between his Austrian and Mediterranean possessions. Finally it was Charles' responsibility to the world to bring about the restoration of peace by the arbitrament of force if necessary. If such motives and ideas seem foreign to modern politics, it is because our conception of political and moral obligations has so greatly changed since the sixteenth century.

There is no point in detailing the battles, sieges and minor treaties of peace, the alliances and counter-alliances which marked the long story of Hapsburg-Valois rivalry in Italy, but certain turning points must be mentioned because on the Imperial reaction to them the course of future history depended.

On February 24th, 1525, Charles' twenty-fifth birthday, Leyva and the Imperial army imposed a crushing defeat on the French outside Pavia. When the Emperor learned of the victory, he repeated the news—'The battle is fought and the King is your prisoner'—as one dazed by surprise and forthwith retired to his room to pray. All the European world wondered what use he would make of his victory. Since Francis was a Christian prince, Charles forbade all rejoicing. But should he invade France and so bring about an unconditional surrender? It is very doubtful whether he was strong enough to do this;[1] but he was in a good position

---

[1] 'If the conquering army held together, it must starve; if it was scattered over a wider area, it fell out of hand, and plundered the Emperor's subjects and allies. The problem solved itself by desertion' (Armstrong, i, 155).

to secure an advantageous peace. He would have done well to have given more detailed attention to the advice tendered him by his able Chancellor, Gattinara. The Chancellor urged that Francis should be kept a prisoner in Italy and that the occasion should be used to prevent any recurrence of French aggression. Charles should treat Francis with the ' magnanimity of the lion and the mercy of God the Father ', but he would only be claiming his just rights if he demanded the whole of his Burgundian inheritance. A stern but just peace would permit the Emperor to destroy Lutheranism and push back the Turk. But Charles preferred a negotiated peace to an Imperial *diktat*. Francis' advisers were very unwilling to surrender Burgundy, which would place the French capital within striking range of Charles' army, but the King quivered at the restraint placed upon his movements. He was advised to appear unwell and was indeed genuinely ill with an abscess on the brain ; illness might move Charles to hurry from his hunting in the Segovian woods to visit the King, but the fascination which Francis knew he possessed for the beautiful women of his court exercised no power over the serious-minded Hapsburg. The surrender of Burgundy might imperil the integrity of the kingdom, but the King placed his wish to return home before national honour. By the Treaty of Madrid, signed on January 13th, 1526, he surrendered his suzerainty over Flanders, Artois and Tournai and ceded his claims to Milan, Genoa and Asti. He agreed to persuade the French Estates to consent to the surrender of Burgundy and swore to return to captivity if he failed in this. Finally, led by the guiding star of Charles' idealism, he promised to go on a crusade with the Emperor against the foes of Christendom.

But could Charles trust Francis ? He took what seemed to him adequate precautions. In the presence of witnesses the French King took an oath on the Gospels after Mass to keep troth, more especially to return to prison if the terms of the Treaty were not observed. Later he pledged his word to Charles again, on parting from him, before a wayside shrine. But the Emperor, with all his knowledge of men, did not truly know Francis. As soon as he reached French soil he shouted ' Now I am King, I am King once more.' ' Charles had let slip his chance. He had lost that one August day which Lannoy, in announcing the victory of Pavia, had declared comes to a man once and once only in his life.' [1] The volatile Frenchman was never greatly concerned with keeping his word. There is indeed no one in fiction whom he so greatly resembles as Kenneth Grahame's Mr. Toad of Toad Hall.[2] He had

[1] E. Armstrong, *The Emperor Charles V*, i, 163.   [2] *The Wind in the Willows.*

the same tactless boastfulness, love of pleasure and splendour, outward charm, exaltation and depression of spirits (in awkward circumstances) and irresponsibility. No episode so well showed the difference in the characters of the two monarchs.

Long before he returned home the reaction in Europe against Charles' great victory had begun, more especially in Italy. Thus Francis' refusal to implement the terms of the Treaty of Madrid and to return to prison made the reopening of war inevitable. On May 22nd, 1526, the League of Cognac was formed between France, the Pope, Florence, Venice and Francesco Sforza of Milan under the 'protection' of Henry VIII of England. Charles' anger is easily understandable. 'Had your King kept his word, we should have been spared this. . . . He has cheated me; he has acted neither as a knight nor as a nobleman, but basely. I demand that if he cannot fulfil his Treaty, the Most Christian King should keep his word and become my prisoner again.' Francis' allies lacked cohesion, resolution and confidence; and a small cloud appeared in the north-east which was soon to develop into a terrifying storm. Frundsberg's German *landsknechts* had crossed the Alps but there was no money to pay them, little enough food to feed them. Their general was a dying man; in his place there was the French noble, the Duke of Bourbon, powerless to control his turbulent hordes. Bourbon had entered the Imperial service in 1523. A great feudatory and Constable of France he had come into conflict with the King and the Queen-Mother over claims which they had made to part of his vast estates. Knowing that he could expect little from the Parlement of Paris, Bourbon had appealed to the Emperor and had entered his service.

Passing by Siena and Florence the gaunt and angry army pushed on towards Rome which was not only a symbol of the enemy but a prize that could supply them with the riches of the world. The horrified Pope suddenly realised his danger. He had not money enough, even by selling cardinals' hats, to buy off the soldiery. The ragged, brutal army lay outside the walls on May 5th, 1527; through the misty morning of May 6th the soldiers mounted the western walls. Bourbon was killed leading his men. In his *Autobiography*, one of the most fascinating works produced by the Italian Renaissance, the boastful and mendacious artist Benvenuto Cellini claimed, probably incorrectly, that he had fired the arquebus which caused Bourbon's death. Uncontrolled, the mutinous army surged into the practically defenceless city. 'Every one fled to seek safety for himself. . . . Some of the fugitives made for the Ponte Sisto . . . others fled to the Castle of St. Angelo, where they found the entrance blocked by a struggling crowd of Cardinals, prelates, officials of the Court, merchants and women . . . at last the bewildered guard with difficulty let down the rusty portcullis and closed the gate. Cardinal Pucci was pushed down in the scramble and seriously injured; but some of his household managed to push him through a window. Cardinal Armellino, who had been left outside, was placed in a basket and drawn up to the top of the castle by a rope. Clement, who was on his knees in his chapel, was warned by the shouts and shrieks of the pursuers and perceived that it was time for flight. He just succeeded in escaping from the Vatican; for 'had he stayed long enough to say three creeds', wrote an eye-witness, 'he would have been taken . . . Paolo Giovio gathered up his train and carried it that he might run faster, throwing over the Pope's head and shoulders his own violet cloak, lest the white colour of the Papal vestments might attract attention.' [1] There was an uncanny horror about the next four days as the city, already plundered by Colonna's raiders in September, 1526, was put to the sack, an event which Charles would have done anything to avoid and which more than anything else damaged his reputation. 'Brutalised by hardships, by poverty, by suffering; of different nations, Germans, Spaniards, Italians; they were', wrote Bishop Mandell Creighton, 'held together by no common bond save that of boundless cupidity and wild desire. Rome was at the mercy, not of a conquering army, but of a host of demons inspired only with avarice, cruelty and lust. . . . The groans of the dying were only interrupted by the blasphemies of the soldiers, and the shrieks of agonising women who were being violated or hurled out of the windows.'

None-the-less the sack of Rome had once again placed the initiative in Charles' hands. Faced with the decision of making the next move he proved irresolute. Gattinara, who had been visiting Italy, advised Charles to deny that he was responsible for what had occurred and to use the occasion to demand a General Council to deal with heresy and to institute much-needed reforms in the Church; but the Imperial counsellors were divided. The Pope surrendered on June 5th, 1527, but in December he escaped through the Vatican gardens to his squalid palace at Orvieto, not perhaps without the connivance of his guards, who disliked having to guard a prisoner who could place their eternal souls in jeopardy. The Imperial situation in Italy was indeed fast deteriorating. The Imperial armies which were shut up in Naples and Milan lacked pay, supplies and ammunition and were surrounded by disaffected

[1] Mandell Creighton, *A History of the Papacy*, vi, 340.

townspeople. Communications by sea were no longer safe since Doria and the Genoese had deserted the Emperor. No money could be raised from Castile or Germany; the rich bankers of Italy were hostile. From this perilous situation Charles was saved not by his friends but by his enemies. Until it was too late Francis did nothing to help Lautrec's forces in southern Italy; his treatment of the Genoese turned Doria from a potential friend of France into an active ally of the Emperor. This volte-face was exceedingly important as it freed the communications between the Spanish ports and Naples and so helped to bring about the surrender of the French army. Returning good fortune culminated in the defeat of another French army under St. Pol at Landriano, which gave Charles full command over Milan and the Lombard plain.

The turn of the tide in Charles' favour sufficed to persuade the anxious Pope to review the situation and to conclude the Treaty of Barcelona with the Emperor. Charles agreed to restore the Sforza to Milan and the Medici to Florence; the Pope recovered certain territory and promised to recognise Charles as King of Naples and to crown him Emperor. There were the usual clauses about combined action against the heretic and the Turk but, significantly enough, nothing about the calling of a General Council of the Church. Far from being the ' Eternal Peace ' that it was proudly proclaimed to be, the Treaty had no permanent importance, but it did help to prepare the way for a general pacification. Negotiations carried on by Francis' mother, Louise of Savoy, and the Emperor's aunt, Margaret, reached a satisfactory conclusion at Cambrai on August 3rd, 1529. In general the terms were much the same as those of the Treaty of Madrid but Charles did not press his claims to the duchy of Burgundy. Francis gave up all his claims to territory in Italy and to Flanders and Artois. The two French princes who had been left behind by Francis as hostages and so had paid the penalty for their father's duplicity by three years harsh detention, were released in return for a large money payment. The Treaty was sealed by the marriage of Charles' favourite sister, Eleanor, the widowed Queen of Portugal, to the French King.

The last episode in this stage of Franco-Hapsburg relations took place in Bologna Cathedral on February 24th, 1530, the Emperor's thirtieth birthday and the fifth anniversary of Pavia, when the Pope placed the Imperial crown upon Charles' head. In appearance the zenith of his good fortune, it was not without ill-omen. Few among those present can have believed that it was the end of Charles' troubles or that the Pope would cease to be the trouble-maker. Indeed the Bishop of Tarbes specifically noted that the latter ' never in his life performed a ceremony which touched him so near the heart, nor of which is less good likely to come to him, for several times when he thought no one saw him he heaved such sighs that heavy as his cope was, he made it shake in good earnest '. And if rumour is to be believed there were many who held that they had watched the last Imperial coronation. And so indeed it proved. No Emperor after Charles received the Imperial crown from papal hands. Bright as may have been the scene at Bologna, the festivities were overshadowed by the precarious nature of the triumph.

Throughout Charles' life he was dogged by a three-fold cycle : victory leading to a reaction which robbed it of its importance, the re-emergence of old problems temporarily shelved, and his own inability to make the best use of a favourable situation. All three factors were present in the history of the next decade. At first he was concerned with urgent problems in Germany arising out of the spread of Lutheranism. Then he had to turn his attention to the Turkish advance against the Empire's eastern borders. Finally he led a successful expedition against the Turkish base at Tunis in 1535 in the hope of stemming the threat to Spanish sea-power in the eastern Mediterranean. His plan for protecting his position in Italy took the shape of a series of personal understandings, supported wherever possible by a family alliance. He restored unreliable Francesco Sforza to the duchy of Milan and gave this ailing and disagreeable Italian his twelve-year-old niece Christina of Denmark in marriage. Nearby Savoy was in practice ruled by the Emperor's devoted and strong-minded sister-in-law, Beatrice of Portugal ; her husband was a weak man whose sole claim to fame was the manner of his demise ; for once there was a man who really got out of bed the wrong side and paid the penalty with his death. The Florentine Duke, Alessandro, was married to Charles' illegitimate daughter, Margaret. Mantua was a duchy ruled by the house of Gonzaga and of great strategic importance. The Duke's heir was married to one of Charles' nieces ; the Duke's brother was a leading Imperial general whom Charles made Viceroy of Sicily in 1535. Genoa was bound to Charles by the profits of the carrying trade with Sicily and Spain as by the fact that its foremost citizen, Andrea Doria, was Charles' best admiral. The three other Italian states were less reliable ; the small duchy of Ferrara, traditionally pro-French, had been bribed to support the Emperor by the cession of Modena and Reggio. Venice was too independent to be drawn into Charles' net, from which Pope Clement VII, as slippery as an eel, was seeking to escape. He could not forget the humiliations that he had endured at Charles' hands and, for all the Emperor's support of his family, he was a Medici, he wanted an understanding with France. Such is the interpretation that must be placed on his journey to meet the French King at Marseilles in 1533 and the subsequent marriage of his cousin, Catherine, to Francis' second son, the future Henry II of France, an event not without future significance for France.

All that Charles had achieved was a precarious equilibrium of forces which might at any moment be disturbed by the complex rivalries which split local Italian politics from top to bottom. That five years elapsed before the next major crisis [1] may be accounted for by the diversion of Charles' attention to more pressing problems and by Francis' reluctance to reopen the war, justified by the impoverishment of his treasury. He did what he could to make Charles' position difficult by coming to terms with the German Protestant princes and with the Sultan of Turkey. And even when war actually began, in March 1536, the military events which followed were so indeterminate that both parties agreed to an armistice, arranged by the subtle Farnese Pope Paul III at Villafranca near Nice on June 18th, 1538. The agreement was, however, no more than a truce in spite of the cordial meeting which took place between the Emperor and the French King in the harbour of Aigues-Mortes. They conversed in friendly fashion. Francis gave Charles a diamond ring and both vowed eternal friendship. ' In truth ', asserted Charles, ' I am full of joy, for I hope that the fortunes of Christianity and of my friends will go right well.'

Neither side wanted war immediately but Francis continued his policy of pin-pricking his enemy, now allying with the Protestant Duke of Cleves, now sending emissaries to the Turk. Charles, hoping to repeat his success at Tunis in 1535, led an imposing expedition against Algiers in the autumn of 1541 which proved a fiasco. Its disastrous outcome encouraged Francis to renew the war. Supported by the Protestant Kings of Denmark and Sweden and in alliance with the Duke of Cleves, his armies invaded Luxemburg and harried Brabant while he besieged Perpignan in the south. Unusually he remained on the defensive in Italy. At first it seemed as if this new anti-Hapsburg combination of powers might carry all before it, but the German princes were embarrassed by the French alliance with the head of the Moslem world; in 1543 Francis handed over the port of Toulon to the Turks and a Franco-Turkish fleet sacked Nice and sold many of its Christian

---

[1] The occasion was again rival claims to the duchy of Milan. As Francesco Sforza died without heirs in 1535, the duchy reverted to Charles as an Imperial fief; but Francis claimed it on behalf of his son, Henry.

inhabitants into slavery. Charles himself believed that if the Pope consented to act with the Turk, he was morally justified in granting concessions to the Protestants if they helped him against the French. Momentarily he agreed at Speyer to a suspension of all measures against the Lutherans and to the demand for the convocation of a general council. This burst of toleration, and the fact that Charles' aunt, Catherine of Aragon, was now dead, made it much easier for the Emperor to come to terms with Henry VIII of England in 1543. About the same time he secured the withdrawal of the Swedes and the Danes from the war by giving up his niece's claim to their respective thrones.

The diplomatic isolation of France had its counterpart in military success. The Imperial army led by Charles himself invaded France and actually threatened Paris. At the same time Henry VIII landed at Calais and besieged Boulogne. Once again final victory evaded the Emperor. In part this was a result of the precariousness of the military situation; the unwillingness of the English to leave Boulogne and march on Paris and the knowledge that he could not depend on the Protestant princes. But it may equally well have been an effect of those overriding considerations which so often shaped his policy. At Speyer he had come nearer to the Protestant princes politically and religiously than he would ever come again; as a result many Catholics had criticised him bitterly. And Charles still realised that the suppression of heresy was his primary task. He was therefore eager to end the wars so that he might once more deal with the religious troubles. This desire for a good understanding is reflected in the generous terms of the ensuing peace.

For the Treaty of Crépy was a remarkably moderate document. Each side agreed to restore the territory which it had occupied since the Truce of Nice. Charles gave up his claim to Burgundy and Francis his demand to suzerainty over Flanders and Artois. There were the usual marriage clauses gilded with the promise of fresh territory. If the Duke of Orléans married Charles' daughter, he would receive the Netherlands, allowing the Emperor the right to act as sovereign while he lived. Francis gave up his claim to Milan. On the other hand, if Orléans married Charles' brother Ferdinand's daughter, he would be invested with Milan. Although the French King also agreed to help the Emperor suppress heresy and to make peace with the Pope, the Treaty lacked the peremptory demands for urgent assistance or for a change of allies which had sometimes figured among Charles' proposals. The Treaty of Crépy represented Charles' acute dislike of war between Francis and himself, an unpleasant necessity foisted on him by the duplicity of his allies, and his belief that his real task lay in the promotion of religious and political unity within the Empire.

The Treaty marked the beginning of the last episode in Charles' long warfare with the Valois, an episode not concluded until Charles was dead. In the years immediately following the Treaty, there was much to cheer the ageing, gout-stricken emperor; the Pope had called a General Council and the Schmalkaldic League had been defeated. But the fruit of victory was soon to turn to ashes. The Pope played false and adjourned the Council of Trent. In Germany Charles had failed to make good use of the victory of Mühlberg, provoking a reaction against him which led to the junction of the Protestant princes with the new French king, Henry II. By the Treaty of Chambord he was promised three Imperial bishoprics, Metz, Toul and Verdun, the 'military keys of Lorraine', for helping them against the Emperor. Henry's entry on the scene changed the situation as it turned an internal conflict into a European struggle. It was symbolic of this new phase in Hapsburg-Valois rivalry that the more important military operations took place in north-west Europe rather than in Italy. The alliance between the French King and the Lutheran princes helped to break Charles and prepared the way for his abdication. And yet neither the King nor the league had a complete victory. It was Charles who negotiated the Truce of Vaucelles with the French representative, Coligny. This was not the end of the struggle which his son, Philip, renewed and which was watched by the Emperor with eager interest from his retreat at Yuste. A year after Charles' death, war-weariness led to the Treaty of Cateau-Cambrésis, signed on April 3rd, 1559.

Although the Treaty did not bring the conflict between the Hapsburgs and the Valois to a close, it represented a significant terminal point. France won the strategically important fortresses of Metz, Toul and Verdun [1] as well as Calais; but gave up its claims on Italy and restored Savoy and Piedmont to Duke Emmanuel Philibert, an exceptionally able prince who did much to make his duchy into a strong, prosperous and well-administered state. Although the French disliked the terms, in appearance they had gained much. Nevertheless the drain of the long Italian Wars on French resources had been such that the country was left facing imminent bankruptcy. During the last half of the sixteenth century

[1] Since the Empire was not a party to the Treaty (signed between France and Spain) no mention was made of the three bishoprics in the Treaty, but their change of rule was tacitly accepted. They remained an Imperial vicariate in name until they were annexed to France by the Treaty of Westphalia in 1648.

the independence of France was to be threatened by internal anarchy
as well as foreign war, to both of which the Italian Wars served as a
prelude. The conclusion of the Treaty of Cateau-Cambrésis freed
large numbers of soldiers to fight in the French Wars of Religion
which were to break out three years later, and did not end the
struggle with the Hapsburgs of Madrid and Vienna.

The Treaty of Cateau-Cambrésis represented a virtual return
to the territorial *status quo* and an abandonment of French claims
in Italy. This helped Spain to counterbalance French power in
the Mediterranean but at the expense of much Spanish wealth and
the squandering of Spanish man-power in useless Imperial enter-
prises.

And what of the state of the Empire at the end of Charles' reign ?
The Italian Wars and the Lutheran problem helped to make the
Empire even more of a political illusion than it had been in the
fifteenth century. So far as Germany was concerned the future
lay with the princes who were to play an increasingly prominent,
if irresponsible, part in the moulding of German history. The
Emperor lacked an army and effective executive power. He was
opposed to constitutional reform and depended for his revenue
on his hereditary and non-German dominions ; Granvelle told the
Diet of Speyer that ' the Emperor has, for the support of his dignity,
not a hazel-nut's worth of profit from the empire '. The Imperial
interests were more and more dynastic and less and less German.
Even the territorial accessions were made to strengthen the dynastic
dominions of the reigning Emperor, not for the good of the *Reich*
itself. Concern for dynastic interests in the fifteenth century had
brought about a reduction in Imperial power in the frontier lands
of the north and east ; Holstein, for instance, was attached to Danish
rule whilst the Teutonic Knights were obliged in 1466 to acknow-
ledge Polish suzerainty. The Swiss, as we have seen,[1] were free
of Imperial control after 1499. It is true that the absorption of
Hungary and Bohemia in the Hapsburg inheritance and the acquisition of the Burgundian dominions as a result of the fortunate
marriage of 1477 strengthened Hapsburg power but at the cost of
diminishing the importance of Germany itself. Thus whatever
hopes the German humanists may have had of a strong and unified
German state around the person of the Emperor faded away completely after 1519 ; ' a mortal disease', Cardinal Nicholas of Cusa
had written as early as 1433, ' has befallen the German *Reich* ; if
it is not speedily treated, death will inexorably ensue. Men will
seek for the realm of Germany and will not find it ; and in time

[1] See p. 106.

strangers will seize our habitations and divide them among themselves.' The frustration which the failure to obtain any constitutional reforms from either Maximilian I or Charles V evoked helps
to explain the spectacular hold which Martin Luther had won over
the whole German people ' in spite of the territorial fragmentation
of Germany '.

But it was not Lutheranism, in any case soon to be challenged
by advancing Calvinism, or Hapsburg Imperialism which were to
determine the future of Germany. This was the task of the territorial princes who grew stronger as the Emperor grew weaker.
They had taken full advantage of Imperial weakness to consolidate
their power over their subjects ; the creation of Frederick of
Hohenzollern as Elector of Brandenburg in 1415 and the bestowal
of the electorate and duchy of Saxony on Frederick of Meissen in
1423 foreshadowed the growth of principalities which were to play
an important part in future German history. The decay of many
of the German towns, arising from foreign competition in the
sixteenth century, fostered the power of the prince, his position
already strengthened theoretically by Roman Law which taught
that the will of the prince could be the basis of the law. In the
fifteenth century the prince, in increasing need of money as a result
of the rising cost of modern armaments and a more extensive administration, had often perforce to come to terms with the local
Estates; but the next century witnessed nearly everywhere an
increase in his power at the cost of the Estates. Struggles
over the control of the purse ended in the victory of the territorial
prince. Thus in Bavaria, Dukes William and Ludwig, ruling jointly
and so restoring the unity of the state, raised general taxes without
the permission of the Bavarian Estates. The rise of Lutheranism
furthered this process as Lutheranism gave the prince control over
the Church as well as over the state. The external complications
of the long reign of Charles V, and the Italian Wars in particular,
led to another increase in the power of the local rulers. Between
1555 and 1618 the German princes strengthened their position
still further by reorganising and modernising their governments.[1]
It was not until the Treaty of Westphalia in 1648 that the Emperor
in fact accepted the practical independence of the princes but the
reign of Charles V had been a landmark in the development of
their power. It was a measure of Charles' failure that as the
champion of universal empire and religious uniformity he had in

---

[1] Influenced by French and Burgundian examples the Emperors
Maximilian I and Ferdinand I had remodelled many of their governmental
institutions. Their example was copied by many German princes.

practice acted as the midwife of national ideas, secular particularism and religious disunity. It was even more disastrous for Germany that the territorial princes proved such unenlightened rulers. ' Every change ', as a recent historian has put it ', . . . in the history of Germany between 1520 and 1648 played its part in confining German political life within the rigid framework of a petrifying territorial absolutism.' [1]

[1] G. Barraclough, *The Origins of Modern Germany* (1946), 389.

CHAPTER X

THE SWISS REFORMERS

1. *Zwingli*

HULDREICH ZWINGLI, the father of the Swiss Reformation, was more the creation of his environment than Luther or Calvin were of theirs. Indeed it is impossible to estimate his significance without knowing something of the background to his early life. Both his father and his uncle held office in the small village of Wildhaus where he was born on New Year's Day, 1484, the one as bailiff or *ammann* and the other as village priest. Zwingli, who was destined for the Church by his uncle, an intelligent man, who had become rural dean of Wesen, was carefully educated. He studied under Bünzli at Basle and Wölflin at Berne; after a period at Vienna University where his fellow-students included the future humanists Joachim von Watt and Heinrich Loriti he returned to Basle where he imbibed humanist ideas from Thomas Wyttenbach. But he was most indebted to Erasmus whose books he greatly admired. He learned Greek and later attempted Hebrew; he read the Fathers of the early Church, finding St. Augustine the most illuminating of the patristic writers.[1] In all this there was little to distinguish him from many other intelligent and studious young men. In 1506 he became priest-in-charge of Glarus but left to become a secular priest of the abbey of Einsiedeln in 1516.[2] Meanwhile he had twice visited Italy while acting as a chaplain to Swiss mercenaries from Glarus; in return for his services he had been granted a papal pension.

In Zwingli's life-story the man's personality and the environment in which he lived are complementary. The trend of Swiss politics, leading to the formation of a series of semi-autonomous unions of cantons, undoubtedly stimulated personal and intellectual freedom. Zwingli's appointment as parish priest of the Grossmünster at Zürich in December, 1518, therefore placed him in a position of special significance because Zürich was a leading Swiss canton

---

[1] But it was not until after 1519 that Zwingli made a close study of Augustine's writings.

[2] The change illustrates Zwingli's ardent patriotism. He had already opposed the French as the nation responsible for seducing the Swiss mercenaries into enterprises foreign to Swiss interests. The decision of Glarus to support the French alliance led to Zwingli's departure to Einsiedeln.

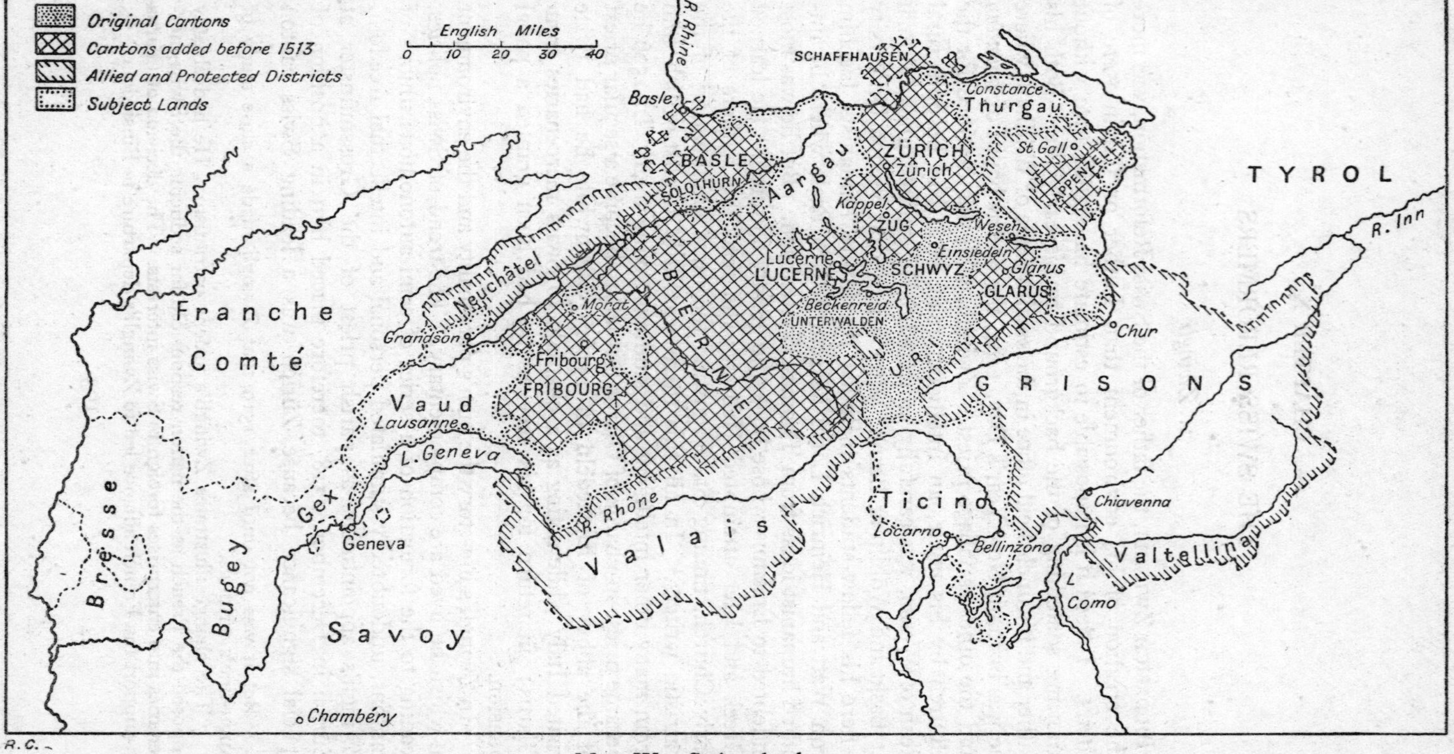

MAP IV.—Switzerland.

TYROL

R. Inn

GRISONS

Chur

Chiavenna

Valtelline

L. Como

Bellinzona

Ticino

Locarno

Constance

St. Gall

Thurgau

Appenzell

Wesen

Glarus

GLARUS

Einsiedeln

SCHAFFHAUSEN

ZÜRICH

Zürich

ZUG

Köppel

SCHWYZ

Morgarten

L. Lucerne

LUCERNE

Sempach

UNTERWALDEN

Aargau

BASLE

SOLOTHURN

R. Rhine

Basle

BERNE

Rhone

VALAIS

Murten

Fribourg

FRIBOURG

Neuchâtel

Grandson

Vaud

Lausanne

L. Geneva

Geneva

Gex

Savoy

Chambéry

Franche Comté

Bugey

Bresse

English Miles

0 10 20 30 40

Original Cantons
Cantons added before 1513
Allied and Protected Districts
Subject Lands

R. C.

which, under its burgomaster Hans Waldmann, had already shown
its desire to legislate in matters affecting Church life. As soon as
he entered on his new office he told the Chapter that he intended
to expound the Gospel of St. Matthew, according to the literal
meaning of the text rather than by reference to the vagaries of
human reason. Unquestionably such a situation placed an eloquent
preacher of strong personality in a favourable position, more
especially when, as in Zwingli's case, he had an ally in the local
printer, Christopher Froschauer, who proved a most enthusiastic
publisher of reformed literature.

Furthermore the development in Zwingli's ideas coincided with
the beginnings of the Lutheran movement. Zwingli himself always
tried to minimise his indebtedness to the German reformer, but
the annotations which he made on the side of his Bible after 1522
show that he had read Luther's writings. But the original impulse
towards the Reformation in Zürich owed little or nothing to Luther.
Like Luther, Zwingli attacked the indulgence system and successfully prevented the entry of the Franciscan preacher of indulgences,
Bernardin Samson, into Zürich in 1519, strangely enough with the
approval of the Bishop of Constance. And he very soon perceived
the significance of Luther's stand, and was soon speaking of the
reformer as another ' David ' or ' Hercules '. Zwingli was, however,
far less emotional and more intellectual. His whole career shows
that he was not introspective ; of all the reformers he was in some
ways the most practical, the most guided by common-sense. Even
when he married the widow Anna Reinhard in 1525, it was not so
much an affair of the heart as an attempt to regularise a dubious
relationship. Yet however different from Luther, Zwingli would
have accomplished little of permanent importance without the
doctrinal cohesion and political backing that the German movement
provided.

So Zürich formed the starting-place of the Swiss reformation.
Zwingli took advantage of the favourable conditions in Zürich to
expound the Gospel to huge congregations, to attack monasticism,
the doctrines of Purgatory and the Invocation of Saints. But such
teaching was not yet directed against the Pope ; the preacher at the
Grossmünster continued to draw his papal pension. It was perhaps
typical that the initial step in the break with the Roman Church
should have been caused by a dispute over the payment of tithes
which Zwingli denounced as without foundation in divine law.
At the same time he condemned the Swiss mercenary system in a
series of patriotic speeches. Partly because of this the Council
forbade the acceptance of gifts from foreign powers and in 1522

prohibited foreign service ; Zwingli as a sequel resigned his papal pension. Simultaneously a number of religious changes were introduced. In practice Zwingli's proposals were sometimes toned down by the Smaller Council of Zürich, more fearful than the reformer of episcopal wrath, but the gap separating Zürich from Rome grew wider. In 1522 some of Zwingli's followers challenged ecclesiastical authority by eating meat in Lent, which Zwingli subsequently justified in a published sermon *On the Choice or Freedom of Food*. The same year the Bishop of Constance was asked to allow clerical marriage, while the burgomaster ordered the clergy of Zürich to base their preaching on the Scriptures. Early in 1523 a disputation was held in the Town-hall in which Zwingli upheld some sixty-seven theses against the Vicar-General of Constance, John Faber, questioning the authority of the Pope and the hierarchy, the Sacrifice of the Mass, the Invocation of the Saints, Purgatory, fasting and clerical celibacy. This was the first of a number of similar disputations which were to mark the progress of reform. Zwingli's teaching was indeed more far-reaching than that of Luther. Whereas Luther in his early days might have been content with the removal of abuses, Zwingli was questioning the Catholic interpretation of the Church almost at the start of his career as a reformer. He placed great reliance on the pulpit as a means of propaganda. Through its medium the people were persuaded to remove all that was likely to remind them of the old order. In the new Communion Service it was ordered that the ' bread be carried around by the appointed ministers on large wooden tranchers from one seat to the next ' and wine in wooden beakers to remove all suspicion of the ceremonial of the Roman Mass. More and more changes were introduced ; services were read in the vernacular ; education was encouraged ; images and statues were removed ; monasteries were dissolved ; the Communion was administered in both kinds. Thus by 1525, the year in which the Lord's Supper at last replaced the Mass at the Grossmünster, the Reformation at Zürich was virtually complete.

The ecclesiastical authorities were slow to take notice of this incipient religious revolution. Zürich was in the diocese of Constance, but the Bishop made only comparatively gentle remonstrations. Even at Rome papal wrath hung fire. As late as August, 1524, the Town Council of Zürich wrote to the Pope excusing their activities on the plea that public opinion was so strong that they could not avoid taking action. Pope Adrian VI in 1523 entrusted a letter to his legate, Ennio Filonardi, speaking highly of Zwingli ; his successor Pope Clement VII himself opened a series of dreary and fruitless negotiations with the city authorities. It is obvious why he did not wish to alienate the Zürichers. The Pope was well aware of the reputation of the Zürich mercenaries and he could not judge when he might require their services.

The next phase in Zwingli's career came with the decision to extend the Reformation to the so-called subject lands.[1] The latter were not the exclusive property of Zürich and in any case jurisdiction in matters of this nature lay with the Federal Diet representing all the cantons, not with Zürich alone. When the Diet met at Lucerne on January 26th, 1524, there was thus a clear division of opinion. In the following April five Catholic cantons, headed by Lucerne and including her neighbours, Uri, Schwyz, Unterwalden and Zug, met at Beckenreid and formed a league to root out heresy. There was also a middle party, led by Berne, which urged that each canton should decide for itself which religion it wished to follow. But Zürich was aggressively Protestant. The intricate situation reveals Zwingli's considerable powers as a statesman. He put forward a plan the object of which was to make Zürich the head or *vorort* of a confederation of Protestant cantons. This would ally with France and Savoy, bribe St. Gall and Thurgau by the promise of monastic property and raise the Tyrol against the Hapsburgs. The spread of Protestantism to other Swiss cities including Berne and Basle furthered Zwingli's plans. However envious the other Protestant cantons might be of Zürich's ascendancy, it was at least unlikely that they would co-operate with her enemies. Thus under the stimulus of theological change and political ambition, Zwingli established a defensive league of Swiss cantons and South German cities, supported by some of the German princes headed by Landgrave Philip of Hesse.

Conflict was the logical outcome of this grouping of powers. For the Christian Civic League, formed by Zwingli, was answered by the creation of another Catholic League enjoying Hapsburg support. The first war was of short duration and was ended by

---

[1] The Confederation of Switzerland was a very complex institution. It consisted of thirteen cantons, Uri, Schwyz, Unterwalden, Zug, Glarus, Appenzell, Zürich, Lucerne, Berne, Fribourg, Solothurn, Basle and Schaffhausen, together with what were known as allied lands and subject lands or ' common bailiwicks '. The allied lands were territories (e.g. the upper valley of the Rhone known as the Valais and three Leagues which made up the Grisons) with which the cantons were in permanent alliance. The subject lands were ruled in a complicated way by the Confederation. They were ruled jointly by a number of cantons ; the cantons took it in turns to appoint a bailiff. Zurich had therefore no right to determine what was to be done in the subject lands without previous consultation with the other cantons (see map on p. 164).

mediation. Zürich's gains were considerable. The religious settlement in the subject lands was to be decided by the will of the majority. The five Catholic cantons agreed to break their alliance with the Hapsburgs and to pay a war indemnity. But as Zwingli fully realised, this first Peace of Kappel (1529) was only an armistice; the terms were so ill-defined that they were certain to be the cause of future contention. Besides, having tasted success, Zwingli had no intention of remaining satisfied with such a compromise; he would not be satisfied until he had thoroughly crushed the Catholic cantons. Theologically these years represented the most uncompromising period in his career; all attempts to reach a uniform agreement with the Lutherans failed. Indeed in his vigour and vitality, broad vision and exemplary energy, Zwingli overtopped all his fellow-reformers, excepting Luther.

War was renewed in 1531. The cantons were again divided over a minor dispute in the Graubunden (or Grisons) which had religious and political implications. Although Zwingli would have preferred an outright declaration of war, his allies under the lead of Berne determined to institute economic sanctions against the five Catholic cantons, in the form of an embargo on the importation of corn, wine and salt, wheat and iron. War, which was the natural result, began on October 4th, 1531. The advance guard from Zürich came into combat with the men of Zug at Kappel. Zwingli, who was among the wounded, was discovered by his enemies under a pear tree, and was slain by a man of Unterwalden.

What Zwingli accomplished appears comparatively slight by comparison with the achievements of Luther and Calvin, but his alert, original mind and his naive yet powerful ambition suggest an imperious personality. The influence which his ideas had on English theological development is clearly revealed in the long correspondence which the English reformers conducted with his son-in-law and successor at Zürich, Heinrich Bullinger. Zwingli differed from Luther in three ways. Where Luther's approach to religion was emotional, Zwingli's was essentially intellectual. Secondly, there was not in Zwinglian thought the distinction which Luther made between the Word of God and the canonical scriptures. Finally he surpassed Luther in shattering the unitary basis of medieval thought, refuting the idea that Church and State were aspects of a single institution and so ' preparing the way for the departmental conception of life which is characteristic of the modern age '.[1]

[1] Rupert Davies, *The Problem of Authority in the Continental Reformers*, 89.

What were the essential characteristics of Zwinglianism? Zwingli identified the Word of God with the Scriptures which he held to be inspired and infallible. 'The Word of God is certain and cannot fail; it is bright and does not let man err in darkness; it teaches of itself, it makes itself plain, and illumines the human soul with all salvation.' 'I will try everything by the touchstone of the Gospel and by the fire of the apostle Paul', he wrote in the *Architeles*, 'What agrees therewith, to that I shall hold fast, what conflicts therewith I shall reject, notwithstanding all the hubbub that is made by those who may feel themselves aggrieved by this maxim.' Like Luther, he held that if a man was a genuine seeker after truth, he would be able to interpret the Bible correctly; God would speak to him just as Christ spoke to Paul on the Damascus road. Confronted with the difficulty of rival interpretations, he replied that other parts of Scripture, the meaning of which was plain, could be used to check and illumine the passage in dispute. This formed the basis of his objections to Luther's insistence on the literal meaning of the phrase 'This is My Body' at the Marburg Conference of 1529.[1] 'The Scriptures', he said, 'are to be compared, and their meanings are to be discovered from the Scriptures themselves.'

Naturally he held that the Church, like everything else, was derived from Scripture. He discarded the conventional interpretation of the Church as a body of professing Christians and replaced it, as Luther had done, by the equally familiar view of an invisible community. 'This Church' he says, 'is nothing but the total of all Christian believers, assembled in the Spirit and the will of God.' But an invisible body required some outward expression. For all practical purposes, the body of believers is divided into a number of congregations, or *Gemeinden*. Technically each *Gemeinde* was autonomous. Although he accepted the 'priesthood' of all believers, he held that in practice each *Gemeinde* must elect its apostles and prophets. 'While the preachers are in office, the message which they preach is to be tested by the *Gemeinde*, and any other preacher whose message does not conform to the proper standard is, of course, dismissed by the *Gemeinde*.'

What was the relation between the *Gemeinde* and the civil authorities? Hating disorder, Zwingli believed that the civil magistrates were ordained of God; it was their duty to help the *Gemeinde*, but the *Gemeinde* should initiate and deal with religious

---

[1] Zwingli himself held that the sacraments are only commemorative signs, *nuda signa*.

questions, only in an emergency calling upon the magistrates to enforce its decisions.

This democratic conception of the Church worked less well in practice than in theory. Until 1525 it was the *Gemeinden* which carried out the reforms in the Church, even when they were initiated and backed by the civil magistrates. But Zwingli soon felt obliged to invoke the power of the secular arm. Thus in 1526 the Council of Zürich ordered that all Anabaptists should be drowned, a striking illustration of the use of the authority of the State for religious ends, justified on the grounds that the Anabaptists were causing civil disturbances.[1]

But Zwingli was more a man of action than a religious thinker. He was regarded, and perhaps regarded himself, as the prophet of Zürich. If the State interfered in the affairs of the Church, the Church through Zwingli began to direct the State. The two authorities had been fused in a single personality. ' The rule of Zwingli in the city of Zürich was the rule of the Word, dominant in worldly and spiritual affairs alike; the Bible is found to contain the law of the State as it had been previously found to contain the law of the Church.' [2] In its unadulterated Biblicism and in its prophetic quality Zwinglianism surpassed both Lutheranism and Calvinism in spite of the fact that sooner or later it was absorbed in one or other of these two reformed systems of belief.[3] Zwingli's death brought the political ascendancy of Zürich to a close, but his teaching formed an important preliminary to the course of events in Geneva.

[1] There were many eccentric forms of Anabaptism, e.g. some taking the text ' Unless ye become as little children ye cannot enter the Kingdom of Heaven ' in St. Gall and Appenzell ' began to conduct themselves like little children, to roll about on the ground, play with fir-cones, etc. The profoundest impression was produced when one of these lunatics, Thomas Schugger, in the presence of his father and his brethren, decapitated his own brother.' (Oeschli, *History of Switzerland*, 91). The teaching of Grebel and Manz whom the Zürichers sentenced to death had communistic leanings.

[2] R. Davies, *The Problem of Authority in the Continental Reformers*, 86.

[3] A personal meeting was held between Calvin, Farel and Bullinger in 1549 leading to the Consensus Tigurinus whereby Zürich accepted Calvin's sacramental system. This in its turn was received by most of the Swiss Protestant Cantons (The Second Helvetic Confession, 1566) and formed the basis for similar credal statements throughout Europe, e.g. Heidelberg Catechism of 1563, Confessio Czengarina of the Hungarian Protestants (1557); but no agreement was reached with the Lutherans.

2. *John Calvin*

Calvinism crystallised the Reformation. Luther and Zwingli had radically changed the old religion but beyond a vigorous emphasis on the Word of God the reformed faiths lacked precise authority, organised government and a logical philosophy. John Calvin supplied them with all this and more. He was one of those rare characters combining thought and action who leave, if they make a mark at all, a profound impression on history. The influence which he wielded from the city of Geneva, which he virtually ruled from 1541 to his death in 1564, spread through Europe and later to America.

Calvin was a Frenchman by birth, born on July 10th, 1509, at Noyon, where his father was notary apostolic and procurator fiscal. His father was a respectable member of the middle class who hoped that his second son, John, would enter the Church; but further back his ancestors had been watermen at Pont l'Éveque on the river Oise. John studied theology and later law at the Universities of Paris, Orléans and Bourges. At Bourges he listened to the lectures of the well-known legalist Alciati and, despite Calvin's own preference for his rival L'Estoile of Orléans, it seems probable that he was much influenced by them. Decidedly his legal and classical studies left a permanent imprint on his mind and may explain the legalistic nature of his theological ideas. His education taught him to think clearly and provided him with a wide knowledge; clarity of thought and expression distinguish his first important written work, an edition of Seneca's *De Clementia*.[1]

How or when Calvin left the faith of his fathers is uncertain. We know little of any emotional crisis, though he wrote later: ' As if by a sudden ray of light I now recognised, as my mind was already prepared for earnest examination, in what an abyss of errors, in what a profundity of filth, I had hitherto been plunged.' Knowing the man it is probable that his conversion represented a profound intellectual change, for which his personal experience provided a fitting background. His father's relations with the cathedral chapter of Noyon were full of quarrels; his elder brother, Charles, was prosecuted for striking a priest. But the primary influences were undoubtedly Erasmus' Greek Testament and Luther's sermons. Both are perhaps reflected in the rectorial address which he probably composed for the new Rector of the University of Paris, his friend Nicholas Cop, at the end of 1533. The Greek Testament showed

[1] This contains no less than 55 quotations from Latin authors and 22 from Greek.

him how far the teaching of the Church had moved away from the Gospel story. Luther's writings emphasised the idea now germinating in his own mind which was henceforth to influence all that he did, that guilt-laden man, standing sinful before the perfectly good God, can only be saved by his utter, unqualified faith in God's mercy. By the winter of 1534 he had left France and was living in the university town of Basle, a gathering place for scholars and humanists from all over Europe.

It was now that he began to write the work which formed the text-book of the Protestant Reformation his *Institutes of the Christian Religion* which contained the fundamental ideas on which Calvinism rested. Within twenty-three years of its publication (1536) its six original chapters had been increased to twenty-four, but the ideas were not themselves sensibly modified. Perhaps no book published in the sixteenth century had such far-reaching effects.

> From coupler-flange to spindle-guide I see Thy hand, O God—
> Predestination in the stride o' yon connectin'-rod.
> John Calvin might ha' forged the same—enorrmous, certain, slow—
> Ay, wrought it in the furnace-flame—*my* ' Institutio '.[1]

While Calvin's ideas were maturing, the religious changes in Switzerland continued to spread. The example of Zürich had been followed at Basle, Berne, and latterly at Geneva. The situation in the last-named city was, however, in many respects unusual. It was situated geographically in the duchy of Savoy; at the beginning of the sixteenth century its citizens owed allegiance to a triplicate authority, the Duke of Savoy who was represented by a Vidomne and who wished to secure absolute authority over the city, the Bishop of Geneva often a tool in the hands of the Duke, and the local municipal government consisting of a series of semi-representative councils. There had been a long struggle between the patriotic citizens and the Duke of Savoy, himself a brother-in-law of Charles V, as a result of which the patriot party, under the lead of Bezanson Hugues [2] helped somewhat reluctantly by Berne and Fribourg had emerged victorious. Almost incidentally this had led to the expulsion of the Bishop, Pierre de la Baume, and to the preaching of the reformed faith by a Frenchman patronised by the Bernese, Guillaume Farel. In May, 1535, he led the image-breaking which was followed by the exodus of the Catholic clergy and the replacement of the Mass by the evangelical service. But the situation remained exceptionally confused. Farel's militant Protestantism

[1] *McAndrew's Hymn*, Rudyard Kipling.
[2] The word ' Huguenot ' has been derived from his name—though with no great certainty. It has also been traced to *Eydgenots* (*Eidgenossen*) or confederates.

naturally aroused opposition, especially among the lighter spirits of the city who did not want Catholicism to be replaced by the new faith. In this dilemma Farel thought of the growing reputation of the young Frenchman who had recently arrived in Geneva en route for Strasburg (he had had to make a detour owing to the presence of Imperial troops on his route). Calvin was not at first eager to accept Farel's invitation, but the ardent reformer would take no refusal. ' You ', he warned Calvin, ' make the excuse of your studies. But if you refuse to give yourself with us to this work of the Lord, God will curse you, for you are seeking yourself rather than Christ.'

Except for three years interval, 1538-41, when the opposition gained the upper hand and expelled Farel and Calvin from the city, Calvin spent the remainder of his life at Geneva. To a later generation he does not seem an attractive personality, even if his affection for his wife and for Farel (which survived the latter's marriage to a girl years younger than himself) as well as the reverence in which his followers held him indicate that his austerity and inhumanity may have been overstressed. The overwhelming difficulty of his task, the grave responsibility which rested on his shoulders as Calvinism spread throughout Europe as well as continuous ill-health, tended to make him rather an isolated and awesome figure. His mind was coldly intellectual; his theology had ever a legal imprint. His regime was undoubtedly severe; no aspect of private or public behaviour was immune from his supervision. Yet if he lacked charm, there can be no question of his burning faith. After his death his friend de Gallars, the pastor of the Huguenot Church in London, wrote of him in glowing terms : ' What labours, watchings and anxieties did he endure ! With what wisdom and perspicacity did he forsee all dangers and how skilfully did he go out to meet them. No words of mine can declare the fidelity and prudence with which he gave counsel, the kindness with which he received all who came to him, the clearness and promptitude with which he replied to those who asked for his opinion on the most important questions, and the ability with which he disentangled the difficulties and problems which were laid before him.'

What were the essentials of his creed ? As with Luther and Zwingli, the Bible, the inspired Word of God, formed the ultimate foundation of all his ideas. All authority is only valid in so far as it is derived from the Scriptures. ' Just as old men, and those suffering from ophthalmia, and all those who have bad eyesight, if you put before them even the finest book, although they recognise that something is written, can yet scarcely put two words together, but if they are helped by the interposition of spectacles will begin to read distinctly, so the Scriptures, gathering together the knowledge of God in our minds which is otherwise confused, disperses the darkness and clearly shows to us the true God.' Although Calvin admitted that Scripture was not wholly devoid of error, he repeated time and time again that ' the Scriptures are the school of the Holy Spirit, in which nothing is omitted which is necessary and useful to know, and nothing is taught except what it is of advantage to know '. ' No one ', he says elsewhere, ' can receive even the smallest taste of right and sound doctrine unless he has become a disciple of the Scriptures.'

It is obvious that Church and State must both derive their authority from Scripture. Like others Calvin distinguished between the visible and invisible Church. The latter consisted of all those who were predestined to salvation. ' We assert ', he wrote in *The Institutes*, ' that by an eternal and immutable counsel God hath once for all determined both whom He would admit to salvation and whom He would admit to destruction. We confirm that this counsel, as concerns the elect, is founded on His gratuitous merit totally irrespective of human merit; but that to those whom He devotes to condemnation the gate of life is closed by a just and irreprehensible judgement.' Calvin's theory of predestination, the most unpalatable of his doctrinal assumptions, arose from his belief in God's unqualified foreknowledge and his firm conviction, fortified by his reading of St. Paul and St. Augustine, that man who is unable to save himself by his own actions can only be saved through the unmerited, freely given grace of God. But if the invisible Church is the circle of the predestinate or elect, it must needs have some visible expression, however imperfect. The Genevan Church, ruled according to scriptural precepts, fulfilling the Word of God, was in Calvin's view the nearest approach to its more perfect but invisible counterpart. Without question he accepted the authority of the Church and condemned the Anabaptists who insisted on the right of private interpretation of the Scriptures and so denied ecclesiastical authority. ' There is ', he wrote, ' no other means of entering life unless she [the Church] conceive us in the womb and give us birth, unless she nourish us at the heart, and watch over us with her protection and guidance. . . . Outside her bosom no forgiveness of sins, no salvation can be hoped for.'

The Church's authority is purely religious just as the State's authority is purely political. Calvin ascribed a god-given authority to the State and called the magistrates the ' ministers of divine justice '. While the Church deals with the life of the ' soul or the inner man ', the magistrates are concerned with ' setting up of civil and external justice of morals '. Ideally the State must not interfere with the Church, though it must do all that it can to help it, but neither must the Church interfere with the State.

This theoretical division into Church and State, each semi-autonomous, largely broke down in practice in Geneva simply because Calvin dominated both. Theoretically he was only a private citizen giving advice; indeed he was not even a citizen of Geneva until 1559, and, except for a place on the constitutional commission of 1543, he was never a magistrate. Yet by the end of his life he held an unchallenged position in the Genevese Church and State. Both formed ' one society, distinct in function but inseparable in being '. Whatever Calvin's theories, in practice Geneva became very like a theocracy with Calvin as the prophet of the Lord.

Geneva thus became the scene of a great social, political and religious experiment. In its secular government Calvin continued to make use of the councils already in existence when Farel invited him to Geneva in 1536. There was the Great Council, consisting of the heads of families, which elected the city's leading secular officials, the Syndics and the Treasurer. The so-called Smaller Council formed an executive committee of the Greater Council. There was also a Council of Sixty which was a larger edition of the Smaller Council and dealt with matters beyond the scope of its powers. The government of the State was distinct from that of the Church, except in so far as it was called to enforce the decisions reached by it.

Calvin's *Ecclesiastical Ordinances* laid down how the Church was to be governed. It had two ruling institutions, the Venerable Ministry and the Consistory. The first consisting of the pastors ' examined those who felt themselves called to ordination, afterwards presenting those whom they had passed to the Council for their approval, studied the Scriptures, listened to sermons on doctrine and acted as moral censors '. The Consistory, a council of six ministers and twelve elders[1] chosen from the three governing councils, was the most significant of Calvin's instruments of government. In theory it was a court of morals, but morality in Geneva had no limits; the Consistory took cognisance of every form of activity, dealing with the gravest vices and the most trivial of offences. Its discipline was strict and the sentences it passed were often but not invariably

[1] The elders (*les anciens*) were to be : ' gens de bonne vie et honeste, sans reproche et hors de toutte suspicion, surtout craigneurs Dieu et ayans bonne prudence spirituelle.'

harsh. Adultery, gambling, swearing, dancing, drinking, sleeping in sermon times and any practice that could be conceivably described as Roman, all came within its purview.

Calvin's Geneva proved relentless in dealing with all who opposed its ideas. The philologist, Castellio, schoolmaster in Geneva, had to resign because he described the *Song of Solomon* as a love-song and criticised Calvin's interpretation of the Apostles' Creed. Bolsec was imprisoned and banished for questioning Calvin's theory of predestination. But the case of Michael Servetus formed the best illustration of Protestant intolerance. Servetus, a Spanish physician, formulated heretical views about the Holy Trinity in a book later published under the title *De Trinitatibus erroribus*. In 1544 he appeared at Vienne under the pseudonym Villeneuve as chaplain and doctor to the Archbishop. He had not abandoned his heretical views and was indeed at this moment writing for publication a little book *Restitutio Christianismi*. The book was published on January 3rd, 1553, and in a devious and fascinating way was brought to the notice of the Inquisition which arrested its supposed author, only, as it would seem, to connive at his escape. Later he was sentenced to be burned over a slow fire, a sentence which could only be carried out on his effigy. What induced Servetus, who had been engaged in acrimonious controversy with Calvin before, to go to Geneva is unknown. Recognised, he was arrested and brought to trial on a charge of heresy which was later changed to one accusing him of subverting religion and society. Before the court concluded its hearing of the case, in which the Ministry represented by Calvin took the part of accusers, the Council stayed its proceedings. Enquiring of the other Swiss reformed churches, it found that they were unanimously of the opinion that Servetus' views were heretical and dangerous. He was accordingly sentenced to death, a fate which he endured under particularly agonising conditions on October 27th, 1553. The whole incident illustrates the close alignment that existed between Church and State in Calvin's Geneva.

Geneva thus became the power-house of the Protestant world, a veritable sixteenth-century Moscow. Protestant refugees from all over Europe found refreshment and instruction within its borders; they returned to their own countries loud in praise of Calvin and full of his ideas. The city soon had a markedly cosmopolitan complexion; on one day in October, 1557, two hundred Frenchmen, fifty Englishmen, twenty-five Italians and four Spaniards became 'habitants' of the city. Calvinist scholarship flourished in its university and in the Academy which Calvin founded in 1559. Literature printed in Geneva flooded Europe, whether through the open market or sold by unlicensed *colporteurs* ; the books and pamphlets were of special portability to avoid detection. Its logical, systematic faith and its excellent organisation, supported by the enthusiasm which only belief in divine election or the acceptance of an inevitable necessity can bring, soon penetrated into nearly every European country. ' Nothing in Europe was safe from the fiery brand with which he set everything in flames.' When he died in 1564 Calvin could at least rest secure in the knowledge that he had created one of the most significant religious and political movements in world history.

3. *The influence of Calvinism*

Calvinism was the foundation of the Protestant movements in France, Geneva, Scotland and Holland, and a major influence in Germany and England, more especially in the colonies which Puritan settlers founded in America in the seventeenth century. The movement's strength arose from the excellence of its organisation and the imposing majesty of its theology. In brief this organisation, modelled on that of Geneva and embracing both laity and ministry, consisted of a series of associations dovetailed with each other ; in France where this included the consistory, the colloquy and the synod it provided the backbone of the Huguenot resistance movement. Elsewhere it was often of such political and social importance as to be a determining factor in the history of the country. In Holland it gave new fire to the rebellion against Spain and overthrew the Arminian critics of precisian Calvinism at the beginning of the seventeenth century.

The Calvinist was undoubtedly strengthened in his struggles against principalities and powers by his sublime faith in the guiding wisdom and merciful grace of God. Far from making men indifferent to virtue (as indeed at first one might suppose), belief in predestination spurred them on to live a good life, sometimes interpreted in a very narrow sense. It followed that the Calvinist who thought in terms of his own damnation was a rarity ; the eighteenth-century English poet William Cowper is the only obvious example. Most Calvinists were convinced of their own election to divine grace. Belief in salvation provided a stimulus to further effort and a feeling of superiority which added to their strength, even if it diminished their humility.

Politically Calvinism opened the gateway to a new world, but its later developments are by no means implicit in the teaching of its master. Calvin upheld lawful authority as the direct instrument

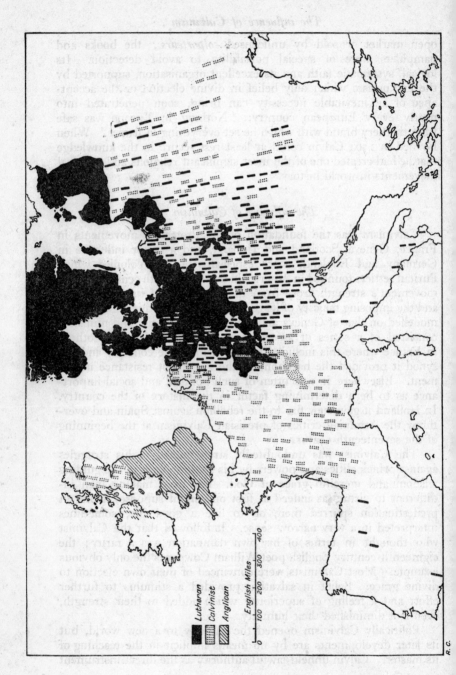

Lutheran
Calvinist
Anglican

English Miles
0   100   200   300   400

of divine rule,[1] but he gave a provisional and very qualified approval to rebellion. Subjects may rebel against a ' usurping power which overrides private conscience '. In his followers' writings this provision was extended into an ultimate characteristic of natural law. If a ruler ' overrode private conscience ', meaning that if he did not carry out his obligation to protect the true Protestant Church, then his subjects were bound to oppose him. Thus both the Englishman Christopher Goodman in a book published at Geneva in 1558 and the fierce Scottish Calvinist John Knox explicitly approved resistance to Catholic sovereigns. ' Though it appear at the first sight a great disorder ', wrote Goodman, ' that the people should take unto them the punishment of transgression, yet when the magistrates and other officers cease to do their duty, they are, as it were, without officers, yea worse than if they had none at all, and then God giveth the sword into the people's hand and He himself is become immediately their head.' Knox's *Appelation*, of the same year, addressed to the Scottish nobility and Estates, was a summons to revolt against an idolatrous sovereign whose overthrow should be the ' duty of every man in his vocation '.

More intellectual and legalistic was the argument developed in Languet's [2] *Vindiciae Contra Tyrannos*, a justification of the Huguenots' rebellion against the French King. He asserted that there was an original contract between God *and* the King and his people. In the union of King and people the people are ultimately the senior partner, since the King is bound by his obligations to serve them. Holding his power from God, the King retains it so long as he uses it for his people's good. If he breaks either the pact between God *and* prince and people or that between prince *and* people he stands condemned as a tyrant and the people are released from their allegiance to him. The *Vindiciae* proved more influential in the disturbed politics of seventeenth-century England than in the author's native France,[3] but it was nevertheless a landmark in the history of political thought.

The Franco-Scottish Calvinist, George Buchanan, one of the most live and interesting of sixteenth-century writers, moved even further away from Calvin's original ideas in his *De Jure Regni apud Scotos*, which he wrote for his royal pupil, James VI, future King of England. Apart from justifying tyrannicide, he affirms that the people under

[1] He had dedicated *The Institutes* to King Francis I of France.
[2] The authorship is by no means certain but modern scholarship attributes the tract to Languet.
[3] It was burned together with the *De Jure Regni* of Buchanan and the political works of John Milton by order of the University of Oxford in 1683.

God must check royal authority; a king only deserves the allegiance of his people so long as he fulfils his duty towards them. And of this, as it would seem, they are the final judge; 'multitudo fere melius quam singuli de rebus omnibus iudicat '.

These illustrations show how Calvinist political thought adapted Calvin's own notions and the medieval idea of natural law to the needs of the contemporary situation in a synthesis pregnant for the future. The seeds sown in sixteenth-century history slowly ripened in the next two centuries. ' It [Calvinism] reinforced the middle-class attempt to throw off the control of the French monarchy and to break the power of the Catholic and aristocratic minorities in Scotland; it toughened the resistance of the Elect and made the Scots more ungovernable than they were before.' [1] It became the source of British and North American Puritanism and so through many vicissitudes was one of the foster-fathers of modern democratic theory.

The economic significance of Calvinism as of the reformed faith in general has been the cause of prolonged controversy.[2] Max Weber asserted that the Protestant faith, through its emphasis on vocation, helped to develop capitalistic enterprise. It is true that he could have pointed to the industrial and commercial capacity of the Dutch Calvinists, of the French Huguenots, Scots business men and British nonconformist industrialists in support of his ideas, but, as his critics pointed out, he had overstated his case. There was a much closer association between medieval economic ideas and the reformers' theories on business enterprise than Weber realised; he paid too little consideration to Catholic teaching on the same subject as well as to Catholic business enterprise. Luther's views on usury, and indeed on business in general, were conservative and medieval, and even Calvin, whose reply to the questions on usury asked by Claude de Sachins in 1545 has been held to mark a new step in freeing usury from ecclesiastical censure, hedged his teaching round with so many qualifications that his economic ideas appear little different from those of the contemporary Catholic Church. It is not in Calvinist teaching but in the practical activities of Calvinist business men, especially in the late seventeenth and early eighteenth centuries, that evidence can be found to show that Calvin's teaching could be adapted to a capitalistic world. Thus the Calvinist emphasis on thrift and industry was soon associated with success (and riches) as a sign of God's election, and failure (and poverty) as an indication of His disfavour. ' And God ',

[1] John Bowle, *Western Political Thought*, 280.
[2] See Appendix I ' Religion and the Rise of Capitalism ', p. 398.

as Tyndale's translation phrased it, ' was with Joseph and he was a lucky fellow.' The strict moral discipline exercised by the New England colonists in the seventeenth century eventually led to the establishment of a bourgeois economy in which the bourgeois virtues became identified with the ethical teaching of the Christian Church.

The social force of Calvinism can be more precisely defined. Calvinism, through the consistory, led to a definite tightening-up of moral standards, especially in sexual relations ; in Geneva adultery was punished by drowning (of women) and by beheading (of men). Its conception of family life was patriarchal and in part borrowed from the Old Testament. The Calvinists adopted an austere attitude towards immoderate extravagance in dress and entertainment. Drama, witchcraft and drunkenness were all censored ; ' thou shalt not suffer a witch to live ' found an eager response from the New England supporters of Cotton Mather. Calvinism patronised a strict and gloomy Sabbatarianism. Although it produced a brand of piety attractive in its occasional humility and gentle devotion, there was much that was rigid and intolerant in sixteenth and seventeenth-century Calvinism. But its renewed emphasis on the sanctity of marriage and of family-life may have done something to improve the morals of a society still affected by the laxity in manners which was a bequest of the Renaissance.

The same austerity affected the culture of the countries where Calvinist influence was supreme, as indeed a glance at the Calvinist interiors of the former Catholic cathedrals of Berne, Basle and Lausanne to-day will confirm. Although it may have contributed to the development of the simple, pleasant mode of building associated with seventeenth-century Dutch and colonial American architecture, it was not architecturally sensitive, nor was its influence much felt in music (except in psalm-singing and in hymns), painting and secular literature. At heart Calvin might have suspected, as did his followers, that art was a product of human vanity ; ' our wisdom ', he said, ' ought to be nothing else than to embrace in gentle docility, and without any exception, whatever is handed down to us in the Sacred Scriptures '.

Calvinism was thus an extremely influential, social, political and religious force, though not always in the way that Calvin himself would have wished, primarily because it taught man to regard life as an integrated whole outside of which nothing could stand. Catholicism took an equally total view of life but even its discipline and enthusiasm paled before this most aggressive of Protestant movements.

CHAPTER XI

THE COUNTER-REFORMATION

1. *The new religious orders*

THE Venetian ambassador, Luigi Mocenigo, writing with the penetrating observation which came so naturally to his country's trained diplomats, stated towards the middle of the sixteenth century that ' in many countries, obedience to the Pope has almost ceased, and matters are becoming so critical that, if God does not interfere, they will soon be desperate. . . . Thus the spiritual power of the Pope is so straitened that the only remedy is a council summoned by the common consent of all princes. Unless this reduces the affairs of religion to order, a grave calamity is to be feared.' Catholics must everywhere have been baffled and dismayed by the great increase in heresy; England, the Scandinavian countries, Switzerland, much of Germany, Poland, and the Dutch-speaking parts of the Netherlands, had accepted the Protestant faith by the middle of the sixteenth century. Headed by non-reforming Popes, whose policy was dictated by family and secular interests, the Catholic Church might well have demanded a miracle if it was to be saved from secular domination and Protestant aggression. It is clear that the Counter-Reformation stopped the rot within the Church, led to an improved standard of life, prayer and scholarship and to a recovery of some of the land lost to the Protestants. If the Roman Church emerged with a diminished following by the middle of the seventeenth century, it was more spiritually alive in 1660 than it had been at the beginning of the previous century.

Every movement begins with a small group of men who think ahead of their contemporaries and often suffer persecution or at least disapproval because of this, and yet finally affect future history far more directly than most of their fellows. If we are to trace the Counter-Reformation to its original source, we need to turn to the so-called Oratory of Divine Love, a society of priests who hoped to deepen their spiritual life by corporate prayer. Established about 1517, the society spread from Rome to other Italian cities, including Verona, Vicenza, Brescia and Venice. Its members gradually gained the attention and even the favour of the papal court. The nepotist Pope, Paul III, raised six of them to the cardinalate, including the Englishman Reginald Pole and the able Pietro Caraffa, the future Pope Paul IV. He also ordered them to prepare a report on the state of the Church which they presented under the title *Consilium delectorum cardinalium . . . de emendanda ecclesia* in 1538. The document was exceptionally outspoken. First it outlined the current abuses, commenting astringently on the conduct of past Popes; ' And this is the source, Holy Father, from which, as from the Trojan horse, every abuse broke forth into the Church . . . more important is it that the Vicar of Christ should never consider himself at liberty to use the power of the Keys for gain.' The commission condemned the non-residence of bishops and parish-priests, the system of papal dispensations and the methods of appointment to Church offices. It attacked simony and commented acidly on the state of some of the monasteries. ' Finally, there are abuses affecting your Holiness as Bishop of Rome itself—the slovenly and ignorant priests, even at St. Peter's, the prostitutes, walking the streets at midday, attended by clerics and members of Cardinals' households—the like of which is never seen in any other city.' But such plain-speaking was inopportune, and the Pope forbade the publication of the report. Yet the episode was significant, because it showed that the necessity for reform had reached the highest quarters of the Church, and that such reform was bound to be stillborn unless the Pope was himself a reformer.

Nevertheless the Oratory of Divine Love had sown its seed well. Reformed or new religious orders, often inspired by its members, were springing up all over Italy. This sort of thing had characterised religious revivals since St. Benedict first established a monastery at Monte Cassino in the sixth century. The tightening-up of old vows and the foundation of new orders designed to put in practice a life of Christian austerity generally betokened the approach of a period of spiritual awakening. Thus the eremetic order of the Camaldolese was revived by Paolo Guistiniani in 1522. Two years later Gaetano di Tiene established a community of secular priests living under rule. Like the Camaldolese, they were patronised by Pietro Caraffa, then Bishop of Chieti and a member of the Oratory, who himself joined the Theatines, as they were soon called, in 1524. The order was important because, being unconfined to the four walls of a monastery, it was specially concerned with raising the standard of the secular clergy. The Capuchins, one of the strictest of the newly-founded orders, was the product of Matteo da Bascio's desire to return to the high ideals of St. Francis of Assisi which his own order, the Friars Observant, had seemed to neglect. If the Theatines enhanced the Church's scholarship by drawing men of learning to their fold, the brown-robed, sandal-shod Capuchins did much to revive the sermon as an instrument of evangelisation; in particular they reinforced the Church's influence among the poverty-stricken peasants of Italy's great landed estates. Surviving the Protestant apostacy of their third Vicar-General, Bernardino Ochino, the Capuchins numbered over 1500 houses by 1619. These orders formed the advance-guard of a new-found religious enthusiasm which reached its climax in Loyola's militant religious Society of Jesus.

2. *The Jesuits*

The opening phrase of the bull, *Regimini Militantis Ecclesiae*, with which Pope Paul III signified his approval of the foundation of the Society of Jesus in 1540 indicates exactly why the Jesuits played so important a part in the history of the Counter-Reformation.

The Society was a militant force, equipped with ' heavenly ' armour and 'spiritual' weapons for the conquest of souls, lost to Protestantism or paganism. The Society, emphatic in the obedience which it owed to its General and to the Pope, was the Church's international force and played a dominant part in extending Catholic rule, in instructing Catholic youth, in attracting the attention and devotion of kings and nobles, as active in the European battlefield of the Catholic faith as in the missions of North Africa, Asia and America.

Ignatius Loyola, the founder of the Jesuits, came comparatively late to his life's work. Born of a noble Basque family at Guipuzcoa about 1491, he served as a soldier until on a spring day in 1521 (May 19th), a cannon ball shattered his leg at the insignificant siege of Pamplona. During his long convalescence, bereft of the chivalric romances which formed his normal reading matter, so far as he read at all, he was forced to turn for entertainment to two medieval devotional works, Ludolf of Saxony's *Life of Christ* and *The Flowers of the Saints*. This reading and the period of quiet meditation which was associated with it led to a reorientation of the whole of his life. He emerged from his illness cured, but for a slight limp, and utterly determined to devote his life to the service of Christ. He made a vow to visit Jerusalem and began to copy excerpts from the books he was now reading ' putting the words of Christ in red ink and those of our Lady in blue '.

The period of preparation now began. Leaving his home he first visited the image of the Blessed Virgin at the monastery of Montserrat and then retired to a cavern outside Manresa. It was here, where he spent some nine months, that he experienced the vision of the Holy Trinity which left a permanent imprint on his

sensitive mind. 'There', says the modern historian of the order,[1]
'he went through the dread mysterious Dark Night of the Soul . . .
and there too he was caught up into Paradise and heard secret words
which it is not granted to man to utter.' 'He thought to himself',
says Diego Lainez who succeeded him as General, 'that, even if the
Scriptures had not been given us to teach us the truths of faith, he
would nevertheless have determined to give up life itself for them,
solely on account of what he had seen with the soul.' His personal
experience thus became the sanction of his dynamic faith. His
manner of life had been one of great austerity but he had no real
calling to the ascetic profession of a hermit and his later life was
characterised by a moderation and common-sense not always associated with sanctity. 'Seeing the fruit reaped from helping
other souls, he ceased from this time from the extreme severities
which he had been wont to practise, and also he began to cut his
nails and his hair.'

It was at this time that he began to write *The Spiritual Exercises*,
a masterly book of devotion and a training manual for the religious
man, not actually published until 1548. During the first week the
meditations are designed to produce so passive a state in the mind
of the reader that in the following week he may perceive afresh the
glories of the Heavenly King and the privilege of serving Him.
The third and fourth weeks are spent in meditating upon the life
and passion of Christ, and the depth of human sin. Finally the
disciple is confronted with the joys of heaven, for which he must
surrender all his liberty in order that he may fulfil his God-appointed
task. All this can only be carried out within the Church, the bride
of Christ. *The Spiritual Exercises* show clearly that with Loyola,
as with his fellow-Spaniard St. Teresa, a mystical experience must
have a practical outcome. And in Loyola's case this became the
incomparably efficient organisation of the Society of Jesus.

Although Loyola's purpose remained fixed, the years that
immediately followed suggest that he had not yet discovered
the medium through which he was to address the world. From
Manresa he went to Jerusalem, thence to Rome and Venice, and
finally to Barcelona. It was characteristic of him that at the age
of thirty-three he decided to make good his scanty education, so
that he might equip himself better for his life's work. Apart from
the obvious difficulty of learning anew at this age, his manner of
life and his preaching aroused the suspicion of the Spanish Inquisition. Barred from the University of Alcala, he found Salamanca no more hospitable and so decided to make his way to Paris.

[1] J. Brodrick, S.J., *The Origin of the Jesuits*, 16.

'By the grace and goodness of God, our Lord, in favourable weather and safe and sound, I arrived in this city of Paris on February 2nd, resolved to study there until such time as the Lord shall otherwise ordain.'

It is unlikely that the ragged, swarthy Spaniard ever met the young classical scholar, John Calvin, who was one of his contemporaries at the Collége Montaigu, but the Paris experience was very significant, not because Loyola eventually received his cherished degree but because it led to the inauguration of the Society of Jesus. On the Feast of the Assumption, 1534, at a Mass celebrated by Favre, the only priest among them, at the chapel of St. Denys belonging to the Benedictine nuns of Montmartre, Loyola and his ten companions took vows of poverty and chastity with the object of going to Jerusalem to convert the heathen.

Practical politics made the fulfilment of this last intention impossible, though it was some time before the members of the little fraternity recognised that this was so. Meanwhile they led lives of disciplined service, 'to tend the patients', so Rodriguez described their work at two Venetian hospitals where they were filling in time in the hope of catching a boat to the Holy Land, 'make the beds, sweep the floors, scrub the dirt, wash the pots, dig the graves, read the services [all, except Salmeron, were now priests] and to bury the dead.' But Ignatius was slowly coming to the conclusion that the Church's more immediate task lay nearer home, in the battle against heresy rather than Saracenic infidelity, even if the latter was an object of which the Jesuits never lost sight.[1] He had already placed himself and his attractive fellow Basque, Francis Xavier, at the Pope's disposal. He now determined to win papal approval for the rule which he had drawn up for his Society. Pope Paul III was willing, but it was only after overcoming much opposition led by Cardinal Guidiccioni that the papal bull was published on September 27th, 1540.

It was in this way that the Counter-Reformation received its greatest impetus. The bull made clear the members' unqualified loyalty to the Pope and to the General of the Society, an office to which Loyola was naturally elected. 'Let us', so it runs, 'with the utmost pains strain every nerve of our strength to exhibit this virtue of obedience, firstly to the Highest Pontiff, then to the Superiors of the Society . . . and let each one persuade himself that they that live under obedience ought to allow themselves to be ruled by divine providence through their Superiors exactly as if

---

[1] At the Jesuit Roman College the students studied Arabic with this object in view.

they were a corpse which suffers itself to be borne and handled in any way whatsoever; or just as an old man's stick which serves him who holds it in his hand wherever and for whatever purpose he wishes to use it.' Loyola felt that obedience was so necessary a virtue that he used metaphors which were liable to be misunderstood by enemies of his Society. ' Altogether I must not desire to belong to myself, but to my Creator and His representative. I must let myself be kneaded, must order myself as a dead man without will or judgment.'

But Loyola was not far wrong in supposing that obedience would give the movement an underlying firmness and strength. Obedience which sometimes cut through ordinary national loyalties was naturally resented by the national monarchs of Europe, not excluding Catholic Kings like Philip II of Spain. The Jesuits were an international body,[1] cutting clean through national loyalties and guided by advice from Rome. They were the more suspect because they were neither monks nor yet secular priests; they were dispensed from signing the monastic hours in choir [2] and from wearing a distinctive monastic garb.

Nothing much of this could be seen in 1540, but the next decade witnessed teething pains. Papal approval was not continuous; Paul IV tried to reduce the privileges of the Society. The other and older orders were often hostile towards it, as was also the Bishop and the Theological Faculty of the University of Paris. ' The Pope ', said Bishop Eustache du Bellay of Paris, ' has no power to approve an order in this country, but only in his own states.' Even the Inquisition at moments appeared to regret that it had let Loyola slip through its clutches. National sovereigns like Philip II gave only a cold and qualified approval to its missionary and educational activities. Nevertheless the progress which it made was steady and solid. By 1545 its members were allowed to preach and to administer the Sacraments without first seeking episcopal permission. The Constitutions which were drafted in 1550 and approved eight years later laid down how the Society was to be governed and

[1] Except in Spain, the Jesuits were hardly affected by national prejudice. ' The Jesuits as a whole sat very lightly indeed to the nationalism which had begun to infect the minds of all European peoples and to dye their histories with blood. In those days, an English Jesuit, Father Adam Brock, was rector of the Polish college in Vilna, a Scotsman, Father Edmund Hay, who spoke bad French with a Highland accent, ruled the Jesuits of Paris while another from Caledonia stern and wild, Father William Crichton, did the same by the Jesuits of Lyons.' (James Brodrick, S.J., *The Progress of the Jesuits*, 272 n.).

[2] This caused contention with the anti-Jesuit Paul IV.

re-emphasised the duty of obedience, which Loyola himself had made plain in a letter written to members of the Society in Portugal in 1553 : ' we may easily suffer ourselves to be surpassed by other Religious Orders in fasting, watching, and other austerities of diet and clothing, which they practise according to their rule, but in true and perfect obedience and the abnegation of our will and judgment, I greatly desire, most dear brethren, that those who serve God in this Society should be conspicuous '.

The full and careful system of training also began to be put in motion. After two years novitiate, the novice either took up some secular work connected with the Order and became a coadjutor temporal, or continued to train for the priesthood as a scholastic. At the end of a further period the Jesuit became a coadjutor spiritual while a few of the members proceeded to yet another grade, the Professed of the Four Vows (i.e. vows of poverty, chastity and obedience to the General and to the Pope) who elected the General. The latter had very full powers but could be kept in check to some extent by the Provincial Congregations, the General Congregation and the Consultors.[1] The prolonged and careful training helped to make the Jesuit a loyal and efficient member of his Society.

What was the Jesuit contribution to the Counter-Reformation movement ? The bull of 1540 defined the Jesuits' main tasks as ' per publicas praedicationes . . . et nominatim per puerorum ac rudium in Christianismo institutionem ac Christifidelium in confessionibus audiendis '—the hearing of confessions, teaching and preaching. As confessors to kings and princes, they exerted an unseen but powerful, and at times dreaded, influence over politics and diplomacy.[2]

As educationalists they were within limits most effective; highly intelligent, enthusiastic missionaries they proved willing and able to use original methods.[3] Loyola had at first intended that the Society should only supply educational facilities for its own members. As a result the famous Jesuit college was founded at Coimbra in 1542 and hostels were established at various Italian and Spanish university towns, including Padua, Valencia, Alcala and Salamanca, but the foundation of the University of Gandia by the delightful St. Francis Borgia, Duke of Gandia, head of a

---

[1] It was the duty of the Consultors to keep watch over the Rectors and Provincials in the interests of the General, and to watch the General in the interests of the Society.

[2] E.g. Fr. Nithard, Confessor to the Spanish Queen-mother, was virtual ruler of Spain in the early part of the reign of Charles II.

[3] The system of marks is said to be a Jesuit invention.

family who did much to redeem its somewhat unsavoury reputation, led to an extension of the original policy. The Jesuits were soon to take their place in the academic world as teachers and lecturers to the laity. They realised that the universities formed one of the key-points in the strategic battle for orthodoxy. It was not long before Catholic Europe was spanned by Jesuit-run colleges, in the main catering for those who were to take their place in the world as men of power and position. Gandia's munificence resulted in the foundation of the famous Gregorian University at Rome (the Roman College). Patronised by the Hapsburgs of Austria and the Wittel-bachs of Bavaria, the Jesuits established flourishing seminaries at Vienna and Ingolstadt, as also at Cologne, these forming centres from which daughter foundations for the reclamation of heretics sprang. A school for young nobles was founded at Prague. A similar educational policy was adopted with marked success in Poland where the Jesuits had an enthusiastic patron in Cardinal Hosius. In France, where the Jesuit-run College de Billom was opened in 1556, they were opposed by the Sorbonne and by the older orders but here as elsewhere they steadily gained ground. A Jesuit college was founded at Lyons in 1563.

This process had a three-fold significance. In the first place it ensured a supply of well-trained, enthusiastic missionaries who would seek to win converts as well as instruct those of the faith in the country where they lived, as the Jesuits who were trained at Douai [1] did in England. Secondly it gave them control over the sons of noble and upper-middle classes at a psychologically receptive age; indoctrinated with the Jesuit view of life their pupils were the more likely to remain stalwart Romanists. Finally they pro-vided, with certain qualifications, a remarkably good education. On the religious side they had a coherent philosophy, or rather theology, of existence which owed much to the discussions of the Council of Trent in which the Jesuit scholar Diego Lainez took a prominent part. But the secular education they provided, especially in mathematics, astronomy and navigation, was equally good. They paid careful attention to the actual organisation of the schools and colleges of which they had charge, ensuring, for instance, that the lower forms of schools had as efficient schoolmasters as did those of the upper part of the school. The eighteenth-century philosopher

[1] Douai, founded by Cardinal William Allen in 1568, was not a Jesuit college, but English Jesuits received missionary training there. From 1578-93, it was established at Rheims. There was also Scots College, first established in Lorraine in 1576, moved to Douai in 1592 and later placed under the Jesuits by Pope Clement VIII.

Helvetius was not indeed far wrong when he asserted that the 'chief crime of the Jesuits was the excellence of their education'. At the same time they carried into the lives of their pupils that watchfulness which by the rules of their Society each member imposed on his brother Jesuit.

They were preachers as well as teachers, whose sincerity won them devoted congregations in the face of much opposition and some disappointment. In France there was Edmund Auger, the author of a *Catechism* of which no less than 38,000 copies were sold in Paris alone, but the most distinguished Jesuit preacher of the sixteenth century was St. Peter Canisius (Peter Kanis of Nimwegen), who did much to reinforce the faith at Ingolstadt. Later he performed great services for his Church as Dean of the Faculty of Theology at the University of Vienna and as the author of a *Catechism*, which a recent Catholic historian has described as 'the most famous book of the entire Counter-Reformation'. The Emperor Ferdinand I, who had the highest opinion of Canisius, made its use compulsory throughout his dominions; 'We have resolved and determined that this your Catechism shall be translated also into our German tongue and taught publicly to youth in all the Latin and German schools of our five Lower Austrian provinces and of our County of Gorz, to the exclusion of any other Catechism, under the severest penalty and the threat of our indignation.'

These activities must be associated with the missionary work of the Society. The fourth vow read: 'I promise special obedience to the Pope regarding the missions' and from the start individual Jesuits worked in India and China, and, at a later date, in South America, the French colony of Quebec and the fabled land of Prester John, Abyssinia. In the first decades the heroic St. Francis Xavier dominates the story and sets the theme which, if it had its sombre patches, was also underlined by martyrdom, suffering and plangent devotion.[1] Xavier went in 1541 to the Portuguese colony of Goa, notorious for its moral laxity, and after doing something to establish a higher standard of behaviour among the colonists he preached the Gospel to the pearl-fishers on the coast of Comorin, to the people of the Malay archipelago and of the fabled land of Cipangu or Japan. It was his great ambition to revive the Christian Church in the Chinese empire, but he died on his way there in 1552. The Jesuit missionary enthusiasm was unquestionable. Father Martinez wrote in 1560: 'I have great strength and health, blessed be God, and

---

[1] Something of this remarkable story can be read in Fr. Brodrick's two books, *The Origin of the Jesuits* and *The Progress of the Jesuits* (1556-1579), more especially Chapters VII and VIII.

I want to spend them both in His divine service, even to the shedding of my blood and the giving of my life. I was sent with the expedition to Oran, and our sufferings on that occasion, which were heavy, have put heart into me for even worse trials. This is what emboldens me to ask you for China.' Three years later a letter from an able young classic, Fernando de Alcaraz, sounded the same note : ' Beyond all comparison with other missions, I feel drawn to the East Indies or China, and for no other reason than that I imagine there will be more hardship and suffering in those countries. I think if I heard of a country that provided a still larger share of the cross, I would transfer my affections to it immediately.'

The Jesuits thus ringed the globe with the mission of Rome.

> ' Let Observation, with extensive view,
> Survey mankind from China to Peru.'

By the middle of the seventeenth century there were signs of the activities and ideas which made them so distrusted by the outside world. The wrath of national governments was aroused by their close identification with the international policy of Rome. Absence of episcopal control and monastic system provoked the ire of many a bishop and the dislike of some of the older monastic orders. Their teaching on moral questions led to the accusation of casuistry ; the blackest picture of all was painted by the eminent Catholic physicist and mathematician, Blaise Pascal, in his beautifully-written *Provincial Letters*. It may be true that individual Jesuits were more inclined to compromise with the world than some of the more conventional moral theologians. ' Loyola ', a modern American sociologist has written, ' came to the conclusion that the Church must fully utilise the existing organs of education, of discipline, even of entertainment ; it must turn pomp and worldliness themselves to its own uses. On these matters Loyola was far more revolutionary than Calvin and Luther ; for whereas they recoiled from the New World that had opened before them, Loyola both figuratively and actually sought to embrace it.' [1]

The Jesuits' unqualified loyalty to the Roman see made them bitterly disliked. One of their greatest and most moderate representatives, Cardinal Robert Bellarmine, claimed that the Christian commonwealth owed its very existence to the God-given authority of the Pope on which ultimately all secular power depended. This view inevitably involved a possible denial of the authority of the temporal prince, more especially as Bellarmine added that ' it is the consent of the people which sets up kings, consuls, and all other

[1] Lewis Mumford, *The Condition of Man* (1944), 224.

governments.' The Spanish Jesuit, Luis Molina, asserted that the people actually have a right to depose a heretical prince. The views of the Spanish teacher of Bellarmine, Juan Mariana, were even more striking, though he cannot be regarded as a typical member of the Society with which his relations were often strained. His book *De Rege et Regis institutione* published in 1598 justified tyrannicide, so long as poison was not used.

The Jesuits were thus the leading craftsmen of the Counter-Reformation. Their real contribution to the Catholic revival came from their teaching, their preaching, writing and scholarship, from their missionary work, perhaps best exemplified in the semi-communistic colony of Paraguay, and from the dynamic vitality of their faith rather than from their occasional casuistry and cruelty.

3. *The Council of Trent*

The Counter-Reformation must ultimately focus itself upon the proceedings at the Imperial city of Trent where, at three meetings held in 1545-49, 1551-52 and 1562-63, the Church grappled with the problems which had split and threatened to annihilate her, her relations with Protestantism, the need for putting her own house in order and for defining her faith more precisely. It was soon apparent that no compromise with Protestantism was possible; the only terms on which the heretics could be re-admitted into the Church were those of unconditional surrender. By the end of the sixteenth century the number of Catholics had been greatly reduced by the secession of Calvinists, Lutherans and Anglicans, but this diminution in numbers was in part counteracted by the successful fulfilment of the Council's other objects. The standard of religious life had been immeasurably improved. The faith had been systematised in a complete and scholarly fashion. The Tridentine revolution, for it was no less, was therefore to have a permanent effect on world history.

There had long been a demand for the calling of a General Council of the bishops of the Church. As early as 1523 the Diet of Nuremberg had prescribed the calling of a ' free Christian Council ' as the best remedy for the divisions afflicting the Church. But although both Catholics and Protestants wanted a Council, their requests were received unsympathetically at Rome. Remembering what had happened at the fifteenth-century Council of Constance, the Pope and the Curia feared a loss of power; besides which they were in no way eager for the removal of abuses in which they had a vested interest or for the initiation of any measure which might increase Hapsburg power at the cost of the Pope. But however long the secular and material interests of the Papacy might delay the calling of a Council, no Pope could hold out indefinitely against the rising chorus of protest which the rapid expansion of the Reformed Religion made the more emphatic. The election of Cardinal Farnese as Pope Paul III in 1534 was helped by his known willingness to summon a Council, if only to avert the calling of national church councils, already threatened in Germany and France. Even so there was some delay before it actually met. Convoked in 1536 to meet at Mantua, it was prorogued by reason of the war between Charles V and Francis I. It was not until December 13th, 1545, that the first session opened at Trent.

Its early proceedings could hardly have given contemporaries much confidence in its outcome. The few bishops present could not be said to represent the Church.[1] There was constant wrangling over procedure. At the fifteenth-century Council of Constance, voting had been decided by national delegations (*nationaliter*) instead of by a majority representing a counting of heads; at Trent it was agreed to exclude the abbots and theologians who had had a vote at Constance and to confine voting to bishops and heads of religious orders. This meant that whereas at Constance the issue had been decided by a majority of the national delegations, to the obvious disadvantage of the many Italian bishops, at Trent it turned on a majority vote of the bishops and heads of orders. Since there were far more Italian than non-Italian bishops, the practical effect of this was to place the council in the pocket of the Pope; this was almost literally true as many of the Italians were so poor that without papal pensions and places they would have found it difficult to live. In intellectual calibre and force of personality they compared unfavourably with their *confrères* from France, Spain and the Empire. There was also a prolonged dispute as to whether reform or doctrine should be discussed first; Cardinal Madruzzo, representing the Emperor, and the Spanish bishops urged that priority should be given to reform, but the legates, knowing that such reform would seriously embarrass the papal court, were only too pleased to accept the suggestion of the Bishop of Feltre that doctrine and reform should be discussed concurrently.

[1] Actually there were one cardinal, four archbishops, twenty-two bishops and five generals of orders, besides various theologians, but the numbers slowly grew. Some were encouraged by the fact that the four French bishops present had bought so much wine that the price had gone up by 25 per cent., thus making a long stay probable.

After these initial difficulties the Council settled down to its real work. Its doctrinal conclusions made any settlement with the Protestants impossible but helped to clarify the Catholic position. Thus the Council agreed that Scripture, which the Church was alone entitled to expound, and Tradition had equal authority in express contradiction to the Protestant emphasis on the Bible. Later it repudiated the Protestant views on original sin and justification by faith. The Imperial representatives were opposed to such an open break which was bound to increase the Emperor's difficulties in Germany. Not unnaturally the subsequent debate caused bitter feeling. A verbal conflict between one of the few supporters of justification by faith, Bishop San Felice of La Cava and Zannetini, Bishop of Chironia, ended by the Bishop of La Cava plucking the beard of his opponent. The influence of the Jesuit theologian, Diego Lainez, helped to secure the rejection of the Protestant doctrine. Of the Council's decisions on justification the Catholic historian Pastor wrote : ' it is a masterpiece of theology, formulating with clearness and precision the standard of Catholic truths as distinguished from Pelagian error on the one hand and Protestant on the other '.

There were many disputes over ecclesiastical reform, but important decisions were reached, insisting that bishops must be properly qualified and should reside in their sees. Other chapters laid down regulations for episcopal visitations, for the repair of churches, and similar matters. The Council's work in this respect was less effective than it might have been because it paid too little attention to the safeguards which would alone have made these reforms operative. It left too many loop-holes of which a still only partly-reformed papal court could and did, through the medium of dispensation, make the fullest possible use.

The Council had by no means completed its work when it became clear that political events were likely to lead to its adjournment, if not to a termination of its proceedings. Some of its more important dogmatic statements on the Sacraments were only in an early stage, even though chapters had been accepted dealing with Baptism, Confirmation and Holy Orders. But the relations between Pope Paul III and the Emperor had become increasingly strained, with the result that the papal legates took advantage of an outbreak of plague to advise that the Council be removed from Trent to Bologna, which lay opportunely in papal territory. The Emperor ordered his bishops to remain in the unhealthy but freer atmosphere of Trent. This division brought the first session of the Council to a close.

The decline in Imperial fortunes and the election of the luxurious and conciliatory Cardinal del Monte as Pope Julius III in succession to the aged and irascible Paul III made the Council's reopening possible. But the second assembly of the Fathers of Trent was relatively short. Nevertheless it added to the number of enactments on doctrine made in the previous sessions, especially in respect of the Eucharist, Penance and Unction. The first of these originally discussed at Trent in January, 1547, underlined the impossibility of reconciliation with the Protestant churches. In clear language it condemned the views which Luther, Zwingli and Calvin had put forward about the Eucharist, and reaffirmed the doctrine of transubstantiation, 'that after the consecration of the elements our Lord Jesus Christ, very God and very man, is verily, really and substantially contained under the species of bread and wine'.[1] It was unable to do much more than this. The Emperor Charles V, a broken and tired man, was faced by a hostile combination which he could not combat successfully. Circumstances did not favour a continuance of the Council, which virtually evaporated.

The decade which followed was full of historic events, the abdication of the Emperor and the accession of his moderate and sensible brother, Ferdinand I, the continued expansion of Protestantism, especially in France, and the end of the line of secular-minded Popes who had for so long acted as dragwheel on the wagon of reform.

It was thus in a changing world that the bishops reassembled at Trent for the final session which lasted from January 18th, 1562 to December 4th, 1563. After an unsatisfactory discussion as to whether the Council was to be regarded as a continuation of the two previous assemblies or not,[2] further important decisions were reached on doctrine and reform. New chapters dealt with the administration of the Chalice and the Sacrifice of the Mass; reasoned decrees were passed concerning Purgatory, the Invocation of Saints, and the veneration given to relics and images. Provision was made for the establishment of seminaries for the training of the clergy in every diocese, a decree which was to have an incalculable influence over the future history and spiritual efficiency of the Roman Church.

---

[1] Vere, realiter ac substantialiter sub specie illarum rerum sensibilium contineri.

[2] The discussion over this had been acrimonious long before the Council was re-summoned. The French (in the main represented by the Cardinal of Lorraine) and the Imperialists wanted a new Council, if Council there must be, while the Pope and the Spaniards wanted the old Council to continue. The French, urged on by Catherine de' Medici, threatened to call a national council.

Even so the Council was rarely a united body. Its bitter controversies resounded throughout Europe; at one time intrigue threatened its very existence. Much of the discussion in effect represented a trial of strength between the Pope and the Italian prelates, and Spanish bishops led by the Archbishop of Granada; the latter would have liked a declaration that the authority of the bishops of the Council was superior to that of the Pope. This dispute eventually centred round the question whether episcopal residence was a divine or merely a papal obligation. The Spaniards and their allies supported the first principle whereas their opponents were tenacious protagonists of the Pope. The papal victory was at last secured by two diplomatic triumphs; the conciliatory Cardinal Morone won over the Emperor to the side of the Pope, and the Pope gained the goodwill of the exceptionally able and influential Cardinal of Lorraine, the leader of the French bishops at the Council, who had been long regarded with suspicion at Rome.

The Pope was unquestionably the real gainer by the Council. By diplomatic skill, not without chicanery, he had managed to overwhelm his opponents. The decrees of the Council depended for their validity on his consent; it was he who summarised the faith in a document which he published in November, 1564, under the title *The Creed of Pope Pius IV*. Whatever chances there had once been of limiting papal autocracy by constitutional means, there was no possibility after the Council of Trent. The struggles which took place in Catholic countries, between the Gallicans and the Ultramontanes in France in the seventeenth century and the Febronians and Ultramontanes in Germany in the eighteenth century formed an apt commentary on the unqualified submission which the bishops of the Council made to the Pope; incidentally, 189 of the 255 prelates who signed the official *acta* of the Council were Italians. The Vatican Council of 1870, together with the bull *Aeternus Pastor* publishing the dogma of papal infallibility, was the true sequel to the *acta* of the Council of Trent. Yet if it could not restore the unity of the faith, and did much to make the breach between the Roman and Protestant communions permanent, it had at least made clear the content of the Roman faith and had declared the necessity for a spiritual discipline among the clergy and laity of the Church.

4. *The Index and the Inquisition*

It is characteristic of the Counter-Reformation that old and tried methods were refashioned. Even the Society of Jesus was medieval in its foundation and object; it was not dissimilar to some medieval crusading order put to a more direct religious use. This is perhaps particularly true of the Inquisition. The very word recalls the acrid dungeon of Edgar Allan Poe's *The Pit and the Pendulum* or the grim oppressors of Charles Kingsley's stalwart Protestant Devonians. Nor can all the white-washing in the world lighten its sinister proceedings, the tedious trial, the atmosphere of secrecy, the unfair criminal procedure, the final sentence which might be consummated in a real *auto da fé*, with its fires watched by crowds of fascinated spectators. But other points demand consideration. Its function can be easily understood if the intolerant nature of sixteenth-century faith is accepted. The Inquisition was designed to protect religion, to save men's souls in spite of themselves. The death of the body by burning, carried out by the secular authorities after the Inquisition had handed over the impenitent to them, was not only a deterrent; it was an act of faith in the power of an invisible judge to save and shrive the soul of the condemned man. Where the Inquisition had failed to convert the heretic, it invoked the supernatural power. Its officials were not tyrannical commissars; they were calm, judicial, even kindly men, sure that what they were doing was right in the eyes of God and the Church. Again, although there was much to condemn in its proceedings, its occasional brutalities including the use of torture, the dread influence which it appeared to wield and the air of mystery and secrecy with which its activities were shrouded have concealed a relative generosity and a certain shrewd common-sense, most marked in the attitude it adopted towards such crimes as witchcraft, hallucination and sexual perversion, all of which lay within its jurisdiction. If its proceedings are closely examined, they will be found to compare favourably with those of many an ordinary secular court.

The Inquisition was mainly a Spanish institution and as such antedated the Counter-Reformation; its origins were indeed medieval. The Spanish Kings used it to repress heresy,[1] including Protestants, suspect Christianised Jews (*Marranos*) and Moors (*Moriscos*),

---

[1] Spain afforded an unfavourable soil for Protestantism which was quickly rooted out. The small Protestant following at Seville was crushed as a result of *auto da fé* held at Seville in 1559, 1560 and 1562. Similar treatment was meted out to the even smaller group of Protestants at Valladolid.

and to deal with their political opponents. No one, not even the primate of Spain himself,[1] was exempt from its jurisdiction. Time and time again under the guise of protecting religious orthodoxy the Crown liquidated genuine or suspected sedition. For this reason the Spanish Inquisition has assumed a prominence in history which its more directly religious activities would never have given it.

The successful working of the Spanish Inquisition so impressed the zealous Cardinal Caraffa, who had been a papal nuncio in Spain, that he suggested to Paul III that he should set up a similar tribunal. The Pope, alarmed by the spread of Protestant ideas in some Italian towns, established the Roman Inquisition by the bull *Licet ab initio*, dated July 21st, 1542. This fulgorous instrument of papal power certainly checked heresy, especially at Lucca, but it was never as popular in Italy as in Spain. After its first triumphant glow, a literal metaphor, the fire burned low and the flame soon lost its ardour. The Inquisitors were to arrest Galileo in the seventeenth and Casanova in the eighteenth century, but the Tribunal had done its real work long before.

The Inquisition was closely linked with the *Index librorum prohibitorum*.[2] Heresy was often a child of book-learning, carried by brave if fanatical *colporteurs* from the printing houses of Geneva and Frankfort. To draw up a list of books which no Catholic

---

[1] A classic instance can be found in the case of Archbishop Carranza of Toledo. A devout Catholic who had given the Last Sacrament to the Emperor Charles V, he had the misfortune to include a few badly-worded statements in his 900 page *Commentary on the Catechism* (1558) which provoked the wrath of his fellow Dominican Melchior Cano. Carranza was arrested by the Inquisition in 1559. ' He disappeared from human sight as completely as though swallowed by the earth ' (H. C. Lea). After a trial lasting seventeen years (1559-76) the Inquisition found him ' vehemently suspect ' of certain errors which it required him to abjure. As Turberville says ' when the King, the Inquisitor-General and the Suprema were in accord, there was as a rule little prospect of success in appealing to Rome ' (*The Spanish Inquisition*, 68).

[2] This is not to be confused with the Spanish *Index* (1558) which did not necessarily contain the same books. There was also an *Index Expurgatorius* (1571 and later), Spanish but not Roman, which contained a list of books which could be read, or published, provided certain passages were deleted, e.g. ' The words in *Don Quixote*, " works of charity negligently performed are of no worth ", were expurgated because they smacked too much of heretical teachings about justification by faith alone.' A Spanish Inquisitor treated an English Catholic bishop of the fifteenth century, Reginald Pecock of Chichester, as an early Protestant. A Roman Inquisitor later confused the works of the physicist Galvini with those of John Calvin. Among other works placed on the *Index* were St. Teresa's *Conceptos del Amor Divino* and Luis of Granada's classic of mysticism *Guia de Peccadores*.

might read was an obvious preventative. As early as 1543 the Inquisitor-General had insisted that no book should be published without the approval of the Holy Office. Sixteen years later (1559) Pope Paul IV issued the *Index*, which still guides Roman Catholics in their reading. The list of books was divided into three sections; one of authors like Erasmus whose works are condemned *in toto* because their authors have erred *ex professo ;* another of authors whose individual books are condemned as likely to lead people into heresy; and finally a list of books containing pernicious doctrines.

These were, of course, purely repressive measures the ultimate validity of which must be a matter of controversy. ' Whoever knew Truth put to the worse ', John Milton wrote in the *Areopagitica* ' in a free and open encounter ', and it was this which the Inquisition and the Index both implicitly denied. Yet there is no doubt that both helped to stem the advance of heresy and so played some part in the Counter-Reformation.

5. *The effects of the Counter-Reformation*

While some time elapsed before the full effects of the Counter-Reformation were apparent, evidence soon showed clearly enough that it had led to striking changes in the life of the Church. This in its turn acted as a stimulus to social and political innovations. There were few departments of life in Catholic countries exempt from its influence. Baroque architecture was one outcrop of this Catholic revival. Its theatrical quality, represented in Carlo Maderna's nave and façade of St. Peter's, Rome, designed in 1606 and completed twenty years later or in Francesco Borromini's church of San Carlo alle Quattre Fontane begun in 1633, was intended to reinforce the liturgical ceremonial of the Church. If the splendid decoration of Baroque interiors, the cream and gold of the plaster and the painted wood and the richly coloured statuary, were designed primarily to give honour to the King of Kings, they were also meant to convert the sceptic and the heretic to the Catholic faith. It was indeed symbolic that one of the first of the Baroque churches was Giacomo Vignola's Jesuit Church of the Gesu at Rome, begun in 1568. ' The innovators ', wrote Peter Canisius, ' accuse us of prodigality in the ornamentation of our churches; they resemble Judas reproaching Mary Magdalen for pouring the precious ointment on the head of Christ.' Literature was affected in a similar manner; Torquato Tasso, whose education was inaugurated at Naples under Jesuit supervision, chose a Christian hero, Godfrey de Bouillon, for his masterly epic poem, *Jerusalem.*

The intensity of religious faith is reflected alike in the paintings of El Greco and the church music of Palestrina, whose Mass of Pope Marcellus is one of the finest pieces of music ever adapted for worship.

A transformed papacy was another attestation of the reality of the Counter-Reformation. Nepotism, once the besetting sin of the Renaissance Popes, tended to disappear, even if favouritism remained. Secular and political ambitions became subject to what hardworking Popes construed as the genuine interests of the Church. With the election of the vigilant and learned Cardinal Caraffa as Pope Paul IV the Counter-Reformation occupied the throne of Peter.[1] His successor, Pius IV, was more conciliatory and more popular but it was a sign of the times that he was once nearly murdered because his life seemed less austere than that of the previous Pope. He re-summoned the Council of Trent and tried to put its findings into practice; ' he combined very happily ', it has been said, ' the ideals of the Counter-Reform with the moderation of the pre-Counter-Reform Papacy '. Pius V, who succeeded him, was the incarnation of the fervid spirit of the Counter-Reformation papacy. A Dominican and a former Inquisitor-General, he instituted important reforms in the government of the papal states, forbidding the alienation of papal territory by the bull *Admonet Nos*. In spite of the policy of caution urged on him by the Catholic Kings of Europe, he excommunicated Elizabeth of England in 1570, and spurred on Philip II of Spain and Venice to form the League against the Turk which led to the great Christian naval victory at Lepanto in 1571. His successor, Gregory XIII, a more mundane character,[2] proved no less ardent. He supported the Irish rebels against Elizabeth and the Catholic League against the French Huguenots. Administrative improvements in the papal states were continued during the pontificate of the Franciscan, Sixtus V, who reverted to the practice of employing his two nephews[3] as his advisers, but

---

[1] Caraffa represents the transition from the Renaissance to the Counter-Reformation papacy in his own person. He was learned, knew five languages and was reported to know Homer, Virgil and the Bible by heart. He had been a favourite of Popes Alexander VI, and Julius II. As Pope he relied far too much on the advice of his nephew, Carlo Caraffa. He disliked the Jesuits and was a bitter enemy of both Charles V and Philip II. Yet his personal life was free from stain and there seems little doubt that he had the best interests of the Church at heart.

[2] The outside world associates him with the reform of the Calendar which bears his name.

[3] These were genuine nephews. The phrase was used sometimes to describe ecclesiastics' sons. Cf. Robert Browning, *The Bishop Orders his Tomb at St Praxed's Church :* ' Nephews—sons mine . . . ah God, I know not ! '

otherwise he was as sternly ascetic and efficient as any of the Counter-Reformation Popes.

Sixtus V represented the apogee of the Counter-Reformation papacy. Secular intrusion, more especially represented by the diverging interests of France and Spain at the elections of the Popes, again began to play an important part in the moulding of papal policy. Nevertheless even so determined a warrior and arch-foe of the Hapsburgs as the seventeenth-century Pope Urban VIII could not have sat happily with his predecessors of a century earlier. Tradition had changed and public opinion required and recognised that the Pope as the successor of Peter should be guided by the needs of the Church rather than by personal caprice or secular ambition.

The canonisation of many of these Popes is itself another proof of the way in which the religious revival had penetrated the Vatican. But there was a veritable superfluity of saints at the end of the sixteenth and beginning of the seventeenth centuries. It is interesting to note the way in which medieval and modern views of life were combined in one religious pattern. Thus the intense religiosity, characterised by a mystical devotion to God underlined by a rigorous asceticism, associated with men like St. Peter of Alcantara and the great mystic St. John of the Cross, seems more medieval than modern. The two strands meet in the person of St. Teresa of Avila. This very matter-of-fact woman, whose religious experiences proved so excruciatingly and even embarrassingly real that they made her ill, was at one and the same time a mystic of the highest order and an extremely practical business woman. The reformed order of nuns, the Discalced Carmelites, which she founded in the face of vigorous opposition from her ecclesiastical superiors at a surprisingly late period in her life, was medieval in its austerity but utilitarian in its practical devotion. The utilitarian aspect of religious devotion was, indeed, a characteristic of Counter-Reformation piety. Many of the more saintly figures of the age realised that their worship must find an outlet in pastoral or social activity.

This was the case with two Italian saints, St. Carlo Borromeo and St. Philip Neri. The first-named was the nephew of Pope Pius IV, who loaded him with high honours at the early age of twenty-two; but unlike earlier papal nephews he had a high sense of responsibility. A scholar and priest, he acted as papal mediator at the Council of Trent, edited the Roman Catechism and took a leading part in preparing new editions of the Vulgate, the Missal and the Breviary. Visiting Switzerland in 1570 he did much to encourage the Catholic cause there; his visit was followed by the introduction of the Jesuits and the Capuchins and the foundation in 1579 of a ' Helvetian ' college at Milan. His piety found a full expression in the work that he did in his archiepiscopal see of Milan. His reforms naturally provoked opposition, especially from the monks, one of whom tried to shoot him as he was saying Mass at the altar. The honour which the Milanese paid to him at his death [1] was a testimony to his goodness. A similar judgment may be passed on his contemporary, St. Philip Neri, the founder of the Oratorians, who did so much to improve the devotional life of the ordinary clergy.

Active Christianity was the keynote of two French representatives of the Counter-Reformation church,[2] St. Francis of Sales and St. Vincent de Paul. The first was a cultured and refined priest who vowed before his ordination in 1593 to remember all day that he must be worthy to say Mass the next morning. He was made titular Bishop of Geneva in 1602 and from Annecy endeavoured to carry out his ministrations amidst a hostile Calvinist people. ' Love ', he said with reference to his own life, ' has a greater empire over souls than, I will not say strictness, but even force of argument.' The spiritual depth of his nature shines through his classic books of devotion, *Love of God* and *The Introduction to a Devout Life*. His contemporary and fellow-countryman, Vincent de Paul, epitomised the social teaching of his Church. After ordination he was captured by Tunisian pirates and his personal experience as a galley-slave made him decide after his escape from imprisonment to devote his life to the alleviation of the misery of the galley-slaves. He spent his time working among the galleys of Bordeaux and Marseilles; at Chartres he established the Congregation of Missions to train preachers to carry on the work of conversion in the French towns. He founded the Sisters of Charity, an order of nuns, especially associated with nursing, whose unstinted heroism and faith cannot be too highly praised.

But the whole point of the Counter-Reformation lies quite simply in the fact that it was a corporate impulse in which many individuals combined to revive the standards of Church life. The instruction of the clergy and the laity was greatly improved by the foundation of diocesan training seminaries and of schools, often run by the Jesuits. The publication in 1566 of the new *Catechism*, drawn up by a committee of Dominicans, provided the laity with a

[1] He lies in state in a sumptuous crypt-chapel below Milan's Cathedral.
[2] ' The French Counter-Reformation, when it came at last to flower, produced a mass of blossoms, unrivalled either in splendour or numbers, to grace the never-wintered garden of Catholic spirituality; but the bursting of the glory was strangely retarded ', H. O. Evennett, *The Cardinal of Lorraine*, 48.

clear and authoritative statement of belief written in sonorous Latin. The reform of the Breviary and of the Missal was equally important. Above all a more emphatic realisation of the meaning of vocation lay at the root of this religious revival.

The immediate result was a full-scale attempt, often backed by armed force and the rigours of persecution, to regain territory and peoples won over by the Protestant reformers. Poland was more or less completely regained for Catholicism. The process of re-evangelisation went steadily ahead within the Empire; individual bishops like Julius Echter von Mespelbrunn of Würzburg and Ernest von Mengersdorf, Bishop of Bamberg, pursued a vigorous policy against heretics, a compound of persuasion and persecution in which the latter predominated. The Jesuits were introduced; devotional activities were increased; churches were built while their flocks were offered the crude alternative of the Mass or exile. Secular princes, above all the Wittelsbach princes of Bavaria, Albert V, William V and the long-ruled Maximilian I, showed a similar enthusiasm. Almost alone among the Catholic princes of Germany the Imperial house showed greater restraint. Having witnessed the dissensions which had at last exhausted and broken his brother, the Emperor Ferdinand I stood by the Religious Peace of Augsburg. Maximilian II was criticised as almost a Protestant. His successor, Rudolf II, the tool of a fanatical half-Spanish camarilla, was more interested in astrology and in searching for the philosopher's stone than in ruling his Empire in the government of which he was at last obliged to associate his cousin, Matthias. Matthias was ambitious but tremulous; he watched the rising tension which was bringing the Empire nearer to the brink of the Thirty Years' War. The Catholic extremists placed their hopes on Matthias' heir, young Ferdinand of Styria, a protégé of the Jesuits by whom he had been educated at the University of Ingolstadt.

Strong as Protestantism remained, the situation seemed to favour the forces of the Counter-Reformation. Italy had been cleared of heresy. Spain was intransigently orthodox. France was indeed divided by religious war and had been obliged to accept in 1589 a Huguenot King, Henry IV, but Henry had shown his appreciation of the situation by becoming a Roman Catholic. The Swedish King, John III, urged on by his Catholic wife, played with the idea of reconciliation with the Roman Church. Protestantism was further hampered by certain inherent weaknesses. It was divided, more especially as Calvinism, unprovided for by the Religious Peace of Augsburg, grew stronger in Germany. The Protestant Churches could not even agree on a common doctrine, let alone a united front against the enemy. In Bohemia which the Hussite tradition made one of the more important centres of European Protestantism there were four different sects, the Utraquists, the Lutherans, the Calvinists and a pietist group known as the Bohemian Brethren. In the field of education the Protestants had suffered an important setback upon which David Ogg has made the shrewd comment: 'The steady decline of the Protestant university of Wittenberg in the sixteenth century and the equally steady rise of the Catholic university of Ingolstadt in the same period provide the most ominous comment on the relative equipment of the two combatants.'

This crusading fervour boded ill for the future. When a Protestant professor, Pareus of Heidelberg, made a plea for the union of the Lutherans and the Calvinists, the Jesuit father Adam Contzen replied by demanding that the Protestants should surrender unconditionally to the Pope; his words 'facile est Europae fidem reddere' represented current hopes among enthusiastic Catholics.

Religious enthusiasm was, however, so closely associated with secular objectives that it is almost impossible to distinguish which was which. The Spanish King, Philip II, who has often been called the armed champion of the Counter-Reformation, was fundamentally more concerned with protecting Spanish interests and with reasserting Spanish hegemony in Europe. The most Catholic of the Hapsburg Emperors, Ferdinand II, was driven by a two-fold motive, the desire to recover souls for the Catholic faith and to reimpose Hapsburg control over the hereditary lands. The same mixture of motive reappears in French history. This indicates the essential weakness of the Counter-Reformation as a religious movement and explains its strength as a political force. Religion was used to cloak political motives by self-interested powers. The Counter-Reformation was in effect an attempt to re-impose a medieval view of religion and life on a society which was slowly separating the two. It implied an admission of certain moral and theological values which current social, political and philosophical developments had already challenged. This explains why the Counter-Reformation had only a limited success and how in attempting to express its ideas in political life it became permeated by secular ambition.

CHAPTER XII

THE EMPIRE OF PHILIP II, 1558–98

1. *Philip II*

WHETHER Philip II was the ' typical Spanish sovereign of all time '[1] is a matter of opinion, but no one in the sixteenth century so influenced the history of his country. Philip epitomised many of the salient trends in contemporary Spanish history. He has been represented as a sinister tyrant so often that it is difficult to know what he was really like as a man. His correspondence with his daughters, Isabella and Catherine, clearly reveals that he was more affectionate than some contemporary documents suggest. Yet there was something inhuman about this graceful, dignified and cultured man the pallor of whose expression revealed both his lack of exercise and his intense concentration on his work. Living in a court governed by a precise etiquette, never mixing on the same terms with his fellow-men, he had grown up outwardly cold and reserved. His family-life, like that of the Emperor Francis Joseph of Austria, was haunted by tragedy. His first wife, Maria of Portugal, died when she was eighteen in giving birth to the heir, Don Carlos. The latter grew up a homicidal lunatic,[2] obviously incapable of wearing the Spanish crown, and his imprisonment, and some thought his death, was ordered by his father. His second marriage to Mary Tudor of England was concluded for dynastic reasons, nor did Philip reciprocate the affection which Mary bore him. His third wife ' the best Queen that they had ever had or could have ' Elizabeth of Valois was deeply mourned by her husband when she died in 1568. His fourth marriage to Anne of Austria was founded on the

[1] The phrase is R. B. Merriman's. Professor J. B. Trend emphasises that Philip was more a typical German than a typical Spaniard and R. Trevor-Davies describes him as ' In appearance . . . . typically German, fair-haired, growing prematurely grey, fresh-complexioned and blue-eyed ' (*Golden Century of Spain*, 117).

[2] Minute in size, physically deformed, Don Carlos suffered from mental disorders from birth. He delighted in cruelty. But a fall which resulted in a brain operation (this seems to be the net effect of what happened) led to more frequent outbursts of homicidal mania. He ' died a natural death as the result of his gluttonous habits and of his sleeping naked on a bed strewn with ice in the draught of a window when the heat of the Madrid summer was at its height ' (*Golden Century of Spain*, 151); but the final verdict must remain unproven.

necessity for a male heir to whom Philip could leave his immense dominions; but the Infante Philip was not of the stuff of which his father was made. ' God ', so Philip is supposed to have said, ' who has given me so many kingdoms has not given me a son worthy to rule them.' ' Philip ', says R. B. Merriman, ' had laid no less than seventeen members of his own family to rest there [in the Escurial] before he had completed his sixtieth year.'

These persistent worries of which few outward hints appeared, for the King possessed iron self-control, must be associated with his extraordinarily high sense of duty. God who had given him his kingdoms expected that Philip would rule them justly and well. Such was Philip's belief and the guiding idea behind his policy. ' Justice ', wrote the Venetian ambassador in 1563, ' is his favourite interest and in so far as its administration concerns him, he does his duty well.' Supremely conscientious, he had also an inherent distrust of other men's motives and so relied on no one but himself. ' Bien es myrar a todo ' (it is well to consider everything) was his favourite phrase, as it had been of his father, the Emperor Charles V. The Spanish government, like that of the Tudors, was conciliar but all final decisions remained in Philip's hands. Even the secretaries of state were little more than royal clerks in whom the King rarely placed full confidence. Night and day he annotated the despatches of state in his spidery handwriting.[1] His reddened eyes were a tribute to his exacting toil. ' Having so many subjects ', again the evidence of the Venetian ambassador, Morosini, in 1581, ' and trusting no one, and insisting that everything pass under his own hand and eye, he is so perpetually preoccupied with this business, with so great labour and toil, that I have heard many people say that they would not for the world be the ruler of so many states as is his Majesty, if it meant living the kind of life he lives.' In spite of the King's industry and excellent memory, the work was really beyond him. It took such an infinitely long time to get a decision from Madrid, that it became a commonly accepted aphorism among his viceroys abroad that ' if death came from Spain, I should be immortal '. The grand almoner, Luis Manrique, did not mince his words when he told Philip that discontent arose from : ' sitting for ever over your papers; from your desire, as they intimate, to seclude yourself from the world, and from a want of confidence in

---

[1] Sometimes he would correct the spelling. On another occasion ' the ambassador in London, knowing Philip's avidity for any and every kind of information, describes at length some minute insects that he has seen crawling over his window-panes. Philip solemnly adds in the margin, " probably fleas " ' (Trevor Davies, *op. cit.*, 128).

your ministers. Hence such interminable delays as fill the soul of every suitor with despair. . . . God did not send your Majesty and all the other kings, his viceroys on earth, to waste their time in reading or writing, nor yet in meditation and prayer.' The situation was not improved by the King's inability to differentiate what was vital from the indifferent and secondary; 'while', as Merriman expresses it, 'Philip was deciding how the sailors on the Armada could best be kept from swearing, Sir Francis Drake raided the Spanish coast.' Philip was not a tyrannical dictator nor a medieval warrior-king; in the history of monarchy he was the arch-bureaucrat.

The Catholic religion formed the spring both of his character and of his policy. 'It is said at court', the industrious Venetian reported, 'that he enquires of his confessor whether it would be injurious to his conscience to do this or that, and on being told that it would be so, changes the plans which he had been advised to adopt'. Except for one brief period, his life was entirely free from vice. His own needs were frugal. From the start of his reign he cut down the expenses of his court; books and paintings were his only extravagances. The splendid *auto da fé* at Valladolid with which his arrival in Spain as King was celebrated symbolised his desire to repress heresy and exalt the Church.

Yet it may be objected that on three scores Philip's policy hardly seemed in accord with his religion. Until the election of a pro-Spaniard in 1591 his relations with successive Popes were almost consistently bad, mainly because questions of foreign policy made the Popes follow an anti-Hapsburg programme. Even on religious issues King and Pope did not always see eye to eye; the Most Catholic King opposed the Jesuits whom the counter-reformation Popes supported. The King showed that he was as determined to be the absolute master of the Church as he was of the State. Henry VIII had little more power over the English Church than Philip had over the Spanish Church. All the major appointments were in his hands; the Spanish Inquisition was his instrument. He constantly forbade the publication of papal decrees in Spain, and otherwise hampered papal nuncios. The Spanish Church seemed more the agent of Spanish political absolutism than the docile tool of the Pope. Finally, time and time again Philip placed the interests of Spain before those of the Catholic Church. 'Wherever', as a recent historian put it, 'political interest and religious zeal clashed, religious zeal almost invariably gave way.'

Even so, his religion remained the fundamental and constant factor in Philip's rule. He had been brought up to distrust papal politics as anti-Hapsburg and to think of Spain as the true bulwark of the Catholic faith. He found it easy to identify the interests of Spain with those of the Church; he could never visualise that there might be a contradiction between the exaltation of the power of Spain and the good of the Church. To be a loyal Spaniard and a good Catholic were for him conterminous.

Nothing so well represents Philip as the palace of the Escurial which he had built in the solitary foot-hills of the Sierra de Guadarrama twenty miles north-west of Madrid. Modelled on the grid-iron on which St. Lawrence was said traditionally to have been martyred, the Escurial was in part a palace and in part a monastery, designed to exalt the monarchy and to give glory to God. Begun on April 22nd, 1563, it was finished on September 13th, 1584. Its outward appearance was austere but its interior was splendid, enriched with jasper and fine marbles and decorated with works of art painted by the greatest masters of the time. But it was a monastery as well as a palace. Day and night the Hieronymite monks chanted the monastic hours; many sacred relics were housed in its church. Even miracles were said to have been performed within its precincts, but in a sense the greatest miracle of all was the King himself. His bedroom was so placed that he could hear the Church services, and it was there at the last, a suppurating corpse in constant agony, yet arranging the details of his funeral with the meticulous detail which characterised all he did, that he died on September 13th, 1598. 'Although change is usually popular', wrote the Venetian ambassador, 'yet nobles and people, rich and poor, universally show great grief.'

The forty years of his reign were overshadowed by his desire to serve God and Spain, a combination in which, unintentionally, Spain sometimes took precedence of God. Heresy must be crushed wherever it appeared, whether in Spain or in the Spanish dominions overseas. The infidel Moor and his compatriot the Turk must be brought to book. All power must be concentrated about the King, whether in Castile and Aragon, the Americas, Italy or the Netherlands. The Valois and the Tudors must be obliged to admit Hapsburg hegemony in Europe. The programme was extensive and neither the King nor Spain had the resources which could alone ensure its successful outcome.

2. *The repression of infidelity*

It is probable that Philip sighed with relief when he realised that he would not be obliged to wear his father's Imperial crown, for the German dominions seethed with heresy whereas Spain was the one country least affected by heretical ideas. The Inquisition, backed by the King, struck rapidly and ruthlessly at high and low, eliminating the Protestant groups at Seville and Valladolid. Philip need never have feared that his own dominions would be seriously infected by prevalent Lutheran and Calvinist ideas.

But one problem caused him grave concern, that of the *Moriscos*, the Moors who had been allowed to remain in Spain as long as they accepted Catholic Christianity. Although they were theoretically Christian, neither the mode of conversion which left them practically uninstructed nor the attitude of the Spanish Christians made them genuine or loyal converts. It is true that Philip had ordered that the *Moriscos* should be better instructed in the elements of the Catholic faith, and at least in 1564 he had tried to make the Inquisition behave less repressively towards the *Moriscos* of Valencia; but he was a man of his time and knew only that the *Moriscos* were suspect of disloyalty to God and to Spain. There was a measure of justification for this belief since continued attachment to Islam necessarily meant pro-Turkish sympathies. Nevertheless nothing can justify the cruel policy which started with the re-enactment in 1566 of the severe edict of 1526, for which the new Inquisitor-General, Espinosa, was largely to blame. The edict of 1526 had forbidden the use of Arabic and had banned Moorish names, dresses, ornaments and baths. Christian midwives were ordered to attend all Moorish births. All *Moriscos* were told to learn Castilian within three years but how they were to learn without teachers the government did not say.

The *Moriscos*, who had believed that the government had abandoned its repressive policy, were indignant and in despair. The captain-general of Granada, Inigo de Mendoza, Marquis of Mondejar, who had not been consulted, remonstrated, as did the Duke of Alva, with Philip's advisers for reviving the edict which he considered unwise. The actual destruction of Moorish baths began in 1567 but it was not until Christmas 1568 that the *Moriscos* revolted. The rebels massacred the Christians wherever they found them, but both sides were equally brutal; ' in this campaign ', wrote a Spanish soldier, ' we were all thieves together, and myself the first of them.' Mondejar, who had practically brought the

rebellion to an end by promises of conciliation, was replaced by
Philip's romantic half-brother, Don John of Austria, who with
some difficulty eventually crushed the revolt. The rebellious Moors
were deported to other parts of the country, only being allowed to
take their families and movable goods; wherever they settled they
lived under irksome restrictions and endured the full rigidity of the
edict of 1566. In spite of this they proved so industrious that their
labours were soon enriching the new districts where they settled.
This was not the end. The *Morisco* problem remained until
Philip's son ordered their deportation in 1609.

The suppression of the *Morisco* rebellion enabled Philip to turn
his attention to their co-religionists, the Turks, whose galleys constituted a permanent menace to the Spanish command of the
western Mediterranean. It was therefore Philip's duty as a champion of the Catholic faith as well as to his interest as a Spanish
sovereign to arrest the Moslem advance. But Philip's vision was
limited in practice to the western waters of the Mediterranean;
he showed no eagerness to be embroiled in the Aegean or the
Adriatic where Venice, the constant enemy of the Hapsburg, engaged alternatively in lucrative commerce and unprofitable war with
the Turk. Despite occasional engagements, such as the great
defeat which the Spaniards suffered at Los Gelves in 1564, Philip's
policy towards the Turk must have appeared vacillating and dilatory
to the remainder of the western world.

When therefore the Sultan again turned his attention towards
the Venetians, instead of sending help to the *Moriscos* of Granada
as his grand vizier advised, Philip took no immediate action. But
the Pope Pius V, a true crusader, persuaded Philip to come to terms
with Venice and to form a Holy League to defend the west against
Islam. Cyprus fell to the Turks before the allied fleet sailed under
the lead of Don John of Austria. In October, 1571, it came into
contact with the Ottoman fleet and in a terrific struggle off Lepanto
virtually annihilated the Turkish galleys. It was the most impressive victory of the sixteenth century, 'the noblest occasion',
as Cervantes wrote, 'that past or present ages have seen or future
ones may hope to see.' The immediate sequel to Lepanto may have
seemed trifling, for Spain and Venice were too much at loggerheads
to remain in alliance for long against the common foe: even the
Spanish capture of Tunis in 1573 was really an anti-climax. But
Lepanto was the end of an epoch in Mediterranean history.
It was the beginning of the close of the Turkish menace in
the Mediterranean as well as the last important battle fought by
grappling and boarding, the battle that inevitably spelt doom for

the galley as a fighting-ship.   Occasional depredations might continue but the Cross, the red cross of Spain on its yellow background, had effectively vanquished the Crescent.

3. *Spanish foreign policy*, 1556-78

In the first half of his reign Philip's foreign policy was really an extension of his domestic programme.   If Philip's intense desire to ' Castilianise ' the outlying provinces of his empire, to centre all power upon himself and to champion the Catholic religion are remembered, the complex story which follows becomes intelligible. Advised by his childhood friend, Ruy Gomez da Silva, Prince of Eboli, Philip wanted to keep peace in Europe through the main-tenance of the *status quo*.   Indeed it was not until after 1578 that Spain took the initiative in foreign affairs.   But Philip failed to realise his object, primarily because of the outbreak of troubles in the Spanish Netherlands, the determining factor in Spanish foreign policy throughout the reign, and the reaction it evoked in the England of Elizabeth and the France of Catherine de' Medici.   The staid and orderly Spanish King had to deal with two capricious women whose day-to-day policy was completely unpredictable.   While Philip's home policy was comparatively straightforward, his foreign policy often appeared curiously opportunist and inextricably tangled.

Philip naturally inherited his father's foreign policy, especially the long conflict with the Valois, when he became King of Spain. Moreover his wife was the Queen of England.   His accession accordingly proved the preliminary to the renewal of war between France and Spain, ended by the Treaty of Cateau-Cambrésis signed on April 3rd, 1559.   France retained Calais recently captured from the English [1] and returned the territories taken from Philip's ally, the soldier Duke Emmanuel Philibert of Savoy.   As Mary Tudor had died in 1558, the new understanding between France and Spain was confirmed by a marriage between Philip and Elizabeth of Valois, the eldest daughter of Henry II.   The Treaty of Cateau-Cambrésis confirmed the Spanish hegemony in Italy, but it could not wipe out the underlying causes of hostility between the two countries. More immediately the conclusion of the Treaty enabled Philip to leave the Netherlands for Spain, a journey postponed from the August 18th to the 23rd because the astrologer Nostradamus ' with his threats of tempests and shipwrecks . . . did put the sailors in great fear '.

---

[1] French retention of Calais was on paper restricted to a term of years but England never regained possession.

Philip was never again to see the Netherlands where rising discontent against Spain was soon to lead to open rebellion. Whether Philip's overtures to Elizabeth or the Treaty of Cateau-Cambrésis could really ensure future peace depended ultimately on the attitude which the English and French Queens were to take towards the revolt in the Netherlands.

Elizabeth of England waited on events as much as did Philip. She had rejected the tentative offer of marriage which Philip had made after Mary's death. She did not want to become a Roman Catholic nor did she wish to go to war needlessly. On the other hand the trouble in the Low Countries provided her with an opportunity for keeping Philip in check. At all costs she wished to avoid a Franco-Spanish *rapprochement* which would automatically be directed against England. She had little real sympathy with the Dutch Protestants either as Protestants or as rebels against authority, but she saw that it was to England's interests to weaken Philip's position in the Low Countries. In brief she wished the revolt to continue but had no wish for either side to win.

The French attitude was very similar but was affected by the confused internal situation which existed on the eve of the outbreak of the French Wars of Religion. Like Elizabeth, Catherine de' Medici, who was the real ruler of France from 1559, did not want the Protestant rebels or Philip II to win. If the former were successful, they would almost certainly help the French Huguenots whom the Queen sought to curb, either by appeasement or by armed force. On the other hand if Philip won, France was obviously placed between the nutcrackers of metropolitan Spain and the Spanish Netherlands.

Spanish diplomacy between 1559 and 1567 formed a prologue to the future. Ominous rumbles in the Netherlands during the governorship of Margaret of Parma announced the coming time of troubles. Alarmed by the policy of appeasement which Catherine de' Medici was adopting towards the Huguenots, Philip did everything in his power to undermine their position in France. An attempt to secure a *rapprochement* reached a climax at a meeting between Catherine and her daughter, the Queen of Spain, accompanied by the Duke of Alva, at Bayonne. Although the Huguenots believed that the Massacre of St. Bartholomew was plotted there, the meeting proved indeterminate; in fact it mainly represented Catherine's desire to see her daughter and it is doubtful if anything dangerous to the Huguenots was discussed. Philip had wanted a ' holy league ' against the heretics, including the Huguenots and his own disaffected subjects in the Low Countries; Catherine cherished a diplomatic marriage. Relations were therefore no more friendly at the end of the interview than they had been at the beginning.

Nor were Philip's relations with England in this period any more conclusive. He never understood England as well as he did France, and throughout his reign underestimated England's potentialities as an enemy. Time and time again his envoys recommended the Spanish King to intervene but the King rarely listened; the part his convoys played in Catholic plots to dethrone Elizabeth did Philip disservice because they made a reconciliation between England and Spain impossible. Furthermore it may be surmised that Elizabeth knew her own mind better than Catherine knew hers. To prevent a reconciliation between the Hapsburg and the Valois she was willing to coquet with both. Philip was angered by the incomprehensible vacillations of English policy. When Philip's ambassador asked Elizabeth to remove the trade restrictions which were hampering the Netherlands woollen industry and so contributing to the rising discontent among the woollen workers, the English Queen characteristically evaded the point. The extension of English privateering was even more irritating to the Spanish Crown. That Sir John Hawkins should sell his West African negro slaves to the colonists in the Spanish West Indies was an undoubted infringement of a more or less divinely appointed economic and political monopoly bestowed by the Pope on Spain. The English were no less annoyed when they heard that Philip's agents had handed English sailors over to the Inquisition as 'corsairos Luteranos'.

The next six years, 1567-73, might have brought the worsening of relations between England and Spain and between France and Spain to a head, but in point of fact they did nothing of the sort. These years coincided with Alva's forceful attempt to suppress the Dutch rebels. Had this been successful it would have so changed the balance of power in north-west Europe that neither England nor France could have long ignored the challenge to their security.

By 1570 the anti-Spanish party was in power in France. The Huguenot leader, Coligny, who had gained great influence over Charles IX and his supporters believed that it might be possible to reconcile the conflicting religious groups in France by a national call for war against Spain. But Catherine did not want war with Spain; she loathed Coligny's influence over her son; and she tried to cut the Gordian Knot by massacring the Protestant leaders on St. Bartholomew's Eve, 1572. It is said that Philip laughed when he heard the news. It was a rare event but he may have done so, for the massacre at least relieved him temporarily of the fear of French intervention in the Low Countries.

Meanwhile relations between England and Spain had drawn dangerously near to war. In December, 1568, Elizabeth had placed the Spanish commander in the Netherlands, Alva, in an awkward position by 'borrowing' the Spanish treasure containing a loan from the Genoese bankers to pay Alva's troops, from merchantmen, which had taken refuge from pirates in English harbours. Elizabeth glibly asserted either that she was keeping the money safe for the King of Spain, or alternatively, she had as much right as he to borrow from the Genoese bankers. During the next two years there were a number of plots against Elizabeth culminating in the Northern Rebellion in which the Spanish ambassador at her court, Guereau de Spes, was clearly implicated. At its Saturday meeting on July 7th, 1571, the Spanish Council of State discussed a plan for assassinating Elizabeth. Yet when the crisis seemed most perilous the English Queen and Alva concluded the Convention of Nimwegen, opening up trade between England and the Low Countries. Furthermore each side agreed to abandon the rebels against the government of the other.

The situation hardly changed during the next five years but there was some heightening of the tension, for the continued success of the Dutch rebels encouraged all Philip's enemies. Catherine de' Medici had once more reverted to a policy of appeasement, thus allowing her younger son, Anjou, to intervene on the rebels' behalf as the so-called 'Defender of the Liberties of the Low Countries', while Philip's relations with England during this period may be summed up in the phrase 'a sordid tale of plot and counter-plot'.

Despite the setbacks which he had suffered, Philip's situation abroad in 1578 was in some ways favourable. England and France were still friends in name. The military situation in the Netherlands had definitely improved within the last few months. The Pope was compliant. The Austrian Hapsburgs were friendly. The Counter-Reformation continued its forward march. There was then something to be said for the more aggressive policy which he was now to adopt. But Philip still did not realise the underlying weakness of Spanish economy on which a successful foreign policy, aggressive or defensive, had ultimately to be founded.

4. *Spanish foreign policy*, 1578-98

The last twenty years of Philip's reign witnessed a change in his foreign policy which after initial successes brought Spain to the

brink of disaster. There was a slow changeover from the defensive
policy which Philip had adopted during the first part of his reign
to a policy of aggression in which the rewards were proportionate
to the gamble involved. He had now a most capable and experienced adviser in the Burgundian cardinal Granvelle.[1] Had he
not died in 1586, it is possible that many major blunders, including
the Armada, might have been avoided, but it is difficult to tell.
Apart from Granvelle, Philip was served by subordinates of more
than average ability abroad, none more capable than the impulsive
Bernardino de Mendoza, expelled from England in 1584 for complicity in plots against Elizabeth and later the King's faithful hench-
man in France. Philip's general in the Low Countries, Alexander
Farnese, Duke of Parma, was probably the finest soldier of his age,
nor was the ruthless Fuentes, who succeeded him, much his inferior.
Spain had a first-class seaman and naval administrator in Alvaro de
Bazan, Marquis of Santa Cruz, whose preliminary work on the
Spanish Armada was brought to nothing by Philip's own niggling
interference and the incompetence of his successor, Medina Sidonia.

Yet ultimately Philip's policy was bound to fail. As Parma
realised, the secret of success in warfare depended on the concentration
of the total force at the King's disposal on a given objective; it was
impossible to carry on a war against the French and against the
Dutch rebels without a dispersal of forces leading to an inevitable
weakening of power. Nor until it was too late did Philip realise
how important it was to have a strong navy; naval power would
have enabled him to protect the long communications upon which the
empire's prosperity depended and would have made a successful
invasion of England more likely. There were other inherent weaknesses, the slowness with which decisions were made, the ingratitude
with which Philip treated his successful generals and the unwillingness with which he gave his confidence to his ministers. Moreover,
it is doubtful if even success could have counteracted the fundamental economic weakness of the Spanish state.

The acquisition of the wealthy and extensive Portuguese empire
in 1580 was Philip's first major success.[2] In ruling this newly-
won empire Philip showed greater wisdom than he had so far displayed in dealing with the dependencies under his direct control.
On his entry into Portugal he dressed in Portuguese costume and
even cut his beard in Portuguese fashion. When he met the

---

[1] He was said to be able to dictate despatches in five different languages
to five different secretaries at one sitting; he had already served the Spanish
interests in the Low Countries (see pp. 243-4, 246).

[2] See pp. 76-7.

Portuguese notables at Tomar, he promised to uphold all the laws, privileges and customs of the state and only to appoint Portuguese to all offices within the Portuguese empire. The economic provisions were also worthy of note; the regulations governing the lucrative colonial trade remained unchanged and the customs at the frontiers of Castile and Portugal were abolished. In spite of minor infractions—the customs, for instance, were restored in 1593—Philip kept the Oath of Tomar, being wiser in his generation than was Olivarez sixty years later. He had in fact gained a vast empire—and additional responsibilities—at a relatively small cost.

The Netherlands, however, still remained the centre round which his foreign policy revolved. Under the lead of the Duke of Parma, there was a steady Spanish recovery as town after town returned to Philip's authority. This in its turn forced the Dutch to rely more and more on outside assistance. They had first turned to the French prince, the Duke of Anjou, but he had proved a broken reed. He returned to France to die only a month before the Dutch leader, William of Orange was murdered by one of Philip's hired assassins. This was a signal if brutal triumph for Philip as it robbed the rebels of their most able commander. In despair the Dutch turned to Elizabeth of England who in her turn allowed an expedition to sail to Holland under the command of the Earl of Leicester. Leicester's expedition of 1585 proved as great a fiasco as Anjou's of 1583, but both French and English intervention were additional proof, if that were needed, of hostility towards Spain. Philip had by now made up his mind definitely to bring both England and France within the sphere of Spanish influence. But this, as Parma realised, required an immediate success to make it effective; a prolonged campaign would only prejudice the future outcome of Philip's war in the Low Countries.

Philip's anger with England was cumulative, though neither he nor Elizabeth really wanted war. Sir Francis Drake, who had circumnavigated the globe between 1577 and 1580, was only one of the many English sailors who raided Spanish ships and possessions. In 1581 the Pretender to the Portuguese throne, Don Antonio, Prior of Crato, for whom Elizabeth's adviser, Sir Francis Walsingham, was a pressing advocate, was given a temporary refuge in England. In November of the same year Elizabeth's former suitor and Philip's opponent in the Netherlands, the Duke of Anjou, arrived in England.[1]

---

[1] ' The air was full of rumours of a Franco-Spanish understanding, and of the possibility that Anjou might wed a Spanish bride. The inference was obvious. Elizabeth must herself lend aid to the rebels in the Low Countries; she must also encourage Anjou's matrimonial aspirations to

On the English side the coming of the Catholic mission in 1580 was unjustifiably associated with Philip while Spanish backing for the constant plots against Elizabeth provided additional provocation. Anglo-Spanish relations had been further confused by the imprisonment of Elizabeth's possible successor, Mary, Queen of Scots. At first Philip had displayed no particular enthusiasm for Mary, all of whose contacts had been pro-French and consequently anti-Spanish, but latterly he had begun to change his attitude. Writing on May 20th, 1586, to the former Spanish ambassador in London, Mendoza, who was then in Paris, Mary had explicitly disinherited her son, James, in Philip's favour. After her execution in February, 1587, Philip could thus regard himself as the heir to a throne, now held by a heretic from allegiance to whom the Pope had freed her subjects by a bull of excommunication published seventeen years earlier. Whereas Philip had in the past deliberately toned down the crusading enthusiasm of the English Catholics, he now—where much besides religion was at issue—claimed that Pope Sixtus V should invest him or his daughter, the Infanta Isabella, with the English crown.

The preparations for the Armada against England, which had begun as long ago as 1586, went forward slowly in spite of Drake's damaging raid on shipping in Cadiz harbour in April 1587 and the death of the great Spanish admiral, Santa Cruz. It sailed at last under the command of the wealthy Duke of Medina Sidonia in May, 1588; all its soldiers and sailors held a certificate to the effect that they had been confessed and shriven, but this could not unfortunately make up for the lamentable deficiencies in munitions and commissariat. Intended to act as a conveyer of Parma's troops from the Flemish ports to the English coast, the Armada was defeated by a combination of English seamanship and climate. What the ships of Lord Howard of Effingham and Drake failed to do, the winds and the waves achieved. Of the original 130 ships, only 11 accompanied Medina Sidonia into Santander harbour on September 22nd, 1588.[1] Nothing can have tested Philip's self-control as much as the news of this unprecedented disaster, but his imperturbability never left him for a single moment.

The Spanish Armada did not bring the war with England to a

whatever extent it might prove necessary, in order to prevent him from seeking another wife. The first she did with extreme reluctance; the second more willingly—for it rather amused her—until Anjou, actually convinced that she was in earnest, forgot about the Netherlands and threatened to outstay his welcome in England; then, indeed, she was hard put to it to get rid of him ' (R. B. Merriman, iv, 503).

[1] In time some 55 of the remaining ships arrived.

close. While its defeat had been a great blow to Spanish naval prestige, it did not mean the end of Spanish power nor did it open Spanish ports to English marauders. In general the initiative certainly remained with the daring English sailors, but the Spaniards raided the Cornish coast in 1595 and helped the Irish rebels in their struggle against the English. The English raids on Spanish possessions were also relatively inconclusive, but in 1596 Howard of Effingham commanded a fleet bearing 10,000 English under Lord Essex, and 5000 Dutch under Louis of Nassau to attack Cadiz. The Duke of Medina Sidonia showed himself as inept in defending Andalusia as he had done in harrying England, and for sixteen days the English plundered Cadiz to their hearts' content. Gorged with booty they returned home on August 8th, 1596. So far as Philip's reign was concerned, this closed the story of Anglo-Spanish relations. The King planned another Armada, but the storms scattered it before it was even ready to sail. 'Truly', wrote Herrera, 'an admiral, like a doctor, must have fortune on his side.'

While Philip continued his unprofitable war against England, he had become involved in the French Wars of Religion. Anjou's death in 1584, no real loss as he was, had made a Huguenot prince, Henry of Navarre, heir to the French throne. Quite apart from the fact that a Huguenot King of France would almost certainly be anti-Spanish, Philip feared that he would give open assistance to the Dutch rebels. At all costs he hoped to prevent Henry's accession to the French throne and, as a first step, he made an alliance with the Catholic Guise family, of whose pretensions he had hitherto been suspicious. The objects of the Treaty of Joinville, signed between Spain and the Guises in 1585, have been summarised as 'a perpetual offensive and defensive alliance for the preservation of the Roman Catholic faith, for the extirpation of heresy in France and in the Low Countries, and for the exclusion of the Bourbons from the French throne'. The murder in 1589 of the French King, Henry III, who by now had broken with both the Guises and Spain and the accession of his Huguenot cousin, Henry IV, gave Philip an opportunity to intervene directly in French affairs. He did not approve of the murder of the Lord's anointed—such precedents in the case of a Catholic King were dangerous—but he must have seen the force behind Mendoza's despatch telling of this event: 'it has pleased our Lord to deliver us by an event so happy that it cannot but be attributed to His all-powerful hand; indeed it gives us reason to hope that we are finished with the heretics.'

For once Philip was quick to seize his opportunity. In company with the French Catholic League he would crush heresy in the neighbouring country and, if he played his cards aright, he might win the acceptance of his own claim or that of his daughter, the Infanta Isabella, to the French throne; Cardinal Bourbon, the Catholic claimant, was an old man without direct heirs who died in 1590. To Parma's distress he had to shelve the campaigns against the rebels in the Low Countries so that the Spaniards might assist the Catholic League by invading northern France. Philip's plans were, however, doomed to fail. As always when he was dealing with problems outside Castile he seemed to lack any real understanding of the situation. The Duke of Mayenne, who had succeeded his brother, the Duke of Guise, murdered by the orders of Henry III in December, 1588, as the Catholic commander, was glad of Spanish help but had no love for Spain and would obviously break with Philip as soon as it was expedient to do so. Parma and his successor, Fuentes, both resented the futile expenditure of men and materials in northern France when they could be used more effectively against the Dutch, but they had to obey the royal orders. Furthermore, however grateful Catholic Frenchmen might be to Philip for helping them against the Huguenots, they disliked his claim to the French throne and had no wish for their nation to be embedded in his vast empire. From 1590 onwards anti-Spanish sentiment in France steadily increased, more especially after Henry of Navarre announced his conversion to the Catholic faith. The capture of Calais in April, 1596, was the only item of good news in a series of military defeats, underlined by another Spanish bankruptcy. Negotiations for peace with France were opened in 1598 leading to the conclusion of the Treaty of Vervins on May 2nd. Philip agreed to surrender Calais and other places remaining to the Spaniards in Picardy and Brittany and to recognise the integrity and independence of France under Henry IV. It was a bitter pill for Philip to swallow, made no sweeter by the story of events elsewhere; one of the French negotiators, Pomponne de Bellièvre, described the treaty as the 'most advantageous that France had concluded for five hundred years'. It was in this depressing fashion that the reign of Philip *el Prudente* came to its close.

5. *Philip's failure*

As Philip lay dying in the Escurial he must have realised that he had only in part fulfilled the objects for which he had laboured so long. With the major exception of the Netherlands he had kept his dominions free from the taint of heresy, but he died without suppressing the Dutch rebels and without bringing his wars with

England and France to a victorious end. He never properly understood that his empire was already suffering from a debility which formed a prelude to the long story of her decline. How far was Philip the victim of circumstances and how far must he bear the responsibility for the disasters of his reign ?

In general, Philip's failure was a result of his environment rather than of his personality, though there is no doubt that he must bear part of the responsibility for Spain's decline. Finance, which formed the main problem of the Spanish monarchy, was curiously enough the one subject in which the King was comparatively uninterested. He inherited a large debt from his father, amounting in all to some fifty million ducats, which handicapped him from the very start of his reign. During the next forty years he was faced with mounting expenses, in part a result of the rising costs of ordinary administration and in part an effect of the extraordinary but constant expenditure made necessary by his foreign policy. The Dutch rebellion so severely strained the King's resources that there were times when he had insufficient money to pay his troops ; it was a financial sponge which had absorbed no less than 110 million ducats by 1598. The Spanish Armada cost another ten million ducats. In spite of all that Philip's Council of Finance (*Consejo de Hacienda*) did to find new ways of raising money, the revenue was never adequate to meet the interest on past loans or current expenses. Many new taxes were imposed. An increasing use was made of monopolies. The sale of offices at home and abroad was greatly extended. Although these new devices may have increased the net revenue, they also helped to cripple commercial and industrial enterprise and often had deleterious social effects. The Spanish empire became overloaded with saleable offices which may have enhanced the dignity of the purchasers but certainly impeded administrative efficiency. In spite of the fact that the amount of the gold and silver from the New World increased steadily throughout Philip's reign, it never sufficed to meet the needs of the national expenditure. At the start of the reign the American treasure amounted at a rough estimate to about half a million pounds, which was only about eleven per cent. of the money due to the royal treasury. By 1580 this sum had increased to about £750,000 and by the end of the century to £1,300,000 but at its height it accounted for no more than twenty-five per cent. of the national needs.[1]

Like his father, Philip was obliged to fall back on loans from the banking houses, thus mortgaging the future. 'The *juros*, and the

[1] On the effect of the Spanish Treasure on European economy, see pp. 237–9.

sums borrowed at exorbitant rates from foreign bankers, mounted by leaps and bounds. . . . Mortgaging the future was the sole policy which he could comprehend—always deluding himself with the belief that the scales were bound to turn. But the great victory which he confidently expected never came, and in the end he left his successor with a debt four times as great as that which his father had bequeathed to him.' [1] On four occasions Philip was forced to repudiate his debts, in 1557, 1560, 1575 and 1596. The decree of 1557 so damaged Philip's credit with the banking houses that he was at first unable to borrow funds. The crash of 1575 obliged them to give him easier terms but caused consternation among the merchants of Antwerp and Genoa. Henceforth the great German bankers and the Spanish monarchy were so closely associated that the bankers could not themselves survive the monarchy's declining fortunes.

Philip was bound in the toils of past policy and an unimaginative economic programme. Even if the King himself had understood finance better he would have had to have been a man of iron-will to change Spain's policy. But Spanish economic policy had a ruinous effect on commerce, industry and agriculture. Thus the silk industry of Granada was crippled by the increase of the *rentas* to which it was subjected. Commerce suffered from the increase in the *encabezamiento* and the *alcabala* after 1577; Seville was the only prosperous port in the kingdom as a result of its colonial trade. Agriculture was in dismal condition, suffering from depopulation and the excessive privileges of the corporation of sheep-farmers known as the Mesta. Philip made the situation worse, especially in Andalusia, by displacing the industrious *Moriscos* from their homes and removing them to another part of Spain after the defeat of the rebellion in Granada.

If Philip was only in part responsible for the fundamental economic weakness of his empire, he had a greater responsibility for the weakness of the Spanish administrative machine. The empire was governed by a series of councils, twelve in number at the end of Philip's reign, headed by the *Consejo de Estado* or Council of State. Philip himself rarely presided but was informed of its decisions by his secretaries. He also used the Council to deploy rival factions against each other, for it was divided between the party headed by the Duke of Alva, who believed in a policy of force, and that of the Prince of Eboli who stood for a policy of peace and persuasion. ' Alva and Eboli ', the Venetian ambassador reported ' are the two columns which support the great machine : on their advice depends the fate of half the world.' In any case the Council's

[1] R. B. Merriman, *The Spanish Empire*, iv, 440.

decisions were only valid if they were confirmed by the King. Under Philip the Cortes of Castile continued to lose power, though it was still allowed to advise and petition the King; the Cortes of Aragon only met once during Philip's reign (in 1592). Every official from the President of the Council to the local *corregidor* was personally responsible to the King's Majesty. The Church was equally subservient to the royal will.

This bureaucratic absolutism, riding rough-shod over local liberties, inevitably created discontent. It was the first and the principal reason for the outbreak of the trouble in the Netherlands. There was constant dissatisfaction in Milan where the archbishop, Carlo Borromeo, fearlessly defended local liberties until his death in 1584; in the latter part of Philip's reign the viceroy, De Velasco, firmly re-established the Crown's authority. Naples gave no trouble but it was a very different story in Sicily where the inhabitants were strongly attached to their local liberties.[1] But it was in Aragon that the conflict between local liberties and royal absolutism came to a head. After his fall from favour in 1579, the King's secretary, Antonio Perez, had been imprisoned and tortured, but in 1590 he escaped and took refuge in Aragon where he appealed to the Justiciar's court. Philip ordered his execution; but the Justiciar stayed the process. Undaunted, Philip, who had other methods if the liberties of Aragon proved too strong, saw to it that Perez was arrested by orders of the Inquisition. Before the grim story reached its climax Perez escaped to France to make the world ring with the infamy of the King. Meanwhile, revolution had broken out in Saragossa under the lead of the new and impulsive Justiciar Don Juan de Lanuza. Naturally Philip won in the end, and the Cortes, which was convoked at Tarragona in June, 1592, ensured that the central government should not be endangered in the future. Philip did not eliminate the 'liberties' of Aragon which had indeed been much abused at the expense of the people by the turbulent nobles, but he had effectively restored the authority of the Crown.

But the picture must not be overdrawn. On the whole the royal authority represented justice, security and order in contrast with feudal misrule. The Spanish administrative machine continued to function efficiently. According to his lights Philip had done his work well. If his foreign policy and what R. B. Merriman has called his 'meticulous paternalism . . . and economic im-policy' contributed to Spain's decline, the real cause of Spain's downfall lay outside the King's control. It lay in the circumstances

[1] This has been described in an able study by H. Koenigsberger, *The Government of Sicily under Philip II of Spain* (1951).

which brought an empire into being by a series of accidents and, perhaps above all, in Spain's lack of creative vitality and of the continuous dynamic energy which empire-building really requires. It is no small tribute to the King that much that he had done endured so long; that the overseas empire lasted until the beginning of the nineteenth century and the monarchy until 1931 was in part an effect of Philip's rule. The Venetian ambassador shrewdly summarised the King's character and reign in the despatch in which he announced Philip's death to his government:[1] 'His Majesty expired at the Escurial this morning at daybreak, after having received all the sacraments of the Church with every sign of devoutness, piety and religion. . . . He was a Prince who fought with gold rather than with steel, by his brain rather than by his arms. He has acquired more by sitting still, by negotiation, by diplomacy, than his father did by armies and by war. . . . Profoundly religious, he loved peace and quiet. He displayed great calmness and professed himself unmoved in good or bad fortune alike. . . . On great occasions . . . he never counted the cost; but he was no close reckoner, but lavished gold without a thought; but in small matters, in the government of his household, in his presents and rewards, he was more parsimonious than became his station. . . . He held his desires in absolute control and showed an immutable and unalterable temper. . . . No one ever saw him in a rage, being always patient, phlegmatic, temperate, melancholy. In short, he left a glorious memory of his royal name, which may serve as an example, not only unto his posterity and his successors, but unto strangers as well.'

[1] Quoted in R. Trevor Davies, *The Golden Century of Spain*, 224-25.

CHAPTER XIII

THE SPANISH COLONIAL EMPIRE

1. *Exploration and conquest*

THE rise of the Spanish American empire is one of the most dramatic stories in world history. For small ships to venture out into the storm-driven deep reflected the dynamic initiative which the Spanish *conquistadores* never lacked. They had to face mutiny on the high seas, massacre by natives, starvation, tropical heat at one moment and the icy cold of the Cordilleras at the next. The leaders' self-confidence was incomparable. With a handful of untrustworthy men Cortes conquered the Aztec empire, whose life-blood was war, and Pizarro annexed the wealth of the Incas. But this story had also many stains; cruelty, inhumanity, treachery and greed formed its constant accompaniment. Idealism played only a small part in the foundation of the Spanish overseas empire. The Cross too often proved a crucifix on which the innocent and ex-ploited native peoples suffered. Yet theoretically few colonial enter-prises have evoked more idealism. The Catholic Kings of Spain sincerely regarded the extension of their empire as a Christian mission in which the salvation of souls counted for more than the extraction of gold and silver. In this they were vigorously supported by the Spanish Church, more especially by the religious orders, represented by a man like Las Casas, and by many leading Spanish jurists.

The story begins with Columbus' voyage in 1492. Having failed to persuade the King of Portugal that an expedition to the western ocean would serve any useful purpose, Columbus went to Spain in 1484 in the hope that he might be received more favourably by Ferdinand and Isabella. After long drawn-out negotiations he was ' granted the rank of Admiral, with all the dignities and privileges hereto pertaining, in such territories as he should discover ', and sailed from Palos on August 3rd, 1492. After many difficulties, he sighted Watling Island in the Bahamas on October 11th and reached northern Cuba which he firmly believed to be the mainland of Asia seventeen days later. On his return to Spain he was well-received and was given permission to lead a further expedition which arrived off Dominica on Sunday, November 3rd, 1493. He then went on to Hispaniola where he found no trace of the settlers he had left behind there. This was the beginning of a series of misfortunes which dogged Columbus' attempt to found a settlement; relations with the Indians became bad nor were they improved by the rough treatment they received from the Spaniards; food grew low; Columbus himself was ill. Leaving his brother in charge he returned home to Cadiz which he reached on June 11th, 1495. He made two further expeditions but he had enemies at court who traduced him to the Catholic Kings. He died in obscurity at Valladolid on Ascension Day, 1506.

Before Columbus made his last voyage in 1502 others continued the work of exploration. Even a list is some guide to the amazing achievements of these years. In 1499 Alonso de Ojeda cruised along the north coast of South America and bestowed the name Venezuela on the native settlement in the Gulf of Maracaibo.[1] In the autumn of the same year Pinzon sailed along the coast of Brazil and discovered the Amazon which he thought to be the Ganges. In 1509 the first attempt at a settlement on the mainland of South America was made when Ojeda established a colony at San Sebastian on the eastern side of the Gulf of Uraba; another Spaniard, a planter from Hispaniola named Nicuesa, founded the town of Nombre de Dios. In 1513 a settler there, Vasco Nunez de Balboa, an adventurous personality who had escaped from his creditors hidden in a cask, led an expedition in search of gold and a western sea—and found the sea which was later re-named the Pacific; ' the other sea so long looked for and never seen before of any man coming out of our world.' Within a few months of Balboa's trek, Juan Ponce de Leon discovered and named Florida, which he believed to be an island, and in February 1516 Juan Diaz de Solis sailed down the coast of Brazil and arrived at the estuary of the Rio de la Plata.

These small beginnings formed the prelude to a period of expansion which took place in the reign of Charles V. Although the Emperor had so many other calls upon his attention, he never lost sight of the work of discovery, even if he hardly understood the purport of much that was happening in the New World. As a Catholic King he desired to propagate his faith, and he saw in his new dominions both a means of saving souls and filling his pocket. Magellan's circumnavigation of the globe heralded the colonial achievements of his reign. After long discussion Charles agreed to furnish Magellan's expedition to the Spice Islands in the West, a Portuguese possession, with five ships and to give Magellan himself a twentieth of the profits of the voyage. Between the departure

---

[1] The native settlement, built on piles in the water, reminded him of Venice. Hence the name.

Spanish Possessions
Portuguese　　"

MAP VI.—Spanish and Portuguese possessions in Central and South America.

of the small fleet on September 10th, 1519, and the return of one of the five ships which originally set sail, the *Victoria* of 85 tons, on September 8th, 1522, there was hardly an uneventful moment. The voyage, as described by Magellan's Italian servant, Antonio Pigafetta, included several mutinies, exploration, near-starvation,[1] fights with the natives in one of which on the Philippines Magellan was killed, and trouble with the Portuguese of Tidor, but the achievement was unparalleled. The cargo of spices which the *Victoria* brought home alone provided Charles with a welcome addition to his treasury. The voyage added much to contemporary knowledge of the world. But as the American historian Merriman has pointed out the results were primarily psychological. ' "Austriae est imperare orbi universo" had already been the motto of the house of Hapsburg for many years past, but hitherto the interpretation of it had been limited to Europe. Now Charles had not only inherited the American lands which had been won under the rule of the Catholic Kings, but he had himself sent forth the first expedition to put a girdle around the globe.'

Although Magellan's voyage was followed by a large number of other voyages of exploration, interest passes to the expansion of the Spanish empire on the mainland, first to New Spain or Mexico and then to New Castile or Peru. The Aztec empire, which had been established around Lake Texcoco towards the first half of the fourteenth century, had a notable and fascinating civilisation; yet basically it centred on fighting that culminated in the horrifying sacrifice of the captives to the bloody deities whom the Aztecs worshipped. Since 1502 the state had been ruled by a brave but vacillating and superstitious prince, the Emperor Montezuma II.

Hernando Cortes, the conqueror of Mexico, was an intrepid, completely ruthless man of thirty-four, an amorous gambler by nature, devout in a superstitious sort of way; he possessed relentless determination and had an amazing capacity for making the most of every opportunity. Since his arrival at Hispaniola in 1504, he had won the respect and later the hostility of his commander Diego Velasquez by the part he had played in the conquest of Cuba. In defiance of Velasquez, he left Cuba for Yucatan and on Good Friday, April 22nd, 1519, arrived at Vera Cruz. Realising that he would get no help from Velasquez he sent a ship direct to Europe with all the treasure he could find and a demand that the Emperor should

---

[1] 'We drank', wrote Pigafetta, 'yellow water that had been putrid for many days . . . and ate some ox hides that covered the top of the mainyard. . . . Rats were sold for one half-ducat apiece, and even then we could not get them.'

confirm his authority; and then he scuttled all his remaining ships, thus making retreat impossible and facing his small force with the alternative of death or victory. If the Tlascalans, whose state lay between Cortes and Montezuma's empire, or the Aztecs had acted with determination they could have rid their shores of the Spanish invaders. But Montezuma could not make up his mind whether the men and the horses which accompanied them were semi-divine agents of friendly disposition, sent by the gods, or a hostile army. The Aztec empire was seized at comparatively small cost by a gigantic piece of bluff.[1] The historic march on Mexico began on August 16th, 1519. The American historian, W. H. Prescott, has told in classic fashion the story of what happened; of Cortes' entry into Tlascala, of Montezuma's inability to make up his mind, of the *conquistadores*' climb up Popocatepetl from which they caught a glimpse far below of the city of Mexico midst the gleaming blue of Lake Texcoco, and of their dramatic interview with the Aztec emperor; 'When I approached', wrote Cortes, ' to speak to Montezuma, I took off a collar of pearls and glass diamonds, that I wore, and put it on his neck, and, after we had gone through some of the streets, one of his servants came with two collars, wrapped in a cloth, which were made of coloured shells. . . . When he received them, he turned towards me, and put them on my neck.' The Spaniards eventually seized Montezuma and overthrew the Aztec idols. Meanwhile the Emperor, Charles V, appointed Cortes governor, captain-general and chief-justice of New Spain (October 15th, 1522); 'Your Sacred Majesty may believe', he wrote in October, 1524, ' that within five years this [Mexico City] will be the most nobly populated city which exists in all the civilised world, and will have the finest buildings.'

But Cortes' early hopes were not fulfilled. The *conquistadores* did not make good administrators or efficient governors, and their arbitrary and ruthless conduct made them many enemies. The appointment of the capable Antonio de Mendoza as first viceroy of New Spain in 1529 [2] marked the virtual end of Cortes' power. He retired to his farm at Cuernavaca but he was treated so unsympathetically by the viceroy that he left for Spain where he died in comparative obscurity, as had Columbus before him, on December 2nd, 1547. While these events were taking place, the new territory was being explored and expanded; if the lust of gold enabled men

---

[1] The tribes in subjection to the Aztecs were not unwilling to help the Spaniards, owing to the quota of victims which their cruel masters required for sacrifice to their gods.

[2] He did not actually arrive in Mexico until 1535.

to endure incomparable hardships it led incidentally to the creation
of an empire. Hernando de Soto's expedition to Florida, though
more remarkable than most, yet typified all. Landing at Tampa
Bay in Florida in May, 1539, like others he sought for gold but
found only trial and trouble; death overtook him as his expedition
moved down the Mississippi river on May 21st, 1542.

Before de Soto died, Charles had won another vast dominion
in the form of the Inca empire situated in the north-western corner
of South America. The Incas were a more attractive people than
the Aztecs with an even more notable culture; their administration
was efficient and socially far in advance of that of many European
states. Their architecture was solid and symmetrical while their
knowledge of agriculture was greater than that of any other American
race. Theoretically the empire was a despotism under the supreme
control of the Inca himself who was regarded as a descendant of
the Sun whom his subjects worshipped. In an evil hour the Inca
Emperor, Huayna Capac, had divided his empire on his deathbed
between his heir, Huascar, and his illegitimate son, Atahualpa. This
disputed succession proved a great help to the Spanish expedition.

Its leader, Francisco Pizarro, was a cruel but intrepid rogue.
'Friends and comrades!' he told his men on the sands at Gallo,
'on that side are toil, hunger, nakedness, the drenching storm,
desertion and death; on this side, ease and pleasure. There lies
Peru with its riches; here, Panama and its poverty. Choose,
each man, what best becomes a brave Castilian. For my part I
go to the south.' This valiant leader, illiterate, ambitious, greedy
and treacherous, did not start on his journey until he had received
a *capitulacion* from Charles V appointing him governor and captain-
general over newly-discovered territory. He and his men had to
undergo experiences similar to those which Cortes had endured
when he conquered Mexico; the changeover from tropical heat to
the cold tempests of the Andes; the hesitant policy of the Inca
Emperor Atahualpa who hoped that he could enlist these warriors
against his half-brother, Huascar; the Spaniards' realisation that
force and treachery would best establish their position and their
demands that the Incas should accept the Catholic faith and admit
the rule of Charles V. Seized by Pizarro, Atahualpa appealed to
the conqueror's cupidity by promising him the most princely of
ransoms, no less than a roomful, twenty-two feet long, seventeen
feet broad and nine feet high, filled with gold, but gold could not
melt Pizarro's heart. Whereas Montezuma died from an accidental
blow, Atahualpa, sentenced to be burned alive at Cajamarca, was
given the more humane but no less unjust fate of the garrote.

The story of the conquest of Peru was unrelieved by any spark of idealism. The riches of the Incas led to disunity and caused civil war between the *conquistadores*. Taking advantage of this, the Inca Manca Cupac maintained a steady campaign of resistance until his death in 1544. The fate of the conquerors matched the fate of the conquered. Atahualpa had been murdered after he had procured the assassination of Huascar; the puppet whom Pizarro pushed on to the vacant throne soon suffered the same fate. Pizarro's accomplice, Almagro, tried to set up a state on his own but was defeated by Pizarro at Las Salinas and garroted. The general did not live long to enjoy his victory; he was murdered by his opponents on Sunday, June 26th, 1541.

Founded on blood and maintained by strife, the story of the colonisation of Spanish South America formed a fitting epilogue to the occupation of Peru. Adventurers in search of gold carried the flag of Spain further and further afield. Under the auspices of the German banking house of Welser, western Venezuela was ruthlessly and callously exploited. De Quesada brought the Chibchas, another of the more civilised of the South American native peoples, into subjection and founded the city of Santa Fé (de Bogotá) in 1538. Three years later Pedro de Valdivia established the city of Santiago de Chile, over which he had himself elected governor and captain-general.

The administration of the Spanish territory outside the West Indies so far had been rudimentary, but this was a situation which the Spanish government could not approve for long. The conflict between the *conquistadores* on the spot and the authorities at home came to a head with the issue in 1542 of the 'New Laws', a humanitarian code designed to eliminate the abuses which had characterised Spanish colonial government. When Blasco Nunez Vela the first viceroy of Peru sent out by the home government arrived, he was faced by a rebellion led by Gonzalvo Pizarro, Francisco's brother, which resulted in his defeat and death on the battlefield of Anaquito on January 18th, 1546. The Imperial government could not condone open defiance of its representative and despatched an unassuming and conciliatory cleric, Pedro de la Gasca, as president of the *audiencia*, to deal with the situation. He overthrew Gonzalvo, and initiated a number of important reforms before he returned to Spain in 1550.

2. *Spanish colonial administration*

In less than fifty years the Spaniards had acquired a great empire which they kept intact for over three hundred years. Their administrative record during this period compares favourably with those of other European nations. Spanish administrators, jurists and churchmen, by contrast with the settlers themselves, were concerned with the moral basis of Imperial power. In part this may have been a rationalisation of the desire to acquire additional territory and wealth. As soon as there was a prospect of Portugal disputing Spain's claims to her newly-found colonies, the Catholic Kings had appealed to Pope Alexander VI who in the bull *Inter Caetera* (1493) granted them the ' islands and mainland . . . towards the west and the south . . . with all their rights, jurisdictions and appurtenances' providing these lands were not in the possession of any other Christian prince before Christmas, 1492. This bull was never accepted by the French and the English, and was long disputed by the Portuguese.[1] Nor were all Spaniards satisfied that papal approval by itself was sufficient to justify the annexation of native territory. Spanish theologians and jurists, soaked in scholastic philosophy, sought a more fundamental justification for the occupation of the American colonies. Thus the Scottish Dominican, John Major, doubtless influenced by the ideas of Aristotle, concluded as early as 1511 : ' In the natural order of things the qualities of some men are such that, in their own interests, it is right and just that they should serve, while others, living freely, exercise their natural authority and command.' In other words the Spaniards had the right to rule over the Indians because the Indians were naturally inferior to them. In his *Democrates Alter* (1542) the jurist de Sepulveda reached a similar conclusion.[2] But popular as were his views with the colonists they weighed little with the home government.

Bishop Las Casas, passionate advocate of Indian rights, was more influential at home than abroad. His emphasis on the duties of the ruler towards his subjects was typically Thomist and medieval.

[1] See pp. 74–5. The provisions were modified by the Treaty of Tordesillas (1494) ; the final line of demarcation was agreed between Spain and Portugal by the Treaty of Saragossa (1529).

[2] ' The special rights and duties of Spain in the New World arose from three causes ; the natural superiority of the Spaniards over the other European nations ; the right of the first discoverer to occupy land (such as the Indies) which had no legitimate ruler, and the decree of the Pope, at once a spiritual commission to convert the heathen, and a temporal grant of legally unoccupied territory ' (J. H. Parry, *The Spanish Theory of Empire*, 39).

He described the colonial *encomienda* as ' onerose, injusta, tiranica y horribile ' on grounds of custom, reason and natural law. A more typical point of view was put forward by the famous theologian and jurist, Francisco de Vitoria, in his *Relectiones de Indis* where he emphasised that the Indians were as much bound by international law, the *jus gentium*, as the Spaniards. The natives ought in justice to receive the Spaniards peacefully and to listen to the Gospel even if they did not wish to accept it.

Thus writers appealed constantly to the natural rights of man and to the responsibilities of the Christian towards native peoples ; though in practice the policy of the man on the spot often counted for more than the decrees of the King of Spain and the Council of the Indies. Thus the *Requerimiento*, a document which every Spanish conquistador was supposed by law to read to the natives before he began to make war against them, calling upon them to accept the supremacy of the Pope and the rule of the King of Castile, exemplifies both the idealism of the Spanish government and its impracticability. This idealism was the basis of the missionary activity which every Spanish King was in duty bound to support. It was implicit in the famous bulls of Pope Paul III of 1537, the most significant of which, *Sublimis Deus*, declared that the Indians were rational beings, perfectly capable of becoming good Christians. Charles V may have been offended by the Pope's interference in a sphere which he regarded as being specifically his own, but the same principles appeared in his own ' New Laws ' of 1542.

The government of the new territories was naturally modelled on that of Castile.[1] Legally each part of the empire formed an independent entity over which the King of Spain reigned as supremely as he did over Castile ; it was an empire which incidentally no Spanish King ever visited. The King's will was expressed through the Council of the Indies. When Columbus returned to Spain in 1493 Queen Isabella entrusted her chaplain, Juan de Fonseca, with a general oversight of colonial business. As the amount of work increased he gathered a number of advisers about him, thus forming what was known from 1524 as the Council of the Indies, which in time had complete authority over every aspect of colonial administration ; the only institution which ever questioned its fiat in colonial matters was the Spanish Inquisition. It passed

[1] Technically the Indies belonged to Castile, not to Aragon whose subjects were not in law given the same rights of emigration until 1596. R. B. Merriman shrewdly points out that one of the reasons why the Catholic Kings bound the colonies to Castile was ' their dread lest the new territories should be contaminated by coming into contact with the " Aragonese liberties " which they had not been able wholly to subvert '.

all laws and decrees relating to colonial government, made all the
leading appointments in Church and State, censored all colonial
publications and acted as a final court of appeal. It worked hard,
meeting from three to five hours every day except Sundays, and was
guided by the best of intentions. If its practical achievements seem
slight, it must be remembered how difficult it was to control territory
separated from the mother country by many weeks of sailing;
furthermore the system of checks and balances which it devised to
protect the royal authority ended by stifling all initiative.

In the Americas the Spanish King was represented by two
viceroys, the viceroy of New Spain ruling from Mexico City, first
appointed in 1529, and the viceroy of New Castile ruling from Lima,
appointed later but taking precedence of his colleague. It was the
normal practice of the Spanish Kings to grant complete power,
usually as governors or *adelantados*, to those who had borne the heat
and burden of exploration and conquest, and to withdraw these
powers as soon as it was possible to exert a more direct authority.
This happened in the cases of Columbus, who was replaced by
Bobadilla and Ovando, Cortes and Pizarro.[1] Each viceroyalty was
divided into a number of districts, presided over by a governor
guided by an administrative and judicial tribunal called the
audiencia.

Although the viceroy's authority might appear to be as absolute
as that of the King himself, it was in fact subject to three different
kinds of control, that of the *audiencia*, of the *residencia* and the
visita. The *audiencia*, one of which was established in the chief
city of each of the main provinces, was a council of state consisting
of a number of judges (*oidores*) over which the viceroy or captain-
general presided *ex officio*. In administrative matters it formed an
executive council; in judicial affairs it served as a court of law in
which even the viceroy had no say unless he was a trained lawyer.
Indeed the relations between the viceroy and the *audiencia* were
often severely strained. The *residencia*, another typically Castilian
mode of procedure, was the term applied to a ' judicial review of an
official's conduct at the end of his term of office '. While these
checks were imposed on the viceroy's authority to promote loyal
and efficient government, it is certain that they hampered enterprise and initiative. ' One of the most apparent results of the
system in America ', wrote Professor Haring, ' was to discourage
healthy initiative on the part of viceroys and governors, and prevent

[1] Columbus' heir, Diego Columbus, was appointed governor in 1509,
less because of his relationship to the great explorer than because he had
married the niece of the Duke of Alva and the cousin of the King Ferdinand.

important political and economic development in the colonies. Always faced with the likelihood of charges by some malicious foe, conscientious magistrates feared to deviate in the slightest degree from instructions composed, often quite ignorantly, by the Council in Spain. Evils of government of which the authorities at home knew little or nothing were perpetuated, and a sort of creeping paralysis ultimately came to pervade the entire political structure of the Spanish empire in the New World.' [1] The *visita* was not unlike the *residencia ;* it was a specific inspection of the activities of any one of the Crown's agents carried out by orders of the Council of the Indies; during his term of office even the viceroy had to comply with the instructions of the special *visitador*. Such was the structure of colonial government under the shadow of which all the many inferior officers, *corregidores* and *alcaldes*, did their daily work.

The relations between the native Indians and the Spanish colonists formed the government's main problem. Although some of the early colonists went to the New World with the object of settling there permanently, the majority were unwilling either to till the soil or work the newly-discovered mines. Even at home the average Spaniard thought that manual labour was a degrading occupation. Thus from the very start the Spanish colonist was forced to depend on native labour, but whether this should be hired or forced slave-labour was an open question. Queen Isabella had been shocked when she heard that Columbus had enslaved native labourers. In 1502 she had ordered the new governor, Nicolas de Ovando, to protect her native subjects who were only to be obliged to work in the Crown mines or in other public works. Ovando replied that the result of trying to put these instructions into practice had been a ' falling-off of tribute, lack of labour and inability to carry forward the work of conversion to Christianity '. The Catholic Kings accordingly agreed to allow forced labour but ordered that the native labourers should be well-treated, given good wages and in all other ways regarded as ' free persons, for such they are '. As a result of this new order two institutions developed, the *encomienda* and the *repartimiento* over the validity of which there was constant controversy. The *encomienda* was in effect an extension of the feudal system into the New World. A group of Indian villages was ' commended ' to a Spanish settler who agreed to provide clergy and teachers and to protect the Indians on condition that they paid him tribute which often took the form of forced labour. The villages 'commended' to the Crown were governed

---

[1] C. H. Haring, *The Spanish Empire in America*, 152

by a different form of labour assessment known as the *repartimiento* by which 'each *pueblo* supplied a definite number of labourers every week, to be employed at a fixed wage by the Spanish settlers, under the supervision of a local magistrate detailed to perform the duty'. Slavery was still illegal but in practice forced labour proved its equivalent. The *encomienda* was bitterly criticised from the first, as a violation of Christian principles in respect of native peoples, especially by the Dominican friars. The Indians' champion was Bartholomew de las Casas who had settled at Hispaniola in 1502 and had received an *encomienda* of Indians. His experience of the system made him into its most determined opponent. He then established a model colony at Cumana on the coast of Venezuela in 1521, but the Indians were unused to distinguishing between good and bad Spaniards and their attacks brought Las Casas' experiment to a disastrous close. After this he became a Dominican friar, ceaselessly urging the Crown to treat the Indians in a Christian and just manner. His influence can be seen in the New Laws of 1542, which forbade all forms of Indian slavery and the granting of any new *encomiendas*. Colonists found guilty of maltreating their Indians were ordered to lose their *encomiendas*. The New Laws caused an immediate outcry in the colonies and civil war in Peru, as a result of which some of the more unpopular measures were repealed in spite of Las Casas' protests.

The dispute over the *encomiendas* not only provides evidence of the Crown's belief in the notion of colonial trusteeship but also reflects the continuous tension existing between the home government and the colonists. Although in practice the home government became more and more inefficient after the middle of the seventeenth century, it remained both vigilant and jealous of its authority. Every conceivable matter, whether of government, trade, religion or censorship, had to pass under its direct surveillance, but it had no real power to see that its instructions were faithfully carried out. Distrusting initiative and original ideas, its officials tended to become bureaucrats, rarely outstanding, sometimes competent but often ineffective and corrupt. The home government tried to confine emigration to the New World to Spaniards with authentic racial purity or *limpieza de sangre*, but it is clear that at a comparatively early period foreigners were actually settling in the colonies, the frontiers of which were extremely difficult to guard effectively. Meanwhile the colonial trade which it tried to restrict to its own nationals passed more and more into the hands of outsiders. Thus the Spanish colonial empire tended to house a static culture and society, which was reflected in a social hierarchy saturated in class-distinction, stretching downwards from the European Spaniards who held all the major secular and ecclesiastical offices through the colonial nobility and merchants to the creoles, the *mestizos*, the Indians, the negroes who were employed more and more as slave labour on the plantations, and the despised part-Indian and part-negro *zambos*. This society possessed fine churches, noble buildings and distinguished universities but was unequal to the task of creating a really progressive civilisation. The dynamic energy which had been so characteristic of the *conquistadores* who founded the empire had very nearly vanished by the end of the sixteenth century. Long before Philip IV died in 1665 the empire over which he ruled was in decline.

3. *The significance of the colonial empire*

The Spanish empire was bound to have repercussions on European life and society. The continuous flow of emigrants may possibly have contributed to the depopulation of Spain, but this was only a symptom of underlying disease. While it is true that Spain's colonial possessions made the country's rise to imperial power and European hegemony possible, in the long run they also helped to bring about its decline and collapse.

In the first half of the sixteenth century the extension of the Spanish empire stimulated the economy of the home country, for it provided Spanish manufacturers with fresh markets for their goods. Since the discoveries coincided with a minor industrial revolution, they might be considered an impetus to Spanish industry, but foreign competition and colonial manufactures, especially in textiles, soon narrowed the market. Even the restrictions which the Spanish government imposed to protect home manufactures could not prevent the decline of Spanish industry.

From the start Spain's economic policy was mercantilistic. The colonies were there to provide the home country with wealth; what fostered the prosperity of the mother country was encouraged, and what threatened it was prescribed. Thus the growing of sugar-cane in Hispaniola was encouraged by the Council of the Indies. At first similar encouragement was given to viticulture but when the cheap wines of Chile and Peru appeared to threaten the Spanish wine industry, restrictions were imposed: much the same thing happened later with the olive-oil industry of Peru. Nevertheless the list of plants produced by colonial America was impressive and obviously had a significant effect on the economic and social life of Europe; it included cinchona, chocolate, sarsaparilla, the pineapple, the tomato, guava, rubber, many kinds of wood and, perhaps most significant of all, tobacco, the use of which was first advocated by the physician Nicolas Monardes on account of its medicinal properties.

From the general standpoint the mining of silver and gold surpassed all else. Silver was first mined in New Spain in 1531 or 1532, but the industry only became of major proportions after the opening of the silver deposits at Zacatecas (in 1548) and Pachuca (1552). Richer deposits were discovered in Peru, the most famous of all, that at Cerro de Potosi, opened in 1545. Mining was even then a great gamble out of which a few men made fortunes and many were ruined. It was undertaken by private enterprise, except in the case of the Peruvian mercury mine at Huanacavelica which was worked directly by the Crown. After the bullion had been transhipped to Spain, the officials of the Spanish treasury subjected it to a careful inspection. It was weighed at the House of Trade at Seville and then placed in chests in the Treasure Chamber. During its voyage the treasure fleet was protected from pirates by special warships equipped from a tax called the *averia* levied on goods carried to and from the Indies.[1]

All the American trade was in theory rigidly controlled through a special office known as the *Casa de Contratacion* or House of Trade set up at Seville in 1503. This soon had a numerous personnel and possessed a very wide authority. It licensed and supervised all vessels, their merchandise and passengers travelling from Spain and received all precious metals. It acted as a court of law for all disputes arising out of the American trade. It provided a school of navigation and trained pilots. Although there was much that was good in this system, it ended by defeating its own ends. Instead of stimulating trade, it helped to stifle it, thus helping to ruin both Spain and her empire. ' And so ', writes Professor Haring in a judicious summary of the position, ' there gradually evolved under the early Hapsburgs a rigid and elaborate commercial system through whose operations a large part of the wealth of America might ultimately be syphoned back to Spain. All external trade of the colonies was reserved to the mother country, Spain furnishing them with all they required from Europe, shipped on Spanish vessels, and the colonies producing in general only raw materials and articles that did not compete with the products of Spain. The export of gold and silver to foreign countries was absolutely forbidden. This

---

[1] Contrary to popular notions losses through piracy were remarkably small. There were only two occasions on which substantial amounts were seized, by the Dutch in 1628 and by the English in 1656.

policy of colonial monopoly was pursued to the very end of the colonial regime.' [1]

Thus, far from enriching Spain, the colonies eventually helped impoverish it. Its own industry languished and could not provide its own subjects, let alone the colonists, with the manufactured articles they required. In practice more and more trade fell into the hands of foreigners who managed to evade the Spanish law forbidding unlicensed commerce. An increasing amount of bullion found its way into Europe partly through the foreign bankers to whom the Spanish Kings were so greatly indebted, and partly through money paid to the army. In 1617 the Cortes asserted that the American treasure ' immediately goes to foreign kingdoms, leaving this one in extreme poverty' and that Castile ' serves as a bridge over which the products of our mines pass to foreign hands, at times even to our worst enemies '. In any case the actual revenue which the Spanish Kings received out of the New World has been vastly overestimated, even if it is remembered that in addition to the ' quint' or fifth of all precious metals to which the Crown was entitled they sometimes took the bullion belonging to private traders as a ' forced loan '. There was therefore an unbalanced trade from an early date which steadily grew more unfavourable to Spain.

Through the import of gold and even more so of silver the Spanish Americas drastically affected the economy of Europe.[2] It formed the chief reason for the rise in prices which was one of the main characteristics of the period, playing its part both in the creation of modern capitalism and in many political movements. Except for the French writer Jean Bodin and the Spanish economist Sancho de Moncada who followed his conclusions some fifty years later (1619), contemporaries were unaware of the main cause of the price rise.[3] In our own day the problem has been studied in great detail by an American historian, Earl J. Hamilton, who has proved beyond all shadow of doubt that the Spanish treasure created rising prices, first in Andalusia, then in other parts of Spain, and finally, percolating over the Pyrenees or from the port of Antwerp or through Genoa and the Mediterranean, throughout Europe. He has shown that for the decade 1601-10 Spanish prices were 3·4 times as high as

---

[1] C. H. Haring, *The Spanish Empire in America*, 314.

[2] At the end of the fifteenth century there had been a famine of precious metals in Europe, in part caused by the stopping of supplies of Sudanese gold ; this was overcome by increased production in the South German mines and by the import of American treasure.

[3] Charles' historiographer, de Gomara, noted the connection between American treasure and rising prices, but his work was not published until the twentieth century.

those of the same decade a century earlier, and other scholars, whose work is still incomplete, have proved that similar increases took place in England (in a ratio of 1 : 2·6, though the maximum increase was not felt until the Civil War), France (1 : 2·2) and in every other European country. The price-rise brought economic and political discontents in its train which contemporaries could neither explain nor control.

Nor were the results of the discovery and development of the Spanish empire on European history purely economic. It is impossible to estimate accurately the social significance of chocolate drinking and tobacco smoking, but nothing can disguise the political sequel to the foundation of the Spanish colonial empire. If the Spanish colonies financed Spain's wars, they also formed the focal point of the European balance of power. Spain's enemies, which in practice meant most of the other European countries, the Portuguese, the French, the English and the Dutch, soon realised that Spanish settlements and colonial trade constituted lucrative pillaging grounds. In their turn they established colonies in the same area. It is not too much to say that the creation of this American empire in time changed the strategy and diplomacy of Europe by shifting attention to American and West Indian waters.

English Miles
0 10 20 40 60

FRIESLAND

Franeker

Groningen Jemminge

Heiligerlee

GRONINGEN

Steenwyk

Koevorden

Alkmaar Hoorn Enkhuisen

Egmont

Zaan ZUYDER
ZEE

Bredenode

Haarlem Amsterdam

Muiden

OVERYSSEL

R. Yssel

Deventer

The Hague

Leyden UTRECHT

Utrecht

Zutphen

Delft

GELDERLAND

ZUTPHEN

Brill

Rotterdam

Loevestein Nimwegen

Dort To
Cleves Cleves

Cleves

Cleves

ZEELAND

Mook
Heide

Xanten

R. Rhine

Breda

Veere

Middelburg Rammeken

Flushing

Bergen-op-Zoom

Turnhout

Ostend Hulst Antwerp

Roermonde

Gravelines

Bruges Sas van Gent

Nieuport Ghent

Dunkirk R. Scheldt

Mechlin

JULIC

FLANDERS

Oudenarde Louvain

Maastricht

Ypres

Courtrai Brussels

Aachen

LIMBURG

Tournai Gembloux Liège

Nivelles Namur

Mons

Meuse

HAINAULT

Valenciennes

Arras

Cambrai

Vaucelles Cateau Cambrésis

Cambrésis

LUXEMBURG

To Liège

FRANCE

Luxemburg

Trier

R.C

MAP VII.—The rise of the Netherlands.

CHAPTER XIV

THE MAKING OF THE NETHERLANDS

1. *The origins of Dutch independence*

THE seventeen provinces,[1] from which modern Belgium and Holland were eventually to emerge, formed a complex congeries of states, disunited by race and language and lacking any unitary authority. While the greater part of the country was Low Germanic by race and language, the Walloon provinces were French speaking. Nor had these states any one ruler until the end of the Middle Ages. There had been four great princes in the medieval Netherlands; the Count of Flanders, the Duke of Brabant, the Duke of Gelderland and the Count of Holland and Zeeland, but none of them had been strong enough to impose his authority over the whole country. Through a series of accidents, this mass of states, cities and seignories had fallen into the hands of one man, the Duke of Burgundy, at the beginning of the fifteenth century. Duke Philip the Good was an able and ambitious prince who aimed to create a national state out of his diverse domains. His court was brilliant and his state was rich, but it remained true that the dynasty was a foreign one superimposed on a native culture which it could not represent and on peoples never thoroughly bound to it by any inherent loyalty. On the death of Duke Charles in 1477, the Netherlands reverted to his daughter, Mary, the wife of the Archduke Maximilian, then to their son Philip, and finally on Philip's death in 1506 to his heir Charles, the future Emperor. Yet, in spite of this particularism, there was a homogeneity of culture and religion which could have formed the foundation for a national state.

Separatist feeling, later helped on by religious disunity, was a prevailing influence throughout the sixteenth and seventeenth centuries. When Charles (V) succeeded his father as Duke of Burgundy in 1506, he became a feudal overlord over provincial magnates, wealthy and extravagant feudal nobles, bishops and abbots, and rich cities like Bruges and Ghent which had a long tradition of constitutional liberty. Each province had its own law-courts, its own nobility and its own traditions. The Duke ruled the

[1] They were actually sixteen until Gelderland became a member in 1523.

provinces through the Stadholder and the Grand Pensionary whom he appointed. The Stadholder had considerable local authority as commander-in-chief of the armed forces, was virtual chief justice and convener of the provincial Estates. Charles himself was brought up as a Fleming, was surrounded by Flemish advisers and cherished the traditions of the Burgundian duchy. Although his later life was spent outside the Netherlands, he retained a warm affection for the Netherlanders which they, in cooler mood, returned. If he had not succeeded one grandfather as King of Spain in 1516 and another as Holy Roman Emperor, the history of the Netherlands might have been very different. For he might have been able to have provided the Netherlands with a centre around which the divergent interests could have grouped themselves in a natural harmony.

But in fact Charles' reign witnessed the development of all the tendencies which brought about the outbreak of the rebellion. Economically the Netherlands was the most prosperous of all his dominions. If Bruges, as a result of the silting-up of the river Zwyn, Ghent and Ypres through English competition, were less prosperous than they had been in the Middle Ages, the 'new drapery', free from the restrictions of the medieval guilds, enriched the merchants of many of the smaller towns as well as the countryside where some of the cloth was worked. The coal and iron mines of Liége, Namur and Hainault were in process of development. The northern provinces were mainly agricultural, but the maritime provinces of Holland and Zeeland throve on fishing and the carrying trade. Amsterdam, the chief city of the northern Netherlands, was a most important corn staple, while Antwerp held a position unique in the economic life of Europe. It was the chief money market and probably the greatest commercial mart in the world, until the civil war brought about its return to Spanish control in the 1580's. This active and shrewd community of merchant-cities not only supplied a proletariat responsive to political and religious agitation but was itself proud of its own privileges and liberties; rebellion against Charles' rule at Ghent in 1540 revealed the citizens' distrust of the Imperial and Spanish policy of the Emperor.

The ground was already fertile for the spread of Protestantism. The Church in the Netherlands was probably as corrupt as anywhere in Europe; the greater nobles used it as a reservoir of offices for their younger sons and illegitimate offspring. The many foreigners who came to trade and to live in the Netherlands made the Dutch cities a changing-ground for religious ideas as well as for the more material goods of life. Anabaptism, the communist ideas of which made a natural appeal to the Dutch working-class, had its birth in the Netherlands where Lutheran teaching soon had a following. Charles, as a good Catholic, was as eager to suppress heresy in the Netherlands as elsewhere, but the introduction of the Inquisition and the growing severity of the *placaten* against heresy, reaching a climax in 1550, aroused the indignation of a stubborn and proud people who had long learned to dislike dictation of any form. It was to men and women of this kind that the stern and militant teaching of Calvinism was to make its insistent appeal.

Nor was the Emperor's anti-French policy necessarily in the true interests of the country, Burgundian as it might be. The continuous war against Francis I constituted a crushing financial burden for the part-payment of which the burghers and nobles of the Netherlands found themselves responsible. Much as they liked the man, they protested more and more vehemently against an Imperial policy which seemed to threaten their cherished liberties. Most of the reforms which Charles tried to institute to bring the provinces closer together, in 1534 and 1535, proved stillborn.

These were rumblings which a wise man might have noted, but the son in whose favour Charles abdicated never showed less wisdom than when he was dealing with his Dutch and Flemish subjects. Haughty and tongue-tied he only wished to return to Spain as quickly as he could. It was soon clear that he was determined to tighten the policy of centralisation and absolutism which his father had followed. By so doing he aroused a growing opposition among all classes of the state.

This resentment first found expression among the greater nobles who realised that Philip intended to push them outside his government and deprive them of any real say in the Council. The Order of the Golden Fleece was to be a mere chivalric insignia, no longer representing the nobles' right to advise their sovereign, the Grand Master. The Council of State was robbed of all real power which remained in the hands of an inner council of three, a churchman, Granvelle, a Frisian lawyer named Viglius and a Walloon noble, Baron von Barlaymont, which received its instructions direct from Madrid. On Philip's behalf it may be urged that the nobility formed a selfish and turbulent group devoid of any sense of re sponsibility to the people, but he could not ride roughshod over the feudal particularism of the nobles or the constitutional liberties of the cities, both of which were bound to conflict with the Spanish King's ideal of political absolutism.

His intended reorganisation of the Church in the Netherlands was another cause of trouble. The Church in the Low Countries was unquestionably corrupt; its lower clergy were ignorant, indolent and sometimes immoral; its dignities were in the hands of noble families who used them as a perquisite carrying wealth and authority. Besides this, the greater part of the Church was under the diocesan authority of foreign prelates the boundaries of whose sees often lay outside the Netherlands. Moreover Philip realised that his father's *placaten* had not halted the spread of heresy and did not suffice to deal with a worsening religious situation. He determined to root out the abuses which helped heresy to spread while suppressing Protestantism with an iron hand. Against the advice of his Council, he introduced the Society of Jesus into the Low Countries. Shortly afterwards a papal bull approved a radical reorganisation of the Dutch Church. In future there were to be eighteen new dioceses, including three archbishoprics, those of Mechlin, Cambrai and Utrecht, under the primacy of a newly-created Archbishop of Mechlin; Cardinal Granvelle was to be the first holder of the title. Other provisions laid down that the right of nominating bishops should in future remain in the hands of the Crown and insisted that those appointed to high office in the Church should be men of good character and skilled theologians, a direct rebuff to the half-hearted worldly prelates with whom the Low Countries was only too familiar. Finally, the new bishoprics were to be endowed from the revenues of the greater abbeys, some of which, like Afflighem, Tongerloo and Marienweerd, were enormously rich.

No measure affronted so many different people for so many different reasons. The great lords disliked losing the invaluable Church patronage which had added so much to their wealth and influence. The abbots were indignant at the loss of power and revenue which the creation of the new bishoprics obviously entailed. The merchant classes, always distrusting ecclesiastical intrusion into their affairs, also criticised the measure; the citizens of Antwerp, perturbed by the idea of a bishop living within their city walls, asked Philip to suspend the reorganisation. Protestants of all descriptions rightly saw that the new order was a threat to their continued existence. Philip may not have been blame-worthy in reorganising the Church but he was certainly unwise to ignore the chorus of protest which it evoked.

What Philip had so far done had been directed chiefly against the higher nobility but the merchant classes and the industrial proletariat were equally aggrieved. The Spanish King inherited a vast debt and an expensive foreign policy, in both of which the people of the Netherlands soon found themselves involved without their interests being at stake. They disliked the Spanish soldiers remaining after the Treaty of Cateau-Cambrésis, not merely as a rapacious and immoral lot of men but as a burden for which in kind or taxes they had to pay. They formed the ' outward and visible sign' of Philip's authority. Furthermore, many Netherlanders believed that just as the King was trying to centralise all authority about himself, so he would also seek to use their economic prosperity for his own advantage by imposing crushing taxation.

In all this there was no real sign of national consciousness or patriotic idealism, nor did the opposition to Philip as yet represent much more than a strident minority of the population. The King's attempt to impose a centralised régime had cut across the sectional interests of nobles, churchmen and merchants, each deriving additional strength from the inchoate discontent of an urban proletariat. A wiser man might have been warned by the course of events, but Philip, in Madrid, never properly understood what was at stake in the Low Countries. Under his incautious and misguided handling the discontent crumbled into open revolt, and the selfish sectional interests took on the aspect of a patriotic nationalism.

2. *The revolt in the Netherlands*

While the story of the revolt described by the American historian John Lothrop Motley in his classic, *The Rise of the Dutch Republic*, requires serious modification, yet the epic quality which Motley emphasised remains authentic. It may be argued that if the Dutch Calvinists had been less implacable, the unity of the Netherlands might have been preserved. It may be claimed—though with much less assurance—that William the Silent was a self-interested noble guided by opportunism who made war, as he made his lucrative marriages, to help pay his enormous debts.[1] Yet the undeniable fact remains that a small but sturdy people, inspired by religious enthusiasm, economic discontent and a wish to preserve their ancient liberties, whether these were constitutional rights or feudal privileges, defied the greatest empire in the world and, in spite of, or rather because of it, it became a strong, rich, enlightened

---

[1] He is described in Trevor Davies' *The Golden Century of Spain* as a coarse and brutal materialist . . . transformed by religious and political partisanship into an angel of light' whose main aim ' is the desire to carve out an independent principality for himself in the Netherlands' (156-7). While William's motives were often mixed and, in his earlier years, not devoid of self-interested ambition, Mr. Davies' comment is clearly injudicious. But his portrait of William affords a useful corrective to the more glowing pen-pictures of J. L. Motley and, more recently, of Miss C. V. Wedgwood.

and cultured nation. And if this story is sometimes stained by cruelty, religious intolerance and treachery on both sides, it is also redeemed by courage of the highest order and by the magnificent leadership of William of Orange.

Philip's policy of centralisation and the discontent which it provoked in the Netherlands provided the Regent, Duchess Margaret of Parma, with problems with which she was not well-fitted to deal. She was not lacking in intelligence but she was inclined to panic in moments of crisis. Although she was nominally advised by the Council of State, consisting of the great nobles of the seventeen provinces, in fact she had come to rely, rather against her will, as her half-brother intended that she should, on the inner council or *consulta*. This form of government challenged the power of men like William of Orange, Egmont, Horn, and Montigny. While they were as yet completely loyal to Philip as their feudal overlord, they held that they were entitled to participate in the government.

It was this group of nobles who first determined to bring pressure to bear on the Regent in the hope that she would enhance their privileged position. In great need of money, Philip had gained the States-General's consent to a subsidy on condition that he recalled the unpopular Spanish troops, but he had so far done little to implement this decision. When William of Orange and Egmont threatened to resign from the Council of State unless the King carried out his promise, an act that would have lessened public confidence in the government, the Regent's leading adviser, Granvelle, told Philip that he would be wise to recall the troops. Their success encouraged the nobles to make a further *démarche*. Offended by Philip's intended reorganisation of the Church which challenged their ecclesiastical patronage, they wanted Philip to countermand or modify his religious policy.

But an outright attack on the King's ecclesiastical programme would most probably defeat its own end, more especially as most of the nobles were still faithful attenders at the Mass and were uninfected by popular Calvinism. They therefore aimed to get rid of Philip's chief representative in the Netherlands, the unpopular Cardinal Granvelle. The King refused to withdraw Granvelle, but the Regent, frightened by a deputation of the Knights of the Golden Fleece, led by William, which asserted that it could not guarantee public order if the Cardinal was not recalled, implored Philip to remove him. Unwillingly Philip suggested that the Cardinal should ask leave to ' see his old mother ', thus saving the Spanish King's ' face '. Granvelle left on March 18th, 1564.[1] ' Certain it

[1] Later he rose high in Philip's favour ; see p. 215.

is ', William had written to his brother thirteen days previously, ' that our man is going; God send that he goes so far as never to come back again.'

But even if the nobles had won the first round, Philip did not intend to modify his religious policy. Indeed as if to underline his previous intentions he ordered the Regent to enforce the decrees of the Council of Trent. As the Council of State informed the Regent, this was a most unwise thing to do in the present disturbed state of the country. The nobles sent one of their number, Count Egmont, to Madrid to explain their objections to Philip personally, but the Count was gulled into believing that all was well, and returning to Brussels at the end of April, 1565, found that Philip had not altered his policy one whit.

It was amidst growing discontent—' It is folly ', William wrote shrewdly, ' to enforce the *Placaten* (against heresy) when corn is dear '—that the lesser nobles took action. The greater nobles were divided, unable to decide on the policy that would best suit their interests, but there was a group of lesser men, headed by Brederode and William's impulsive brother, Louis of Nassau, who wanted popularity and were willing to risk an open conflict with Spain. Later dubbed the Confederates, these men drew up a document known as the Compromise, demanding that Philip should change his religious policy. They presented a petition to the tearful Regent on Friday, April 5th, 1566, an audience made memorable by Barlaymont's sneering remark ; ' Quoi, Madame, peur de ces gueux?' The name ' gueux ' or ' beggars ' was to stick and was later to sound unpleasantly in Spanish ears. Margaret temporised and promised to send a deputation to Philip at Madrid.

The policy of indecision was doomed to fail because it never grappled with the underlying problem. If the nobles' cause should fuse with the more popular agitation, there would be no holding back the opponents of Spanish rule. Many of the cities had large numbers of workers who, like the dockers of Antwerp, suffered from seasonal employment. They formed a potential source of trouble. The preaching of enthusiastic Calvinists and other Protestant sects found an increasing response among the middle and lower classes. In such an explosive situation a policy of indecision was fatal, and on August 19th, 1566, the explosion occurred. In town after town, at Antwerp, Delft, The Hague, Utrecht, Veere, Oudenarde and Valenciennes, the people sacked the churches, broke up the sacred images, tore the hangings, smashed the glass and maltreated the clergy. The Regent capitulated believing that the situation was beyond her control and unable to recognise that she might still appeal to the greater nobility to suppress mob violence. She issued the *Accord*, granting the Protestants liberty of worship and suspending the laws against heresy. Conceded under the threat of force, the *Accord* only had meaning while the sanction of force remained. Within a few months Margaret was hoping to withdraw it and reimpose Philip's policy, while the lesser nobles, realising that they would be the first to pay the penalty for their active disobedience, plotted revolt.

At this juncture (March, 1567) Philip decided to tighten his policy and bring his rebellious subjects to their senses by sending a soldier, the Duke of Alva, to command a Spanish Army despatched for this purpose. Alva entered Brussels on August 22nd, 1567; Duchess Margaret resigned on September 8th. Well-intentioned but weak, she was not a fit mistress for the likes of Alva. His six years' governorship was not unnaturally regarded as the dark night of Spanish rule. He believed in the iron policy of repression, unrelieved by any conciliatory measures. Given a subservient people he might have been a just and efficient ruler. Given the circumstances he could be, and was, a remorseless tyrant. Egmont and Horn were placed in detention as hostages for the good behaviour of the greater nobles; William had wisely retired to his estate at Dillenburg outside the Netherlands. The unpopular inner council or *consulta* was replaced by a more sinister group which the Dutch called the Council of Blood; its most influential members were three Spaniards, Jeronimo de Roda, Luis del Rio and the bloody-minded Juan Vargas. With scientific persistence Alva arrested suspects and hanged heretics in the hope that the peoples of the Netherlands might learn that treason did not pay.

By 1568 William of Orange was the real leader in the resistance to Spanish rule. Born the son of a minor German prince thirty-five years before, he had inherited a vast fortune and great estates from his cousin, René, Count of Nassau and Prince of Orange, a principality in the south of France, in 1544. Fortune favoured his youth. The Lutheran boy became a Catholic young man, magnificent, handsome, popular, extravagant, a favourite of the Emperor. But in the next twenty years he was to change from a noble into a popular leader. He was not at heart a profoundly religious man but he grew to love his country. The publication of his *Justification* in 1568 showed that while he was still asserting his loyalty to Philip and attacking his evil councillors rather than the King, he was clearly opposing Spanish policy.

But the armed revolt against Spanish rule did not yet prosper. 'We have come', William's brother, Louis of Nassau, told the townspeople of Groningen, ' with the help of the mighty and eternal God, for the welfare and protection of the entire Netherlands, to drive out the intruding, foreign and shameful tyranny of these cruel ravishers and persecutors of Christian blood, to bring back your old privileges and to maintain them ; to give comfort, help, safety and support to the scattered and fearful Christians and patriots.' And the rebels had full need of divine assistance. It is true that on a Sunday afternoon in May, 1568, Louis of Nassau defeated a Spanish band at Heiligerlee but Heiligerlee only made Alva more determined than ever to scarify the rebels.* The skirmish was fought on May 23rd ; Egmont and Horn, innocent of disloyalty but representative of the greater nobility, were executed at Brussels on June 5th. Louis' army was not much better placed. It had already alienated the peasants by its indiscipline and plunder before Alva crushed it at Jemmingen on the Ems on July 21st, 1568.

It is doubtful whether Alva understood the problem he was tackling much better than Philip himself. Brute force had brought about a return to nominal order. Alva supposed that he could wither potential resistance by a series of fiscal measures. To give him his due these formed an almost inevitable result of the crushing economic burden which Spain was carrying, in this particular made the more formidable by Elizabeth's ' borrowing ' of money intended to pay Alva's troops.[1] It seemed ludicrous to Alva, as to Philip, that some of the King's wealthiest subjects did not contribute more to the expenses of government. Alva was less to blame for imposing these new taxes than for failing to see the volcanic nature of the whole problem. Repressive taxation formed a natural stimulus to further armed rebellion, the more impressive because the merchant classes gave their support to the greater nobles. In spite of agitated protests from all his advisers, Alva imposed a capital levy of one per cent., a levy on goods of five per cent. and a purchase tax of ten per cent., already familiar to Spaniards as the *alcabala*. The attempt to levy the last-named tax at once provoked passive resistance, for it was peculiarly destructive of the economic life of a people who lived by commerce. Once again economic unrest fused with religious discontent to create trouble for Spain.

The event which caused a renewal of armed revolt came from an unexpected source, the seizure of the port of Brill by the Sea-Beggars, a ruffianly crew of semi-pirates licensed by William of Orange to fly his flag and for the moment refused asylum by Elizabeth. The hoisting of the Orange tricolour over the walls of Brill was an example soon followed by other towns. ' Men jested that the Duke

[1] See p. 214.

of Alva had lost his spectacles [the Flemish word *brill*=spectacles] on All Fools Day.' Louis of Nassau seized Mons in the south; in the north the rebellious cities recognised William as their Stadholder and commander-in-chief. The Spaniards recaptured town after town but Philip had begun to doubt Alva's capacity and replaced the efficient if ruthless soldier by a conscientious, conciliatory but rather ineffective grandee, Don Luis de Requesens.

Requesens' rule lasted from November, 1573, until typhus carried him off on March 5th, 1576. The new governor, more conciliatory than Alva, lifted the tenth penny and did something to regain the loyalty of the Catholic nobility. The war itself ebbed and flowed but Spain steadily gained ground. Although the Sea-Beggars won a signal success by capturing the port of Middelburg on February 18th, 1574, the rebels suffered one of their worst defeats at Mook Heide the following April where Louis of Nassau and three of his brothers lost their lives. William was himself ill that summer, weighed down by sorrow and strain, made the heavier by the heroic defence of Leyden besieged by the Spaniards and saved by the breaking of the dykes, an epic story which received a worthy memorial in the foundation of Leyden University. ' Leyden was ' indeed ' in travail for the birth of Holland.' But during the next year Spanish troops regained further lost ground and the situation remained grave for the rebels when Requesens died in 1576.

Requesens' death was followed by an interregnum during which Spanish fortunes deteriorated. William of Orange had long felt that the failure or success of his policy depended ultimately on foreign assistance but so far the Protestant powers had received his overtures coldly. He now considered placing the Netherlands under the protection of the ambitious young Catholic prince, the Duke of Anjou,[1] son of Catherine de' Medici. But before the negotiations were concluded the ' Spanish Fury ' had broken at Antwerp. Kept short of money, the Spanish troops had suddenly revolted and spoiled both friend and foe. ' They neither spared age nor sex ', wrote Gascoigne, ' time nor place ; person nor country ; young nor old ; rich nor poor . . . they slew great numbers of young children . . . and as great respect they had to the Church and churchyard as the butcher hath to his shambles. They spared neither friend nor foe, Portingal nor Turk. . . . Within three days Antwerp, which was one of the richest towns in Europe, had now no money nor treasure to be found therein, but only in the hands of murderers and strumpets.' The ' Spanish Fury ' had done what

---

[1] Known as the Duke of Alençon until 1574.

all William's eloquence had failed to do, for it had united sixteen out of the seventeen provinces, Catholic as well as Protestant, in a great effort to expel the Spaniard.

Requesens' successor, the courageous but self-centred half-brother of Philip, Don John of Austria, was thus placed in a difficult and dangerous position when he arrived in the once loyal province of Luxemburg. The Pacification of Ghent, a proposed settlement of all outstanding problems, had been worked out by delegates from all the provinces under the lead of William and was proclaimed on November 8th, 1576; it suspended all edicts against heresy and demanded that the Spanish troops should be expelled from the Low Countries, while asserting the provinces' loyalty to the Spanish Crown. What could Don John do ? The victor of Lepanto was a grandiose dreamer. He visualised the rebels defeated, England invaded and himself as the husband of Mary, Queen of Scots, but he did not keep his head permanently in the clouds. He knew that religious intolerance endangered the union of the northern and southern provinces, for whereas the south was still firmly Catholic, many of the northern provinces were intolerantly Calvinist. The Catholic nobles of the south headed by the Duke of Aerschot were jealous of the authority exercised by William of Orange and suspected his motives. Don John, knowing this, exerted all his natural personal attraction to win over the waverers and to sow discord among the rebels. His first move was to win their confidence by agreeing to the Perpetual Edict by which the Governor declared that he would remove the Spanish soldiers and respect the ancient constitutional liberties of the people. William realised that this was really a trick on the Governor's part to gain time but only the Estates of Holland and Zeeland refused to accept it. With the Perpetual Edict in his knapsack Don John could enter Brussels in proper ceremony as the duly-recognised Governor.

Instinctively Don John knew that he must sooner or later revert to a policy of force, for, as he himself put it, ' only a renewal of the war could make the situation bearable, only by possessing Holland and Zeeland and thereby commanding the trade of the Netherlands, can one be Governor of the Netherlands in reality.' He acted on impulse, seizing the citadel of Namur in July, 1577, whence he demanded the punishment of William the Silent.

His action was both mistimed and misguided, mistimed because the forces at his disposal were as yet inadequate and misguided because its first effect was an enthusiastic reaction in favour of Orange. But Don John was helped by the fact that popular as Orange was, he never had full command of the situation. He could neither control the religious intolerance of his Calvinist supporters nor gain the loyal co-operation of the southern nobles. He was convinced that foreign support was necessary for success but on each occasion that he sought for foreign aid he was forced to compromise. Thus he was obliged to accept the effete and colourless Hapsburg prince Matthias as the anti-Spaniard Governor to conciliate the Catholic party. Time soon showed that Matthias lacked any real following in the Netherlands.

Thus, misguided and mistimed as Don John's action at Namur may have been, it was not disastrous. Reinforced by 3000 Spanish troops, he routed the rebels at Gembloux in January, 1578, and might have recovered further ground had not Philip shown unnatural reluctance to send reinforcements. In fact, Philip, ever jealous of success, was about to recall Don John when news reached him of his death.

The interval which ensued before the arrival of his successor, the able Alexander, Duke of Parma, gave the rebellious states time to organise their defences. The religious divisions were now more marked than ever. The northern states, except Gelderland, were Calvinist; the Walloon provinces were predominantly Catholic. Questions of defence forced Catholic Gelderland into union with the six other provinces at Utrecht on the 23rd January, 1579. The union meant that conduct of military affairs would be henceforth more efficient and that in practice Catholicism would be suppressed. Much as William might deplore this, circumstances forced him to accept the settlement.

Meanwhile the Walloon provinces formed the Union of Arras, making it clear that they would recognise Spanish rule as long as Philip respected the constitutional terms of the Pacification of Ghent. Parma, in every way a greater man than Don John, seized the opportunity with open arms. He guaranteed the provinces' constitutional rights and agreed to withdraw the Spanish troops. The southern half of the Netherlands returned to the fold of Spain with which its fortunes were to be linked until 1713.

Parma's governorship began well for Spain and badly for the rebels. To a greater extent than ever before William and his friends relied on foreign aid but experience so far had hardly justified their hopes. The Archduke Matthias, now to be quietly shelved, had proved an incompetent nonentity. Another auxiliary, John Casimir of the Palatinate, had harmed rather than helped the Protestant cause by the rapacity and indiscipline of his troops. Two possible sources of help remained, England and France. Elizabeth's policy had been so far both insular and capricious; she showed no sign of giving any substantial assistance to the rebel cause. There was less to hope from England's mean, majestic Queen than from the Valois line of France, more especially from the unpleasing and selfish Duke of Anjou with whom William re-opened negotiations in the autumn of 1580. Eventually William agreed to recognise Anjou as virtual sovereign of the rebel provinces, but the move was fraught with difficulties. His Calvinist subjects naturally suspected a Valois and a Catholic; 'they had', the Protestant ministers asserted, ' to expect no help or blessings from the said Duke, seeing that he was of contrary religion, and that God promises His help to Kings and Lords who walk in fear of Him'. Anjou, lacking military success, justifiably mistrusted by the Netherlanders, followed the Valois tradition by trying to solve his problems by a sudden and treacherous *coup d'état*; disregarding all his promises he tried to gain control of Antwerp by force in January, 1583. But the ' French Fury' proved a dismal fiasco and irretrievably damaged Anjou's standing in the Netherlands. He retired to France where he died on June 10th, 1584. Exactly a calendar month later, July 10th, the cabinet-maker's apprentice, Balthasar Gérard, accomplished what others had long tried in vain to do; he killed William with a shot from a pistol bought with money given to him by his victim. ' Mon Dieu, ayez pitié de mon ame; mon Dieu, ayez pitié de ce pauvre peuple ' were William's dying words. There was a spontaneous outburst of grief at this dastardly action. The inscription over his grave in the New Church at Delft, where his faithful dog, Kuntz, lies ever on guard at his feet, reads 'To the Glory of God and to the everlasting memory of William of Nassau, Father of the Fatherland, who valued the fortunes of the Netherlands above his own.' It is a faithful mirror of his character and of the part which he played in the struggle for Dutch independence.

All these events helped the Duke of Parma in his attempts to recover the lost provinces. While he would not tolerate Protestantism, he was averse to persecution and did more than any previous governor to reconcile the southern provinces to Spanish rule. Military success formed a fitting accompaniment to sensible diplomacy.

In these circumstances the States-General once more renewed its search for foreign help. Critical as it had been of William's collusion with Anjou, it swallowed its pride and appealed to Henry III of France, but the King was himself so perilously placed that he was obliged to decline. There remained Elizabeth of England. While her policy had hitherto been to keep Philip embroiled in the struggle rather than to secure the victory of his enemies, she was so disturbed by Parma's recent successes that she agreed to make a treaty. In return for the cession of Brill and Flushing as cautionary towns to England, she promised to send a force of 4000 infantry and 400 cavalry under the command of the Earl of Leicester. Such help came in the nick of time, for Brussels, Mechlin and Antwerp had all surrendered to Parma.

Leicester's expedition may have checked Parma's victorious advance but it was nevertheless a failure. The 'governor-general' was a Protestant, but he was a poor soldier and a worse politician. He became involved in an internal struggle between the so-called Precisians, who identified Church and State, and the Libertines who disliked ecclesiastical interference and represented the rich province of Holland. Leicester unwisely supported the Precisians and so provoked the hostility of the Hollanders. He made Utrecht the centre of his administration and confined his favours in the Council of State to its English members and two Flemings, Van Meetkerke and De Borchgrave, while Holland's leading delegate, Paul de Buys, was imprisoned. Naturally enough Holland, led by the purposeful Oldenbarneveldt, was not slow to respond to this shabby treatment. Whether Leicester was in effect ready for an open conflict is doubtful. He came back to England in November, 1586, but returned the following summer just as his mistress began to negotiate with Parma. Another attempt to reduce the power of the Estates of Holland proved so dismal a fiasco that Leicester left for England, never to return.

All things considered, it is surprising that Parma did not sweep all before him, but factors outside his control limited his success. Geography played a pre-eminent part in the creation of an independent Netherlands. Except at Ostend, and Bergen-op-Zoom, the Spaniards had now reached the Dutch natural defences, whether canals, lakes or marshes, which Parma's armies could not easily penetrate. Four other factors explain the limited nature of his success. In view of Philip's plans for defeating England, Parma was forced to divert troops to Dunkirk and Nieuport where they were to be embarked on the invincible Armada. No sooner had the Armada proved that it was not invincible than the accession of the Protestant prince, Henry IV, to the French throne made Spanish interference in France inevitable. Again he had to divert his troops from an all-important attack on Holland and Zeeland to campaign in northern France. In the third place the repeated failure of foreign help was a lesson not lost on the two intelligent rebel leaders, van Oldenbarneveldt and William's son, Maurice of Nassau. In 1589 Oldenbarneveldt persuaded the Estates of Utrecht, Gelderland and Overyssel to offer Maurice, who was already Stadholder of Holland

and Zeeland, the Stadholderate in their provinces. As Maurice's cousin and brother-in-law was already Stadholder of the one remaining province of Friesland, military command was placed beyond dispute in the hands of one man, Maurice of Nassau. A capable soldier he took Breda in 1590, failed before Nimwegen but captured Zutphen and Deventer in 1591, Steenwyk and Koevorden the next year. Parma's last impediment was the one constant factor in the Spanish Government, the King. Jealous of success, he continued to expect more of his subordinates than they could give, and sometimes grudged them the help they required. Death in 1592 freed Parma from probable disgrace.

In spite of the fact that Parma's virtual successor [1] was a harsh but capable soldier, Alva's brother-in-law, the Count de Fuentes, Maurice and the Dutch made steady progress. While the Spanish army was entrenched in France in 1597, Maurice won a spectacular victory at Turnhout which gave him control over the eastern provinces.

Philip II's death in 1598 opened a period of military stalemate. His successor, Philip III, had no more idea than his father of relaxing his hold over the Netherlands or of tolerating any other religion but the Catholic. The end of the wars with France (1598) and England (1604) enabled his commanders to concentrate all their military forces on the reduction of the United Provinces. And although Maurice had successfully 'closed the fence' which had made an attack on Gelderland and Overyssel continuously possible, the eastern frontiers were still insecure; three times in the ensuing decade, in 1593, 1605 and 1606, they were the target of Spanish forces. Furthermore discontent with Spanish rule in the south, widespread but never profound enough to cause a rising, diminished after 1598 as a result of the conciliatory rule of the Archduke Albert and his wife who were left as effective sovereigns. Finally, the Spaniards had again secured a great commander in the Genoese, Ambrogio Spinola, in whom Philip III soon placed great trust.

The military history of the period 1598-1609 is thus mainly a story of siege warfare but so bald a summary demands some qualification. Maurice at least won a great victory over the Spaniards at Nieuport in 1600 which he failed to follow up. But the long wars had so exhausted both combatants that the Truce of 1609 was

---

[1] Parma's immediate successor was a Flemish nobleman, Count Mansfeld who was soon succeeded by a Hapsburg prince, the Archduke Ernest, brother of the reigning Emperor (and of the Archduke Matthias) and destined to marry Philip's daughter, Isabella. When the Archduke died, his brother Albert succeeded both to his wife and to the governorship. This represented Philip's desire to strengthen Hapsburg power in north-west Europe.

as good as inevitable. The truce, which was to last twelve years, has an importance far outstretching its particular terms. On nearly every disputed point the south gave way to the north. There was no definite prohibition of Dutch trade to the Indies, nor was the Scheldt thrown open to permit trade with Antwerp. The Catholics living in the north received no explicit protection. The north was in fact left in a far stronger position than the south. Whatever the future held in store, the Truce of 1609 amounted to a virtual recognition of Dutch independence; if the forty years struggle had not yet actually reached its final stage, it had at least come to a decisive result.

3. *The causes of Dutch success*

The epic quality of the long struggle in which seven provinces successfully defied the mightiest of contemporary empires demands an explanation. The military factor was, of course, primary; that, and that alone, determined that the split between the north and the south should remain permanent. But the military capacity of William and Maurice cannot ultimately explain why the Dutch endured and achieved so much. It is possible to point to the stolid patriotism and toughness and persistence, which were characteristic of the Dutch people, beside which a foreign army, however well-equipped and well-led, billeted in a land where it was often regarded with hostility, was placed at an obvious disadvantage.

Geography helps to explain the Spanish failure to reconquer the rebellious provinces. ' In the trial of strength between Spain, based on the wide perimeter on the Netherlands—from Grevelingen (Gravelines) over Nivelles, Leuven (Louvain), Maastricht, and Roermonde to Groningen—and the revolt, based on the maritime provinces of Holland and Zeeland ', writes a modern authority, Professor Geyl, ' the geographical configuration of the country, in particular the inestimable strategic importance of the great rivers, was to be the determining factor.' The waterways constituted a natural defence line for the Dutch, but their enemies had to suffer the disadvantage of long drawn-out communications.

Religion, more especially Calvinism, also played its part in bringing about victory. It is true that by the end of the sixteenth century there were signs of a cleavage between the Precisians and the Libertines but it was not yet serious enough to imperil national unity. The confidence and enthusiasm which the Calvinist idea of election afforded its followers was an impetus to the religious fervour that long endurance in rebellion required. Calvinism also

supplied the Dutch with a theoretical justification for their revolt
against a divinely-appointed feudal overlord. Finally Calvinism was
an important unifying factor in a state or rather a series of states
deeply permeated by separatist tendencies. Wherever the army
occupied a town the Reformed Church was not slow to follow;
the local Catholic church was whitewashed and ' purged ' of undesirable elements. ' The Protestantisation of the people ', writes
Dr. Geyl, ' was considered as an indispensable guarantee of their
loyalty to the states régime.'

But, basically, Dutch success was made possible by the almost
miraculous economic development of the country. The Dutch had
long been experienced sailors, engaging in the herring fishery.
The decline of the Hanseatic fish trade, an improved method of
preparing herrings for salting and the use of largish boats (*busses*)
which made possible fishing in the rich spawning banks off the
English coast, all contributed to make the herring one of the foundations of future Dutch wealth. ' The herring keeps Dutch trade
going, and Dutch trade sets the world afloat.'

Holland and Zeeland, immune from attack since 1576, were
thus able to develop their economic life, of which the other provinces were always envious, in comparative security. Their sailors
watched the Flemish ports from which pro-Spanish privateers
sailed, and Dutch merchant fleets carried Dutch merchandise
further and further afield. By the middle of the sixteenth century
they had already taken over much of the Baltic and Scandinavian
trade from the Hanseatic League. They had developed a profitable
traffic with Lisbon, Cadiz and the Mediterranean but the outbreak
of war with Spain cut this short and forced them to look for other
fields.

Colonial enterprise was thus a natural sequel to the Spanish
War and an outgrowth of European trade. The Dutch were soon
engaged in an illegal but lucrative commerce with Brazil, a Spanish
possession from 1580, while in a desire to circumvent the perils of
the voyages to the Indies (which was more or less under Portuguese
control) attempts were made to find a north-east or north-west
passage to the East. The cargo of pepper and spice which Cornelius
Houtman brought back in 1597 for the Amsterdam merchants who
had subsidised his voyage proved that it was possible to defy the
Spaniards and the Portuguese with impunity and profit. Twenty-
six ships sailed for the Indies in 1598 and thirty-six the next year.
From the purely military and commercial point of view individual
enterprise was less fruitful than co-operative activity. Oldenbarneveldt put forward a plan for joining the individual ventures in

I

a United East India Company in 1602. It was fully capitalised and was given a monopoly of all trade between the Cape of Good Hope and Cape Magelhaes as well as full sovereign authority over any land that it colonised within these limits. From the start it prospered; its dividends regularly reached 15 per cent. to 25 per cent. and sometimes far exceeded that amount.

Trade brought wealth which stimulated industry and agriculture in the home country. The capture of Antwerp by Parma's troops ruined the port's prosperity since the Dutch continued to control the river Scheldt. As a result many of its merchants transferred their business activities to Amsterdam which soon became one of the leading financial and trading centres in Europe. Its Bank, founded in 1609, formed a reservoir of wealth from which foreign states as well as Dutch merchants were able to draw money on loan. Harbours were improved and rebuilt. Many thousands found work in shipbuilding, especially in the Zaan region. Work was begun on the reclamation of the land. Linen and woollen workers left Flanders for Haarlem and Leyden. A contemporary wrote truly: ' In the command of the sea and in the conduct of the war on the water resides the entire prosperity of the country.' It was on such foundations that a brave and hard-working people conducted their war against Spain and built an independent nation.

CHAPTER XV

THE FRENCH WARS OF RELIGION

1. *The political and social background*

FRENCH history in the last half of the sixteenth century was almost continuously strife-ridden. Although the coming of Calvinism to France was the spring which released the mechanism of revolt, the time was ripe for change and trouble. The lowering of the prestige of the monarchy contributed to this.[1] Fundamentally Francis I, King from 1515-47, was a secular-minded man who had tried to repress heresy in rather a half-hearted manner because heresy challenged the royal authority. Towards the close of his reign the spread of Protestantism made him act more rigorously; his son and successor, Henry II, followed suit until he died of a wound acquired in a jousting match at the Tournelles in July, 1559. His death proved the signal which plunged France into anarchy, for his sons inherited the weakness and vicious character of the Valois stock rather than the Italian cunning and physical sturdiness of their mother, Catherine de' Medici. The eldest son, Francis II, a sickly boy married to Mary of Scotland, was a tool in the hands of his uncles of the house of Guise. When he died in 1560 he was succeeded by his ten-year-old brother, Charles IX who, with one brief interval, clung to his mother's apron strings until death removed his shadowy figure on Whitsunday, 1574. He had two brothers. The younger, Francis, Duke of Alençon (and after 1574, of Anjou), Elizabeth's ' Frog ', was an intelligent and wholly unscrupulous fop; this scented puppy proved a persistent nuisance as he sought to fulfil his ignoble ambitions. His elder brother, Henry III, was probably the shrewdest but most degenerate of Catherine's sons. Clearly a psychological case, he delighted to mince in eccentric and macaroni-like fashion in company with the sophisticated and vicious dandies of his court. ' The King ', wrote a contemporary, ' goes every night to balls and does nothing but dance. During four whole days he was dressed in mulberry satin with stockings, doublet, and cloak of the same colour. The cloak was very much slashed in the body and had all its folds set with

[1] It should be made clear that although the French monarchy was weak in this period, none of its adversaries challenged the monarchical idea. It is probable that the mass of Frenchmen remained loyal to the Crown, even under the most ineffective of the Valois kings.

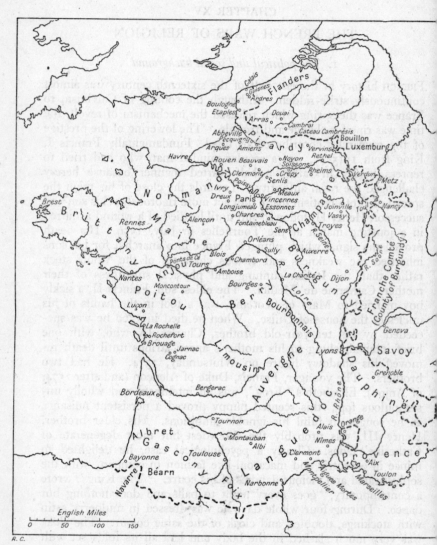

MAP VIII.—France in the sixteenth century.

buttons and adorned with ribbons, white and scarlet and mulberry, and he wore bracelets of coral on his arms.' Like the Spanish Hapsburgs, this prince was liable to fits of remorse as a result of which he would flagellate himself and indulge in religious austerities. But he had some political wisdom and was less under the thumb of Catherine, whose favourite son he was, than his brothers had been.

Catherine's own impact on the history of the period was supremely important. During her husband's lifetime she had had to take second place to his mistress, Diane de Poitiers but with his death came her great opportunity. Inheriting the shrewdness of her mercantile ancestors, the Medici dukes of Florence, she yet lacked their foresight. Bereft of principle, she was often guided by temporary or even by trifling objectives, more especially by her excessive love for her children. Vital, vigorous and maternal, she was astonishingly superficial. The bewildering shifts of royal policy can only be explained by the unprincipled opportunism of the Queen-Mother. Her death in 1589 removed a dominant figure in French history in the last half of the sixteenth century.

In every respect the monarchy was weak. It had no real popular support, for none of the Kings until the coming of Henry of Navarre had the type of personality which could grip the popular imagination. Its finances were in a fantastic state as a result of the reckless extravagance of Francis I and had to be reinforced to an increasing extent by short-term loans. In 1555 Henry II had drawn a volume of credit to his support by renewing his vast loans at Lyons at the extravagantly high interest of 16 per cent. but the Great Deal, as it was called, could not be sustained. The King defaulted, thus admitting virtual bankruptcy. As the expenses of the religious wars mounted, as less and less revenue passed from the long-suffering peasants to the Crown, as Henry III danced and feasted, so the financial state of the monarchy grew worse and worse.

An enfeebled, shiftless and bankrupt monarchy was inevitably the prey of noble factions at court. The great noble families, in some respects wealthier and more influential than the Crown, were proud and ambitious. The Lotheringian house of Guise, of ancient lineage, was closely allied to the royal house by marriage. In 1559 it was headed by a gallant soldier, Francis, Duke of Guise, and by a singularly fertile diplomat, Charles, the Cardinal of Lorraine.[1] The Bourbons were more closely related to the royal

[1] The power and position of the Guise family is worth emphasising. The Duke of Guise owned estates worth 53,000 livres a year as well as numerous titles. His brother, Charles, Cardinal of Lorraine, was even richer and as titled. He was Duke of Rheims and Chevreuse, Bishop of Metz (and as

house. Their actual leader was Louis, Prince of Condé, an ambitious, hot-tempered prince, far-outmatching in ability his supine and irresolute elder brother, Anthony, King of Navarre. The third of the great noble families, that of Montmorency, had less royal blood but was no less influential. Guise influence was strongly Catholic and mainly confined to their extensive estates in eastern France. The chief Bourbon princes were Huguenots, but their objects were more political than religious; their influence was greatest in western France. The Montmorencys, whose lands lay chiefly in central and southern France, were divided by religion, for whereas the head of the family, Constable Anne de Montmorency, was a fervent Catholic, his three nephews, Gaspard de Coligny, Odet, former Cardinal de Châtillon, and Francis d'Andelot (incidentally buried in Canterbury Cathedral) were sincere Huguenots.

Apart from this highly-complex situation at the French court, which was to be so fertile of trouble, all social classes were permeated by growing discontent. While the greater nobility, already in part divested of governmental responsibility, were factious and unruly, the lesser nobility suffered to an increasing degree from the effects of rising prices, the division of their landed estates among their many sons and, since the ending of the Italian Wars, from lack of employment. Custom precluded their entry into trade. Restless and penurious, they were only too ready to take advantage of civil strife to benefit themselves; on the analogy of their English compeers they were attracted by the hope of winning Church land. Growing industry, more especially the development of the silk industry at Lyons, Tours and Nîmes, was not immune from the steady rise in prices, followed at a much slower speed by wages, which created discontent among the industrial workers. Economic discontent mixed with religious agitation in a town like Lyons to create an ugly situation. And what of the peasantry who formed

such a Prince of the Empire), Bishop of Verdun, Abbot *in commendam* of St. Rémi-de-Rheims, Gorze, Cluny, St. Paul-de-Verdun, St. Martin-de-Laon, St. Urbain, Montier-en-Der, Cormery, Fécamp, Marmoutier and St. Denis. His full income has been estimated as 300,000 livres a year. His younger brother, Louis, the Cardinal of Guise, was Bishop of Troyes and later of Metz, Archbishop of Albi, Sens and Bordeaux. The Guise family possessed a vast secular and ecclesiastical patronage. In his excellent *The Cardinal of Lorraine and the Council of Trent* (1930) H. O. Evennett comments : ' The Guise tentacles penetrated to all corners of Europe. In addition to the ordinary state diplomatic servants the Cardinal of Lorraine had his own system of private agents, which he developed to a very high pitch of efficiency, the skilled politician and administrator existing, in his person, side by side with the grave scholar, the seductive courtier and the austere man of God ' (11-12).

the majority of Frenchmen? The revolution in prices had forced many of the nobility to sell land to wealthy *bourgeois* from the towns[1] who often took advantage of the changeover to exact higher rents from their tenants and to insist on a more rigorous observance of their feudal rights. But it was, as Arthur Young found two centuries later, impossible to generalise about the French peasantry. The peasants bore the fiscal burden of the state on their broad backs, unwilling and yet, except in moments of desperation, apathetic victims of the more powerful influences in the state.

France was thus devoid of financial, political and social stability by the middle of the sixteenth century. The Crown was bound to fall a victim to the impassioned ambitions of disputing factions, and when these factions were imbued, sincerely or otherwise, with opposing religious ideas, it was impossible to prevent the outbreak of civil war. What the situation required was a spark which would set the inflammable tinder alight; and this was the purpose which Calvin's agents served.

2. *The rise of the Huguenots*

The French Church was probably in no worse state than that of any other European country at the beginning of the sixteenth century, but the movement which sought to reform its abuses lacked any real stimulus. The list of abuses is long and tedious; non-resident prelates, pluralists like Cardinal du Bellay who at one time enjoyed the revenues of five bishoprics and fourteen abbeys, a low standard of conduct and discipline, ignorance and immorality, all betrayed a lack of real vocation which weakened the Church's spiritual strength and diminished its ability to withstand the world, the flesh and the devil, habited, as a Catholic would have it, *in forma Lutherana.* Nor had the Concordat of Bologna in 1516 in any way improved the situation, since it had virtually placed all the higher offices of the Church in the King's patronage, enabling him to use them as rewards or bribes. Spiritual worth was in fact a less important qualification for high office than political service. The Concordat impeded the calling of provincial and diocesan synods which could not be summoned without royal permission. It also tended to emphasise the persistent Gallicanism which made

---

[1] The extent to which the price revolution affected the landed nobility has led to controversy. Recent evidence suggests that in most Mediterranean countries the seigneurial class was least hit by prevailing economic tendencies and that it may even to some extent have benefited from rising prices. See Braudel, *La Méditerranée et le Monde Méditerranéen*, 403, 625-9.

each French King suspect the policy pursued by the Pope of Rome. Thus just as Francis I fluctuated in the policy he adopted towards the Huguenots, so his son, Henry II, opposed the recalling of the Council of Trent by Julius III in 1551, and his daughter-in-law, Catherine de' Medici, placed more faith in the 'national' Colloquy of Poissy than in the continuance of the Tridentine discussions.

In spite of this the French Reform movement made at first very slow headway. Its early leader was the scholarly Jacques Lefèvre who had been converted to a Lutheran view of Justification by reading St. Paul's Epistles, but he was already an elderly man when he first published in 1512 a Latin translation of St. Paul's Epistles with a commentary. Eleven years later a revised French translation of the Four Gospels was published. French reform was thus mainly Erasmian and Lutheran but it lacked emotional intensity or a vigorous social appeal. Among its followers it numbered administrators like Lefèvre's former pupil, Guillaume Briçonnet, Bishop of Meaux, scholars, and even for a time a member of the French royal family, Margaret, Queen of Navarre, Francis I's sister.

The French government, allied to the Catholic Church, could not ignore the slow growth of Protestantism. Persecution was at first sporadic rather than persistent; Jean Leclerc, a woolcarder, was burned in 1525; a scholarly squire, Louis de Berquin, died at Paris four years later. But these men were forerunners of the new order rather than of the old which was better represented by Margaret and her chaplain, Gérard Roussel, Bishop of Oloron, who retained Catholic ceremonial and at the same time accepted certain Protestant ideas. Had this been all, French Protestantism would soon have been smothered by the Counter-Reformation. Yet in small degree it fertilised the soil in which Huguenotism was to take vigorous root. What it wanted was a leader, a vigorous message and an effective organisation. And this was what Calvin was able to give it.

Although Geneva was Calvin's spiritual capital, France was his intellectual home. He had been trained in French universities; his *Institutes of the Christian Religion* had been originally dedicated to Francis I of France in the hope that that peculiarly un-Calvinistic monarch would champion the reformed cause in France. Unable to secure royal support, Calvinism turned naturally towards the Crown's hereditary opponents, the nobles, whom it invested with a theoretical justification for rebellion. Geneva's contiguity to France made the country an ideal mission field. Calvin, in fact, transformed the French Protestant movement by giving it an abiding sense of mission, sustained always by a belief in divine election to grace. If Calvinism appealed to the political ambitions of the French nobility who wished to check royal absolutism, it also had much in common with the economic doctrine of self-interest with its implicit appeal to the French merchants, while its social teaching did not prove unattractive to the French working-class.

Above all Calvin endowed the Reformed Church in France with an extraordinarily efficient organisation. As in Geneva the consistory was the first link in a chain of authorities culminating in a national synod representing all the Calvinist congregations throughout France. Above the consistory there was the colloquy, not unlike an English rural deanery since it consisted of representatives, including laymen, of a number of churches in a particular district. Meeting less frequently and comprising wider areas were the provincial and national synods.

The spread of Calvinist teaching coincided with the adoption of a more rigorous policy by the French state. Francis I, advised by Cardinal de Tournon, issued a harsh edict for the suppression of heresy which the French parlements were not unwilling to enforce. The next few decades witnessed a number of martyrdoms. While there were some distinguished victims, including the scholarly theologian, Etienne Dolet, the greater number were men and women of the middle and lower classes. In 1547 a special criminal court of the Parlement of Paris, appropriately called the Chambre Ardente, was set up to try cases of heresy, and Henry II would have introduced the Inquisition had not the Parlement objected to the setting up of an institution which might overrule its own jurisdiction.

In spite of this policy Calvinism spread quickly throughout France, less so in Paris than elsewhere. Persecution had the effect of discouraging the half-hearted, but Calvin's enthusiastic missionaries whipped up the zeal of humble artisans and rich merchants in city after city; Calvinism, incidentally, never had any real hold over the French peasantry. Advancing from the university cities along the river valleys, it never lacked patrons in high places. Imprisoned by the Spaniards, Gaspard de Coligny and Francis d'Andelot had had time to reflect on their religious beliefs and had emerged high-principled Huguenots. Other converts of even higher rank, but less respectability, included Anthony, King of Navarre, and his brother, Condé. The spread of Calvinism was cellular. Small groups, like that at Paris under the lead of Jean le Macon, organised a consistory which was in course of time linked up with the colloquy and the provincial synod. The first national synod was held in conditions of secrecy at Paris on May 26th, 1559. It accepted a Confession of faith drawn up by Calvin two years earlier and drew up a ' Discipline ' on which the conduct and the procedure of members of the Reformed faith were to rest. With justifiable exaggeration Calvin wrote that there were now 300,000 Huguenots in France. In spite of the hostility of the Crown, the Church and the Parlements, congregation after congregation established new churches, meeting together to sing Clement Marot's translations of the Psalms with inspiring enthusiasm. Calvinism had indeed become an *imperium in imperio* which no government could long endure. The faction-ridden French monarchy required all the spiritual and physical force at its disposal if it was to face and overcome a crisis more serious than that of the Hundred Years' War.

3. *The Wars of Religion*

The Wars of Religion, which lasted on and off from 1562 to 1598, are inextricably confused, tedious if considered in detail, on some occasions dramatic, occasionally revealing intense devotion to principle but more often complete lack of it, frequently throwing into grim relief the depths of human treachery and greed. If they were fought over the right to worship according to the dictates of conscience, the Crown's ability to maintain its absolute authority depended on their outcome. Calvinism threatened the political power of the King as well as the religious supremacy of the Church. In the long run it was obliged to rationalise and justify its policy of disobedience, as the significant *Vindiciae contra Tyrannos* amply illustrates. ' There are two contracts,' wrote the author of this lucid tract, 'one between God and the King and people by which God contracts to endow the nation with prosperity so long as the people serve him and abstain from idolatry ; the other is between the King and the people.' The people agree to obey the King providing he grants them good government ; ' bene imperanti bene optemperatur.' Huguenot opinion was much more inclined to emphasise the breach of the first contract than the second, but there was no disguising the fact that the rise of the Huguenot movement was an implicit challenge to the absolute authority of the Crown.

The accession of Francis II in 1559 really opened the period of civil war. The new King, a weakly boy of fifteen and a half, relied on the Guise faction, but rising unemployment and growing religious passion made its rule unpopular. This gave the Guises' rival, Louis, Prince of Condé, a handle to his own ambitions. He planned to seize the King and the Guises while the court was at Amboise in March, 1560, but the plot went awry. Nevertheless, Condé, who had found a scapegoat in a lesser noble, La Renaudie, for the Conspiracy of Amboise, planned a further coup d'état, but was caught out and arrested on a charge of treason. At this juncture the King died.

The new King, Charles IX, was only nine and a half years old, thus making a regency necessary. Condé's brother, the King of Navarre, had the best claims to the regency, but the accession to power of so violent an opponent of the Guises would have made the outbreak of disorder inevitable. It was now that Catherine decided to assert herself. Young Charles' bed was brought into her own room. By a series of skilfully manipulated moves she managed to conciliate the Bourbon faction, including Condé who was released from prison, as well as the Guises and to secure the regency for herself.

She had now to decide what policy should be adopted towards the religious disputants. Like Elizabeth of England, her temperament was secular rather than religious; in dealing with religious problems she always showed less than her usual foresight because she was unable to comprehend the depth of religious passion. In any case she believed the Huguenots to be much less strong than they actually were, and for the moment she was convinced that it would be possible to reach a compromise which would satisfy both parties. Although she had little intention of following a policy of toleration permanently, she believed that it would be possible to gain time by granting an amnesty. The immediate effect was to encourage the Huguenots and to alienate the Catholics but she persevered with her plan, hoping to settle the whole problem by a general council of the French Church which would institute necessary reforms and discuss doctrinal differences. It was the mirage which had beckoned Charles V to disaster. Unfortunately the recall of the Council of Trent, which had been dealing with similar problems, forced Catherine to modify her intentions. As a result she called together representatives of both sides in the Colloquy of Poissy.[1] This should have revealed to Catherine the underlying dangers and weaknesses of the policy of appeasement on which she had now embarked. The sole result of the Colloquy was to stimulate Catholic distrust of Catherine, made the stronger by the marked favour she had shown to the outspoken Protestant leader, Beza, as well as to the Huguenot leader, de Coligny. Neither side really wanted either toleration or comprehension, and each was fundamentally contemptuous of Catherine's well-meant intentions. Instead of healing the breach Catherine had widened it, and

[1] For the full significance of the Colloquy of Poissy see H. O. Evennett, *The Cardinal of Lorraine and the Council of Trent*, 283-394.

unhappily placed the Crown in the centre between the two disputing parties.

Catherine was in fact sitting on a keg of gunpowder to which a burning fuse was already attached. But with skill and consummate optimism she persisted in her policy. In January, 1562, she issued an edict, allowing the Huguenots to worship freely in the suburbs of towns [1] and in the countryside. The Duke of Guise, irritated by this move towards toleration, retired from court to sulk in high dudgeon on his estates, while Anthony of Navarre, specious as ever, decided to return to the Catholic fold. The edict was indeed generally unpopular and was only registered by the Parlement of Paris after prolonged discussion. Alarmed by Catholic hostility, Catherine made a false move. Through Coligny Catherine appealed to the Huguenots to support her with their armed forces if Catholic powers invaded France.

The incident which brought about war was comparatively slight. On Sunday March 1st, 1562, the Duke of Guise, who was staying at his château of Joinville, preparatory to returning to court, went to dine at Vassy where he came across a Huguenot service being held in a barn within the town walls contrary to the provisions of the edict of January. In the ensuing riot Guise's armed retainers slew thirty of the Huguenots and wounded about one hundred and twenty more. When news of this reached Paris the turbulent Condé called the Huguenots to arms, and, defying Catherine's appeal to him to protect the King, opened hostilities. Condé had not in fact handled the situation well; by refusing Catherine's offer he had decanted both her and Charles IX into the open arms of the Catholic triumvirate of nobles of which Guise was the head.[2]

Begun in this unpromising way the first of the religious wars yielded Catherine better dividends than she could possibly have hoped for. Two of the chief leaders, the Huguenot Condé and the Catholic Montmorency, were captured by each other's armies. The luckless Anthony of Navarre and a second triumvir, the Marshal de St. André, were killed in battle. Guise was murdered by a young Huguenot who confessed, under torture, that Coligny had instructed him to do the deed. The young Huguenot was pulled in pieces by four horses, and the Catholics from this time onwards sought to avenge the murder, of which Coligny was really innocent. The disintegration of the two rival armies served Catherine well as it

[1] To have permitted the Huguenots to worship freely in the centres of towns would have encouraged rioting and disorder.

[2] The Catholic triumvirate consisted of Guise, Montmorency and St. André.

enabled her to negotiate a peace and to drive out the English, whom Condé in an unwise moment had introduced into the country as his allies. The war was closed, if but temporarily, by the Pacification of Amboise, signed in March, 1563, which allowed the Huguenots liberty of conscience but seriously restricted their right to worship.[1] It was symptomatic of Catherine's shrewdness—and shortsightedness —that the Protestant nobility were to be exempt from these restrictions.

The next four years were an uneasy period marked by growing violence. ' I have often heard my mother say ', wrote a Huguenot later, ' that just before I was born, she several times had the greatest difficulty to save herself from being drowned like others of all ages and sexes by a great lord of the country, a persecutor of religion. He had them thrown into a river close by his house, saying that he would make them drink out of his big saucer.' The Queen-Mother temporised, ingraining distrust in Catholic and Huguenot alike by her sheer opportunism. Convinced by now that France was Catholic at heart she had abandoned appeasement, but had no intention of restoring the Guises to power. The Huguenots were naturally alarmed by the restrictions imposed on their liberty by the Peace of Amboise and by the increasing pro-Catholic trend of Catherine's policy, made doubly ominous by Alva's arrival in the Netherlands in 1567, and by a meeting held at Bayonne between Catherine and Philip two years earlier.[2] These fears may explain, if they do not justify, another wild-cat scheme initiated by Condé to seize the young King at Meaux during the festivities of St. Michael's Eve in 1567. The plot failed, because the Catholics held the one bridge across the Marne over which the Huguenots had to pass *en route* for Meaux but it was followed by the reopening of hostilities.

The second war was of short duration and served as a preliminary skirmish to a more embittered conflict. The Peace of Longjumeau which ended it in March, 1568, confirmed the agreement of Amboise, but it was only a truce. Enraged by Condé's attempt on the King, which aroused her strong maternal feelings, Catherine planned to safeguard him by arresting Condé and Coligny at Noyers in Burgundy ; but they learned of her intentions and fleeing through hill and forest between the Loire and Saône reached La Rochelle. The third war was the natural sequel.

[1] Protestant worship was limited to Huguenot towns or to the suburbs of one town in each bailiwick ; no Huguenot meetings were allowed in Paris.

[2] In fact, Catherine went to Bayonne to meet her daughter, Elizabeth, Philip's wife, and to try to heal the strained relations with Spain by a further diplomatic marriage. See p. 212.

This war was marked by the great savagery shown by both sides. No quarter was given to man, woman or child. ' At Auxerre ', Professor J. E. Neale has written, ' one mob killed a hundred and fifty Huguenots, stripped their bodies, dragged them through the streets and threw them into the river or into the sewers.'[1] But the war did not go well for the Huguenots. Condé was defeated and killed at Jarnac. Coligny, so much more attractive as a man, suffered a similar disaster at Moncontour, but in a typically Italianate way Catherine was still trying to hold the balance between the conflicting forces. Few women in history have allowed policy to be so influenced by personal caprice, but there was more sense in her determination to reach a compromise than in her fervent wish to rid herself of the Guise influence, represented by the powerful Cardinal of Lorraine. Behind the feverish gaiety of the Louvre there was the sinister spectre of financial instability, made the worse by a threatening business depression. Backed by the moderates she negotiated the Peace of St. Germain, signed in August 1570, allowing the Huguenot nobles practically full freedom to worship but otherwise restricting the places of worship to towns where it was already practised and to two towns in each of the administrative districts of France. The Huguenots were also granted certain judicial privileges and given the right to hold four towns, La Rochelle, Montauban, Cognac and La Charité, for two years as a guarantee that the terms of the peace would be carried out.

The peace, which was much criticised by the Catholics as unduly favourable to the Huguenots, represented the rise of a new party in French politics which attracted Catherine's support, the *Politiques*. Catholic in religion, they yet resented foreign interference and were above all concerned with the peace and prosperity of the kingdom. They ' preferred the repose of the kingdom and their own homes to the salvation of their souls; who would rather ', as a hostile witness put it, ' that the Kingdom remained at peace without God than at war with Him.' The *Politiques* included the former Chancellor, Michael L'Hôpital,[2] the Constable's son, François de Montmorency, and many others who resented the Guise influence at court. The projected marriage of Catherine's daughter, Margaret, to the young Huguenot prince, Henry of Navarre, represented the high hopes which the *Politiques* had of reconciling the conflicting parties. At the same time national feeling against Spain was

[1] J. E. Neale, *The Age of Catherine de' Medici* (1943), 72.
[2] He was an able and intelligent man who had been dismissed from office in 1568 and replaced by a tool of the Guises, the bitter anti-Protestant Morvilliers, Bishop of Orléans.

spurred on by proposals for an English alliance, for which purpose a Valois prince was despatched to woo the English queen. Momentarily all went well and a defensive alliance was signed between England and France at Blois in 1572. Within two years this house of cards had been thrown to the four winds by the passions arising out of the Massacre of St. Bartholomew.

The train of events explains why the policy of conciliation proved so disastrous. The *Politiques* and the Huguenots placed great hopes on war with Spain which, they believed, might unite the nation. It was the traditional policy of the Valois house and, as some would argue, in the obvious interests of France to prevent Spain from encompassing France on every side. Now that Spain was deeply involved in the Netherlands it was the obvious time to strike. But Catherine, as cautious a politician as Elizabeth, doubted the wisdom of the policy which Coligny and the Huguenots as well as Damville and the *Politiques* were pressing upon her. An expensive war would add to the crippling debts of the Crown and oblige her to send an army to help the Calvinist rebels in the Low Countries, a precedent which did not appeal to the Queen-Mother.

There was also a personal issue involved in the change of policy. She watched with patent maternal anxiety the growing influence which the Huguenot, Coligny, was exerting over the young King. This languid prince, whose delicate features stare out dully from Clouet's masterly portrait, had for once escaped from Catherine's possessive affection. Catherine was thus enraged on two points, the alienation of her son's affections by Coligny and the danger to France involved in a war with Spain which Coligny advocated. She decided to rid herself of the influential Huguenot. Her method of approach to the problem was as always Machiavellian. Thinking in terms of the factions that divided French politics she decided to make use of the Guise desire for vengeance on Coligny. If the young duke was willing he could avenge his father's murder, leaving Catherine above suspicion.

Paris in festive array was full of young Huguenot nobles gathered together for the marriage of their leader, Henry of Navarre to the princess, Margaret of Valois. Four days after the marriage (August 22nd, 1572) someone fired a shot at Coligny, wounding but not killing him. As everything pointed to the complicity of the Guises, the Huguenots demanded justice from the King, himself tearful and angry at the attack on his favourite. What should Catherine do ? To save herself from guilt and the possible loss of her son's affections she decided to steep France in blood. Persuading the King that the angry Huguenots were plotting to murder and dethrone him, she gained his consent for a general massacre of all the Huguenots at Paris. By eliminating the Huguenot leaders at one blow she might indeed hope to solve the religious problem, but this act of cauterisation was fundamentally an amateurish essay by a highly-strung woman who did not perceive the full consequences of her action.

At the sounding of the tocsin on the early morning of August 24th, St. Bartholomew's day, bands of armed men led by the Guises and other Roman Catholic nobles, started the grim work of killing the Huguenots; Coligny, still suffering from his wound, was speared by a pike, flung out of the window, cruelly mutilated and affixed by his heels to the gibbet at Montfaucon. The Huguenots living on the south side of the river Seine heard what was happening and fled, but of the others no one was allowed to escape, except Henry of Navarre and Condé both of whom were obliged to profess Catholicism. The lesson of Paris was repeated all over France.

The fruit of Catherine's action was as yet uncertain. In general Catholic powers greeted it with paeans of joy. Pope Gregory XIII ordered a *Te Deum* to be sung and a medal struck in honour of the event. Philip of Spain smiled grimly as he wrote to his mother-in-law that the massacre ' was indeed of such value and prudence and of such service, glory and honour to God and universal benefit to all Christendom that to hear of it was for me the best and most cheerful news which at present could come to me '. On the other hand the Emperor and some of the German Catholic princes disapproved. Naturally the Protestant countries were aghast both at the apparent treachery and obvious brutality, more especially as they supposed—wrongly—that Catherine had long planned the events of St. Bartholomew's Day.

What were the results on France itself? Momentarily Catherine might have appeared to have done a very clever thing, for she had rid herself of the leading Huguenots. Coligny's death removed the ablest as well as the most honest of the Huguenot nobility. Both Henry of Navarre and Condé were virtual prisoners of the court and obliged to attend Mass. The more timid of their followers returned to the Catholic faith, finding in the Mass the security for life and property which they wanted. But in the darkest moment Huguenot morale remained exceptionally high, especially among the rank and file. A renewal of the war was an obvious sequel to the massacre. The resistance of La Rochelle was a symbol of resurgent Huguenotism, fortified by new arguments to justify resistance to crowned authority. The notion of a contract between the King and people which is broken when the King acts

tyrannically makes its appearance in Huguenot writings. Finding
that she was once again faced with a broken kingdom, Catherine made
the best of a bad job and in July, 1573, concluded the fourth war by
the Peace of La Rochelle which provided for full liberty of conscience all over France and for liberty of worship in La Rochelle and
certain other towns.

But if Catherine thought that a return to a policy of appeasement would effectively solve the religious problem, she was reckon-
ing without her host. The difficulties of her position made it
unenviable. Henry of Navarre was not indeed far wrong when he
urged later: ' What could a woman have done, with her husband
dead and five small children upon her hands, and two families who
were scheming to seize the throne—our own and the Guises. I
am astonished that she did not do even worse.' The abandonment
of the policy represented by the *Politiques* had effected a junction
between the Huguenots, many of whom were still under arms
against the meagre concessions granted to them at La Rochelle,
and the powerful moderate party who put the well-being of France
above religious strife. Moreover, the *Politiques* had been strengthened by the adhesion of Catherine's youngest son, Alençon, the
playboy who had courted Elizabeth and befriended Coligny and
was drawn by his selfish ambitions to intrigues in the Netherlands
as well as in France. To prevent the situation from deteriorating
further, Catherine, who was never wanting in initiative, retained
Henry of Navarre and Condé in detention, sent the *Politique* leader,
François de Montmorency, to the Bastille and placed Alençon under
surveillance. This latter move was wise for it coincided with the
death of Charles IX. As some time must elapse before Henry III
could arrive from his distant kingdom of Poland,[1] Catherine had
made doubly sure of the regency by imprisoning Alençon.

Neither for the first nor last time Catherine had been too clever.
Within a few months she was faced with a dangerous situation.
Although he might at times appear enlightened and liberal, the new
King, surrounded by a troop of sophisticated young men whom
contemporaries dubbed ' princes of Sodom ' and followed by a
galaxy of lap-poodles, was even less likely than Charles IX to win
the loyalty of the mass of Frenchmen. Moreover his mother had
alienated both the Catholic Guises and the *Politique* Montmorency
as well as the Huguenot leaders all of whom managed to escape from

[1] He had been elected to the throne of Poland in June, 1573, but was so
desirous to leave that he fled by night from his kingdom, travelling by
the southern route in order to escape those who would otherwise have held
him.

court in 1575-76. Catherine had effectively divided France into two great factions and had left the Crown powerless to decide the issue without joining one or other of the sides. Such was the situation when Henry III returned to France.

The war was not of long duration. Through the organising ability of Damville, a practically independent republic had been established in Languedoc with a council of state and the other appendages of efficient government. The Crown could make no real headway against so well-organised an opposition, and the Peace of Monsieur, signed in 1576, was in effect an admission of the Crown's failure to subdue the rebels and a repudiation of the policy of St. Bartholomew's Day. The peace gave the Huguenots full religious liberty with guarantees that the terms would be carried out.

But too many hands had been washed in blood for the stain to be wiped out by one document. Neither Henry III nor his mother was satisfied with a treaty which so humiliated the monarchy, but where was the Crown to turn ? It was the essential weakness of the French monarchy in these years, made all the more obvious by the anarchic state of its finances, that it could never rely on itself. It was regularly forced into the hands of one or other of the parties ; even Catherine who loathed such a policy could not for long avoid it. The Guises and the extreme Catholic party, with Spanish backing, had now formed the Catholic League with the intention of reversing the terms of the Peace of Monsieur. By what might have been a skilful move the King averted this threat to his authority by placing himself at the head of the League. The war restarted, but the Huguenots, weakened by the defection of Damville and Alençon (or Anjou as he had now become), were willing to accept a modification of the generous terms given them by the previous treaty. Such was the Peace of Bergerac signed in September, 1577.

Although only one short obscure war broke out in the following eight years, there was little relaxation of tension. A demoralised and burdened people acquiesced in the breakdown of law and order, and in business stagnation. The outward gaiety and luxury of the King's court disguised a morass of bankruptcy, both in respect of finance and policy ; Catherine was as active as ever but age and gout were playing havoc with her intriguing spirit. The Guises, dominant in the state, were still dissatisfied with the freedom enjoyed by the Huguenots, while the latter resented the limits placed upon their religious liberty. Anjou, who had been invited to help the Dutch rebels against Philip of Spain, retired to France to die in 1584 after he had tried to sabotage the liberties which he had come to defend. His death proved as great an irritant to France as his life had been, for it made a Huguenot prince, Henry of Navarre, direct heir to the French throne.

The prospect of a heretical King was bound to cause trouble. In the interests of the monarchy Catherine urged Henry to become a Catholic but as yet he was unwilling to take so decisive a step. Meanwhile the Guises had come into closer contact with Philip of Spain who astutely agreed to help destroy Protestantism in France and to recognise the aged Cardinal Bourbon as the heir, in the hope that on Bourbon's death the crown might pass to himself or to his daughter, the Infanta Isabella. Moreover the Catholic League had now a big following throughout France; priests and regulars had whipped up the religious enthusiasm of the people. The unfortunate last of the Valois was so placed that he could only capitulate to this powerful weapon of the nobility and of the Church. By so doing he made the Crown a pawn of the Guises who were allied with France's natural enemy, Spain. In July, 1585, in accordance with the League's demands, he withdrew all religious concessions, condemned heresy and offered the Huguenots the alternative of conversion or exile. Henry of Navarre commented that one half of his moustache turned white when he heard the news.

Thus began the war known as the War of the Three Henries.[1] Its military history is relatively uninteresting but behind the scenes the Queen-Mother and her son tried once again to save the monarchy from its degrading subjection to the Guises. In May, 1588, the League ordered the popular Duke of Guise to Paris. In spite of Henry's disapproval, he entered the capital to the cheers of 30,000 Parisians. Powerless against the barricades of Paris, raised to isolate those who remained loyal to him, the King fled, only to swallow his pride and admit that the ' King of Paris ', Guise, was Lieutenant-General of the Kingdom and head of the Catholic League whose advice was now inseparable from the policy of the Crown.

Such a situation could not go on for ever. Catherine was ill in bed, not far from death. Whatever his vices the King was not unintelligent. He realised that the recent defeat of the Spanish Armada relieved the immediate threat from Spain, and, taking a leaf out of his mother's book, decided to rid himself of the Guises. Guise and his brother, the Cardinal, were ordered to attend a meeting of the Council at the Château of Blois on the early morning of December 23rd. As he was called to the King's presence the royal bodyguard murdered him in the ante-chamber. A day later the Cardinal met with a similar fate. But if Henry supposed that

[1] I.e. Henry III, Henry of Navarre and Henry, Duke of Guise.

he could drown his foes by blood he was mistaken. Paris lashed its monarch. ' Children ', says J. E. Neale, ' marched through the streets of Paris, led by their curés and others, all carrying torches, which, from time to time, they dashed to the ground, crying " So may God quench the race of Valois." ' [1]   Within a few months of his mother's death, the King had been forced to ally with the Huguenot leader, Henry of Navarre.   And then a Dominican friar, Jacques Clément, feeling that he was a divinely appointed agent, stabbed the King to death on August 1st, 1589, in the camp outside Paris, leaving France to face the fact that a heretic, Henry IV, was now its ' Most Christian King '.

The new King was placed in a difficult but not an impossible position.   The Catholic League, now led by Guise's brother, the Duke of Mayenne, was indeed still strong and was supported by Spanish arms, but paradoxically this was in some ways its greatest weakness, for even good Catholic Frenchmen had little love for the domineering Spaniard.   This feeling grew stronger after the death of the aged Cardinal Bourbon gave Philip an opportunity to put forward his own claims to the French throne.   Besides this, Henry had three other things to his credit.   In the first place he was immensely likeable.   Brought up in a tough school, he had no veneer or polish to hide his intrinsic honesty.   He was affectionate, perhaps over-affectionate if his immense number of love letters give any clue to his character, brave and capable.   He was a King such as France had not known since Louis XII and was never to know again.   His bearded, freckled, sun-burned countenance, homely manners and clothes contrasted favourably with the epicene Valois whom he had succeeded.   Then, secondly, he was a good general. Adversity had taught him military lessons which he applied with increasing success ; the victories of Arques and Ivry formed a prelude to a war in which he gained more and more support from nobles and populace alike.   Finally, Frenchmen had wearied of a war which interrupted both business and harvest.   The ordinary Frenchman was more and more convinced that only a French King, independent both of Spain and of noble factions, could restore stable government.   The country had been brought to its present pass because monarchical authority had fallen into disuse.   A King who could restore the prestige and power of the Crown would go far to win the loyalty of the French peasant and merchant.

There remained the one great impediment to success, Henry's religion.   Catholic France would never recognise a Huguenot King.   Henry himself was a religious man in a conventional way

[1] J. E. Neale, *The Age of Catherine de' Medici*, 99.

but, like so many sixteenth-century monarchs, political convenience came to count more with him than religious belief. Yet he would not desert those who had died and suffered on his behalf. His previous conversion to Catholicism had taken place under duress. He would only accept the faith again when his position was strong enough to defend his followers. It was not, therefore, until 1593 that he bewildered his adversaries by returning to the Catholic faith. On July 25th, 1593, the Archbishop of Bourges absolved him from past error and he heard Mass at the Abbey of St. Denis. The way was now open for the papal absolution, his coronation— and final victory.

But this was not the end of the religious wars, though very nearly so. Paris accepted its King while the Spaniards were pushed back in the north. Genuine loyalty or self-interest, accompanied by bribes, led to an increasing number of desertions to Henry's side. On September 25th, 1597, Amiens, the last great stronghold remaining to the enemy, surrendered. ' When ', Henry had said, ' I have recovered Amiens, Calais and Ardres, I shall be prepared to speak of peace.' Exhausted, disappointed and ailing, Philip II agreed to negotiate ; the Peace of Vervins signed on May 2nd, 1598, was a virtual recapitulation of that of Cateau-Cambrésis concluded nearly forty years earlier. At the beginning of 1598 only one major district of France had remained against Henry, Brittany where the Duke of Mercoeur and remnants of the army of the Catholic League reinforced by 5000 Spaniards still held out against him. But the King was more interested in reconciliation than in vengeance and was willing to pay Mercoeur some four million livres for his loyalty and to grant an amnesty to his troops. With the conclusion of this treaty at Ponts de Cé on March 20th, 1598, the religious wars were very nearly ended.

It was appropriate that Henry should issue from Nantes, which Mercoeur had held to the end, the edict which provided for the future of the Huguenot religion. There had already been grumblings among the King's Huguenot supporters at the way in which their interests had been neglected. But the edict which was more a treaty between two equal powers than a royal decree went far to satisfy them. They were granted complete liberty of conscience and freedom to worship wherever such worship was now in existence and at two places in every *bailliage* or *sénéchaussée*. They received support for their colleges and schools as well as full civil rights and protection ; they were afforded special chambers known as *Chambres de l'Édit* in the local Parlements for the trial of all cases touching their interests. Nor was this all. The Huguenots had often been placed in a perilous position in the past by the Crown's failure to implement its agreements, and they were determined that such a situation should not recur again. With the King's consent they could now hold religious synods and the political assemblies which could form a basis for organisation and the formulation of policy. Finally they were allowed to hold for a stated period, extended in 1612, a number of fortified towns, including strongholds of strategic importance such as La Rochelle, Montauban and Montpellier. In this way Henry was able to reconcile his former co-religionists to his rule without alienating his fellow-Catholics.

3. *The effects of the Religious Wars*

The religious wars vitally affected the future development of the French monarchy. The Crown had been shackled with a debt from which all the fiscal devices of Sully and Colbert could never effectually free it; the house of Bourbon in the person of Henry IV started off with a handicap which became more and more pronounced as each successive monarch plunged into war after war. This does not mean that the financial instability of the French monarchy in the seventeenth and eighteenth centuries was only or wholly caused by the Wars of Religion, but it does indicate the disadvantageous financial position in which the Crown was placed at the beginning of the seventeenth century.

Town and countryside had both suffered from the economic stagnation which the wars had helped to create. It is true that the actual distress caused by the comparatively small armies engaged in fighting was localised to certain districts, but the dislocation of communications, the insecurity of credit and the general lawlessness helped to diminish the amount of business and commerce.[1] The wars also accentuated directly and indirectly the misery of the peasant's life. A new seigneurial class arose in some districts, in part replacing those who had been killed in battle or who had been forced to sell their estates, keener on maintaining feudal obligations and, to an increasing extent, divorced from land-holding. The peasants continued to pay the greater part of the French taxes

---

[1] An event which illustrates this occurred in 1562 when the Huguenots led by Condé threw the paper mills at Essonnes, near Paris, into the river on the pretext that the workmen were controlled by the Catholic rector of the Sorbonne. The collapse of the French salt trade to the Baltic in the latter half of the century, following the Huguenot seizure of the Biscayan salt, also illustrates the economic dislocation caused by war. By contrast the cloth trade of the near-by province of Poitou grew in the same period, as did the trade of ports as far apart as Marseilles and Le Havre.

from which the privileged classes were exempt and which had been partly imposed to meet the expenses of the Crown arising out of the wars. Until Turgot was appointed in 1774 no minister contemplated any effective remedy to these serious economic problems.

Nor had the Edict of Nantes closed the Huguenot question. The edict was not a permanent solution for while it restricted the Huguenots' religious freedom, it gave them political rights which enabled them to defy the authority of the Crown with impunity. No minister could for long endure this permanent threat to the peace of the realm. Thus the uneasy calm which continued while Henry was alive ended during the regency of Marie de' Medici. Richelieu, frightened by the prospect of a renewal of civil strife, decided to deal with the problem once and for all, by taking away the Huguenots' political privileges while confirming their religious liberty. Less than sixty years later Louis XIV revoked the Edict of Nantes, thus divesting the Huguenots of their remaining privileges. The edict represented the continuing influence of two factors, the fear lest a powerful minority party might challenge the royal power, and the religious intolerance of the French Catholics. Even on the eve of the French Revolution, the French clergy were deploring Turgot's advocacy of toleration and urging Louis XVI to stamp out heresy as his ancestors had done.

Finally the religious wars had vindicated the necessity for a strong monarch. The futility and weakness of the last Valois Kings had forced France into the hands of faction, represented by the great noble houses. A strong and popular King had now emerged victorious. The Crown now had an opportunity to re-assert its authority over all its possible challengers, more especially over the nobility, an opportunity which Henry IV, Cardinal Richelieu and Louis XIV were not slow to grasp. And that the end of the wars placed the French monarchy in a position to make itself an absolute power was probably the most significant result of all.

CHAPTER XVI

THE RECONSTRUCTION OF FRANCE, 1598-1660

1. *Introduction*

By the end of the seventeenth century France had become the greatest power in Europe. Quite apart from the successful wars in which Louis XIV had involved his country, France was the arbiter of taste, the centre and even the exemplar of contemporary civilised behaviour. Its resources had been strained by continuous warfare, and the mass of the French labourers had a penurious existence; but these fundamental weaknesses cannot conceal what had been achieved. Indeed in 1661 an Italian visitor to France could state: 'To establish the grandeur of the French monarchy Heaven itself has given the nation almost miraculous gifts . . . fertile land . . . excellently situated upon two oceans, watered by many navigable rivers . . . well populated . . . rich in wealth and in soldiers.' A first-class army and an efficient navy had been created. The middle class continued to grow daily in wealth and power and resented noble privilege increasingly. A colonial empire, the richest part of which lay in the sugar-producing islands of the West Indies, was in process of foundation. France was an absolute monarchy, the tentacles of which gripped all branches of administration, but the central government had not yet been so overloaded with business that it could not differentiate what was of primary from what was of secondary importance. By comparison with other European countries France was the strongest, the richest and most civilised, and to some extent one of the best-governed, of all European countries.

This picture appears the more remarkable if it is contrasted with a corresponding description of the state of France at the accession of Henry IV in 1589. The nightmare of the religious wars had led to the complete debilitation of French finances and indeed of French economy generally; civil strife formed, as it always does, an ideal setting for industrial decay and administrative inefficiency. Ravaging bands had brought about a decline in the amount of cultivable land, leading to a drop in food production, all the more serious because parts of France were liable to be affected by famine if the communications were interrupted. The prestige of the monarchy which had grown in the period following the conclusion of the Hundred Years' War had been damaged, though to a less extent than is sometimes supposed, during the reigns of the last monarchs of the house of Valois.

The King had therefore to impose his authority on an arrogant nobility which had taken advantage of disorder to usurp power. Technically subordinate to the Crown, it had been able to challenge the King himself. The nobles held all the greatest offices in the royal household and in the government of the provinces, Condé in Berry, Vendôme in Brittany, Longueville in Normandy, Luynes in Picardy, Nevers in Champagne, Chevreuse in Auvergne, Soissons in Dauphiné, Guise in Provence and Montmorency in Languedoc all had considerable influence. The nobles were largely untaxed, drew seignorial dues from their tenants, held the chief offices in the royal council, influenced the States-General and dominated the Assembly of Notables. Their faction fights and constant duels disturbed France which they robbed without serving.

Clearly this aristocratic conception of government had to be modified if it was to be adapted to the needs of the new monarchy. The English Tudors and the Spanish Hapsburgs had to some extent drawn the teeth of feudalism by reducing the nobles' power and by placing great reliance on the royal council in which men of middle-class origin had come to play a leading part. If Louis XI and his immediate successors had done something along the same lines the religious wars had prevented any further development. It remained to Henry IV and to the two cardinals, Richelieu and Mazarin, to chain the nobility to the monarchy as well as to make as docile as possible the other *corps intermédiaires* which had challenged monarchical authority in the past.

In the main the rehabilitation of the monarchy forms the theme of French history in the first half of the seventeenth century. The theoretical build-up was provided by writers who were willing to use every casuistical argument to justify the Divine Right of Kings. What Henry IV began, Richelieu and Mazarin completed. Noble opposition flared up again in the Fronde but it was the last significant flicker until the eve of the Revolution. Tamed, the nobles shone at Louis XIV's palace of Versailles as the brightest jewels in the King's crown.

The religious problem was closely intertwined with all this, partly because the factious nobles had used religion as a cloak for their ambitions, and partly because religious heterodoxy represented a challenge to the royal authority. By asserting their privileges, the Huguenots implicitly criticised the absolute power of the Crown in the Church as in the State. Every intelligent man must have

realised that the provisions of the Edict of Nantes could not last for
ever. Richelieu eliminated the more obvious political danger
represented by the Huguenots, but it was left to Louis XIV to
place the corner stone on the edifice of absolute monarchy by
revoking the Edict of Nantes and by expelling some of the more
industrious and loyal of his subjects in the interests of political and
religious uniformity.

Finally by the end of the sixteenth century the French monarchy
lacked the most essential of all requisites, reserves of power. According to contemporary economic ideas such power fundamentally
consisted of actual bullion, represented by an excess of imports
over exports. The more intelligent French ministers understood
that a flourishing economy, healthy agriculture, regulated industry
and good communications formed the natural foundation of a
strong country. For only a wealthy country could fight a successful
war and overcome, as every French monarch from the beginning
of the sixteenth century wished, the pretensions of the Hapsburgs
of Madrid and Vienna to supremacy in Europe.

2. *Henry IV of France*

Henry IV was the most popular of the French Kings, partly
because of what he was as a man and partly because of what he did
for the kingdom. His Béarnais upbringing had saved him from
the adulation and social isolation which hedged most contemporary
monarchs from their cradles; his virtues as a courageous soldier
and faithful friend as well as his vices as a self-indulgent lover
attracted the loyal affection of his people. But he was a genuine
patriot. Even his acceptance of Catholicism represented his conviction that this drastic step alone could save the country from re-
curring foreign invasion and civil war. He intended to use the
resurrected authority of the Crown to restore order, and to give
prosperity to France. Not only through his long apprenticeship
but also as a King he knew Frenchmen in a way that no other Bourbon
monarch ever approached. Madame de Stael's comment that
Henry was ' the most French King that France ever had ' was both
just and wise.

The conclusion of the Treaty of Vervins and the publication of
the Edict of Nantes solved two fundamental problems, if only for
a period, but left several others untouched. If peace had at last
been signed with Spain, and if the Huguenots had been granted the
privileges which they had long sought, Henry still to undertake
the work of reconstruction in a country long rent by war and dis-

order.   Circumstances at first forced him to conciliate and even to
bribe the nobles, but this was conditional on their loyalty.   If
they dared to raise the standard of revolt, Henry crushed them with
appropriate harshness.   In governing France he relied largely on
royal councils, and in particular upon his Huguenot friend,
Maximilien de Béthune, Duke of Sully.   He did not consult the
States-General and the Assembly of Notables was only called once,
at Rouen in 1596.   The absolute character of his rule may have
been less obvious than that of Richelieu and Louis XIV, but the
principles upon which it was based were much the same.   When
noble faction reared itself, as it did in the case of an ambitious noble,
Biron, Governor of Burgundy and Marshal of France, Henry struck
decisively : in spite of his influential position Biron was executed in
July, 1602.

How far the restoration of France's economy was the work of
Henry and how far the work of Sully cannot now be determined.
In his *Memoirs*, written during his thirty years' retirement, Sully
was not unwilling to overestimate the part he had played in con-
temporary history.   He was in many ways a fit foil to Henry.
Although younger than his master, he lacked his engaging qualities ;
he was humourless and austere where Henry was gallant and gay.
Although he had not been averse to enriching himself during the
Wars of Religion, he proved a singularly honest Superintendent of
Finances in a corrupt age, and his shrewd judgment was exactly
what France wanted.   Thus Sully and Henry proved an excellent
partnership, though the responsibility for what industrial advance
there was rests with the King rather than with the minister.

Sully realised that poverty was the main weakness of the Crown
and so made an increase in the royal revenue the chief object of his
administration.   But he made no attempt to revolutionise the
burdensome French fiscal system.   To have done so would have
brought him at once into conflict with the nobles and other authorities exempt from the chief taxes.   He was satisfied with removing
some of the worst abuses and with making the existing system work
more effectively.   This was no mean achievement, as the French
finances had practically broken down during the last half-century ;
many of the tax-collectors had been so corrupt that only a proportion
of the taxes raised reached the royal exchequer.   Although Sully
did not abolish the system of tax-farming, he tried to make the
actual collection of taxes more honest and more effective.   He instituted a system of book-keeping which, primitive as it appears by
comparison with modern methods, at least gave him some idea of
what money he had at his disposal.   He was indeed one of the very

few financial ministers of the *Ancien Régime* who had any understanding of the incredibly complex system of French finance. He was able to prevent the squandering of royal money on the relatives of favourite mistresses and importunate courtiers, while he enriched the Crown by ensuring the return of some of the property and fiscal rights which had been alienated by it in its years of weakness and turmoil.

But apart from this he did little directly to increase the revenue. The clergy were once more obliged to grant the *don gratuit* which had fallen into abeyance. The increase in the unpopular salt tax or *gabelle* brought in more money at the cost of greater suffering to the peasants on whom its incidence mainly fell. Sully continued to make use of the sale of offices, and the one new tax which he imposed revealed his innate fiscal conservatism. This was the *paulette*,[1] a payment which secured the transmission of judicial and administrative offices from father to son.

The general success of his policy was unquestionable. The country, which had been practically bankrupt in 1598, was in a position to enter a major war in 1610. In round figures, trivial as they may appear to the citizen of a modern state, Sully's accomplishments were considerable. He had even been able to reduce the *taille* on three occasions in spite of the fact that his economic policy as a whole required some capital expenditure. But ultimately the financial rehabilitation of France could only have occurred as a result of the restoration of order and the general expansion of trade.

Trade depended on the encouragement given to improved communications, and to the development of agriculture and industry. As Grand Voyer or Director of Communications, Sully did much to repair and build new roads, to provide a better system of posts and to begin the building of the canals joining the Seine to the Loire and the Loire to the Saône. But on the whole Sully was far less willing than his master to spend money on capital projects for which he could not foresee a fairly immediate visible return. He believed as did the King that agriculture was the foundation of the country's wealth and, within certain limits, he was willing to do everything possible to encourage it. Thus he ordered the nobles to avoid trampling over ripening cornfields and through vineyards

---

[1] Recent research indicates that the *paulette* was more important in giving security of tenure than in establishing hereditary right. (R. Mousnier, *La Venalité des Offices sous Henri IV et Louis XIII*). So-named after Charles Paulet to whom it was farmed out when it was first instituted in 1604.

when they were out hunting, and he encouraged farmers to use new crops and to reclaim the soil by drainage. But it was the King who patronised the two Huguenots, Olivier de Serres and Barthélemy Laffemas, who wanted to build up a French silk industry in central and southern France by planting mulberry trees. These achievements must not be over-emphasised. De Serres' textbook *Théâtre d'agriculture et mesnage de champs* (1600) in the main fell on stony soil. The King required the co-operation of the nobility, but France always lacked the agrarian-conscious nobles who did so much for English agriculture in the seventeenth and eighteenth centuries. The French nobles remained much keener on their hunting rights and the collection of their seigneurial dues than on scientific farming. However much Henry may have desired to improve the peasants' lot, he could accomplish little without changing the French social system. Even the schemes for cultivating silk imposed a new burden on the peasants since they had to bear the increased cost of the *taille* with which this venture was financed.

Henry's plans for encouraging industry proved less fruitful, for Sully, who regarded the cultivation of silk as an unnecessary luxury, looked even more askance at the Council's plans for stimulating other luxury industries, as carpets and tapestries, glassware and gold thread. Rich brocades offended his Puritan spirit as well as his economic sensibility. Nor in practice was the encouragement given to these nascent industries exactly what was wanted. There was too much emphasis on regulation and restriction, as is well illustrated by the series of rules drafted by Laffemas for the Chamber of Commerce in 1601, and far too little encouragement was given to enterprise and initiative.

Yet it is clear that whatever the underlying defects of French economy, Henry had given his kingdom a much-needed measure of order and prosperity, even if such prosperity was incidental to the fulfilment of his foreign policy. In his *Memoirs* Sully attributed to Henry a scheme which he called *Le Grand Dessein*. This involved the formation of alliances with foreign powers with the object of crushing the Hapsburg supremacy in Europe, and safeguarding the future of world peace through the creation of a series of councils. Six of these were to have dealt with local and national affairs, while the seventh, representing all the allies, was to discuss major questions of European policy and administration. It was to possess an armed force to see that its decisions, which incidentally included European disarmament, were obeyed. Whatever its authorship, this wise and eirenic scheme proved the forebear of many other designs for perpetual peace none of which has yet borne fruit. Indeed it bears the hall-mark of Sully's patient mind rather than the military practicality of Henry IV.

Henry was mainly concerned with the first of the objects attributed to him in the *Grand Dessein*, the formation of an anti-Hapsburg coalition of powers which would end that family's domination of central Europe and the Spanish peninsula, and so free France from the ever-present threat of encirclement. His reign was free from major wars but its minor incidents formed a prelude to the outbreak of the Thirty Years' War. There was, for instance, the all-important question of Hapsburg communications in Italy, involved in the relations between France and the Duke of Savoy. A pro-Hapsburg duke might permit the Spanish troops to pass through his duchy, thus enhancing the possible success of a direct Spanish attack on France. As the Duke, Charles Emmanuel had failed to carry out the terms of a recent treaty with France, French troops occupied the old Savoyard capital, Chambéry, with the result that the French gained Bresse,[1] Bugey and Gex, thus strengthening France's south-eastern frontier. This, however, still left Savoy a small slice of territory through which the Spaniards could, if necessary, pass *en route* for Franche Comté, then in their possession.

There was another potential danger to France, arising out of Spanish control over the Alpine passes, providing the Spaniards with another entry into the Franche Comté. One Alpine valley, the Valtelline, linking the Milanese in Spanish possession with the Protestant Grisons, formed a fruitful storm centre of European diplomacy ·for the next few decades. Henry manoeuvred for position without taking drastic action. Thus treaties of friendship signed with Venice, Florence and Savoy were intended to counteract Spanish power in Italy while another treaty with the Dutch proved a foil to the Spanish Netherlands.

But Henry's eyes were mainly fixed on events in Germany where there was gradually rising tension between the Catholic and Imperialist princes and the Protestant authorities. The German Protestant princes who had formed a defensive league looked to Henry IV to afford them support and protection, nor was the King unwilling to interfere. By 1609 a pretty problem had arisen which looked as if it might give rise to a major war.[2] The Duke of the small but strategically-important west German state of Cleves-Jülich had died without direct heirs, leaving two claimants to his

---

[1] A most important gastronomic region; Brillat Savarin was born, appropriately, at Belley. See map on p. 164.

[2] See pp. 310-11.

estates, the Elector of Brandenburg and the Count of Neuburg. Before either could get possession of the duchies, the Emperor sent Imperial troops to occupy the disputed lands on the grounds that he was entitled to judge between the claimants. This gave Henry his opportunity. He made a formal alliance with the Evangelical Union at Schwabisch on February 11th, 1610, and prepared for war against the Imperialists.[1] But fate intervened in the person of a fanatical Catholic schoolmaster, François Ravaillac. The schoolmaster's narrow mind was perturbed by the possibility of a Catholic sovereign fighting side by side with the heretical Protestants, and as Henry's coach, coming from the Louvre to visit Sully at the Arsenal, was halted by a straw cart in the Rue de la Ferronière, the fanatic stabbed the King. Thus ignobly and undeservedly perished Henry of Navarre, for all his faults one of the noblest Kings of France and the best of the Bourbon line.

3. *The rise of Richelieu*

It is possible to be in two minds about Cardinal de Richelieu, to be repelled by his authoritarian ruthlessness or to be fascinated by his sheer ability. But whatever the point of view of the individual historian, none can deny that Richelieu contributed more than any other Frenchman to the creation of a strong monarchy in the seventeenth century.

The work already accomplished by Henry IV and Sully provided Richelieu with a foundation on which to build, but Henry's murder was followed by a chaotic period in which much that he had accomplished vanished. As his successor Louis XIII was only a child of nine, power remained in the hands of Henry's widow, his second wife, the Italian princess, Marie de' Medici, advised by a small inner council. The Regent was a singularly foolish woman who, as Rubens' voluptuous portraits suggest, deserved the scathing comments passed recently upon her by Aldous Huxley.[2] She loved power but was completely unfitted to use it. She was the prey of her Italian foster-sister, Leonora Galigai, and of her

---

[1] There is a view that Henry's intervention arose as a result of one of his many love affairs. Charlotte de Montmorency, with her husband Condé, fled to Brussels, where they sought the protection of the Archduke Albert, to escape the King's advances—and that this made Henry eager to open hostilities against the Hapsburgs.

[2] 'The portraits of Marie de' Medici reveal a large, fleshy, gorgeously bedizened barmaid; and the records of her administration prove her to have been even stupider, if that were possible, than she looked . . .' (Aldous Huxley, *Grey Eminence*, 97).

adventurer-husband, Concino Concini who soon cloaked his singularly euphonious names under the titles of Marshal of France and Marquis d'Ancre. The financial reserves that Sully had built up were soon dissipated, while Henry's friends were horrified by the growing influence which the Spanish ambassadors seemed to wield over the moulding of foreign policy. The Queen-Mother reckoned that friendship with the Hapsburgs served French interests better than enmity and war, and arranged a double marriage to cement the new-found amity, while the Cleves-Jülich problem was relegated to the background. The Huguenots, who could not easily forget the help which Spain had given their adversaries in the Wars of Religion, were equally if not more horrified by the trust which Marie appeared to give to the papal nuncio and the Jesuits. Furthermore the removal of a strong King provided the nobles with an opportunity to regain their ancient rights and take once more the prominent but disturbing position that they had once held in French political life.

There were soon signs of imminent disorder. The leading nobles presented a virtual ultimatum to the Regent which Concini tried to meet by inviting them to share in the spoils of the court. The surrender only postponed a serious crisis. Another clique of nobles headed by the King's cousin, Henry of Bourbon, Prince of Condé, forced the Regent to summon the long-quiescent States-General in 1614. Either as a salve for France's wounds or as a spur to the fulfilment of noble ambitions, the meeting proved equally futile. It was chiefly important for the jealousy between the orders which prevented the nobles from gaining their objects, and for Richelieu's debût and brilliant valedictory speech. One other noble rising, in which the Huguenots were implicated, was brought to a close by bribes in 1616.

It was at this opportune moment in French history that Armand Jean du Plessis de Richelieu, Bishop of Luçon, made his appearance. In 1615 he was thirty years old, the third son of a minor French noble and a lawyer's daughter. It was originally intended that he should enter the army but his brother's decision to become a monk led to a change of career. The Richelieu family had a lien on the bishopric of Luçon, which had been earmarked for Armand's elder brother. Richelieu was persuaded to change the profession of soldier for the habit of a priest at the rather unpropitious age of seventeen in order that he might eventually take his place at Luçon. He would have been a good soldier and in a sense the military character remained with him, but he bowed to his mother's decision, writing ' God's will be done. I will accept all for the good of the

Church and the glory of our house.' He was ordained and in due course became Bishop of Luçon.

How sincere was Richelieu ? Like Strafford and Laud, all that he undertook deserves the epithet ' thorough '. He proved a good bishop in a poor and neglected see. He bought new vestments for the cathedral which he had repaired, visited his parishes, compiled a catechism and interested himself in the conversion of the Huguenots. He was assiduous in his attendance at Mass and patronised the reforms carried out in the French Church by men of very different stamp to himself such as Cardinal Bérulle and St. Vincent de Paul. Even at the height of his power, he was not merely a secular states-man clothed in sussurrating cardinalatial purple. Yet he was ruthless, unbending and Machiavellian. How was he able to recon-cile Christian principle with the ' reason of state ' which governed all his public actions ?

While nothing can satisfactorily explain this underlying dicho-tomy, yet his friendship with Father Joseph may indicate a possible solution. The Capuchin, whom contemporaries were to dub ' l'éminence grise ', was one of the most actively religious men of his day. He was the spiritual adviser to the order of nuns which he had founded ; he was a mystic living a disciplined life of incredible austerity. And yet he became the principal agent of Richelieu's amoral statecraft. For he had become convinced that just as Hapsburg ambitions formed a negation of God's will, so the for-warding of French power might become the vehicle of divine justice. There is no reason to doubt that this may well have been Richelieu's attitude, but it is equally unquestionable that the Christian bishop was often submerged in the militant statesman and the ruthless if able opportunist.

Richelieu was an ambitious young man. The constant ill-health from which he suffered could not break his iron will and may incidentally account for the uncertainty of his temper. His attacks of migraine were sometimes so severe that on occasions he would shut himself up in his room and neigh like a horse. The States-General of 1614 gave him his chance, as the first Estate, representing the clergy, chose him to compose the address to the throne. This brought him to the attention of Marie de' Medici who gave him a place on the Council of State as Minister for Foreign Affairs. But 1616 was not a propitious year. The ill-feeling against the Regent's corrupt and feeble rule mounted to a climax. The King, a neurotic and sulky youth of sixteen, was persuaded by his favourite the Duke of Luynes who had originally attracted his attention by his skill as a falconer and huntsman, to approve the arrest and death of Concini.

When he heard that this had been accomplished he stated with unwonted passion from the top of a billiard-table ' I am King now '.

But the seven years which followed the seven lean years of the Regency were far from being full and fat. Louis XIII was a curiously complex character. He was never a mere cipher, and where military topics were at issue he often took an intelligent and original line of his own. But he was more interested in hunting than in any other activity. In his relationship with his intimates he remained strangely impersonal. He had a limited love for his mother, Marie, but little affection for his wife, Anne of Austria ; his friendship with young men and women seem to have been entirely platonic and pure. He grew to esteem and to admire Richelieu. It is difficult to estimate his significance, but it is probably true to say that he had little capacity for continuous work. Nor were the men to whom he entrusted office in the seven years between 1617 and 1624 much more fitted to rule than Louis himself ; the problems which confronted the Regency remained to face Luynes who died in 1621, Sillery and La Vieuville.

The fall of the Queen-Mother had been disconcerting for Richelieu and potentially dangerous, but he had played his cards carefully. More and more use was made of his services, despite Luynes' open dislike ; he was used as an intermediary to bring about a reconciliation between the King and his mother. But he saw that Marie was a falling star and linked his fortunes with those of the Crown. In April 1624, he was given a seat in the Council and eleven days after Vieuville's fall, August 24th, 1624, he became the real head of the French government, a position which he was to hold until his death in 1642.

4. *The rule of the Cardinal*

The Cardinal set himself four tasks, to check the power of the nobility, to destroy the political privileges of the Huguenots, to exalt the authority of the King, and to make France respected abroad. The next eighteen years show how faithfully Richelieu pursued his objects. Nor was the task which he had set himself easy to carry out. If, for the purposes of writing history, what he did appears to fall into neat, carefully sealed divisions, it is all the more necessary to remember that throughout his ministry he was forced to turn his attention to a new or recurrent problem before he had completed dealing with any one question. Except during the historic Day of Dupes in 1630, he had the King's confidence, but Louis was not physically strong and until 1638 he was childless. This fact indicates Richelieu's astonishing courage. His power depended entirely on the King's life and on the King's will. At court he was faced by enemies, by the stupid, intriguing Queen-Mother, by Louis' temperamental and jealous wife, Anne of Austria, and by the heir-presumptive to the throne, Louis' brother, the fickle, scheming, cowardly Gaston, Duke of Orléans. He was a menace from whom Richelieu was never completely free; too near the throne to be sent the way of the nobles whose plans he betrayed to serve his own interests, this unpleasing specimen of the Bourbon line flits through Richelieu's life like some vicious insect. Behind Gaston there were many leading nobles who engaged continuously in schemes to rid France of their hated enemy, while the Huguenots, frightened by the possible loss of their privileges, never relaxed their intrigues against the Cardinal until La Rochelle had fallen.

A great minister needs to be well-served. Richelieu in general inspired fear rather than affection, and only one man can be properly called his close friend, the singular Capuchin Father Joseph. Born François Leclerc du Tremblay, he had become a friar at the age of twenty-two after reading *The Rule of Perfection* written by the English mystic, Father Benet of Canfield. The would-be saint and practising mystic paradoxically emerged in history as the friend and political adviser of Richelieu; while never deserting his spartan mode of life he became the minister's principal diplomatic agent and political confidante. Jogging along in the coach which under dispensation he had reluctantly agreed to use, saying his Breviary and imagining the Sacrifice of Christ, he was likely to be *en route* for some conference where he would represent the Cardinal's materialistic and amoral policy. For him, as probably for Richelieu, the will of God had become identified with the interests of the state.

Richelieu himself never had the remotest doubt that reasons of state afforded the best justification for every political action. Politics rather than religion made him a determined opponent of the Huguenots; 'So long', he wrote, ' as they have a foothold in France, the King will not be master in his own house and will be unable to undertake any great enterprise abroad.' The Huguenots were themselves alarmed by the appointment of the Cardinal as first minister as well as by the growing strength of Catholic missionary activity, but their first revolt was singularly ill-timed. For Richelieu, acting in alliance with Venice and Savoy, had just expelled the papal garrisons from the Valtelline with the intention of restoring this strategically situated valley to the control of the Protestant Grisons. By revolting, the Huguenots not only sank most of Richelieu's new fleet at Blavet but forced him to withdraw French troops from the

Valtelline and so freed the Spaniards to send reinforcements to Germany and Holland. The Huguenots had placed the Cardinal in a precarious position. Although he managed to extricate himself with some skill, the episode impressed upon him the dangers which the political and military force of the Huguenots represented.

A short breathing space followed the conclusion of the Treaty of La Rochelle in 1626 until war broke out between France and England the next year. This gave Richelieu the chance he wanted for dealing with the Huguenot problem once and for all. The egregious Duke of Buckingham who had once intended to help Richelieu against the Huguenots now decided to assist them against the Cardinal. Knowing that they could expect no mercy from the Cardinal and hoping against hope that the English fleet might yet succour them, the people of La Rochelle prepared for a long siege, but even heroism has its limits, and after fourteen months of acute suffering the fortress-town surrendered to its conqueror. Shortly afterwards Condé brought the southern rebels to heel.

In dealing with the future of the Huguenots Richelieu showed his exceptional statesmanship. The Rochellois had been severely punished; their privileges and their fortifications had been abolished, and their churches had been handed back to the Catholics. The Huguenots as a whole might have expected similar treatment. To their surprise Richelieu concerned himself only with depriving them of their political privileges; they were allowed to continue to worship freely. The Cardinal was in effect much more concerned with their potential danger to the royal government, represented by their own fortresses and law-courts, than with the threat to orthodoxy implied by their heretical doctrines. Time proved how expediently he had acted. If he never earned their gratitude, his successor, Mazarin, found them during the Fronde among the most loyal, as well as industrious, of the King's subjects. Naturally the Catholic victory encouraged the Catholic extremists, some of whom were disagreeably surprised by the Cardinal's tolerance, to found schools and missions in Huguenot districts, thus paving the way for the revocation of the Edict of Nantes in 1685. But for the time being Richelieu had solved one of the problems which had tended to weaken the Crown abroad as well as at home.

The end of opposition from the Huguenots may have helped to check the power of the nobility, some of whom had been prominent in the Huguenot ranks, but throughout his ministry Richelieu was never free from the peril of the over-mighty subject. The trend of his policy was revealed by the edict of 1626 ordering the destruction of all fortresses not necessary for defence against the country's natural enemies. The nobility's reaction was swift, if, as in most noble plots, also confused and amateurish. The conspiracy was headed by Gaston, angry at being forced into a marriage with Mademoiselle de Montpensier whom he disliked, helped by the Queen's friend, Madame de Chevreuse, the King's half-brothers and a number of lesser nobles. Richelieu got wind of the plot. Gaston confessed all and on August 5th, 1626, 'was solemnly joined in wedlock to the lady he had vehemently rejected by the Cardinal whom he had planned to murder: a curious sacrament'.[1] The lesser breed alone suffered the full penalty of the law; Chalais, whose loquacity had originally revealed the plot, was executed.

Richelieu's answer and warning was another edict, prohibiting duelling under pain of death. The duel, a profound social nuisance, had been forbidden before but the nobles had never paid attention to former royal decrees. They were therefore the more horrified when Montmorency-Bouteville, a young scion of one of the oldest families in France and a great exponent of sword-play[2] who had had the temerity to fight a duel under Richelieu's window in the Palace Royale, was arrested and sentenced to death. 'It may be said with truth', Richelieu told his master, 'that His Majesty and his council will have to answer for all the souls which may be lost in future by this devilish fashion if they pardon a convicted duellist.'

The nobles glowered but were not curbed. They knew that they had many friends at court and that if the minister lost the King's favour he would be ruined. For a few hours on November 30th, 1630, it seemed as if their hopes were justified. The Queen and the Queen-Mother working in an unusual alliance thought that they had persuaded Louis to dismiss the Cardinal; Richelieu also believed that this was so. He meant to leave Court when Louis sent him a note requiring his presence at Versailles where he had a hunting-lodge. He went to the King, knelt before him and in silence the King raised him. For Louis knew in his heart of hearts that his royal authority depended on the Cardinal's will. 'I shall have no greater happiness in the world', he wrote to the King that evening, 'than in making known to Your Majesty by ever-increasing proofs that I am the most devoted subject and the most zealous servant that ever king or master had in this world.' Within a year Marie de' Medici was in exile while Gaston pursued his campaign of vilification from the safety of Lorraine. Again it was the less guilty Maréchal de Marillac who was sentenced to death on an unjust charge in a trial of doubtful legality.

[1] C. V. Wedgwood, *Richelieu and the French Monarchy*, 59.
[2] He had already killed twenty-two men in duels.

Only death would end Gaston's intrigues. He had conveniently drawn the Duke of Lorraine into his web by marrying his daughter, and he had persuaded yet another great noble, Henri de Montmorency, the Governor of Languedoc, to lead an armed rebellion against the Cardinal. Why these nobles allowed themselves to serve the purpose of this high-born mischief-maker on whose words they could not place the least reliance is a mystery. Personally courageous, Montmorency went to the scaffold as yet another reminder of the futility of feudal intrigue. Even if Gaston did not yet give up hope, the failure of Montmorency's rebellion gave the Cardinal a breathing-space. Apart from the fact that his own measures for counteracting noble power were beginning to take effect, many nobles soon found employment in the French armies fighting against Spain from 1635.

But Richelieu had to face one more conspiracy, in some ways the most dangerous of them all. Its initiator, naturally patronised by Gaston, no longer heir to the French throne since the birth of the Dauphin in 1638, was a young and inexperienced favourite of the King, Henri d'Effiat, Marquis de Cinq Mars. He believed that it would be possible to overthrow the Cardinal and to persuade Louis to appoint him to his place. Ironically Richelieu, knowing the King's liking for young men, had himself been instrumental in introducing Cinq Mars to Louis. The King, genuinely infatuated, had showered favours and honours on this rather unpleasant aristocratic puppy. Now, driven by ambition, he began to weave a great intrigue; all the old gang supported him, as ever willing to sacrifice their country by intriguing with Spain to gain their end. Yet the Cardinal, who was ill and indeed on the verge of death, showed himself an expert in unravelling the design and pitiless in his treatment of the miscreants.

Cinq Mars' death was perhaps symbolic of Richelieu's achievements. he had not completely fulfilled his object of subjecting the nobles to the royal will, he had at least made such progress that the Crown was able to withstand the baffling conspiracies of the Fronde in ten years' time. But his answer to the challenge of noble power was not to be found only in edicts against duelling nor in the mere suppression of plots. He did not wish to eliminate noble privileges but he was determined to subordinate the nobility to the royal will.

Throughout his ministry he determined to do what he could to increase the power of the Crown and to centralise all government about the King and his immediate advisers. Like the English Tudors, he used the instruments already at his disposal to effect this end. The Royal Council grew more and more to represent the royal will—or rather the Cardinal's policy. To prevent possible rebellion Richelieu changed the governors of the French provinces, often great nobles, at fairly frequent intervals. Special provision was made for the trial of rebellious subjects with whom the ordinary courts would have been powerless to deal. The Parlements, often fractious, were brought to heel by the use of the *lit de justice*. Three of the French provinces known as the *pays d'état*, Burgundy, Dauphiné and Provence, which by custom had had preferential treatment in fiscal matters, were henceforth to be treated like the rest of France in the interests of governmental uniformity. It is, however, an indication of Richelieu's ability to assess any given situation that he did not force the three remaining *pays d'état* into line. Moreover he made good use of an official known as the intendant whom he made the direct link between the Crown and the provinces, so cutting out dangerous feudal intermediaries. The intendant, with whose work he is specially connected, became responsible for the collection of all revenue except that farmed out to special collectors, as well as for all the other numerous aspects of administrative activity once largely carried out by noble governors, who were now reduced to an honorary position without real power. The Cardinal truly described his own work when he wrote : ' The first thing I considered was the majesty of the King, the second was the greatness of the kingdom.'

He thus deserves the title ' founder of the modern French monarchy ' because he had subjected everything to its service. ' Public interests ', he wrote, ' must be the unique end of the Prince and his counsellors.' *Raison d'état* was an argument used to justify his every action. He supported a news-sheet, Renaudot's *La Gazette*, on condition that he could ' la dominer absolument '. Truth was to be subservient to his authoritarian dictatorship. But he was above all, as his *Testament Politique* indicates, the practical politician. In his own mind he identified the King with the State, and so made the State rather than the individuals of whom it was composed the object of his hard work. Medieval as some of his conceptions may appear, he was yet one of the founders of the modern totalitarian state. ' The theory behind it (the *Testament Politique*) is really that of the *Leviathan* of Hobbes, for all the conventional garb of God and Reason with which it is clothed. . . . His motives were disinterested but he is the classic example of the power addict on a great scale.' [1]

Nevertheless his rule had serious limitations. He wanted France

[1] J. Bowle, *Western Political Thought*, 307.

to be a prosperous nation, but he knew little about economics and the schemes which he initiated to develop French wealth rarely succeeded.[1] He founded a number of trading and colonising companies; but they infrequently came to maturity, partly because he sought to over-regulate them. That he failed to grasp the inter-relation which exists between politics and commerce is revealed by another incident. Spain was the main purchaser of French goods but Richelieu did not realise the effect that war with Spain might have on French commerce. The outcome was so disastrous that Richelieu was obliged to lift the ban on French trade with Spain in 1639, even though the countries were still at war. ' Je confesse tellement ', he told the appropriately named Superintendent of the French Finances, Bullion, in 1635, ' mon ignorance de finances '. On occasion he may have enriched his relatives, but under his rule the state's finances continued to deteriorate.

His lack of interest in the French people was perhaps his most fundamental weakness. He served the state well but he ignored the people. They are hardly mentioned in the mass of his letters; he expressed sincere anxiety on the rare occasions when their de-pressed condition was brought to his notice, but he never did any-thing about it. If in statesmanship he was far superior to Henry of Navarre, in human sympathies he was greatly his inferior. ' All politicians agree ', he wrote coldly, ' that when the people are too comfortable it is impossible to keep them within the bounds of their duty . . . they must be compared to mules which, being used to burdens, are spoiled more by rest than by labour.' But it was the ' mules' ' toil which produced the *sous* from which the French armies received their pay and on which basically the monarchy rested. While the Cardinal was building up the power of the *Ancien Régime* with such loving care, he was at the same time helping to dig the grave into which less than a century and a half after his death it was to totter.

5. *Richelieu's foreign policy*

It is undesirable to separate foreign policy from home affairs, but it is advisable to deal with the fourth point of Richelieu's pro-gramme, ' the greatness of the kingdom ' abroad, by itself to clarify the general picture. His foreign policy was traditional, being based on the desire to abase the Hapsburgs in the interests of French

[1] There is some disagreement over Richelieu's aptitude for economics—which some historians believe to be underestimated. For a modern view see Hauser, *La pensée et l'action économiques de Richelieu* (1944).

security. ' It is necessary ', he wrote, ' to have a perpetual design to arrest the progress of Spain, and while this nation has for its goal to augment its dominion and extend its frontiers, France should think only of fortifying herself, and of building bridgeheads into neighbouring states to guarantee them against the oppression of Spain if the occasion should arise.'

The fortification of France in the last resort meant an army, a navy and a strong treasury. When Richelieu took over in 1624, France lacked all three, nor was he ever able to give her financial stability. But he expanded the army and modernised it. The navy was in some way his noblest creation. In 1626 he made himself *Surintendant général de la navigation et commerce*, and by the *Ordonnance de la Marine*, perhaps the most radical of all his measures, he deprived the privileged owners of their coastal rights, thus bringing the whole of the French coast-line under the control of the French state. Shipyards, arsenals and foundries were set up at Brouage, La Rochelle and Brest. Before he died he had created effective Atlantic and Mediterranean fleets which changed the strategic situation in those waters for the better. France was too weak in 1624 to intervene in the great European struggle which had begun six years earlier. Indeed it was only after the Huguenots had been defeated and the power of the nobles had been checked and an effective striking force had been created that the Cardinal was able to enter the war as the Hapsburgs' leading opponent.

This indicated that Richelieu was mainly concerned with the second of his objectives, the ' building of bridgeheads into neighbouring states ' in the first few years of his ministry. With the aid of gifted diplomats, Charnacé, Feuquières, Servien, Avaux and the indispensable Father Joseph, he wove a web to ensnare the Hapsburgs. Communications between the Spanish Milanese and Hapsburg territory in Austria and Germany depended on the control of the Valtelline valley, and so ultimately upon the attitude of its rulers, the people of the Protestant Grisons. The outbreak of the first of the Huguenot revolts had spoiled the Cardinal's first gesture here, as it obliged him to withdraw the French troops which had occupied the valley. Richelieu managed to extricate himself from a dangerous situation with fair skill by agreeing to admit the independence of the Catholics of the Valtelline in return for which the Spaniards consented to recognise the independence of the Grisons and to destroy their fortresses in the Valtelline. But this Treaty of Monzon, which had been negotiated without consultation with France's allies, Venice and Savoy, had grave disadvantages for France, since it left the passes giving access from Italy to Central Europe and the Low Countries in effect in Spanish hands.

For the next eighteen months the Cardinal's attention was concentrated on war with England and the Huguenot revolt, but as soon as victory was assured in both he once again turned beyond the Alps, where a first-class crisis was brewing. Chameleon-like, his former ally, the Duke of Savoy, had rejoined the Hapsburgs, deeply perturbed by the succession of a Frenchman, Charles, Duke of Nevers, to the strategically-significant duchy of Mantua. Nevers, enraged by the way in which the Hapsburgs tried to prevent his succession, appealed to Richelieu thus paving the way for a number of expeditions designed to force the Duke of Savoy to return to his former alliance and to secure Nevers' enthronement at Mantua. This was achieved by the Treaty of Cherasco, signed in July, 1631, which left the Duke in possession of his duchy and ceded to the French the key-fortresses of Casale and Pinerolo.

Richelieu now turned his attention from Italy to north-east Europe as a more fruitful field for indirect French intervention in the Thirty Years' War. Too insecure to enter into the struggle herself, France was raising Europe against the Hapsburgs by her labyrinthine diplomacy. Thus Richelieu sent an ambassador, Brulart, accompanied by Father Joseph as 'theological adviser', to the meeting of the Emperor and the Catholic Princes arranged at Ratisbon in 1630. The French used the Diet to get the Mantuan succession settled in their favour [1] and to check Imperial power.[2] After the Danish King had proved a weak reed, Richelieu opened negotiations with Gustavus Adolphus of Sweden who was as eager for French money as the French were for him to intervene in Germany. De Charnacé was sent to conduct negotiations which were concluded successfully at Bärwalde, some six months after Gustavus had actually landed on the island of Usedom. The French agreed to subsidise the Swedish King as long as he kept his army in Germany against the Hapsburgs. He also promised that he would not molest the Catholics, the only safeguard that Richelieu could get to persuade the *dévots* at the French court that he was not sacrificing the interests of the Church for a purely political objective.

Successful as this phase of his diplomatic activity may appear, it was not as advantageous to France as Richelieu wished. Gustavus would be no man's catspaw and sweeping all before him paid scant attention to the religious provisions of the Treaty of Bärwalde.

---

[1] In fact Richelieu disowned the settlement as he was able by the Treaty of Cherasco to secure better terms than those agreed on at Ratisbon.

[2] See pp. 318–19.

The Cardinal, who felt that Gustavus was becoming too powerful and therefore potentially dangerous, cannot have been entirely displeased to hear of his death on the battlefield of Lützen in November, 1632. Able as was Oxenstierna, the man with whom Sweden's future rested, he could not match the diplomatic skill of the French representative, Feuquières. He was thus persuaded into recognising the decision of the League of German princes, known as the Heilbronn League, to place themselves under the protection of France as well as of Sweden, and into such a revision of the Treaty of Bärwalde that the Swedish army virtually became French mercenaries.

The way was thus open for full intervention in the war, but it is doubtful if Richelieu would have taken this step had not events more or less obliged him to do so. The Spanish general, the Cardinal-Infante Ferdinand, joined the Imperialists after passing through the Valtelline and imposed a crushing defeat on the Swedes at Nördlingen, forcing Bernard of Saxe-Weimar and his Protestant army back to the Rhine. As quick to take advantage of disaster as of victory, the Cardinal forced a favourable treaty on the German princes; he agreed to send 12,000 troops as well as money on condition that they ceded the fortresses of Schlettstadt and Benfeld in Alsace and the bridge-head over the Rhine at Strasburg to France. The Germans agreed but Oxenstierna and the Swedes demurred until Richelieu promised to declare war against Spain in 1635.

With the beginning of the war against Spain French foreign policy entered a new phase. Open conflict paid less dividends than the cold war, for the drag on the French finances became greater than ever, and the country's prosperity suffered by the loss of the Franco-Spanish trade. Furthermore the French army, less prepared than Richelieu supposed, had to defend frontiers vulnerable from the Pyrenees to the Low Countries. The Cardinal was himself so sunk in despair that he lost his habitual power of decision and it was the King who left for the front—the Spaniards were at Corbie not far from Paris—instead of deserting his capital as Richelieu had advised. ' Do not behave ', Father Joseph told his master, ' like a wet hen ' (*une poule mouillée*). The tide only turned slowly in favour of the French. Bernard of Saxe-Weimar remained grimly inactive; the Protestants of the Grisons under the lead of Jürg Jenatsch having secured a guarantee of their religious freedom from the Spaniards forced de Rohan and his Frenchman to withdraw. But the French army and navy were both growing in confidence and strength; under their gallant leader, Henri de Sourdis, archbishop of Bordeaux, the French ships imposed a major defeat on the Spanish fleet in 1638. Then Bernard of Saxe-Weimar besieged and captured Breisach, an important fortress which dominated the Rhine. Richelieu's delight [1] was, however, soon modified when he learned that the victorious general intended to keep the captured town himself. Even Bernard's loyalty to France became suspect, but providence, and some said poison, though without any evidence, removed him from the scene during the warm summer of 1639.

The remaining three years of Richelieu's life saw his chickens coming home to roost, even if the final victory was not achieved in his lifetime. It is not easy to measure his achievement but in fifteen years he made France the greatest power in Europe. He had checked and indeed shattered the Hapsburgs, for the Treaties of Westphalia (1648) and the Pyrenees (1659) were founded on his work. By the summer of 1642 he was clearly a dying man. With funereal slowness he was carried from place to place, in agony but with a mind as clear as crystal. He travelled up the Rhone on a state-barge, laying on a bed hung with purple taffeta, guarded incessantly by soldiers. He came back to Paris in early November, 1641, was fed by the King with egg-yolk, received the sacrament from the parish priest of St. Eustache, the parish in which he had been born and in which he died on December 4th, 1642. 'The torment and the ornament of his age', wrote a contemporary Englishman, 'France he subdued, Italy he terrified, Portugal he crowned, Lorraine he took, Catalonia he received, Swethland [Sweden] he fostered, Flanders he mangled, England he troubled, Europe he beguiled. Then shalt thou admire that he is shut up now dead in so small a place, whom living, the whole earth could not contain.' Both the execration and the tribute were just.

6. *Cardinal Mazarin*

Richelieu's successor, Jules Mazarin was less attractive as a man but no less capable. The Cardinal, himself a keen judge of character, had no doubt that Mazarin was well-fitted to succeed him. His past career had given him a rich and varied experience. Neither the lowly-born seminarist (in fact through his mother he was connected with the princely house of Colonna) nor the professional pickpocket that his detractors once set out to make him, he had, however, carved a career for himself by a skilful use of his own talents. Trained canonist and shrewd diplomat, he was less of the churchman

---

[1] Represented by the words with which he tried to cheer the dying Father Joseph: 'Breisach est à nous', though in fact Breisach had not yet fallen.

than Richelieu. He was, in fact, never ordained priest, remaining a deacon all his life. His diplomatic qualities attracted the Cardinal's attention and won his praise. Now (1643) in his forty-third year he appeared a smooth ecclesiastic in whose mouth butter would not melt, but his mind was as tortuous and subtle as that of the proverbial serpent. His private vices were more petty than those of the Cardinal. He did not scruple to enrich himself and his friends at the cost of the state, but at times he could be intolerably mean.

His objects differed little from those of Richelieu, and he showed the same unrelenting determination in following them. He wished to make his adopted country the arbiter of Europe's fortunes and to reap the victories the seed of which his predecessor had already sown so well. He was as keen as Richelieu in maintaining the absolute authority of the Crown. Nor was his understanding of public finance much more developed ; under his guidance and that of the brilliant but unscrupulous Fouquet the finances of the state thundered down the road to ruin. Mazarin's attachment to Richelieu's aims explains why he was faced with rebellions which threatened to bring his own authority, and perhaps even that of the King, to an untimely end.

From the very start of the reign[1] Mazarin aroused the hatred of the nobility, in part by so effectively playing off Condé against Orléans that he virtually secured the dismissal of the Council of Regency and the proclamation of the Queen-Mother, Anne of Austria, as Regent with absolute powers. Anne, who held the Cardinal in great esteem and may even have been secretly married to him, herself played a prominent part in this manoeuvre. The nobles, relieved from the pressure of Richelieu's iron hand, were naturally in a fractious mood and hoped to depose the minister and so gain a restoration of their own lost powers ; as early as 1643 a plot headed by the so-called *Importants*, led by the Duke of Beaufort, a grandson of Henry IV, the object of which was to murder Mazarin, was only just foiled in time ; nor was it to be the last.

The nobles were not alone in expressing their dissatisfaction with Mazarin's rule. The expenses of war had brought the Treasury to the brink of bankruptcy and had caused several new and unpopular taxes to be imposed. If the Treasury had been more efficient and if the tax-collectors had been more honest, discontent might have been much less, but corruption and injustice were the order of the day. The Parisians were affronted by the revival by the finance minister, Particelli D'Emeri, of an old law banning the

---

[1] Louis XIII died in 1643. His son and heir, Louis XIV, was only five years old.

building of houses in the suburbs of Paris; it led to a rich but
unpopular haul of fines from those who had broken the law. An
attempt to manipulate the *rentes* further alienated the middle class
from the Cardinal's rule. Mazarin defaulted on the interest; this
led to a depreciation enabling him to buy cheap. The payment of
interest then caused a rise and a profitable sale. This smouldering
discontent soon found expression through the resistance of the
Parlement of Paris to the Regent's demands. Although this so-
called 'parliamentary movement' occurred at the same time as the
Civil War in England, it had little in common with it,[1] being in the
main concerned with the defence of its own corporate privileges.
But the question of fairer taxation provided it with a battle-cry and
an enthusiastic following.[2] As soon as the first or Parliamentary
Fronde [3] had ended, or seemingly so, fresh trouble occurred as a
result of the nobles' rebellion. There were, in fact, two Frondes,
the *Fronde parlementaire* and the *Fronde princière* sometimes in
co-operation, sometimes not, but only combined by their united
hatred of the minister.

The course of events illustrated three points, the very confused
nature of the whole business, the real danger with which Mazarin
was faced and the calculated shrewdness with which he at last overcame it. The trouble itself began with a warning against unpopular taxation, made by Omar Talon the advocate-general of the
Parlement of Paris, leading to virtual passive resistance to the Crown
and the exile of some of the leaders of the Parlement in June, 1648.
Whether Anne of Austria and Mazarin were strong enough to
withstand a popular movement was doubtful, and the Cardinal,
hoping that a policy of conciliation might temporarily appease his
opponents, advised Anne to grant the demands which the Parlement
had made at the Chambre de St. Louis between June 30th and
July 12th, 1648. These were very far-reaching and had they proved
successful they might well have launched France on the path to constitutional government. But the news of Condé's victory over the

---

[1] In his study *The Fronde* (1935), P. R. Doolin analyses the arguments
put forward by the opposition to Mazarin in great detail (111-166) and asserts
'that this movement rested upon a constitutional theory according to which
the will of the King is not law . . . To the reason of the absolutists, which
was that the end of the state is peace or power, they opposed a rationalisation
of the constitution, which was that the end of the state is justice, and the
Catholic life.'

[2] Among other things they asked that the intendants should be removed,
that no taxes should be levied without their consent, that the administration
of the finances should be fairer and more honest.

[3] The word *fronde* came from the sling with which the guttersnipes of
Paris pelted their enemies with mud.

Spaniards at Lens put new heart into Mazarin and immediately after the *Te Deum* which celebrated it had been sung he tried to pinch the head of the revolt by arresting the leaders, Broussel and Blancmesnil. This proved a disastrous and precipitate action, since it provoked at once a popular uprising in the streets of Paris and produced a leader in the person of a singularly unprincipled and irreligious cleric, Paul de Gondi, coadjutor to the Archbishop of Paris whom he later succeeded.

Mazarin was not at the moment prepared for a renewal of the conflict and agreed to accept the Declaration of St. Germain, of October 22nd, 1648, which confirmed all the Parlement's previous demands.[1] ' You ', so a contemporary addresses the Parlement, ' are now masters of the battlefield ; you will know how to make good use of the victory won, and the honour of the triumph.' Time showed that such hopes were not prophetic. The minister had no intention of allowing the Crown to lose its absolute authority without a struggle. The terms of the Treaty of Westphalia, signed at Münster as recently as October 24th, represented a triumph for his diplomacy. Although the war with Spain went on, his prestige was high and two great nobles, Gaston, Duke of Orléans and the Prince of Condé, had promised to support him. At the start of the new year (January 7th, 1649), the Regent ordered the Parlement of Paris to leave for Montargis. This was tantamount to exile and was accepted by the supporters of the Parlement as by the Paris mob as a declaration of war.

Thus began the first Fronde. While it may be regarded primarily as a constitutional movement, it had many nobles among its leaders, including Conti, Longueville and Beaufort, some of whom undertook the defence of Paris against the royal troops which were besieging it. The insurrection was brought to an end by the Treaty of Rueil by which the Regent agreed to accept most of the provisions embodied in the Declaration of St. Germain.

The uneasy [2] interval which followed preceded the renewal of the civil war, in the shape of the Princes' Fronde. This had its

[1]The fifteen articles disclose the apparent extent of the victory of the Parlement. Important changes in taxation were promised. The last article read : ' We desire also that none of our subjects of whatever quality and condition, be treated criminally in the future except in accordance with the forms prescribed by the laws of our Kingdom. . . .'

[2] Apart from the continual propaganda there were several incidents which showed the tension in Paris. The following is typical. On June 18th, 1649, some supporters of the government, headed by the Comte de Jarzé, dined at Renard's in the Tuileries Gardens. The Duke of Beaufort, who had a big following among the Paris mob, strode into the room, rudely

roots in the ambitions of the arrogant but able soldier, the Prince of Condé, who supposed that he was indispensable and aimed to persuade the Regent to appoint him chief minister in place of Mazarin. Aware of his intrigues Mazarin eventually had him arrested, imprisoned at Vincennes and later transferred to Le Havre early in 1650. This was the signal for a number of noble risings in the provinces,[1] made the more dangerous by the treasonable negotiations into which their leaders entered with Spain. Moreover the intriguing de Gondi brought additional strength to the cause by arranging an unusual and precarious alliance between the Parlement and the nobility. Unable to overcome such a combination by sheer force, Mazarin left France on February 11th, 1651, leaving Anne and the young King to the mercy of the victorious *Frondeurs*. Although the situation seemed desperate all was not lost; the Cardinal's hope lay, as he realised, in the fact that a continuance of a united front was unlikely. The *bourgeoisie* and the Parlement were soon offended by the manners and policy, or lack of it, of the aristocratic leaders, and withdrew their support.

Thus although the nobility were still placed in a strong position, the Crown was steadily regaining ground. Mazarin felt that the position was satisfactory enough to return to France in January, 1652, and won over to the royal side the best of the opposing generals, Turenne; the rebels were also strengthened, if temporarily, by the support of Orléans, whose daughter, Mademoiselle de Montpensier, held the capital for the *Frondeurs*. The series of minor military engagements which followed represented a continuance of disorder which peasant and *bourgeois* alike must have dreaded. If Mazarin could only bring about a restoration of order, he would go a long way to gaining the country's support. The Prince of Condé, seated precariously in Paris, had had Orléans proclaimed Lieutenant-General of the kingdom and in order to consolidate a position, which he was fast losing, came to terms with France's enemies, the Spaniards. A Spanish advance towards Paris once more obliged Mazarin to leave France, if only to prove to his enemies that it was not only his continued presence which caused disorder. In the early autumn Condé definitely went over to Spain, thus providing the Regent

asked Jarzé whether he had his violins ready as he and his companions were about to dance, and then picking up the table cloth emptied the dishes over the diners.

[1] 'Mme de Longueville went to Normandy, the Duke de la Rouchefoucauld to Poitou, the Duke de Bouillon to Turenne, and his brother, the Maréchal de Turenne, to his fortress Stenay, on the northern frontier. The Count of Tavannes attempted to raise Burgundy, the government of the Prince of Condé' (Doolin, *The Fronde*, 36).

and her young son, Louis XIV, who had been declared of age in 1651, with an opportunity to re-enter Paris in triumph and to revoke all the concessions granted to the Parlements and to the nobles. In February, 1653, the Cardinal was once more reseated at the Queen-Mother's side.

The Frondes were much more than a mere nuisance. They had undone some of the good work accomplished by Richelieu by reviving the power of the nobility and diminishing the authority of the Crown. On the other hand the irresponsible behaviour of the nobles had done much to alienate the *bourgeois*. Abroad they had interfered with the conduct of the war against Spain and had reduced France's prestige.

France therefore needed a period of economic and political rehabilitation, but this Mazarin was in no position to grant it. Following Richelieu, he never saw his task in economic terms, but in degrees of prestige and the extent of spheres of influence. With certain reservations the Treaty of Westphalia had been a brilliant diplomatic victory; France had her possession of the three bishoprics of Metz, Toul and Verdun confirmed [1] and gained the sovereignty over the greater part of Alsace. But the war with Spain had still to be won. For five years Mazarin had been haunted by the spectre of French civil war. Freed from this, he was able to turn his attention to the employment of all means towards the subjection of the Spanish Hapsburgs. However much he may personally have disliked the idea of uniting with a country headed by a regicide, the commercial understanding which he had signed with Cromwell and the English in November, 1655, was turned into a full military alliance on March 3rd, 1657. At the same time his agents in Germany worked to prevent any possible reunion between Spain and the German Catholic princes; a weapon lay ready to his hand in the recently constituted League of the Rhine of which France became a full member in August, 1658. Diplomatic isolation of Spain coincided with military defeat—Dunkirk which fell to the former *Frondeur* Turenne in June, 1658, was one of England's gains from the alliance—which pressed so hard on the shattered Spaniards that peace became an overriding need.

This resulted in the Treaty of the Pyrenees, signed on an island in the middle of the Bidassoa river, after protracted negotiations between France and Spain on November 7th, 1659. Spain recognised the French right to Roussillon, Artois and a number of Flemish towns as well as to Montmédy in Luxemburg. The King pardoned the Prince of Condé who was also given back his estates. To avoid

[1] See p. 159.

any disputes about the future succession to the Spanish throne, the Spanish princess, Maria Teresa, who was to marry Louis XIV, agreed to renounce all claims to the Spanish throne in compensation for which she was to receive, within eighteen months of the marriage, a dowry of half a million crowns. As the dowry was never paid, Louis XIV held that his wife's repudiation was invalid, thus preparing the way for the outbreak of the War of the Spanish Succession forty years later. The marriage took place amidst extravagant pomp in June, 1660.

Mazarin did not himself long survive the consummation of his plans, dying on March 9th, 1661. More than any other great minister of the time, he had helped to draw the frontier lines of western Europe. He handed over an absolute monarchy intact to a young man who was to be its very incarnation. He had left France strong and respected in spite of the Frondes, but he had not left the Crown rich or the country prosperous. Without a radical improvement in the government's finances the absolute monarchy of the Bourbons could never know true security. Richelieu had prepared the way, Mazarin had followed in his footsteps but the end of the road was nearly a century and a half later—in 1789.

CHAPTER XVII

THE THIRTY YEARS' WAR, 1618–48.

1. *The origins of the War*

EVERY war is so rooted in past history that it is difficult to ascertain its real causes. The Thirty Years' War, which is really a series of wars rather than one single war, occurred because a number of different developments converged to produce a situation as a result of which peoples were plunged by an accidental and even trifling incident from a ' cold ' war into the violence of full-blooded conflict. The latter was thus preceded by many decades of ' cold ' warfare during which mountains of propaganda piled up from the sixteenth-century printing presses. Protestants and Catholics alike turned to their God to justify their ways and indict their opponents of ir-religion, heresy and self-seeking.

Religious differences formed a predisposing cause, as the history of the events which followed the Treaty of Augsburg of 1555[1] has already shown. In particular the ecclesiastical reservation clauses of the treaty were so vague that both Catholic and Protestant inter-preted them as they thought fit. The intrusion of Calvinism into German religious life had led to more bitter doctrinal controversy, but it had also helped to stiffen resistance to the aggressive Catholicism of the Counter-Reformation. In spite of some decline, Protestantism, for secular as well as religious reasons, remained firm and determined to press back any move made against it by its enemies.

The Counter-Reformation had, however, brought about a change in the German religious scene. The Catholic Church had re-conquered much that had been lost to Protestantism[2] by the per-suasion of missionaries like Peter Canisius as well as by the forceful methods of its patrons; of these Maximilian the Catholic of Bavaria was the most outstanding. Neither an idealist nor an enthusiast his practical political skill made him the leading prince in Germany. Successive Hapsburg Emperors had been less forward in their championship of the resurgent Catholic Church, but the Catholics placed great hopes in the young Archduke Ferdinand, a *dévot* who became Emperor in 1619. He took his faith with narrow seriousness, and it was as a genuine champion of the Church that he entered the

---

[1] See p. 150. [2] See pp. 203–4.

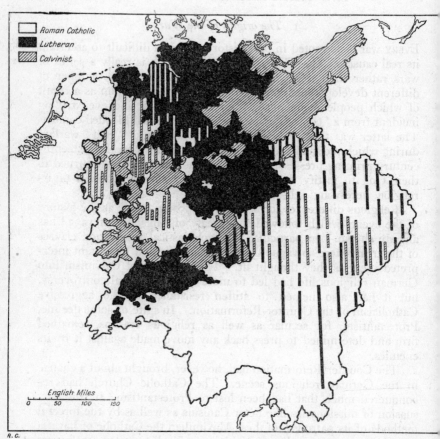

R. C.

MAP IX.—Religious divisions in Germany at the beginning of the Thirty Years' War.

war. Neither victory nor defeat affected his profound but rigid beliefs; ' even the bitter cold of the winter did not deter him from his devotions, and the Empress, waking sometimes in the night, would find him kneeling at the bedside deep in prayer and, stretching out her hand to take his, would implore him in vain to rest '.[1]

But it is impossible to detach the advancing tide of militant Catholicism and the breakdown of the Religious Peace of Augsburg from political motives. The Protestant princes had always used the religious struggle as means by which they could win their independence of the Emperor. Some, at least, having tasted the revenues of secularised bishoprics, were not averse to expanding their domains and the Protestant faith at one and the same time. Similar motives moved some of the Catholic princes. To reconquer and annex territory in the name of the Church, and so gain at the same time extra revenue on earth and a golden crown in the next world, was indeed to build barns with half an eye on heaven. The case of Elector Maximilian of Bavaria was in some ways typical. A devout Catholic he became the champion of the Catholic cause against the Lutheran and Calvinist, but political requirements led him to two volte-faces at least as a result of which he ended as a determined opponent of the Catholic Emperor. Even the Pope himself was not immune from this combination of motives; the head of the Catholic Church opposed the Catholic Emperor with unrelenting hostility. The more secular minded of Imperial counsellors, of whom Wallenstein was the chief, dreamt of a revival of Imperial power which need not be exclusively Catholic, but it is doubtful whether the pious Emperor ever saw his task in that light. Yet, with his advisers, he was naturally eager to reassert the traditional rights of his house which had been long whittled away by the subject-princes.

But the struggle was not a purely Germanic one. From the start it was a European conflict and before it had ended there were few European countries of any significance which had not taken part in it. Foreign intervention showed clearly enough that whatever part religion may have played in the opening stages of the struggle, its influence over the course of events grew less and less. Thus while both the Danish and Swedish intervention in the war might be interpreted as due to religious zeal, a more penetrating study shows that the political motive was the real compelling agent. Gustavus Adolphus of Sweden was strongly attached to the Protestant cause, but it was as an anti-Hapsburg politician that he entered the war. Moreover his desire to gain the ' dominium maris

[1] C. V. Wedgwood, *The Thirty Years' War*, 409.

Baltici' in turn had brought him into conflict with Protestant Denmark, Catholic Poland and Orthodox Russia, quite apart from the Imperialists. Such secular motives were most conspicuous in the case of France which had the strongest reason for entering into the war, even if internal history delayed this until 1635. A Catholic country governed by a cardinal might have been expected to have helped its co-religionists against the common foe, but France had been fighting a long struggle to defeat the encircling Hapsburgs since Charles V's day.

The long-rising tension between Catholic and Protestant is revealed by the Donauwörth episode of April, 1606. In defiance of the town's Protestant magistrates the Abbot of the local monastery had led a religious procession through the streets which had clashed with the local Protestants. The riot was reported to the *Reichshofrat* which placed the town under an Imperial ban without reference to the Diet. To the indignation of the stout-hearted burghers of Donauwörth the execution of this ban was entrusted to Maximilian of Bavaria, the head of the Bavarian Circle rather than to the Duke of Wurtemberg, the director of the Swabian Circle. A Catholic majority was forced into the Council; the Protestant Church was restored to the Catholics and the town was placed under Bavarian rule. As a result, a storm of protest spread through Lutheran and Calvinist Germany.

The incident at Donauwörth was soon followed by the formation of rival political unions of Catholic and Protestant princes. The Protestant or Evangelical Union was founded at a meeting of princes headed by the Elector-Palatine, Frederick, at Ahausen in May, 1608; it agreed to press for the inclusion of Calvinists in the religious peace and in general to defend the Protestant cause. It had a protector outside Germany in the French King, Henry IV. The Catholic League was founded a year later by Maximilian of Bavaria and the three Rhenish Elector-Archbishops who were perturbed by the threat of trouble from France. The League in part owed its genesis to the Spanish ambassador to the Imperial court, Zuniga, and from the start was assured of Spanish help.

Nor was a *casus belli* long in coming. The death of the half-witted Duke of Cleves-Jülich without direct male heirs left two Protestant princes as claimants to his estates, John Sigismund, the Elector of Brandenburg and Philip Louis, the Count of Neuburg. The possible extension of Protestant rule in the Catholic stronghold of the Lower Rhine constituted a grave danger to the Spanish Low Countries as to the Catholic Elector-Archbishops. War seemed inevitable, especially after the Emperor had ordered the sequestration of the disputed territories; this helped to bring into being a firm alliance between the Evangelical Union and the French King who began actively to prepare for war. Nevertheless the promised conflict hung fire, partly because the Emperor Rudolf was not eager to increase the power of the Catholic League but mainly because of the murder of Henry IV in 1610. Realising that they had lost their chief supporter, the Protestants decided to temporise. The Cleves-Jülich problem ended in a welter of intrigue and petty warfare as a result of which, by the Treaty of Xanten, signed in 1614, Philip Louis (or more accurately his son, Wolfgang William, a convenient convert to Catholicism), gained Jülich and Berg while Cleves and Ravensburg went to the Elector of Brandenburg.

The Imperial policy at this time was hardly consistent. Pious as the Emperor Rudolf might be, he had proved a weak and incapable ruler. In 1609 fear of rebellion had made him grant the so-called Letter of Majesty to the Bohemian Protestants, guaranteeing the right of the Lutherans to worship freely. Indeed for some years before Rudolf ceased to be Emperor, he was only a solitary and helpless figure in the Hradschin Palace at Prague more attached to his pet lion Ottakar than to any human being; the greater part of his territory was ruled by his younger brother Matthias who became Emperor in 1612. Matthias, as earlier history has suggested,[1] was only one degree more capable than Rudolf; he was dominated by the unattractive Cardinal Khlesl, who at once showed the German trend of his policy by trying to make Vienna rather than Prague the centre of Imperial rule. Thus the difficulties of administering the Letter of Majesty increased, more especially as it had never in fact protected the rights of the two other important Protestant groups, the Calvinists and the Bohemian Brethren. The Archduke Ferdinand, the Emperor's heir, who was elected King of Bohemia in 1617 with his cousin's approval, swore to observe the Letter of Majesty. While the Hapsburg forces were gaining in strength, anti-Hapsburg feeling in Bohemia, always anti-Germanic and Slavonic in character, race and literature, rose to fever heat. In March 1618 an Imperial decree prohibited Protestant meetings. On May 22nd, the Calvinist noble, Henry Matthias of Thurn, with Ruppa and Fels, made their way to the Hradschin Palace where they found the Imperial regents, Jaroslav Martinitz and William Slavata. After a fierce altercation, the rebels hoisted the two men and pushed them, together with their secretary Fabricius, out of the window. They fell fifty feet to the courtyard below. ' Let your Mary save you if she can ', an onlooker shouted, and then, as Martinitz crawled

[1] See p. 252.

311

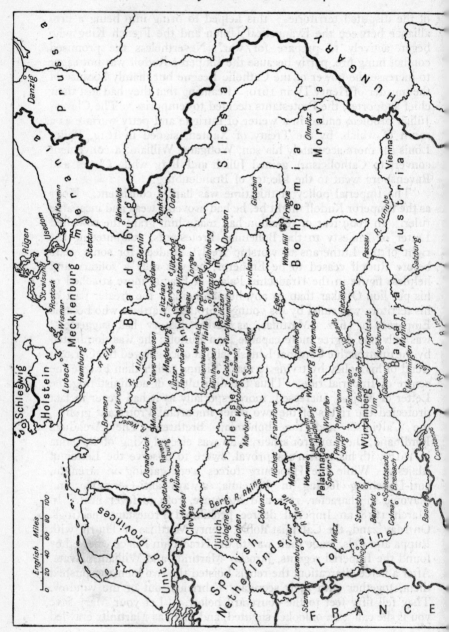

away he exclaimed ' By God she has ! ' The implications of this
dramatic if trivial incident were profound ; it made a Bohemian
rebellion inevitable and a European war likely.

2. *The War*

The Thirty Years' War was rather a series of struggles than a
continuous conflict, which circumstances outside the control of the
combatants served to prolong.   There were a number of occasions
when the logic of events should have made the end of the war
probable ; but time and time again French diplomacy made the
conclusion of peace impossible.   From its very start the war promised to be a European rather than a German struggle.   It was
never confined to a single locality.   It flared up all over Europe,
now in the Low Countries, now at sea, now in the Lombard Plain
or in the Valtelline Valley, now in Saxony and the Rhineland.   Its
ubiquitous character only makes the war the more difficult to un-
ravel.   Yet it is probably true that the intervention of Catholic
France and Protestant Sweden against the Hapsburgs was to prove
the most vital event in its history.

Neither the defenestration of Prague nor its sequel the Bohemian
rebellion need have made a general war inevitable.   The Emperor
Matthias, who was still on the throne in 1618, hoped that the conflict
could be localised.   Even the rebels themselves preserved the fiction
that the Bohemians were loyal to the Emperor and were only con-
cerned with the carrying-out of the Letter of Majesty.   But it was
soon apparent that the Bohemian rebellion was a serious rising.
This was proved by the willingness of the Elector Palatine, Frederick
V, to accept the Bohemian crown previously conferred on the
Emperor's heir, Ferdinand of Styria ;[1] Frederick's incapacity and
Calvinist faith, which made him unpopular with the Bohemian
Lutherans, were counterbalanced by the ability of his adviser,
Christian of Anhalt, and by the support which he hoped he might
win from the German Protestant princes and from his father-in-
law, James I of England.   Already in November, 1618, the vigorous
mercenary leader, Ernst von Mansfeld, had captured Pilsen, though
actually at the behest of the Catholic Emmanuel of Savoy who
thought that disturbance in Imperial territory might strengthen his
own chances of the Imperial crown.   For the Emperor Matthias
died in March, 1619.   His successor as Emperor was his Catholic
nephew, Ferdinand of Styria, elected on August 28th, two days
after the provisional government set up by the Bohemian rebels

[1] See p. 311.

had proclaimed Frederick their new King. The new Emperor was to be most concerned with the rehabilitation of Hapsburg and Catholic fortunes.

Despite its initial threat to Hapsburg power the Bohemian rebellion did not last long. Frederick's position was weak. Although a number of Protestant states congratulated him on his election, they sent no help; James I of England disapproved of his action. In Bohemia the King and his beautiful wife, Elizabeth, had done much to alienate their new subjects; Frederick, we are told, wore a 'bright red cloak with a yellow feather stuck jauntily in his hat' and 'bathed stark naked in the Moldau before the Queen and all her ladies', thus offending the staid burghers of Prague. His only ally, the semi-barbaric prince of Transylvania, Bethlen-Gabor, a Calvinist in doctrine and a hedonist by reputation, did indeed co-operate with the Bohemian army to besiege Vienna in the early summer of 1619; but this was only a flash in the pan. In the words of Pope Paul V, Frederick found himself in a 'foul labyrinth in which he will certainly lose himself'.

The suppression of the Bohemian rebellion was not, however, the sole work of the Imperialist armies. It is an instructive commentary on the character of the war that neither side was ever so governed by a single head that it could win a straight fight. The greatest of the German Catholic princes was Maximilian of Bavaria, a man whose jealousy of Hapsburg authority was only a little less than his desire for spoils. In July, 1620, the Emperor agreed to a secret treaty, conferring the Palatine electorate on Maximilian in return for military assistance. As a result Maximilian invaded Bohemia and on November 8th, 1620, defeated the rebels at the White Hill, a few miles outside Prague. Frederick and his wife went into exile, living first on the crown jewels and later on the generosity of their Dutch hosts. 'Seldom', Miss Wedgwood has written, 'has the insignificance of one man had so profound an effect upon his period.'[1]

As a result of the Imperial victory a Catholic reaction, as harsh as it was thorough, obliterated the liberties of the Czech people. After a series of executions, a grim reminder of the penalties of treason, the victors proceeded to profit from adversity under the lead of the niggardly and undistinguished Karl von Liechtenstein, the newly-appointed governor of Prague. Estates belonging to 'treasonable' families were confiscated and distributed among loyal Catholics. The coinage of the country was withdrawn from circulation and reminted at half the value of the old, a financial

[1] C. V. Wedgwood, *The Thirty Years' War*, 103.

speculation of peculiar dishonesty. The Jesuits entered the country and took over virtual control of education, while many Protestant professors were deprived of their posts; among these was Comenius, one of the most notable scholars of his time. The whole weight of the Counter-Reformation was in fact thrown against the unfortunate country; Protestant churches were closed and even the Czech hymn tunes were replaced by German. The Letter of Majesty was torn up and the Imperial constitution of 1627 provided that the crown of Bohemia should henceforth be hereditary in the Hapsburg house. ' Thou shalt break them with a rod of iron; thou shalt dash them to pieces with a potter's vessel ' had been the text which a Capuchin Friar had selected after hearing of the victory of the White Hill. The flame of Czech nationalism never died but it quivered perilously low after 1620.

The Imperial victory did not, however, mean the end of the war. Its very completeness aroused a reaction against the Hapsburgs in Europe. Although Frederick was now a King in exile and an Elector in disgrace, he remained a focal-point for the anti-Hapsburg forces. The bluff Danish King, Christian IV, feared that a Protestant defeat in Bohemia might encourage the Hapsburgs to revive their authority in Germany; he also wanted to annex the secularised bishoprics of Halberstadt and Osnabrück. The United Provinces, with which Christian had recently opened negotiations, welcomed Frederick and urged Mansfeld to transfer his battered army to Dutch service in the foreknowledge that the Spaniards intended to reopen the war as soon as the Twelve Years' Truce ended in 1621. The Emperor's own position was made the more difficult by the fact that his victory had largely been won by Maximilian of Bavaria. Lack of money made it impossible for him to repay Maximilian, with the result that the Bavarian troops continued to occupy Upper Austria. The continued existence of these standing armies in itself invited the reopening of hostilities; but it was the widening diplomatic issues which turned an internal rebellion into a great European conflict.

Such was the setting for the next five years of war (1620-25). The mercenary leader, Mansfeld, ravaged the Rhineland, but he had a foeman worthy of his steel in the austere Catholic general, Tilly. The latter defeated the Elector's allies: the Marquis of Baden-Durlach at Wimpfen and the gallant Christian of Halberstadt (wearing the glove of his ill-fated cousin, the Queen of Bohemia, on his helmet) at Höchst; and occupied Heidelberg and Mannheim, the chief towns in the Lower Palatinate. In the following year Tilly entered Dutch territory where Christian had retreated and defeated him at Stadtlohn; Mansfeld's own defeat at Freisoythe did much to damage further his already tarnished military reputation. This completed Frederick's discomfiture; even his library had been sent to Rome. As to his electoral dignity, this was formally conferred on Maximilian for life on February 23rd. It is important to notice that the elevation of the Bavarian Wittelsbach was vigorously criticised by some of the Catholics as well as the Protestant German princes, and by the Spaniards who did not wish to alienate the Elector Frederick's father-in-law, James I. But these were comparatively small crumbs of comfort to the anti-Hapsburg world.

It is, however, an invariable lesson of history that victory is never final. The very year that witnessed the apparent triumph of the Hapsburgs also saw the rise of the man who was to be their greatest enemy, Cardinal Richelieu, appointed first minister in 1624. From now until his death in 1642 he was to prove the most inveterate and insidious opponent of Hapsburg plans. His first essay in this direction, an attempted occupation of the strategic valley of the Valtelline, proved indeed a failure;[1] but the Emperor was nevertheless faced by an increasing number of difficulties as 1625 ended. James I of England, alienated by the Spanish treatment of his favourite, the Duke of Buckingham, had decided at last to support his son-in-law. The Danish King, Christian IV, incidentally a brother-in-law of James I, and the Swede, Gustavus Adolphus, both dreaded an extension of Hapsburg power along the Baltic coast; but they were too suspicious of each other to collaborate. It was therefore a question of which monarch would intervene first. The Swede was already involved in Poland, so that it was the Dane who actually decided to champion the Protestant cause.

That Mansfeld and the Danish King should both have suffered defeats within a few months bear witness to a revival of Imperial fortunes which Christian cannot have foreseen. Christian's forces were shattered by Tilly, but Mansfeld was faced by a new antagonist who was to play a significant part in the events of the next few years. This was Albert von Wallenstein, or Waldstein, a Bohemian by birth, forty years old in 1625 and above all else a selfish and determined careerist. He had already deserted Protestantism for Catholicism and would doubtless have accepted any other faith if it had offered him a rich enough reward. His life suggests that he was a neurotic, subject to ungovernable tempers and beset by a childish faith in the stars. He had had the good fortune to marry a wealthy widow, Lucretia von Wishkow, who had died shortly afterwards, leaving him with a substantial fortune. He had used this

[1] See pp. 297-8.

in a business-like way to develop and to expand his estates and to
engage in the corn trade supplying the Imperial armies, thus becoming an exceptionally wealthy man. Wealth was the natural harbinger
of political ambition. He offered to raise and equip an army at
his own expense, an offer which the Emperor accepted.

Wallenstein's appearance on the scene was to make all the
difference to the war. This was not because of his generalship but
because he brought a new and in some sense an original vision to
the situation. He has been credited, but only by straining the
evidence, with leanings towards the creation of a unified German
state, or at least with ideas of pan-Germanic unity. Yet he certainly
believed that it was to the Emperor's interest to focus his attention
on German and Austrian problems to the virtual exclusion of
matters that were primarily Spanish or dynastic. He believed that
the Hapsburg territories, if combined with north-east Germany,
could form a powerful Imperial block and be the basis of a strong
military state. This is revealed by the direction of his military
efforts. Mecklenburg was occupied and granted to him by the
Emperor who was now deeply in his debt. Allying with the free
cities of Hamburg and Lübeck, he captured Rostock and Wismar ;
but the Baltic fortress of Stralsund withstood him. In thus ven-
turing his armies in northern Germany Wallenstein was stimulated
by more than a mere desire to drive Christian IV out of the war,
an object achieved through the Treaty of Lübeck signed in 1629.[1]
He believed that the Baltic coast could be made a starting-point for
the restoration of Imperial fortunes ; it provided opportunities for
helping the Polish King, Sigismund, to assert his claims to the
Swedish throne, and for making alliances with the Hanseatic ports.
Although the latter were no longer as prosperous as they had once
been when their well-laden ships dominated the Baltic and North
Seas, they were still rich ; there were resources which could be
used to replenish the ever-empty Imperial treasury.

But Wallenstein was soon to discover that neither his diplomacy
nor his strategy were exactly what the Emperor wanted. He never
really understood the jealous nature and powerful affections of the
Emperor Ferdinand II. The Imperial court distrusted the plans
of the self-made bourgeois opportunist who had risen so high in
Imperial favour. The Spaniards were repeatedly making calls on
the Emperor for reinforcements which his close kinship with Philip
IV made him unwilling to refuse. Since 1628 he had been involved

---

[1] ' Denmark ', commented the Imperialist Aldringen, ' will now be given
the last unction notwithstanding the royal worthy holds this sacrament in
no esteem.'

in the War of Mantuan Succession as a result of Spanish opposition to the enthronement of a French prince as Duke of Mantua.[1] The Spaniards demanded that 30,000 Imperial troops be sent to help them in Italy. But Wallenstein opposed a move that might imperil his Baltic policy. ' I wage ', he complained, ' more war with a few ministers than with the enemy.'

Even before this trouble a new source of friction had arisen. The Emperor Ferdinand was a sincere Catholic, much given to prayer and religious processions, placing great reliance on his Jesuit Confessor, Father Lamormaini. He felt that the restoration of lands taken from the Catholics by the Protestants was a matter of conscience as well as of Imperial policy. He had to pay God a dividend out of the proceeds of Imperial victory. There is every reason to suppose that Wallenstein was much dismayed by the news that Ferdinand proposed to issue an Edict of Restitution, ordering that all Church property secularised since the Religious Peace of Augsburg should be restored to the Catholic Church. Wallenstein, a superstitious rather than a religious man, foresaw that the edict would arouse the fury of the Protestant princes, more especially of those who, like John George of Saxony, had so far remained neutral; for the restoration of the secularised bishoprics in northern Germany would lose the Protestant princes their territorial supremacy there. Moreover many Catholic princes regarded the measure as inopportune on the grounds that it might further extend Hapsburg power and Jesuit influence, which they disliked.[2] It was ironical that the only man in high office who was probably a believer in religious toleration should have been ordered to enforce the edict.

The situation in 1630 was thus confused. The extent of the Imperial victories had been considerable but dissatisfaction in Germany had been heightened both by the Edict of Restitution and by Wallenstein's continuance as Commander-in-Chief. The Diet of German princes, in practice representing the Catholic side, which met at Ratisbon in July, 1630, illustrated these tendencies. The Catholic princes, under the lead of Maximilian of Bavaria, prevailed upon Ferdinand, albeit reluctantly, to dismiss Wallenstein. The princes were, however, unwilling to elect Ferdinand's son as King of the Romans and to permit the sending of Imperial troops to

---

[1] See p. 298. Wallenstein was a friend of the French claimant, the Duke of Nevers, against whom the Hapsburgs were making war.

[2] The appointment of a Hapsburg prince, Ferdinand's second son, to the important archbishopric of Magdeburg shows there were grounds for this suspicion.

help the Spaniards against the French in Mantua; this last refusal hastened the conclusion of the Treaty of Cherasco (in July, 1631), in effect a French success. French activities at the Diet were of the highest importance, even though superficially disavowed by Richelieu. The latter's leading agent, Father Joseph, accompanied the French envoy, Brulart, to the Diet, ostensibly to look after French interests in respect of the Mantuan Succession but in practice to do whatever was possible to alienate the Catholic princes from the Catholic Emperor. The net result was a secret treaty with the Duke of Bavaria and his associates, by which the latter agreed not to help the enemies of France nor to make any breach of Dutch neutrality. Wallenstein's dismissal, coming at this vital moment, was all the more inopportune, since the tortuous French diplomacy at Ratisbon was really a prelude to the Treaty of Bärwalde, signed in January, 1631, between Richelieu and King Gustavus Adolphus of Sweden.

Gustavus' entry into the war, which occurred in 1630, vitally influenced its future course. In the first place it helped to prolong it. If the Swedes had come earlier, the war might have been over by 1630, but Swedish distrust of the Danes had prevented any effective co-operation between the two Protestant countries. Nor, in fact, did the collaboration between the Catholic Cardinal and the Protestant King bear as much fruit as it might have done. This was in part a result of Richelieu's inability to dominate Gustavus Adolphus and his subsequent suspicion of his designs. Secondly, Gustavus' arrival on German soil made the war beyond all question a European struggle, since it represented the conjunction of Baltic Protestant imperialism and the French fear of Hapsburg ambitions.

Moreover Gustavus was the greatest single personality of the war. As a King [1] he had already shown his love of his country the resources of which he had done much to develop. He was intelligent, courageous and unselfish, and was greatly and deservedly loved by his soldiers. He brought to the war a wider policy and a new conception of warfare. He believed in the expansion of Swedish territory and influence as the surest protection against Hapsburg and Polish aggression. 'Pomerania and the Baltic coast', he wrote 'are the outworks of Sweden—they are guarantees against the Emperor.' But he was sincere when he claimed that he came to restore the displaced Protestant princes and to defend the political and religious liberties of Germany. Whether such plans were in fact practicable or suited Swedish interests was another matter. Many German princes, Protestant as well as Catholic, distrusted the Swedes; and time showed that the Swedish army was to burden both the territory

[1] See pp. 335–8.

on which it was billeted as well as the Swedes who had to support it. Finally Gustavus was the greatest general of the war. Mansfeld, Tilly, Pappenheim, and Wallenstein were all his inferiors. He had an army that was well-disciplined and well-equipped; his generalship was marked by effective tactics and he placed a greater reliance on speed and mobility than did his adversaries. Many prominent generals in the next hundred and fifty years were indebted to Gustavus for his new notions of warfare. It was hardly surprising that to many Germans his army appeared as a whirlwind, reaping destruction as it marched through their countryside.

The first few weeks after his arrival on the island of Usedom off the Baltic coast in July, 1630, gave little impression of his fighting strength. He took Stettin, occupied Pomerania and in April, 1631, marched into Frankfort-on-Oder. But two events soon occurred which decisively affected the future history of the war. The first was the Swedish alliance with France to which allusion has already been made.[1] By the Treaty of Bärwalde Gustavus agreed to invade the Empire with 30,000 infantry and 6000 cavalry on condition that France paid him a subsidy of 400,000 thalers. The Cardinal hoped to assuage the *dévots* of the French court through the inclusion of a clause by which the Swedish King agreed that he would not interfere with the exercise of the Catholic faith in any territories that he might occupy. The other event was the spectacular sack of Magdeburg by the Imperialists under Pappenheim on May 20th, 1631. The city, a rich Hanse town and for long a Protestant centre, was treated with the greatest brutality by a mad-drunk soldiery. Even in an age not unduly soft the sack sent a shiver of apprehension and disgust throughout Protestant Europe, which helped to strengthen Gustavus' position. An alliance with the United Provinces had been signed on May 31st. Before 1631 had ended many of the German princes, who had up to now favoured a policy of neutrality, made alliances with the Swedes, among them the two Electors, George William of Brandenburg and John George of Saxony.

The full meaning of Gustavus' invasion was revealed by his crushing victory over Tilly at Breitenfeld on September 18th, which displayed the superb quality of the Swedish fighting force to all Europe. The victory freed Gustavus either to strike at the Austrian lands or at the rich ecclesiastical electorates of the Rhineland. He preferred, perhaps foolishly, to seek a decision in Germany rather than in Austria. Leaving the hesitant and unreliable John George of Saxony to invade Bohemia he marched towards the Rhine; by

[1] See p. 298.

320

the winter he was firmly established at Frankfort and Mainz. The Swedish army in full flood was a force which Richelieu could not control; the Cardinal's irritation at the extent of Gustavus' success was profound, especially as the Swedish alliance had cost him the neutrality of Maximilian of Bavaria. Meanwhile the Emperor, in desperation, had been forced to recall Wallenstein to the command of the Imperial armies. Wallenstein turned back the Swedish King before Nuremberg, and then with Pappenheim was himself attacked by Gustavus at Lützen. That misty November day in 1632 lived long in Swedish history. Although his troops were victorious, Gustavus lay dead on the field. So died the 'evangelical Joshua' as the protestant burghers of Nuremberg had described him in the previous April. 'When His Majesty fell', wrote one of his subjects, 'the sun lost his splendour, and shone no more thereafter by the space of four weeks.'

If his active intervention in the war had been unfortunate, Gustavus' death was doubly so. His throne passed to his young daughter, Christina, and his place in the state to his Chancellor, Oxenstierna, who, however able, lacked the impulsive warmth and the command of strategy which his master possessed. Thenceforth the Swedish army became little more than a body of mercenaries largely under the control of Richelieu.

There was one other critical event which might have made the conclusion of a general peace possible, the Imperial victory at Nördlingen in 1634. After his defeat at Lützen, Wallenstein had deteriorated into an embittered, gout-stricken neurotic, eager for revenge on the master who had once dismissed him. Taking into account Wallenstein's futile strategy and treacherous diplomacy, no one can blame the Emperor for ordering his arrest, either alive or dead. The general left his army at Pilsen on February 22nd, 1634, with a thousand men, intending eventually to join the enemy; but he was murdered three days later at Eger. 'Presently', wrote a contemporary, ' (they) drew him out by the heels, his head knocking upon every stair, all bloody, and threw him into a coach where the rest (of his associates) lay naked close together . . . and there he had the superior place of them, being the right hand file, which they could not do less, being so great a general.' Wallenstein's death injected the Imperialists with renewed hope, which his successor, the incompetent drunkard, Gallas, should hardly have raised. But in the summer of 1634, the young Cardinal-Infante Ferdinand joined his cousin, the King of Hungary, at Donauwörth and imposed a shattering defeat on the army of Bernard of Saxe-Weimar and the Swedes at Nördlingen on November 6th.

In a few hours the Swedes had lost nearly all they had won, their land and their military reputation, and the Emperor had once more regained the initiative.

The Treaty of Prague, signed in May, 1635, was the more immediate sequel to Nördlingen and might well have seemed the start of the much-desired general peace. By its terms Protestants and Catholics were to remain in possession of all the lands they held on November 12th, 1626; all territories taken since 1630 were restored to their owners. Lusatia was given to the Elector of Saxony and Pomerania was promised to the Elector of Brandenburg if he accepted the peace. The Treaty was originally negotiated between the Elector of Saxony and the Emperor, but it was hoped that other German princes would follow suit, thus preparing the way for a general pacification. If anyone thought that this would happen they were soon to be disillusioned. ' Saxony ', wrote Richelieu, ' has made his peace but that will have no effect on us save to make us renew our efforts to keep all in train.' Nine days before the publication of the terms of the Treaty of Prague, the French declared war against Spain with old-world ceremonial.

The history of the last thirteen years of the war proves singularly unrewarding to the historian; but one theme was constant, French determination to push the war to a successful close. Alliances were signed with Sweden, the United Provinces and the Duke of Savoy. After a depressing start the scale tipped more and more in favour of the French, now ruled by Richelieu's successor, Mazarin. Nothing typified this better than the seizure of Rocroi, a Spanish-held fortress in the Ardennes, after a brilliant victory in 1643 which destroyed the legend of Spanish invincibility. The victory gave the French generals, Enghien (later Prince of Condé) and Turenne, control over the Rhine. But Rocroi was in one sense exceptional. For the most part victory ebbed and flowed in favour of all the combatants, thus prolonging unduly the peace negotiations which had been opened at Münster and Osnabrück as early as 1643. War continued whilst the peace-makers engaged in wordy battles. By the strange irony of history the war finished where it had begun, in Bohemia; the news of the long-awaited end saved Prague, which the Swedes were storming, from the terrible fate which had overwhelmed Magdeburg sixteen years previously.

3. *The Treaty of Westphalia*

The long-protracted negotiations, carried on at Münster and Osnabrück, expressed the high hopes and the major difficulties of the peacemakers. Even the choice of the two places where the discussions took place concurrently indicated the nature of the problem, for the Swedes would not give precedence to the French nor the French to the Swedes, thus making the choice of two distinct places a necessity. Negotiations between the French and the Emperor were conducted at Münster whereas the Swedes met the Imperialists at Osnabrück. In general the embassies were led by noble figure-heads, who quarrelled incessantly over trivialities, while the real work was undertaken by their subordinates, the members of the trained diplomatic services which the congresses of Westphalia did so much to create. Jealousy and tension, between allies as between enemies, were accentuated by the shifting nature of the news from the different centres of war. Yet it would be unjust to assume that the delegates were not in their own way concerned with giving war-torn Europe an enduring peace based on universally accepted frontiers.

The last question constituted the most obvious problem. Thus the Elector of Bavaria, now an ally of France, hoped for the cession of the Rhineland fortresses of Breisach and Philipsburg whereas the Emperor was determined to yield only one of these. The Swedish claims were complicated by the aged Oxenstierna's desire to prolong the war in order that he might remain in office and by his young mistress's equal determination to finish the fight as soon as possible so that the Chancellor might retire. The Swedes wanted a ninth electorate. The Emperor did not want to tolerate the Protestant religion in his hereditary lands. This multitude of conflicting voices was suddenly stilled by the totally unexpected news that the Spaniards and the Dutch had at last reached agreement at Münster on January 7th, 1648. This bilateral treaty so jolted the noble negotiators that they set to work on their treaty with greater zeal after excluding Spain, Lorraine and the circle of Burgundy (which comprised the Spanish Low Countries) from future negotiations. The two definitive treaties of Münster and Osnabrück, known collectively as the Treaty of Westphalia, were confirmed and signed at Münster on October 24th, 1648.

The Treaty is of the utmost significance in European history, in some ways more so than its terms might suggest. But even these were impressive enough. France was confirmed in her possession of the three strategic fortress towns of Metz, Toul and Verdun, as well as of Moyenvic, Breisach and Philipsburg on the Rhine and Pinerolo on the frontier of Savoy and France; the landgraviate of Alsace, except for Strasburg, also became French, but the clauses relating to Alsace were so obscure that they were bound to be a source of trouble in the future. These gains were a testimony to the tireless diplomacy of Richelieu and Mazarin. France's ally, Sweden, received as Imperial fiefs western Pomerania, Bremen and Verden, Wismar and Stettin together with some territory at the mouth of the river Oder. Brandenburg, whose Elector had been singularly lacking in both loyalty and courage, won more than any other German state. The Duke of Bavaria held on to the upper Palatinate as well as his electoral title; the son of the Elector Frederick, Charles Louis, was recognised as Elector Palatine. Bohemia continued as one of the hereditary dominions of the Empire, and Upper Austria, so long retained by the Bavarians as a pledge of the Emperor's debts to the Duke, returned to Hapsburg rule.

The religious clauses of the Treaty were a virtual repetition of the Religious Peace of Augsburg of 1555, except in so far as the Calvinists were to enjoy the same privileges as the Lutherans. It is sometimes asserted that the Treaty represented the victory of the forces of toleration, but this is a mistaken view. The Emperor was under no obligation to permit religious toleration in his hereditary dominions while the reaffirmation of the *cujus regio ejus religio* clause only replaced the whole question in the hands of the local prince, irrespective of what people or Churches wanted. So far as Church property was concerned, the Edict of Restitution of 1629 was naturally abrogated and it was decided that all Church land was to remain in the hands of whoever had it on January 1st, 1624, a date which in fact favoured the Catholics rather than the Protestants.

The implications of the Treaty were epochal. It was shown clearly enough that the Empire was in decline; indeed the Austrian character of the Empire became henceforth its dominant feature. The Treaty implicitly recognised the sovereign rights of the German princes who had long acted independently of the Emperor. In theory they were still bound by Imperial law and were unable to make alliances which were not in accord with Imperial policy, but in practice the Emperor had no control over them. Any direct intervention in their affairs was impracticable. This victory of the princes over the Emperor, to which the history of the past two hundred years had been leading, had significant after-effects.

It meant that in the future Germany was to be an artificial conglomeration of two hundred and thirty-four states, lacking national consciousness, varying greatly in size and power, ruled by selfish men who were only very rarely concerned with the true interests of their people. In the years immediately following the Treaty the princes were able to re-establish firm government and to modernise their administrations; but their petty absolutisms were never rooted in popular loyalty. The energies of the German middle class were now to be devoted more to the stifling routine of the bureaucratic administration of a small state than to the promotion of commerce and industry; political and economic life were muffled by a moribund conservatism. The condition of the German peasant was even worse than that of the townsman, especially in north and north-east Germany where the secularisation of Church lands had given the German *Junkers* an opportunity to form large landed estates, worked by peasants burdened by servile dues.

Brandenburg-Prussia was the German state to benefit most from the Treaty. The Hohenzollern Elector had already won Cleves in west Germany in 1614; four years later he had become by inheritance Duke of Prussia (to be freed from Polish suzerainty in 1657). The Treaty of Westphalia brought the Elector, Frederick William, new territorial gains in the shape of the eastern half of Pomerania, and the bishoprics of Magdeburg, Halberstadt, Minden and Kammin. Though not yet even of the rank of a second-class power, Brandenburg-Prussia, under a succession of able Hohenzollern rulers, was to do much to determine the future history of Germany.

The Treaty also revealed the declining prestige of the Papacy. Although an exceptionally skilful papal diplomat, Cardinal Chigi, had acted as the mediator at Münster, the Pope, Innocent X, had nevertheless condemned the final Treaty in the bull *Zelo Domini Deus*, issued in November, 1648, as ' null, void, invalid, iniquitous, unjust, damnable, reprobate, inane, empty of meaning and effect for all time.' But the papal repudiation of the Treaty caused such a small stir that it was clear that papal influence in European politics was decidedly on the wane.

The Treaty was indeed centred about the national state. Sweden and France were the immediate arbiters of Germany's future. The French historian, Sorel, has rightly called the Treaty ' la grande oeuvre européene de l'ancienne France ', for more than anything else it paved the way for Louis XIV's policy of territorial and personal aggrandisement—largely at the expense of German disunity. Beyond all question the Treaty marked the end of the medieval conception of Europe which had been long a dying and the emergence of the modern state. It represented the beginning of a period, as far as history can be divided into periods, dominated by the national sovereign state which two great wars in the twentieth century have not yet brought to an end.

4. *The War in Germany*

The Thirty Years' War had not only established the future course of European history by breaking forever the possibility of Hapsburg hegemony in Europe, thus opening for France the most aggressive stage in her history; it also had notable effects on German history. Yet these have often been misinterpreted. It was to the interest of the ambitious Elector of Brandenburg and his historiographer Samuel von Pufendorf to exaggerate the sufferings which Germany had undergone as a result of the war in order to explain and justify the achievements of his own reign, thus suggesting that Brandenburg was the most effective guardian of German liberty against the Hapsburg and the foreigner. Furthermore much of the historian's information about the more violent and unpleasant aspects of warfare comes from the records of the middle class who were the most affected by them.

Some of their sufferings were not necessarily the result of warfare. Modern research suggests that the decline in the prosperity of the German towns and the deterioration in the condition of the peasantry, for which some have assumed that the war was responsible, were the result of economic movements which happened to coincide with the war. Thus repeated Spanish bankruptcies had already hit the German mercantile bankers before the war actually began, while the trade of the Hanse towns was very materially damaged by the sack of Antwerp in 1585, the tremendous expansion of Dutch trade and the closing of the London Steelyard in 1598. This business depression was accentuated by the currency inflation of the years 1619-23, of which the Emperor and some of the German princes took full advantage. Wallenstein was himself one of those who made a fortune out of shrewd speculation in the landed property that was changing hands at this time. Even so, the economic crisis came to an end; and a recent writer has asserted that ' on the whole, the national income, productive power and standard of living were higher about 1650 than they had been fifty years earlier '.[1]

[1] S. H. Steinberg in *History* [Vol. xxxii, No. 116], 98.

The peasantry on the other hand were worse off. Rising prices, especially in corn, had led to the creation of large farms at the end of the sixteenth century, leading to the eviction of peasants from their holdings and a general increase in rents. This process was probably accentuated by the conditions of war, for the war spurred on the process of requisitioning which gradually replaced the unsystematic pillaging of earlier armies. Either way the peasant suffered, both from the policy of the big landlord and from the rapine of foreign armies.

Certain other effects of the war usually accepted also require significant modification. It has been stated that the war was responsible for so marked a depopulation of Germany that the country never recovered until the nineteenth century. This legend, so useful to Hohenzollern propagandists, has been in part disproved. Although it is difficult to get reliable statistics the death rate seems to have differed little in areas outside the battle area from those which were the seat of conflict, and the general increase in the population was much the same all over Europe. It is true that pillage and destruction, and occasional epidemics, did cause pockets of depopulation, and the move from the countryside to the towns, which was occurring in many parts of Germany, may have done something to give the appearance of depopulation to the superficial observer.[1] Nor is there much reason to suppose that the war affected the cultural life of Germany to any marked extent. Long before the war had ended the temporary stagnation in German literature and scholarship had given way to a period rich in artistic and literary achievement.

It may indeed appear as if the Thirty Years' War did not greatly affect Germany. But small as were the armies engaged in the war,[2] the picture must not be unduly lightened. Certain districts which were of great strategic importance were devastated

---

[1] Yet there are strong arguments in favour of depopulation, which cannot be disregarded. J. U. Nef writes : ' According to the most reliable estimates, the number of persons living in those regions which were to form the German Empire of 1871-1919 diminished in the hundred years 1550-1650 from almost twenty-one millions to about thirteen and a half millions.' It is indeed certain that there was an economic depression which the long war made worse.

[2] The Catholic League had an effective strength of about 15,000 men ; Gustavus Adolphus landed in Germany with 15,000 men ; the Imperial army under Wallenstein may have exceeded 20,000 men ; Bernard of Saxe-Weimar received French subsidies for 18,000 men ; Condé's army in 1645, the strongest French contingent to be employed in Germany, numbered 12,000 men.

time and time again by opposing forces.[1]   In any case the material damage and the physical suffering were probably less important than the coarsening of manners which long campaigning inevitably brought.   The absorption of the soldiers who made a profession of warfare into the civil population created, as it always does, a significant and difficult social problem.   It seems undeniable that in some ways the war was unusually brutal.   Callot's grim pictures are supported by a wealth of evidence which suggests that the Thirty Years' War gave rise to atrocities which Europe was not again to experience until the twentieth century.   A soldier who accompanied the armies, Hans von Grimmelshausen, later embodied some of his experiences in a work of fiction entitled *The Adventurous Simplicissimus*.   Whatever the exaggeration, the underlying note of disorder and rapine cannot be disguised.   Frenzy and ferocity, depopulation, pillage, torture and rape marched in the rear of the conflicting armies.   Few narratives in history are so tedious or disgusting as that of the Thirty Years' War, and none a better pointer to contemporary political morality.

[1] ' The Rhine crossings of Breisach and Wesel, the Leipzig plain, the passes across the Black Forest and the roads to Regensburg and the Danube valley.'

CHAPTER XVIII

THE RISE OF SWEDEN

1. *Swedish independence*

THE rise of Sweden to imperial status was one of the striking features of seventeenth-century history but it was not historically inevitable. The formation of an independent Swedish nation under Gustavus Vasa, the adoption of the Lutheran faith and the steady development of the country's natural resources gave no hint of a Baltic empire. It is only as one perceives the historic circumstances, the continuous dread of the Hapsburgs as a Catholic and Imperial predatory power and the success of the defensive policy against Russia and Poland that one also sees how propitious conditions were for the extension of Swedish power, if only there was a statesman great enough to initiate the struggle. In Gustavus Adolphus the man and the hour met, if some minutes too late. His nephew, Charles X Gustavus, defied the majority of European states with impunity. But time had its revenge on Sweden during the reign of his grandson, Charles XII, when the country was gradually divested of its imperial domains.

The story of sixteenth century Sweden forms a necessary prelude to this heroic national venture. The reign of Gustavus Vasa, the first independent Swedish King since the Union of Calmar of 1397, was important for three things : the creation of a strong state ; the increase in the power of the monarch ; and the foundation of a national Protestant Church. Towards the end of the Middle Ages the Swedes had successfully defied the Danes under national leaders like Sten Sture the elder, Svante Nilsson and the younger Sten Sture, but the Danes had been unwilling to grant the Swedes freedom from their rule. The Danish King, Christian II, acting with the new Archbishop of Upsala, Gustavus Trolle, who was a personal enemy of Sten Sture, invaded Sweden in 1520 ; Sten Sture was mortally wounded and the Danes entered Stockholm in triumph. To consolidate their victory, Christian and Archbishop Trolle arrested the leading opponents of their régime and had them executed in the market-place of Stockholm. This indefensible ' Blood Bath ' of Stockholm, as it was dubbed, alienated the mass of the Swedish people from their Danish monarch and formed a direct prelude to the national revolt which broke out

MAP XI.—Northern Europe.

a few months later. The lead in this was taken by a young Swedish nobleman, Gustavus Vasa, who was helped financially by the German Hanse towns as well as by a convenient rebellion against Christian's rule in Denmark itself. On June 6th, 1523, he was proclaimed King of Sweden ' To the praise, honour and glory of God and to the lasting benefit, protection and strength of all Swedish people, spiritual and temporal '.

His position was highly uneviable, as the new state was surrounded by potentially hostile powers. The Danes, who controlled many of the large river mouths, were favourably situated to attack the east coast of Sweden and to break Swedish communications with Finland. Finland, which was Swedish territory, was an obvious target for Russia soon to be ruled by Ivan the Terrible. Nor could the Swedes free themselves from the fear of Hapsburg power in the north under the young Catholic ruler, Charles V. Even the allies of Sweden were in some ways more of a loss than a gain. In return for their help against Denmark, the Hanse towns, led by Lübeck, had forced Gustavus to grant them valuable economic privileges by the Treaty of Strängnäs which practically made Sweden dependent on the Hanse. Many of the leading nobility were jealous of the way in which one of their equals had risen to the position of a king and were not averse to intriguing with the Danes. Finally the King himself was the ruler of a poor and undeveloped country. Yet by the time he died in 1560 he had created a compact and relatively prosperous state. How did he manage this ?

Like Henry VIII of England Gustavus took advantage of the prevailing religious troubles to strengthen the royal power. If he accepted the Lutheran faith, he was bound to alienate some potential allies and make every Catholic prince in the north his enemy; but there were significant compensations. Thus although Lutheran teachers had already reached Sweden, the Swedish Reformation was primarily political. It represented the King's urgent need of money and his desire to attach the nobles to his cause. The opening scene was laid at a meeting of the *Riksdag* held at Västerås in June, 1527. After a bitter altercation in which the Catholic bishop, Hans Brask of Linköping, and one of the disaffected magnates, Ture Jönsson, led the opposition to the King's proposals, it was agreed to confiscate monastic property, to reduce episcopal and cathedral incomes and to secure the restoration of all property alienated or given to ecclesiastical foundations since the middle of the fifteenth century. This Recess of Västerås, as it was called, thus helped to fill the coffers of the Crown, and to bribe the nobles to support the King by promising them the return of all land granted to the Church by their families since 1430. The matter was clinched by the final clause which allowed the teaching of the Lutheran faith.[1] A doctrinal reformation was the natural sequel. Olaus Petri, an eloquent preacher, had already translated the New Testament into Swedish. Together with his fellow Lutheran, Laurentius Andreae, he worked to reform the service books and to eliminate the abuses which had undoubtedly characterised the Swedish Church in recent years. A confession of faith, denouncing the worship paid to saints, transubstantiation, the Mass and monasticism, was decreed at Örebro in 1529. Although the episcopal government was retained, Sweden had become a Protestant country. But it was a form of Protestantism in which the King remained supreme. One incident illustrates this. When Olaus Petri and Laurentius Andreae tried to limit royal interference, they were arrested by the King's orders (1539), tried and sentenced to death for high treason; the sentence was not carried out but both it and the royal pardon showed the unquestioned supremacy which the King enjoyed in the Church.

The political and economic development of Sweden was closely associated with the growth of the royal power and of the personal prestige of the monarch. Gustavus continued to call the *Riksdag*, which strengthened his position by making the Crown hereditary, but he never became subservient to it. He did everything possible to raise the revenue by increasing the extent of royal property and by encouraging farming. Since Swedish economy was still backward and most of the Crown's revenue was collected in kind, he did what he could to improve its administration and to punish waste. German miners were introduced into the country to exploit copper at Falun, silver at Sala and iron at a number of other places. The free flow of Swedish trade was, however, hindered by Danish control over the outlets

---

[1] Like the Swedes the Danes had become Lutherans. During the reign of Christian II's successor, Frederick I (1523-33), the Crown had brought the Danish bishops under its control and with the help of the nobles had launched an attack on Church property. The lead in doctrinal reform was taken by Hans Tausen (1494-1561), who had studied at Wittenberg and was a disciple of Luther; he became Frederick's court chaplain and later (1542) Bishop of Ribe. Frederick's successor, Christian III (1533-59), was a convinced Lutheran and at once decided to impose the reformed faith on his subjects. He was opposed by the peasantry (and the town of Lübeck) led by Count Christopher of Oldenburg but with the help of Gustavus Vasa of Sweden emerged victorious. As a result Lutheranism became the official faith of Denmark and Norway. For further details see E. H. Dunkley, *The Reformation in Denmark.*

from the Baltic and by the exacting conditions imposed by Lübeck and Danzig. The first of these obstacles for long remained a fruitful source of discord. The second led to war when Lübeck under the lead of the ambitious Jörgen Wullenwever tried to regain economic supremacy in the Baltic. The Swedes and the Danes joined forces and imposed so crushing a defeat on Lübeck and their own disaffected subjects that Swedish trade was free from control in Baltic waters.

If Gustavus I played no part in European politics, this was primarily because he was chiefly concerned with consolidating his position in Sweden. He had to suppress a number of risings and to prevent Christian II from regaining his lost dominions, which now included Denmark itself. Since his deposition the Danish King's court in the Netherlands had become a storm-centre of all discontent in Scandinavia ; he had been induced to return to the Catholic faith by the promise of Hapsburg support and Spanish treasure. Accordingly in 1531 he made a vain effort to reconquer his lost kingdoms but only had a temporary victory in Norway ; elsewhere Gustavus of Sweden and Frederick of Denmark were easily able to suppress the rebels. When Gustavus died in 1560 he left a strong and vigorous state ; the greatest of his successors, Gustavus Adolphus, rightly apostrophised his work : ' This King Gustavus was the true instrument by which God again raised up our fatherland to prosperity.'

The half-century which followed his death forms a rather tedious anti-climax. His immediate successor, Eric XIV, was arrogant, extravagant, ill-tempered and mentally unstable. His short reign was fraught with trouble. The absorption of Esthonia into the Swedish state in 1561 anticipated the policy of building up a Swedish empire in the Baltic, but its immediate consequence was to alienate his near neighbours, Denmark and Poland. As a result Denmark, Poland and Lübeck attacked Sweden ; the Swedish navy held the seas, but the Danish army, largely consisting of German mercenaries, ravaged Swedish territory. Eric's disastrous foreign policy, his continued alienation of his younger brothers, the powerful Dukes John and Charles, his passionate rages and acute melancholia, the favour he showed to an upstart of low birth, George Persson, and his marriage to his mistress Karin Månsdotter [1] completed his undoing. A rebel army under Dukes John and Charles captured the King who was deposed, imprisoned and probably (in 1577) poisoned.

[1] He had been one of the many princes who courted the English Queen, Elizabeth.

Whether his successor John III was really better fitted to govern is doubtful. Lacking military skill, the new King was a learned theologian with leanings towards Catholicism. His wife, a Polish princess of strong personality, was a Roman Catholic; his son and heir, Sigismund, was brought up in his mother's faith. It is not therefore surprising that the King conceived that his main task was to find a formula which should reconcile the contending parties, which found expression in the historic Red Book of 1575. The King's efforts, excellent as they were in intention, proved disastrous in effect, since they alienated all parties. More especially his policy made an enemy of his vigorous younger brother, Duke Charles of Södermanland, who was alarmed by the encouragement which the King had given to the resurgent Catholicism of the Counter-Reformation in its apparent designs on Lutheran Sweden.

The evil inheritance which John left behind him showed up forcibly in the reign of his son Sigismund. Since 1587 he had been King of Poland now largely cleared of Protestantism. As he could not immediately leave his other kingdom, his uncle acted as regent. This incident in effect crystallised the problem of his reign; an ardent Catholic, ruling over a Protestant country, who was also a young and inexperienced statesman was faced by a ruthless and ambitious noble, many years his senior, and fervently attached to the Protestant faith. In such circumstances a struggle was sooner or later inevitable. Breaking out in 1598, the war soon ended in a victory for Duke Charles. King Sigismund was deposed from the Swedish throne but it was laid down that his son was to succeed him if he were brought to Sweden and educated as a Protestant. Charles was to act as regent for the time being. Since Sigismund not unnaturally refused to comply with these conditions and since all opposition had been ruthlessly liquidated, the Duke was proclaimed King Charles IX at Norrköping in 1604.

2. Swedish imperialism

It was in these rather unfavourable circumstances that Swedish imperialism really had its birth. Sweden had a footing on the other side of the Baltic through its possession of Esthonia and of Finland, but it was faced by a ring of potential enemies. The Danish King, Christian IV, who had not forgotten that he had a claim to the Swedish throne, was determined to retain control over the Sound. The dispossessed monarch, Sigismund, was naturally unwilling to forgo his claim to the Swedish crown and had strong backing in Poland, both from Polish natives and from Swedish nobles opposed to Charles IX. In the background, as yet immersed in the rightly-named Time of Troubles which formed the birth-pangs of the Romanoff dynasty, there was Russia.[1] Thus Sweden's safety, even her continued existence as a power, lay in the creation of a strong-armed state which could determine the balance of power in northern waters. Thus in what appeared to be the defensive policy of Charles IX can be seen the seeds of the aggressive plans of Gustavus II and Charles X.

Charles' reign was a prelude to the more successful rule of his son, being in the main a period of uncertainty. The new King was able but tactless and was soon involved in war with his nephew of Poland. Realising that he must prevent Polish troops from gaining a foothold on the Swedish mainland, he crossed the Baltic but with no great success. Fortunately the period of anarchy which opened in Russia gave both the Swedish and Polish Kings an opportunity to try to place their respective candidates on the Russian throne. Neither was successful, but the Swedish intervention was one of the factors which led Czar Michael Romanoff to recognise Swedish control over Ingria and Kexholm by the Treaty of Stolbova in 1617. Before the Russian War ended Charles was involved in conflict with Christian IV of Denmark.

At this juncture (1611) he died, leaving his throne to his seventeen-year old son, Gustavus Adolphus. The new King was built on the heroic mould. He had been carefully coached for his office by the cultured John Skytte. If not a scholar he was never lacking in intellectual curiosity. He knew something of

---

[1] Although its history is fascinating, Russia played very little part in the European history of the period. Its more important rulers consolidated and increased the power of the monarchy. Thus Ivan III the Great (1462-1505) greatly extended Russian territory, annexing the rich trading republic of Novgorod ; he married Sophia, the niece of the last Byzantine emperor. His successor, Basil or Vasili III (1505-33) continued his policy, annexing Pskov as well as other lands. Ivan IV the Terrible (1533-84) ascended the throne at the age of three but soon showed that he was an exceptionally able if a cruel and an unbalanced ruler. He too greatly extended Russian territory and was the first Russian ruler to call himself Czar. He tried to bring both the Church and nobility under his control. During his reign trade was opened with the west ; Richard Chancellor visited Moscow in 1553. On his death, the Czardom fell on evil days and there was a ' time of troubles ' which gave Sweden and Poland an opportunity to intervene in Russian internal politics. In 1613 Michael Romanoff became Czar and under Michael and his successor Alexis (1645-76), the ground was prepared for the far-reaching changes of Peter the Great (1689-1725). For further details see Sir Bernard Pares, *History of Russia* and B. H. Sumner, *A Survey of Russian History*.

ten languages and carried Grotius's learned work with him for recreational reading. He was physically a fine figure of a man; in reference to his tawny hair and beard the Italian mercenaries called him ' il re d'oro ', which makes his English nickname ' The Lion of the North ' more easily understandable. He had great powers of leadership and endurance which won his soldiers' deep affection. ' He would sweat and starve ', Miss Wedgwood wrote of him, ' freeze and thirst with his men, and had stayed fifteen hours at a stretch in the saddle.' He inherited the fierce Vasa temper, and was equally feared and loved by all around him. He had a reliable collaborator and a loyal friend in his Chancellor, Axel Oxenstierna, whose cooler judgment and wide knowledge of affairs sometimes counteracted his master's impulsive ardour.

From the start of his reign the King was a man of large schemes. How soon the grandiose idea of making Sweden the dominant Baltic power took root in his mind it is difficult to say. At least in his early years his policy was partly governed by the fact that he was already involved in three wars, with the Danes, the Poles and the Russians. The Danish War, in which the Swedes had not so far distinguished themselves, was ended through the good offices of the English King, James I, the son-in-law of the Danish King Christian IV, at Knäred in 1613. The Danes insisted that the Swedes should pay a monetary compensation before they ceded the territory around Alvsborg which they had occupied, but they agreed to exempt from the payment of tolls all Swedish ships passing through the Sound. The Russian War, which ended four years later, gave the Swedes additional territory on the Russian side of the Baltic. The Polish War, a series of episodes rather than a persistent struggle, continued until 1629, providing Gustavus Adolphus with military experience which served him in good stead when in 1630 he entered the main battle against the Haps- burgs. He had realised by 1630 that the issue of Swedish security depended more upon the defeat of the Emperor than of King Sigismund. With French and English mediation an armistice was arranged which allowed Gustavus to champion the Protestant cause—and Swedish imperialism—in Germany itself.

It must not, however, be supposed that Gustavus was merely a warrior King. The economic and constitutional development in which he took a deep personal interest was probably more important than the spectacular campaigns he fought, for whereas the results of the latter were in the long run comparatively barren, the former laid the foundations of modern Swedish prosperity. The Vasas as a whole were not great administrators. They had

had only infrequently the simultaneous goodwill of the greater nobles represented through the *Råd* or Council and the *Riksdag* in which the townsmen and peasants were represented as well as the nobles and clergy. Gustavus was, however, able to win and retain the loyalty of both. His father, Charles IX, had won the backing of the *Riksdag* in his fight against his Catholic nephew, Sigismund, but at the cost of alienating many members of the *Råd* who took refuge at the Polish court. The accession of a young King gave the nobles an opportunity to try to regain their lost powers which they were not slow to take. Under the lead of Axel Oxenstierna they presented a royal charter to Gustavus by which he promised to maintain the Lutheran faith, to safeguard the interests of the lower Estates and to give all the leading appointments in the government to nobles. It was in this way that the *Råd* hoped to dominate both the *Riksdag* and the King. Gustavus did indeed use the members of the *Råd* in his government, sensibly making Oxenstierna his Chancellor, but he transformed their functions. They ceased to be merely the self-appointed defenders of a privileged class and instead became the loyal civil servants of the King. Far from destroying their privileged position the King did much to uphold and even to extend it, but he bound them to the Crown by giving them responsible positions in the state. Thus an ordinance of 1626 gave the nobles an organisation and a meeting place, not yet constructed, in the shape of the Riddarhus.

This successful treatment of the nobility was closely associated with another important administrative reform, the establishment of *Kollegia* or government departments, headed by a president who became one of the leading officers in the state. Each of the five ministers, the Chancellor, the Admiral, the Treasurer, the High Steward and the Marshal, became the head of an efficient machine, all the instruments of which worked so well that Gustavus could leave the country on long absences in the knowledge that the government would continue to function efficiently. Of these departments the Chancery (*Kansli*), under the indefatigable Oxenstierna, became the focal-point of Swedish administration.

Other reforms took place affecting the *Riksdag*. All the Swedish Kings since Gustavus Vasa had made good use of the *Riksdag* to win public opinion to their side, but it was still an unbusiness-like assembly with unco-ordinated powers and an uncertain procedure, an institution which ' had hardly emerged from its medieval swaddling-clothes '. The *Riksdagsordning* of 1617 regulated its future procedure both in respect of its own meetings and its relations with the King. Henceforth it was to consist of four regular estates, nobles, clergy, townsmen headed by the burgomaster of Stockholm and the tax-paying peasants (*skattesbonder*). While the relations between the King and the *Riksdag* had been governed hitherto by written documents, there was in future to be more personal contact. Thus the *Riksdag* was admitted to be the main Swedish representative institution and was strong enough to withstand the move towards bureaucracy which characterised the reigns of Gustavus' immediate successors. It was also in his reign that increasing reliance was placed on a ' secret committee ' of the *Riksdag* which discussed foreign affairs. The Swedish representative system had certain intrinsic weaknesses. Under a weak King the position of the *Råd* could be used to reinforce the power of the nobility while the *Riksdag* was likely to suffer from the limited nature of its authority, including its inability to initiate legislation. Nevertheless Gustavus' constitutional achievements, most of which were embodied in the constitution or *Ars Regeringsform* of 1634, were considerable. The *Råd*, the *Riksdag* and the King worked in harmonious co-operation in the interests of the country as a whole. Without such administrative stability Gustavus could never have indulged so freely in his foreign ventures.

He also realised that the growing complexity of the government and the heavy demands of war made an increase in the Crown's revenue and the country's prosperity doubly necessary. He did what he could to stimulate trade and commerce in the cities, seaports and market towns ; if the results fell short of Gustavus' expectation, they at least included the foundation of Gothenburg on the western coast—which greatly encouraged Swedish trade with the English and the Dutch to the irritation of the Danes. Both the English and the Dutch were big buyers of Swedish timber which they used for shipbuilding, and the Dutch invested much surplus capital in Swedish industry. It was a Dutchman, Louis de Geer, who largely developed Swedish mining, including the ironworks at Finspong and Leufsta and the brass-foundry at Norrköping.[1]

Ultimately Gustavus thought of power in terms of military might to which economic and political programmes must be

---

[1] De Geer actually came from Liége but as a Calvinist made Amsterdam his headquarters. ' Swedish iron exports increased more than tenfold, from some 1600 tons in 1548 to approximately 5,000 tons annually in the early 1620's and then to some 20,000 tons in the early 1650's. Swedish copper exports increased from 100 tons in 1548 to 2,600 tons in 1650.'

subordinate. But, as we have seen,[1] it was doubtful whether his intervention in the Thirty Years' War really served his country's interest. His own conviction that he came to defend Sweden and Protestantism cannot conceal the ripening of Swedish imperialism which in time showed itself to be impracticable and ruinous. The King himself fell a victim at Lützen, but his entombment in the Riddarholm at Stockholm, where the inscription reads ' moriens triumphans ', meant no interruption of the policy which he had planned to carry out, only the removal of its ablest interpreter. His successor was a young girl, Christina, but Swedish domestic and foreign policy still remained in Oxenstierna's capable hands. No one grudged the Swedish successes in Germany more than the Danish King, Christian IV, who took advantage of an alleged breach of the Treaty of Knäred (1613) to renew the war. Denmark's defeat led to a speedy treaty of peace, signed at Brömsebro in 1645. As a result the Danes agreed to surrender their claim to levy tolls on Swedish ships passing through the Sound. In pledge of this they handed over the province of Halland to Sweden for thirty years as well as Ösel and the former Swedish provinces of Jamtland, Harjedalen and Gottland. Three years later the Treaty of Westphalia awarded Sweden further territorial gains including western Pomerania, the port of Stettin, the city of Wismar and the secularised bishoprics of Bremen and Verden.

Was Sweden fitted to govern or defend this growing empire ? After Lützen government remained in the hands of the ageing Chancellor and members of the *Råd* or Council which inevitably tended to raise the power of the nobles at the cost of the monarchy. As Queen Christina grew up, it was obvious that she was an exceptional personality, fond of scholarship and the arts, in many ways more masculine than feminine, willing to defy convention and disinclined to rule Sweden. In 1654 she resigned her crown to her cousin, Charles X Gustavus, left the country and became a Roman Catholic, in future following a career which would have—and indeed has—satisfied the most ardent romanticists of Hollywood before she died in 1689. Beneath the apparently healthy constitutional and economic development of the country, certain weaknesses may be discerned. The trend towards the predominance of the aristocracy continued in the reign of Charles X who was too concerned with continental campaigns to pay much attention to the day-to-day government of Sweden. The finances had in fact become dangerously unstable, for the expedients which the government used to raise extra revenue, whether by granting monopolies or

[1] See pp. 319-21.

raising taxation, were unpopular and insufficient. The sale of Crown land, to which Christina had given reckless approval, brought a temporary relief but in the long run helped to undermine the royal revenue. Charles X had done something to secure the return of some of the alienated land, by the so-called *fjardepartsraftsten*, but the return was not proportionate to the loss. Thus the disquieting symptoms of economic collapse and political sterility appeared to threaten Swedish Imperialism.

The seriousness of this trend for the future of Swedish history is revealed by the expensive but impressive campaigns of Charles X. A soldier of the calibre of Gustavus Adolphus but lacking his sure judgment, he soon found an opportunity to try his fortune in the lottery of war by crushing the claimant to the Swedish throne, Sigismund's son, John Casimir of Poland. Taking advantage of internal trouble in Poland he marched from Pomerania through Brandenburg into Polish territory where he captured Warsaw and Cracow. But this victory was too complete. The shrewd Elector Frederick William of Brandenburg had been obliged to dance to Charles' tune, but it was a forced measure. In any case the Swedish army was unable to control or to curb the amorphous Polish state. Attacked by wandering Polish guerillas the Swedish army became demoralised. The Elector, who had cast covetous eyes on Swedish Pomerania, was therefore very ready to listen to the overtures of Frederick III of Denmark, himself only awaiting an opportunity to revenge the Treaty of Brömsebro. In 1657 the Danes declared war, hoping that Brandenburg would follow suit. The most dramatic of lightning campaigns was the sequel. Charles withdrew to Pomerania, captured the fortress of Fredericia on Jutland and then in January, 1658, taking advantage of a severe frost crossed over the ice of the Little Belt to Fyen. He then embarked on a still more daring exploit, no less than to take some 5000 men with guns and waggons across the narrow channel of the Great Belt beneath which there were strong and treacherous currents to Sjaelland. The surprised and defeated Danes were forced to accept the Treaty of Roskilde, signed on February 26th, which brought additional territory to Sweden—Skane, Bleking, Halland in perpetuity, Bohuslan and Trondhjem's Iän.

Neither Charles nor his people were immune from hubris. Frederick of Denmark had been defeated but he was not crushed. Arrangements had been opened even before Charles' winter campaign for Dutch naval assistance, nor had they been suspended. Charles was soon ringed by a new and powerful alliance of powers, Denmark, the United Provinces, Brandenburg and Poland. The

King was not, however, to live to see the end of the storm he had raised, for he died in 1660 leaving his throne to a small child. The Regency naturally determined to end the war on the most favourable terms that it could obtain. A treaty signed with Denmark at Copenhagen confirmed all the gains which Sweden had won at Roskilde except Trondhjem's Iän. Another treaty, concluded at Oliva, closed the struggle with Poland and Brandenburg along the lines of the existing *status quo.* By a skilful manipulation of events Brandenburg had managed to secure full sovereign power over East Prussia.

The pacification of the North led to a lull which gave Sweden an opportunity to restore her damaged economy and to prepare for the next and last round in the struggle for hegemony around the Baltic Sea.

CHAPTER XIX

THE UNITED PROVINCES

1. *Introduction*

THE first half of the seventeenth century has been rightly termed Holland's Golden Age, for it was then that the United Provinces rose to the status of a world power, nor was this pre-eminence based mainly, as was that of Sweden, on war and conquest. The Spaniards were indeed at long last compelled to admit Dutch independence at Münster in 1648, but it was in the realms of commerce and culture that the Dutch particularly excelled. Through their shrewd business men they gained a mastery in world finance which they did not wholly lose until the middle of the eighteenth century,[1] and through their traders they won a colonial empire. Their culture was many-sided and rich, but it was not only in cartography and navigation, the making of optical instruments and in engineering, pursuits closely allied to their economic development, that the Dutch genius revealed itself. In their poetry and scholarship, in their simple but attractive style of architecture, and in their landscape painting they provided a pattern for all Europe.

At no other period of history did they so markedly influence Europe's development. There were an innumerable number of points where Britain and Holland made contact. Dutch refugees from Spanish intolerance found a refuge on English soil where they played an important part in developing the ' New Drapery ' just as at a later period English Puritans fled from Laud's heavy hand to Amsterdam and Leyden. English divines, led by the Bishop of Salisbury and the Archdeacon of Taunton, attended the Synod of Dort in 1618. How far the English poet John Milton was indebted for *Paradise Lost* to the Dutch poet, Joost van der Vondel's *Lucifer* remains an open question, but in their humanism and dislike of theological intolerance the two men had much in common, though one was a Puritan and the other a Catholic. Cornelius Vermuyden, who was a Dutch engineer knighted by Charles I, in 1629, helped to drain the Cambridgeshire Fens. Flemish and

---

[1] In his notable *Anglo-Dutch Financial Relations in the Eighteenth Century* (1940), Mr. C. H. Wilson has shown clearly that the Dutch did not lose their financial pre-eminence as has sometimes been asserted until the end of the Seven Years' War.

Dutch painters were repeatedly patronised by England's Stuart Kings, with whom the House of Orange was closely associated by marriage. Nor were other nations immune from Dutch influence. Grotius, one of the greatest Dutchmen of his time, found a refuge from his government's intolerance at Paris and Stockholm. Another Dutch engineer, Humphrey Bradley of Bergen-op-Zoom, drained French marshes in the reign of Henry IV, and it was a Dutch family, Robais from Middelburg, who developed the textile industry of Abbeville some years later. The capitalist, Louis de Geer, played a prominent part in the development of Swedish mining and was equally at home at Stockholm or Amsterdam. All nations came to Amsterdam as the world's premier exchange, somewhat scathingly mentioned by the English poet Andrew Marvell as a fountain of potential schism :

> ' Hence Amsterdam, Turk, Christian, Pagan, Jew,
> Staple of sects and mint of schisme grew :
> That bank of conscience, where not one so strange
> Opinion but finds credit and exchange. '

In spite of its political instability, this was probably the most notable period in the history of the United Provinces.

2. *The Calvinist supremacy*

The seventeenth century in Holland opened with a bitter religious controversy of far-reaching importance which ended with a victory for the rigid Calvinists at Dort in 1618. This meant far more than the triumph of a particular creed. Although the victorious Calvinism did not swamp Dutch literature or life, yet its political and social consequences were considerable. It resulted in the triumph of the party which wanted the renewal of war with Spain and was utterly opposed to conciliation with the southern provinces now under Spanish and Catholic rule. In these circumstances there could be no possible hope of maintaining the union of the Netherlands. Triumphant Calvinism did much to shape the Dutch character and mould future Dutch society. ' The ultimate result of this persistent pressure of the Church in the new order of things brought about by the revolution of 1618-19 was that the middle-class and peasantry in the Northern Netherlands acquired an unmistakably Reformed and Puritan cast of thought and conduct.' [1]

The dispute was caused by the criticism of Calvin's rigorist views of predestination and allied subjects by Arminius, or Harmensz, a professor at Leyden. His followers argued that the Calvinist view

[1] P. Geyl, *The Netherlands Divided*, 82.

as it stood did not accord with God's mercy and illogically made
God the author of sin; 'the dreadful doctrine of predestination
renders useless all remonstrance and punishment and destroys all
zeal for godliness'. Arminius, a mild, learned consumptive, died
in 1609, but the cause which he had generated continued to inflame
clerical and lay opinion. In an attempt to test or try the Arminians,
who had a stalwart leader in Uytenbogaert, the rigorists demanded
that a national synod be called, but the States-General had no wish
as yet to divide the country on a religious issue.

But the matter was not specifically religious. The theological
assumptions upon which the two parties depended were profoundly
philosophical and drew forth a vast literature, but even so, they were
closely related to the all-important question of the power which the
State had in respect of Church affairs.[1] Moreover Arminius'
opponents taunted him with papalism and treason. If he criticised
the doctrine of the elect as Calvin had set it forth, he was asserting
that Jesus Christ died for all men. To suggest that Jesus Christ
died on the Cross to save the Spaniards as well as the Dutch Calvinists was surely tantamount to treason. The danger appeared the
more real as everyone knew that there were Catholic missionary
priests at Cologne and Louvain who would readily assist the
Arminians to defeat the Dutch Calvinists. The matter was further
confused by the fact that the Arminians were supported by the Grand
Pensionary, Oldenbarneveldt, and some of the Estates of Holland
who wished to prolong the truce which had been signed with Spain
in 1609. The very fact that the Estates' rights were involved in a
religious dispute made the discussion the more troublesome as such
rights appeared to challenge the federal authority. Far from being
a mere academic dispute the Arminian controversy epitomised many
of the problems which made the government of the United Provinces
so unstable in the first half of the seventeenth century.

The first significant step occurred in 1609 when the Arminian
leader, Uytenbogaert, in company with Oldenbarneveldt, drew up a
Remonstrance, stating their views on justification by faith and asking
for the protection of the Estates of Holland. The Estates of Holland,
never unwilling to extend their authority, agreed to do this, but urged
restraint on both sides, especially in respect of those questions
'which are at present, God help it, all too much in dispute'. This
was like throwing a stone into a wasp's nest. Arminius' opponents,
led by the implacable Plancius of Amsterdam and Festius Hommius

---

[1] The problem has been discussed in great detail by Douglas Nobbs
in his *Theocracy and Toleration, A Study of the Disputes in Dutch Calvinism
from 1600 to 1650* (1938).

of Leyden, drew up a Counter-Remonstrance, vigorously asserting the infallibility of the Calvinist view of election. But as yet everything seemed to favour the Remonstrants. The Estates of Holland were obviously willing to turn a blind eye to what in some instances was a virtual persecution of the Contra-Remonstrants. And then in 1614 they actually defined the teaching of the Reformed Church by taking a middle standpoint, condemning both the view that 'God the Lord created any man unto damnation' or 'that man of his own natural powers or deeds can achieve salvation, both tending to God's dishonour, and to great slandering of our Christian Reformation, and conflicting with our good judgment.'

However sensible such conclusions might seem to a later generation, at the time they only added fuel to the flames. The Contra-Remonstrants were indignant that the Estates of Holland should even try to prescribe what the Church should believe. It was even more serious for the Remonstrants that Oldenbarneveldt's strong advocacy of their cause in the Estates of Holland should have lost him the goodwill of the rich commercial city of Amsterdam. The burghers of Amsterdam were bitterly opposed to the peace policy for which the Grand Pensionary stood, believing that a prolongation of the truce with Spain would damage their plan for establishing a Dutch West India Company, the chief object of which was the pillage of the Spanish trade in the West Indies. Once again politics and economics had been intruded into what was professedly a religious dispute. The Remonstrants had one further disadvantage, the enmity of the Stadholder—and leader of the war party—Maurice of Nassau. Maurice was not a particularly religious man but he had gradually grown to dislike Oldenbarneveldt. Believing that a strong Catholic but anti-Spanish government suited the Dutch better than a France split asunder by civil and religious strife, Oldenbarneveldt had opposed the Stadholder's plans for supporting the Huguenots. This was enough in itself to get Oldenbarneveldt and his supporters branded as papists. James I's representative at the Hague, Sir Dudley Carleton, had also been told to use his influence against the Grand Pensionary, for it seems that the 'wisest fool' was more moved by the rivalry of the Dutch East India Company and by the way in which Oldenbarneveldt had made him evacuate the 'cautionary towns' which England had held since 1585 than by the merits and demerits of the theological questions under discussion.

A crisis could not be long delayed. With passion mounting and violence increasing, the States-General agreed to summon a national synod to deal with the religious dispute, the Estates of Holland alone dissenting to this decision. The Grand Pensionary was so irritated by this proposal that he pushed matters perilously close to civil war by persuading the Estates of Holland to approve the townships' rights to employ special troops—the Waardgelders—for the protection of law and order. It was asserted that the regular troops stationed in the same district were obliged to co-operate with the Waardgelders whatever their previous instructions. The ' Sharp Resolution,' as this was called, was an act of defiance flung at the unitary authority of the State and at the federal army headed by Maurice of Nassau. With pamphlet and pulpit literature reaching new heights of scurrility the Resolution was little less than an ultimatum to the States-General. By the beginning of 1618 the Contra-Remonstrants had prevailed on a willing Stadholder to use his authority to dismiss Remonstrant magistrates in a number of places in Gelderland and Overyssel. Following his lead the States-General ordered the disbandment of the Waardgelders. As Utrecht, which had hitherto supported Holland, was forced to comply with this decree, Holland, a divided state at best, was left isolated. Supported by the States-General, Maurice ordered the arrest of Oldenbarneveldt and other notable Remonstrants including the well-known jurist Grotius, and by displacing their supporters from the Estates secured unanimous approval for the trial of the arrested men. The monstrous miscarriage of justice which passed for a trial ended in Oldenbarneveldt's execution which took place at the Binnenhof on May 12th, 1619, and in the sentence of his accomplices to varying terms of imprisonment. ' Is this ', the great statesman asked, ' the wages of the three and thirty years' service that I have given to the country ? '

Meanwhile the Synod of Dort had met in November, 1618, to deal with the theological aspect of this dispute. An attempt to give the Synod a more representative character by inviting members of foreign Churches to its deliberations failed to conceal the fact that it was dominated from first to last by the Contra-Remonstrants headed by the Frisian Bogerman who was elected its president. After long debates the Remonstrants were ignominiously expelled and condemned and the Calvinists' views were accepted as the only valid doctrines.

What did the Calvinist triumph mean ? At first there was a spirit of persecution abroad which came inappropriately from a country which had once suffered from the Spanish Inquisition. Remonstrant ministers were ejected from their livings and in some cases expelled from the State. The leading universities, Leyden, Franeker and Groningen, were purged of professors who deviated from the party line. But this attempt to canalise the country's culture into the pure waters of Calvinism soon failed. Yet it was the Calvinist triumph which made impossible any future reconciliation with the Catholic south, and, as we have seen, fastened on to the country the puritanical outlook represented by the action of the local consistories.

The struggle between the Remonstrants and their opponents illustrated the conflict between the Federal and State authorities and was not yet at an end. The Synod of Dort formed a prelude to the renewal of the war with Spain, which for the time being was to strengthen further the Stadholder's power in the State.

3. *War and the Stadholderate*

While the victory of the Calvinist and pro-war party made it certain that the truce with Spain would not be renewed when it came to an end in 1621, war represented something that was more important to the Dutch as a whole than division over controversial doctrine. Even the gap created by the decisions of the Synod of Dort was partially closed by the end of the truce, for whatever his religious views no Dutchman would have willingly accepted the Spanish terms, viz.: freedom of worship for the Catholics, the opening of the river Scheldt and the evacuation of the East and West Indies. These conditions would have struck at the commercial and religious independence of the country and have made its political independence dubious.

By 1621 religion and war had divided two peoples who might in other circumstances have remained one nation. The negotiations for possible reunion opened between 1631 and 1635 never had any real chance of success. Under the patronage of the Archduchess Isabella hopes of peace were raised, but the southern delegation sent to the Hague reported that if it agreed to the Dutch terms ' the King (Philip IV) would keep only the bare title, as he is King of Jerusalem; and that they would therefore find it difficult to accept them '. It is hardly surprising that the Spanish Netherlands, steeped as they were in a rather stiff Catholic culture, should have slowly atrophied under the unenterprising Spanish rule which excluded their merchants both from the Brazilian and East Indian trade. Thus whatever the issues involved in the reopening of the war, it was already in 1621 extremely improbable that the Southern and Northern Netherlands would be united again.

The war also had significant repercussions on the Dutch political situation. The Stadholder, besides being a good soldier, realised that his authority depended either on the continuance of or fear of war; as Admiral and General of the United Provinces he had powers in war which he was unlikely to retain for long in peace. When Maurice died in 1625, he was succeeded by his half-brother, Frederick Henry, who was equally convinced of the necessity for carrying on the war against Spain. Urged on by his ambitious wife, Amalia von Solms, and his virulent and intriguing adviser Francis van Aerssens, he hoped to increase his authority as Stadholder and to centralise the government. Such a threat to the traditional republicanism and separatist sympathies of the provinces could not go unchallenged, especially when it was linked with policies which many Dutch disliked. Since war made an understanding with Catholic France imperative, Frederick Henry stood for the Franco-Dutch alliance; indeed the culture and conversation of his court was wholly French. The Calvinist and Republican sympathies of the Dutch clashed on many points with the French and monarchical ideas of the Stadholder. This uneasiness became the more marked as the prince began to plan dynastic marriages with the tottering Stuart House of England. Finally as the war continued an anti-war party again began to rear its head in the rich commercial province of Holland.

The story of the war between 1621 and 1648 itself bore witness to the growing importance of these trends. Although the war soon became little more than a series of rather dull sieges, there were occasional crises worthy of record. The capture of Bois-le-duc by Frederick Henry in 1629 brought important additional territory to the United Provinces and spurred on an anti-Spanish reaction in the Southern Netherlands directed against the unpopular Cardinal de la Cueva. This resulted in a reopening of negotiations. It was therefore unfortunate that no freedom of religion was granted to the Catholic inhabitants of the captured town. A Spanish official, living at Brussels, summed up the position : ' If the Prince of Orange and the rebels were not kept by their fanatical intolerance from granting liberty of worship and from guaranteeing of churches and Church property to the priesthood, then a union of the loyal provinces with those of the North could not be prevented.'

The failure of these negotiations, inevitable as it was, perhaps formed a kind of climacteric in the war. Gustavus' death at Lützen, followed by the Imperial victory at Nördlingen in 1634 won by the new governor of the Spanish Netherlands, the Cardinal-Infant Ferdinand, encouraged the Spaniards and forced the United Provinces towards the French alliance. Although the Stadholder had at first stood rather aloof from the discussions, he was soon identified with the pro-French party which had grown enormously since the distribution of bribes by the able French diplomat, Charnacé. But there were those who already murmured that the rising power of France endangered Holland more than the declining power of Spain.

The war years between 1635 and 1644 were thus more important as a commentary on the growth of the peace party, anxious for the recognition of Dutch independence by Spain and the end of the French alliance, than for the details of the campaigns. Meanwhile Dutch shipping, which had greatly expanded of recent years, suffered repeated damage from privateers who sailed from Spanish-held Dunkirk. All efforts, whether by the sending of convoys or by reprisals, proved inadequate to stem the losses for which the Stadholder's incompetent naval policy was in part to blame. That was why Tromp's great victory over the Spanish fleet of D'Oquando in English waters in 1639 constituted a major landmark in the history of the war. It showed the Dutch that they were superior to the Spaniards at sea and freed them from the fear that Spanish naval supremacy might damage irretrievably their trade. The victory naturally encouraged the party which hoped that Spain could be persuaded to recognise Dutch independence.

Such hopes were furthered by the story of military events and by the Stadholder's unpopular foreign policy. The French victory over the Spanish infantry at Rocroi in 1643 reinforced the lesson that the French might be potentially more dangerous than the Spaniards. Meanwhile Frederick Henry himself had taken Sas van Gent (1644) and Hulst (1645), thus opening the way to Antwerp, but the peace party began to wonder whether Antwerp was so desirable a capture after all. It would serve the interests of the merchants of Amsterdam and Rotterdam better as a derelict port in Spanish hands than as a flourishing commercial rival.

Such feelings confirmed the rumour that the Stadholder aimed to overthrow the semi-republican constitution of the state and replace it by a centralised monarchy. His attitude to the English Civil War was certainly out of accord with that of his people as a whole. Whereas the Dutch Calvinist merchants sympathised with the Puritans in their struggle against the Stuarts, the Stadholder and his court openly favoured Charles I, giving his sanction to a marriage between his heir William and the English King's daughter, Mary. A similar difference of opinion occurred over Dutch relations with Sweden and Denmark between whom war had broken out in 1644. The Dutch had many interests in Sweden and wanted the Danes to lower the tolls on Dutch shipping passing through the Sound. Knowing that the English royal house placed some hopes on Danish intervention, the Stadholder unwisely tried to block the close understanding which had hitherto existed between Sweden and the United Provinces. Nor was the Stadholder's position in any way strengthened by his inevitable surrender to the demands of the Estates of Holland, the conclusion of an armed alliance with the Swedes and the subsequent reduction in the dues which the Danes levied on Dutch ships passing through the Sound by the Treaty of Christianopel. The collapse of the English cause after Naseby (1645) was yet another setback for the Stadholder.

The last years of the Stadholder's life were thus darkened by the growing shadow of the Estates of Holland. The plans for attacking Antwerp were shelved. The death of Frederick Henry and the accession of William II reinforced the peace party, now as heavily bribed by the Spaniards as the war party had previously been by the French. In spite of French opposition, in April 1648 the States-General decided to ratify the terms which the plenipotentiaries had reached at Münster. The Treaty of Münster was the culmination of the long struggle which had opened eighty years earlier. King Philip IV acknowledged that the ' Lord States-General of the United Provinces, and the respective Provinces thereof, with all their associated Territories, Towns and dependent Lands are free sovereign States, Provinces and Lands '. The Spaniards also recognised the permanent closure of the rivers Scheldt and Zwyn, thus assuring the continued economic pre-eminence of the United Provinces. The death of William II in 1650 and the seizure of power by the republican elements in the Estates seems almost an anti-climax after this; but it is significant that just as the ending of hostilities with Spain led to the virtual abolition of the Stadholderate, so did the war with the French bring about its restoration twenty-two years later.

4. *Economic supremacy*

The rise of the Dutch to economic pre-eminence in Europe is a fascinating subject, made the more astonishing by the fact that the population of the country was never more than $2\frac{1}{2}$ million people. War did no particular disservice to the Dutch since it involved the closing of the northern port of Antwerp and the transfer of much of its trade and business to Amsterdam. War was indeed one of the causes which led the Dutch to search for markets outside Europe and so brought about the foundation of a colonial empire. Furthermore from the days of the Sea-Beggars, the sea had been one of the theatres of warfare on which the Dutch had been able to hold their own against the Spaniards.

And it was on the sea rather than on warfare that Dutch commercial greatness was really founded. The Dutch herring fisheries gave their sailors invaluable experience and were the foundation for an expanding coastal trade.[1] Growing Dutch hold over the European carrying trade was undoubtedly assisted by the low cost of shipbuilding in Holland. Plenty of timber could be obtained from Germany—the oak was floated down the Rhine—and from Scandinavia. As the material was bought in bulk the prices were moderately low, and in any case the low rates of interest in Holland made shipbuilding there a cheaper process than in other countries. The Dutch had even achieved a primitive kind of mass production which enabled their shipyards to produce the *fluitschips* at a comparatively rapid rate. A further economy, both in respect of bulk and speed, was gained by making such ships merchantmen pure and simple instead of something between a merchant and a war vessel.

Thus the coastal traffic flowed into the Mediterranean as well as into the Baltic. Levantine goods and Sicilian corn passed to Holland in exchange for Dutch fish, cheese and other manufactures and continued in spite of the war with Spain. Spanish trade was so precariously balanced that the Spanish Kings had often to turn a blind eye to commerce between the two countries after a definite rupture had been made in their relations. Nevertheless, as we have noticed,[2] Spanish command over the Straits of Gibraltar, the closing of the ports of Lisbon and Cadiz to Dutch shipping limited the extent of Dutch trade in the Mediterranean area and was one of the reasons which led Dutch sailors to cruise further afield.

The Dutch colonial empire was not unlike the British in that it was an accidental outcrop of commercial needs, but there the analogy ends. During the sixteenth century the Portuguese had monopolised the spice trade on which every other western country had cast covetous eyes. The desire for the ' rich spicery ' was one of the reasons which led sailors to try to find a north-east and north-west passage by which the Portuguese controls might be evaded. The absorption of the Portuguese empire into that of Spain naturally made Portuguese shipping a legitimate prey to the Dutch. Dutch interest in Portuguese India was further stimulated by the publication in 1595-96 of the *Itinerario*, an invaluable travel book written by a Dutchman, Jan van Linschoten, who had been in the service of the Portuguese archbishop of Goa. Linschoten's book formed the basis for Houtman's voyage to the East, a useful reconnaissance which formed the prelude to a great burst of maritime activity.

[1] See p. 257.   [2] See pp. 257-8.

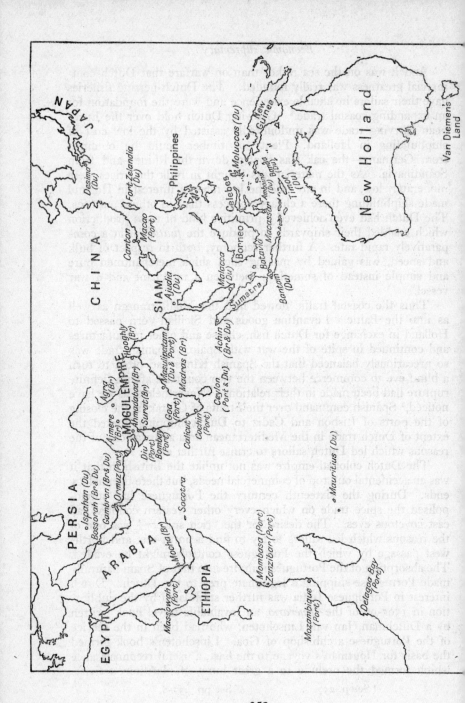

Japan

Desima (Du)

Fort Zelandia (Du)

New Guinea

Moluccas (Du)

New Holland

Van Diemen's
Land

Philippines

CHINA

Canton

Macao (Port)

Celebes

Borneo

Amboina (Du)

Macassar (Du)

Ternate (Du)

Timor (Du)

SIAM

Ajudia (Du)

Malacca (Port)

Sumatra

Batavia (Du)

Bantam (Du)

Achin (Br)

Hooghly (Br)

Agra (Br)

Masulipatam (Du & Br)

Madras (Br)

Ceylon (Port & Du)

MOGUL EMPIRE

Ahmadabad (Br)

Surat (Br)

Ajmere (Br)

Goa (Port)

Calicut (Port)

Cochin (Port)

Diu (Port)

Bombay (Br)

PERSIA

Ispahan (Du)

Bassorah (Br & Du)

Gambroon (Br & Du)

Ormuz (Port)

Socotra

Mauritius (Du)

ARABIA

Mocha (Br)

Massowah (Port)

ETHIOPIA

EGYPT

Mombasa (Port)

Zanzibar (Port)

Mozambique (Port)

Delagoa Bay (Port)

In the following years a number of voyages, financed by syndicates of rich merchants, sailed to the East, greatly damaging the Portuguese who had never been popular there. Apart from their business efficiency which made them select goods suitable for the eastern markets, the Dutch brought back merchandise at a lower price than could the Portuguese.

The establishment of the Dutch East India Company by the States-General was a logical development of this growing activity. If the various companies already engaged in the eastern trade were amalgamated, it would prevent trade rivalry, create a valuable monopoly and provide the new institution with overwhelming political and economic strength. The capital of the new company was immensely greater than that of the English East India Company, founded two years earlier, and was subscribed by leading merchants from all over the United Provinces. The government gave it very wide powers, a virtual monopoly of all trade from the Cape to Magellan's Strait, the authority to garrison and fortify such settlements as it might make, to seize foreign ships and even to make peace and war. The States-General retained a general right of supervision, especially over the Company's finances.

Commercial expansion seemed the sole governing factor in the astonishing and ruthless story which followed. All other considerations, moral or political, were placed at the mercy of the profit-motive. The expansion of the colonial commerce and the foundation of colonies were both closely associated with the war against Spain, but in the view of many a shrewd Dutch merchant both war and religion were subordinate to trade.

This necessarily involved the elimination of possible trade rivals and the continuance of Dutch control over such commercial settlements as might have been established. Like the Dutch company, the youthful English East India Company had been founded originally to acquire some share in the Portuguese spice trade; hence the foundation of an English settlement at Amboina. Until the conclusion of the truce with Spain Dutch and English traders worked side by side, if in no great amity at least without obvious hostility, but the signing of the truce, coinciding with James I's conciliatory policy towards Spain, freed the Dutch from any need to remain friendly with their English rivals. As soon as a governor-general arrived at Bantam in 1611 plans were evolved for pushing out the English from the East Indian trade, resulting in 1623 in the arrest of a number of English merchants by the Dutch, a mockery of a trial and their execution, followed by a funeral in which the Dutch charged for the palls on the coffins of the tortured and decapitated

M

victims. Horrified as were the English, James I did not wish to go to war; in effect the English East India Company had been turned out of the Moluccas and incidentally began to concentrate its attention on its as yet unimpressive Indian settlements.

The Dutch had still to face Portuguese competition, even though Portugal was in decline. As early as 1601 the ships of the two peoples had come into conflict in the roadsteads of Bantam to the discomfiture of the Portuguese. By 1623 the Dutch had acquired control, uncertain in some districts, over the Moluccas of which Batavia became the focal-point. Eighteen years later Governor Van Diemen captured Malacca, the last centre of Portuguese trade in East India, thus giving the Dutch complete control over the western Java Sea. A year earlier the Dutch gained a foothold in Ceylon by allying with the native King of Kandy against the Portuguese, but it was not until 1658 that they won effective control over the island. But as Ceylon was important as one of the controlling centres of the trade of the Indian Ocean, its conquest was another sign of Dutch pre-eminence.

It was one thing to establish bases and another to maintain them in the face of Portuguese, Spanish (who held on at Tidor in the Moluccas until 1663) and English interlopers, not to speak of treacherous and difficult native sultans. Considering the small population of Holland and the country's relatively poor resources, the Dutch had undertaken a major operation. Nor were the merchants of the East India Company at first eager to undertake a policy of territorial expansion. They believed that the heavy expenses in which this had involved the Portuguese was one of the reasons for their decline, but conditions in the East soon made such a policy inevitable. If the Company wished to create a monopoly of the whole of the trade between Asia and Europe, as well as the inter-Asiatic trade, fortified settlements were essential in order that such a complex commercial network could be satisfactorily protected. Thus commercial enterprise generated imperial dominion.

The steady expansion of Dutch territory in the East became one of the most important factors in seventeenth-century history. The lead in this was taken by a man of outstanding personality and ruthless determination, Jan Pieterszoon Coen who, without much cooperation from the authorities in Holland, had founded Batavia, drove out the Portuguese and the English and so laid the foundations on which his successors could build a stable dominion. The subject sultans on the fringe of Dutch settlements were gradually brought under Dutch protection. In general, Dutch colonial administration was practical and devoid of idealism. Direct Dutch rule was confined to a relatively small area of territory but there were many subject states where Dutch-appointed Regents protected the Company's interests. The native princes were allowed considerable autonomy as long as they obeyed the commercial regulations imposed by the Company. There was no missionary work nor indeed any real racial discrimination, but the Dutch insisted that although mixed marriages were allowed those who indulged in them should not return to Holland. Incidentally, while the Dutch colonists tolerated Islam, they would permit no Christian rival to the Dutch Reformed Church in their settlements.

Thus trading profits dominated the East India Company's policy from start to finish. Its colonial settlements were only commercial outposts established with the sole object of bringing wealth to the Company and its shareholders. When Coen captured the Banda Islands in 1621, he divided the land among the Company's servants who agreed to sell all the spices produced thereon to the Company at a rate fixed by it. Similarly a quarter of a century later the Dutch obliged their chief native rival, the Sultan or *Susuhunan* of Bantam, to sell all his produce to the Company. Next year (1647) native mercenaries were actually despatched to Amboina to cut down clove trees to keep the price of spice high in the European markets. A similar system of economic regulation appeared in the terms of the treaty which the Dutch negotiated with the Sultan of Ternate in 1657; the latter was forced to ban the growing of spices in the islands under his control, thus leaving the monopoly to the Dutch. Had the Dutch been primarily interested in colonial expansion, they would have made more use of the discovery of New Guinea and North-east Australia by Janszoon in 1606, the voyages of Hartogszoon and Houtman in 1616 and the remarkable voyage of Tasman in 1642 which took him to Tasmania and New Zealand. It is hardly surprising that the Dutch were the pioneers in the science of mapmaking. The only colonial settlement in the real meaning of the word was made at the Cape of Good Hope in 1652 by Jan van Riebeck, primarily as a provisioning station for ships sailing to the East Indies.

The story of Dutch enterprise in the west was more chequered and less successful, mainly because the Dutch West India Company, founded by Usselinx in 1621, was as much a means of conducting war against Spain as of getting profits from plunder and trade. But its invested capital was large and its monopoly of trade seemed as valuable as that of the East India Company as it included the very lucrative commerce in negro slaves. But some of the Dutch merchants preferred the more profitable, unlicensed trade with the Spanish colonists, while the Company's resources proved unequal to the heavy burdens of maintaining new possessions in a state of continuous preparedness against attack. Thus whereas the East India Company continued to operate until the eve of the French Revolution, the West India Company closed its doors in 1674.

Nevertheless the dramatic story of its activities in the first half of the seventeenth century showed the significant part it played in defeating the Spaniards and the Portuguese and in enriching the United Provinces. Its ships sailed into the very heart of the Spanish empire; Piet Hein's fleet in 1628 achieved one of the most brilliant of naval victories at Matanzas Bay where the greater part of the Spanish Treasure Fleet was either captured or sunk. This daring exploit took place four years after the beginning of the Dutch invasion of the rich sugar-producing region of Portuguese Brazil. They managed to secure a hold over the strip of coast-line stretching from Bahia up to the Amazon, and under the greatest of Dutch viceroys in the west, John Maurice of Nassau, it seemed likely that this might become the centre of a flourishing Dutch empire. But the Company was reluctant to sink money in a colonial enterprise the expenses of which were by no means covered by the profits from the trade in sugar. After John Maurice's recall the colony languished and a native rising following the Portuguese rebellion against Spain resulted in the expulsion of the Dutch from Brazil by 1654.

Dutch power in the West Indies still remained considerable. They kept Surinam and in 1634 captured Curaçao which was an ideal centre for illicit trade and depredations; moreover it was rich in natural salt, which could be used in the herring industry.[1] By the middle of the seventeenth century they also had a small settlement called New Netherland on the coast of North America, valuable as an outlet for the fur trade (it was at the mouth of the river Hudson) and as a base for Dutch shipping. For the actual trade of the Dutch colonies in the west was not so profitable as the carrying-trade between the colonies of all the European powers. In any case it was already problematical whether the Dutch would be able to retain their hold over this in the face of the growing hostility of maritime powers like England and France. Nothing, however, had so contributed to the wealth of Holland.

The word 'Holland' has been used advisedly, for it was to the seaboard states of Holland and Zeeland, and the city of Amsterdam in particular, that the profits of the colonial trade and the carrying trade flowed—though such wealth was naturally to some extent distributed all over the country. The East India Company for

---

[1] This, incidentally, had been originally imported from Portugal.

years paid a substantial dividend which had no equal in contemporary history. Capital was thus available for the expansion of Dutch industry, but such industry as there was was restricted by the nature of the raw materials available. Thus the sugar-refining industry at Rotterdam represented colonial interests in Brazil and the West Indies. The making of silk yarn at Amsterdam originated with the capture of two Portuguese galleons carrying Chinese raw silk in 1606. Interest in oriental china led to the development of the famous blue-and-white Delft ware. Exiles from the Southern Netherlands extended the woollen industry of Leyden[1] and the linen industry of Haarlem. Two other industries revealed the Dutch genius for making the best use of talent within their reach and adjusting it to the country's economic needs, those of printing and the making of optical instruments. The Dutch printing houses published books and pamphlets in foreign languages, thus enabling the Calvinist Republicans to maintain touch with their fellow-sympathisers abroad. The development of the diamond cutting industry and the manufacture of optical instruments illustrated the way in which economic needs fathered scientific invention. Indeed a similar integration between the scientific outlook and economic productivity found expression in Dutch agriculture, in the reclamation of land from the sea by skilled Dutch engineers, in the building of dikes and in improved agricultural methods (which included specialisation in dairying), all of which helped to make Dutch agriculture the most advanced of the century.

This vital economic life was centred on the great city of Amsterdam where were to be found many of the characteristics of the modern money-market. Its supremacy in the world of currency exchange remained practically unchallenged until the middle of the eighteenth century. The Bank founded in 1609 served as a bank of deposit and dealt in foreign exchange and bills, frequently lending money to the East India Company as well as at a later date to foreign governments. The Bourse or Stock-Exchange became the principal money-market of Europe; ' it was the currency and banking centre, the repository of economic experience and commercial intelligence, the one place in Europe where a buyer could always be put into contact with a seller or *vice-versa* '.[2] Even the cyclical depressions, so typical of the modern capitalistic world, affected Amsterdam's economic life. There was a severe economic crisis in 1636 arising out of a boom in tulips, the craze for tulips led to a fantastic rise in

[1] So the output of cloth at Leyden increased from 26,620 pieces in 1584 to 109,560 pieces in 1619.
[2] C. H. Wilson, *Holland and Britain*, 22.

shares but the bubble of profit was quickly pricked and led to a ruinous collapse of the stock market in February, 1637.

This economic supremacy which enriched the country and fostered the renaissance of art, learning and literature had its disadvantageous side, for it tended to replace moral values by commercial standards. But it was the precariousness of the foundation which made Dutch pre-eminence such a temporary phenomenon. The Dutch may have continued to hold the keys of the richest coffers in Europe until the middle of the next century, but money could not alone overcome the military might of France and the naval and commercial rivalry of England. Its rulers were often surprisingly unimaginative in their more general policies. Yet within the limits of the period the rise of the United Provinces was an astonishing story only matched by its achievements in every form of activity.

5. *Dutch culture*

Although the splendid culture of seventeenth-century Holland may be described as a late flowering of the Renaissance, it was in the main a rich indigenous product. Broadly speaking Dutch art reflected the life of the people. It was rarely stimulated by religion or by profound emotion. Dutch pictures, like so much Dutch literature, were full of accurate detail and domestic complacency. Ruysdael's windmills turn against a sky full of clouds drifting over a calm and fertile countryside. A bunch of flowers, the warm interior of a rich merchant's dwelling-house, or sailing ships in evening light characterised a people who were not in general given to mysticism or passion, reflecting a mundane culture such as one would expect in so wealthy a country.[1] The wealthy Dutch burghers bought pictures for their homes but they never flaunted their riches like the Italian patrons of the Renaissance. The republican simplicity of the Dutch mercantile aristocracy compared favourably with the ostentatious luxury of the Francophile court of the Stadholder Frederick Henry. There is a sombre magnificence about Rembrandt's picture of the Syndics, but it only throws into relief the essential shrewdness of the business men whose portraits the artist was preserving for posterity. Thus Dutch culture was bourgeois rather than aristocratic, practical rather than idealistic,

---

[1] There was also a rich cultural renaissance in the Southern Netherlands, more especially linked with the painter Rubens; but it was essentially Catholic and in the main baroque, and had comparatively little influence over style and taste in the United Provinces.

forthright rather than evasive, simple rather than elaborate, Puritan without being purely secular or rigidly religious.

Dutch literature of the period reflected all these characteristics. There was the cultured group which used to meet at the turreted castle of Muiden overlooking the orchards to the Zuyder Zee. Other writers frequented the bourgeois society of Amsterdam or found patronage at the brilliant court at the Hague. Some foreigners of distinction preferred the orderly but stimulating atmosphere of the Netherlands to the semi-feudal society of their own countries, among them the philosopher Descartes. Thus contemporary literature was many-sided. Jacob Cats represented the powerful pietist and Calvinist tendency in Dutch society. His poetry, more especially his longer poems, is marred by excessive moralising and didacticism, but he was a great master of the Dutch language. He remained the most influential figure in popular literature until the end of the nineteenth century. His contemporary, Constantyn Huygens, the father of the famous scientist, was as stiff a Protestant but his work was more intellectual, more sensitive, metaphysical and obscure. His style is terse, personal, sometimes difficult but in general permeated by a rich humanity. Hooft, on the other hand, wrote in lighter vein and was an infinitely finer poet ; his poetry is lyrical, serene ' perfect in form and structure, in rhythm and music ', full of feeling and grace. Nor did Hooft, who was the leader of the cultured circle known as the *Muidenkring*, confine himself to poetry ; later in his life he wrote history in modern style, admirably descriptive and penetrated by his stoical, aristocratic but wholly patriotic philosophy.

All these writers were overshadowed by the greatest poet of contemporary Holland, Joost van der Vondel. The ninety-one years of his life were full of infinite variety. Starting life as a Calvinist he ended it as a Roman Catholic and was yet elected the master-poet by the guildsmen of St. Luke at their annual festival in 1653. He was the friend of Grotius and attacked the Contra-Remonstrant opponents of Grotius and Oldenbarneveldt in a play *Palamedes* whose form owed much to Greek tragedy. Whether he was as representative of Dutch culture as was the ever-popular Cats is much more debatable. Nevertheless his poetry, effortless, harmonious, and stimulated by his love of beauty and truth, reached heights where his contemporaries could not follow.

To mention a few of the more outstanding writers in this way may create a false impression, for learning was widely spread in seventeenth-century Holland. The universities, where rigid Calvinism found its strongest supporters, were staffed by some of the greatest scholars of the age, more especially in those subjects where controversy was confined to pedantic philological points involving no confession of religious faith. The classical scholars, Daniel Heinsius and Salmasius, Gerard Vossius and Caspar Barlaeus had a European reputation.[1] Voetius was the greatest of contemporary theologians, erudite, doctrinaire, an intense and even a fanatical upholder of the rigid Calvinist point of view. If his moral theology struck even his contemporaries as old-fashioned, it is unquestionable that Voetius probably did more than any of his contemporaries to perpetuate the Puritan strain in Calvinist teaching in Holland. It is instructive to note that he opposed equally usury and organ-music as un-Christian and refused to accept either Harvey's theory of the circulation of the blood or the discoveries of Galileo.

The universities did not, however, embody all the intellectual activity of the country. In spite of their prosperity, their intellectual outlook tended to restrict free-speaking. Thus the greatest mind of his time, Hugo Grotius, was eventually obliged to flee from the castle of Loevestein, where he was imprisoned, concealed in a parcel of books. His ideas on international law, formulated in his famous *De Belli ac Pacis*, were closely connected with the economic development of his country. It was to the obvious interests of the Dutch merchants that he should argue, as he did, in his *Mare Liberum* that the seas should be free to all. ' Between us and the Spaniards the following points are in dispute : Can the vast, the boundless deep be the appanage of one Kingdom alone, and it not the greatest ? Can any one Nation have the right to prevent other nations which so desire from selling to one another, from bartering with one another, actually from communicating with one another ? ' Written originally to refute Spanish and Portuguese claims, such theories involved the Dutch in controversy with the English. But Grotius had to spend the remainder of his life in the Swedish diplomatic service. Some lesser minds were also affected by the intolerant intellectual discipline which was as opposed to the abandonment of the Galenic and Aristotelian systems as it was to the Pope and the Catholic Church.

This was perhaps the more surprising as the Dutch played an outstanding part in the scientific revolution of the seventeenth century. The optical and glass industries of Amsterdam provided a stimulus to work of first-class importance, more especially as a sea-going people like the Dutch required good navigational instruments, telescopes and binoculars. The telescope was almost

---

[1] Both Vossius and Barlaeus were Remonstrants and had to leave Leyden for that reason, but they continued to teach at Amsterdam.

certainly the invention of a Dutch spectacle-maker, Lippershey of Middelburg, who was paid 900 florins by the States-General for his work. That he was a craftsman reflects the close association between the Dutch optical industry and scientific discovery. The polishing of lens gave Leeuwenhoek the ideas that led him to construct the first simple microscope. It was amidst such a fertile and ingenious community that Christiaan Huygens flourished. The son of the poet and statesman and the friend of John Donne, he undoubtedly possessed one of the best minds of the century. His scientific work was essentially practical, but with profound bearings on theory. He was only twenty-six when he discovered the fourth satellite of Saturn and observed the nebula of Orion. There followed the pendulum clock, claimed also by the English scientist Robert Hooke, significant improvements in the telescope, the micrometer, and a newly-invented air-pump. Later he was responsible for the enunciation of the laws governing the collision of elastic bodies, the wave theory of light and the theory of the polarisation of light, all of which place him on the same plane as Sir Isaac Newton. This studious, cheerful bachelor symbolised the magnificent achievement, the inventive genius and the shrewd practical nature of the seventeenth-century Dutch scientist.

Similar circumstances brought into being both a literary revival and a distinctively Dutch school of painting. Whereas in the Southern Netherlands the superb paintings of Rubens and his pupils, among them the precocious Van Dyck, stand firmly in the European tradition, Dutch art was far more native and in keeping with the character of the people in subject-matter and style. Franz Hals, brought up in Haarlem, was primarily an interpreter of ordinary men and women. He has bequeathed to us a matchless portrait-gallery in which that society itself lives on, with all its self-confidence, its positiveness, its zest for life, its unconscious swagger. Just as Hals interpreted character, so others depicted the natural beauty of the country itself, whether in the poplar-lined avenues of Ruysdael and Jan van Goyen, or the red-roofed towns and luminous water of a Vermeer.

The greatest Dutch artist of the period cannot, however, be confined to a category. Like Vondel in literature, Rembrandt was a European genius. At its best his work has never been surpassed, either in the sombre richness of its colouring or in the play of light and shadow so well illustrated in his famous painting *The Night Watch*. This miller's son, who became wealthy and yet died poor, who refused to visit Italy lest his style be affected by the Italian manner of painting, infused his own dynamic and egoistic emotional experience of life into his art. But it is not only his comprehensive and dramatic treatment which gave him fame. His etchings, probably unequalled in his own line, show his ability to size up a subject in a deft and masterly fashion. European in genius, there remains something instinctively Dutch in his bold and forceful approach to his subject-matter, nor can any one else so well represent the Golden Age or *Roemrijke* of the country where he lived.

CHAPTER XX

THE SPANISH EMPIRE IN DECLINE, 1598-1665

1. *The decline of Spain*

SPANISH history in this period was full of contrasts. At the beginning of the seventeenth century Spain's imperial greatness was more obvious than its decline, whereas by 1700 the world regarded Spanish decadence as a recognised fact. Disputes as to the ultimate reason for this decrepitude have gone on interminably, but no one cause can explain why the Spanish empire lost its original vigour. In the first half of the century paradox was never far away from its history. When Philip II died in 1598 the Spanish universities were crowded with students and staffed by professors of international fame ; there was a healthy Church life and much to suggest deepened spiritual perception in the country as a whole, leavened indeed by superstition and intolerance. The government was relatively efficient. The empire was one of the richest and most extensive that the world had ever known. There had been considerable economic progress during the sixteenth century. Spain possessed the second largest merchant marine before the union with Portugal in 1580 gave it shipping which enabled it to outstrip all its rivals. Industry had developed as the growth of centres like Burgos, Segovia and Toledo clearly indicate. Moreover that the population of peninsular Spain should have increased by 15 per cent. during the sixteenth century in spite of emigration to the New World and the necessity for maintaining garrisons in many parts of the world is a further proof of economic advance. But, to accompany all this, there were signs of decaying industry, a poor agriculture, repeated bankruptcies, an extravagant court ruled over by kings tainted in blood as in mind, in a phrase, an empire dangerously near to degeneration. As time passed the victory of inertia over energy, of decay over progress, became more and more apparent.[1]

[1] But it is necessary to guard against too much emphasis on the Spanish economic decline. In Professor Earl Hamilton's words : ' Strong biases . . . have infused into economico-historical literature an exaggeration of Spanish economic decadence in the seventeenth century. The Germans have tended to magnify the extent of the collapse in order to glorify the Emperor Charles V through contrast ; the French in order to exalt the economic policy of the first Bourbons ; and the liberals of all countries in order to place absolutism, the Inquisition, the persecution of minorities, and the Moorish expulsion in a more unfavourable light.'

The decline was indeed symbolised in the personalities of the Hapsburg line of kings. Philip II's son and heir, Philip III, was an affable and pleasure-loving monarch. He was indifferent to the responsibilities of government which, unlike his father, he was willing to leave in the hands of his favourites, the most important of whom was the courtly Duke of Lerma, a mediocrity who used his power to enrich himself rather than to prevent the impoverishment of Spain. On his disgrace, his son, the Duke of Uçeda, filled his position with a curious lack of filial obligation but with no greater success. The feeble Hapsburg king hovered in the background, more and more concerned with the condition of his soul as ill-health began to dog his weary limbs. The most dramatic incident in his monotonous life was the scene at his death-bed when the relics of former saints were pressed in gruesome fashion to the dying King's side in a vain effort to save his life. He bequeathed his state to an attractive but incompetent King, his son, Philip IV, familiar to so many through Velasquez' magnificent portraits.

Philip's character forms a fascinating and significant study. His good intentions never faltered and were never fulfilled. As his father had fallen under Lerma's influence, so the new King, devoid of will-power, was soon under the control of Olivarez; but when that much-hated minister was at last disgraced, Philip quickly gave up the idea of governing Spain himself, with which he had played momentarily, and gave his confidence to Count Luis de Haro. The King was a strange mixture. He was a cultured aesthete, generous, charming and elegant, possessed of a sense of duty which troubled his conscience the more he tried to stifle it. He was abnormally self-indulgent and sensual, finding relief from tedious wives in low intrigues. The King himself was well aware of all this, so well aware that on occasions the strain of religious fanaticism and melancholy, often found in the male members of his house. vanquished the epicurean pleasure-seeker. His correspondence with the abbess whom he consulted on moral problems, Sor Maria de Agreda, is a minor religious classic. He alternated between dissipation and degrading remorse, a remorse which was all the more terrifying as he believed that Spain's woes were God's judgment on his own immoral life. In this at least he was wrong. They were the result of his inheritance rather than of his defective character. He died in 1665, leaving his empire to an epileptic child, Charles II, around whose bed the vulture-like courtiers and foreign ambassadors were to gather in anticipation of his decease for the next thirty-five years.

Some would argue that the fatal flaws in the line of Spanish Hapsburg kings in fact represented the Spaniard's own ineptitude for imperial dominion. At that time and later it was asserted that the Spaniard's natural disinclination to work, the familiar procrastination summed up in the word *mañana*, was the real reason why Spain failed at the last in the race for empire. And, it is added, the Spanish hidalgos' racial pride led them so to despise mercantile activities that they preferred to starve amidst splendour than to soil their hands with honest toil. There is an atom of truth in both generalisations, but it is so slight that it is hardly worthy of credence. The history of Spain has shown that if indolence is a national failing, willingness to labour is also a characteristic of the Spanish people. Much nonsense is talked about the decline of the Spanish empire. The empire lasted for nearly three hundred years, and might have lasted longer if Napoleon had not brought the unworthy Bourbon line to a close by invading Spain and so loosening the contacts between metropolitan Spain and her dominions overseas ; nor was it badly or oppressively governed. If it is true that the Spanish *hidalgo* scorned trade, he never scorned its profits. The reason for the decline in the economic productivity of the empire is to be found elsewhere.

Protestants seeking to explain the decadence of a great Catholic power have sometimes found a fundamental and to them a pleasing explanation in the Spanish devotion to Catholic orthodoxy. Spanish liberals like Ramon y Cajal, often anti-clerical, have also made much of this point of view. With some justification they argue that the sombre traditionalism of Spanish learning atrophied all new ideas and scientific developments. The Englishman, H. T. Buckle, came to a similar conclusion : ' everyone believed ; no one inquired ', a process which Cajal summarised as ' spiritual encystment '. Yet it is doubtful whether this apparent intellectual isolation and paucity of scientific study were wholly due to the pressure of an intransigent Church ; if Italy and France, two other Catholic countries, could produce savants and critics, there is every reason to suppose that Spain could have done the same. It is, however, undeniable that the Spanish Church was more intolerant of new ideas than contemporary Churches in other Catholic countries. The policy of the Church undoubtedly impeded progressive thought but it cannot account for the decline of Spain, any more than the large numbers of nuns and priests per head of population explain the reason for the decline of the population in the seventeenth century when the population of every other country was growing.

Others traced the decline of Spain to the expulsion of the Moors, a process begun by Ferdinand and Isabella, carried further by Philip II and completed by his son, Philip III. Even if some of the Moors intrigued with their co-religionists, the Barbary Corsairs, their expulsion was a wicked and unjustifiable act perpetrated in the name of religion and patriotism. The Moors had suffered from continuous ill-usage, were misunderstood and subjected to exceptionally heavy financial burdens as well as other disabilities. The Council did indeed try to protect the *Moriscos* on their journeys to the coast, but that much suffering was caused cannot be doubted; even Richelieu, who was not ordinarily an unduly sympathetic man, described the expulsion of 1609-14 as the ' most barbarous stroke ' in human history. All the same the economic and social effects of what took place have been over-estimated. Many *Moriscos* continued to live in Spain in spite of the edicts, sometimes with the connivance of their landlords who did not wish to lose good tenants and hard-working farmers. It is in any case probable that the economic decline of eastern Spain where most of the *Moriscos* lived had started before their expulsion. Contemporaries were thus given a false impression by the fact that the expulsion coincided with an economic depression. There is little evidence to suggest that the expulsion of the Moors had much immediate effect on Spanish agriculture. Their departure may well have made the economic crisis worse but it did not cause it.

The economic decline was much more fundamental. On all sides there is abundant evidence for the collapse of the incipient industrial revolution, the impoverishment of agriculture and the fall in exports. Naturally these three trends were closely inter-related. The reduction in manufactures, which obliged Spain and its colonies to rely more and more on goods imported from foreign countries, helped to create an unfavourable balance of trade. It is an astonishing fact that in an age of almost continuous warfare the Cortes should have had to petition the Crown to import artisans to sustain the Spanish armaments industry. The fall in the number of ships engaged in carrying goods to and from Spanish ports, both in the mother country and in the colonies, was a sinister characteristic of the country's unbalanced commerce. It has been reckoned that from the last quarter of the sixteenth to the last quarter of the seventeenth century the tonnage of ships carrying goods between Spain and her empire had fallen by 75 per cent. Much of this trade had passed into foreign hands. Complaints about declining industry were unending. If Spain's inability to develop its industries resulted from the government's failure to subsidise them the government's faulty currency policy was even more responsible for Spain's commercial decline.

Agriculture also showed signs of withering, in part because of the privileges bestowed on the wealthy corporation of sheep-farmers, including owners of large and small migratory herds, which caused the arable land to languish. The sheep-farmers had the right to trim or even to cut down trees for fences, fire and other purposes during the periodic migrations of their herds. Moreover the owners of both migratory and sedentary herds (on the increase in Spain during this period) indulged in the practice of burning the land in the autumn to produce good Spring pasturage for the sheep. The Mesta had also used all its influence to prevent the enclosure of arable land. At the same time large estates were in process of formation, mainly for sheep-grazing. But it may be suspected that the landlord's unwillingness, and even inability, to enrich a naturally infertile soil, from which the Spaniards tried to wrest so inadequate a living, as they still do, was a more significant reason for the failure of agriculture to develop than the privileges of the Mesta. Some evidence at least suggests that the Crown viewed the Mesta with increasing disfavour, and it is certain that the number of migratory herds fell very sharply in the seventeenth century. Spanish agrarian policy, or lack of it, was a fatal legacy from which the country still suffers.

These were symptoms rather than the causes of the underlying disorder. If we would seek further for the reasons of Spain's decline, we will find them in the economic policy of the government and in the politics involved in Spain's rise to imperial dominion. Wealth continued to flow from the Spanish-American mines, though at a steadily decreasing rate, into the mother country, but the greater part was already ear-marked for the Crown's debtors. Spanish silver had been passing from the mother-country to Flanders and Italy in return for loans for many years. Until its fall in 1585 Antwerp had been the main source from which the American treasure was redistributed in the direction of Germany, northern Europe and the British Isles, but after this more and more silver had passed to the Genoese bankers. So that Spain suffered from the rise in prices [1] without even enjoying to any great extent the use of the gold and silver which caused it. In these circumstances the government should have tried to stimulate production in the hope that by so doing it could create a favourable balance of trade. But there was no minister during the reigns of Philip III or Philip IV who had the least understanding of his country's real needs, or indeed even

---

[1] The Spanish government sought, if rather unsuccessfully, to keep the bullion in Spain itself. This mercantilistic policy had, in the view of Professor Hamilton, 'raised prices and costs above the level in other European countries, and thus handicapped industries, naval construction, and navigation.'

the ability to cope with its many economic problems. The ineptitude of ministerial control throughout the seventeenth century forms a strong contrast with the conscientious administration of Philip II. Whatever action was taken to order economic and social life normally made the situation worse rather than improved it. With the decline in revenue and the rise in costs, minister after minister had to devise some expedient to fill his treasury. The great banking houses like the Fuggers and the Welsers had themselves fallen victims to the Spanish crown's repeated inability to pay its debts and some, at least, had gone bankrupt; the King had killed the goose that laid the golden eggs. The heavy burden of taxation, from which the nobles were exempt, fell on a poverty-stricken peasantry[1] and a middle-class of merchants and traders increasingly unable to make both ends meet. The Crown had long ago resorted to the sale of offices, orders and titles, for which the Spaniard had an unhealthy and inordinate passion. It could now play with the currency, indulging in the debasement of the coinage and the issue of vellon money which Philip II had always refused to consider in spite of demands for it from some of his advisers. This in its turn reduced credit, helped to cause business crises, created discontent and decreased the amount of trade.

All these things, incompetent kings, selfish and short-sighted ministers, a declining economy, were perhaps ultimately subservient to the circumstances of history. If the Spanish Crown had ordered its resources better initially, the situation might have been less critical, but the wars in which Spain was involved would still have made it dangerous. War has been so rarely profitable that governments should have learned the lesson that it is the most vicious of luxuries. The ministry of Lerma fortunately coincided with a period of peace; war with France had been ended by the Treaty of Vervins in 1598; war with England, where Spain's only first-class diplomat Gondomar was to serve his country well, came to an end in 1604; the twelve years' truce was signed with the United Provinces in 1609. But this much-needed breathing space did not coincide with a period of economic rehabilitation nor did it represent a change of heart on the part of Spain's governors. Philip IV's favourite, Don Gaspar de Guzman, Count-Duke of Olivarez, introduced some reforms in the administration at the start of his ministry, but he soon put the interests of his family before that of the nation. Even the one aspect of his policy which could be called constructive led to unmitigated disaster. He aimed to break down the

[1] Thus heavy taxation, rather than the expulsion of the *Moriscos*, accounts for the ruin of the sugar industry of Granada.

deep-founded Spanish provincialism by administrative and legal uniformity. This provoked a rising among the Basques, the most independent-minded of the Spanish races, and much more serious trouble in Catalonia, where the rebels were helped by the French, which it took the Spanish Crown twelve years to suppress. The same sort of thing caused trouble in Portugal, again stimulated by Richelieu's intrigues. The Portuguese, whose liberties and virtual autonomy Philip II had promised to preserve, watched the selection of Spaniards to rule them with growing indignation. The rebels found a figure-head in the leading claimant to the throne, Don John de Braganza, and in a long and epic struggle of twenty-six years won their independence from Spain.

The early victories of the Portuguese awoke the King from his apathy, if but temporarily, and brought about Olivarez' disgrace and retirement, but his successor Don Luis de Haro was no more successful in his conduct of affairs. In addition to the risings in Portugal and Catalonia, Spanish rule was severely challenged by the outbreak of a rebellion in Naples where discontent with Spanish maladministration had been growing for some time. With the object of raising a revenue to prepare a fleet to guard Naples against threatened French attack, the Spanish viceroy decided to impose a tax on fruit which at once led to disturbances; soon the fruit with which the Neapolitans pelted the tax-collectors was replaced by more dangerous missiles. The lead was taken by a young and energetic fisherman, Masaniello, who quickly gathered a force big enough to demand that the Spanish viceroy comply with the rebels' demands. Success went to the fêted rebel-leader's head; all who did not obey his least whim lost their lives. The gross indiscretions and eccentricities of Masaniello clearly showed that he was insane; but his murder by assassins in the pay of Spain far from ending the rebellion led to a show of popular feeling rare even in that city. It is said that 100,000 people attended his funeral, and that 4000 priests took part in the last rites, but when the same contemporary adds that the dismembered head joined the trunk and blessed the excited congregation, credibility gives way to distrust. It was not until the Spring of 1648 that the Spaniards regained control over Naples.

The French had played a significant part in fomenting internal dissension in the Spanish empire, and it is legitimate to argue that the rivalry of the French Bourbons and the Spanish Hapsburgs was as potent a reason as any for the heavy burden of war-expense which was crushing the country. From 1635 to 1659 the two countries were at war, but this does not disclose the full extent of Spain's war obligations. Long before the French declaration of war Richelieu had done everything possible to reduce Spanish influence in Italy and to prevent Spanish-paid troops from marching through the Valtelline to help the Austrian Hapsburgs in the Thirty Years' War. He had also done what he could to hinder the success of Spanish arms against the Dutch with whom war had recommenced in 1621. Olivarez indeed worked under the delusion that if the rebellious Netherlands could be reconquered Spain could replenish its empty treasury with Dutch money; but the sole result of the long twenty-seven years' conflict was to drain the resources of the Spanish exchequer still further, stifle the economic recovery of the Spanish Netherlands and ruin the military reputation of the Spanish army, at Rocroi where the infantry was practically annihilated, as well as to defeat the Spanish navy at the battle of the Downs.

Thus the final years of Philip IV's reign were clouded by storms which were shaking the Spanish monarchy and empire to their very foundations. Spanish history was indeed characterised by the heavy demands of war; increasing administrative inefficiency; the fulsome display of a dissipated and luxury-loving court; the decline in justice; the impoverishment of agriculture and trade; the fall in recruitment for the armed forces. All this and much else was to grow worse during the reign of the physical wreck who succeeded Philip IV in 1665. It is indeed possible to argue that it was this period of Spanish history which effectively removed Spain from the ranks of the first-class powers and which helped to create many of the problems from which it has since suffered. The country was certainly a ' Colossus with feet of clay '.

2. *Spanish culture*

There was, however, a bright side to so gloomy a picture. That this decline permeated all branches of Spanish life cannot be doubted, but it was slower and only came into being after the middle of the seventeenth century in the realms of art and learning. There was much in early seventeenth-century Spain of exceptional intellectual and cultural value, even if it was naturally limited by the demands of orthodoxy in religion and race which Spain as a nation regarded as fundamental. Thus there was never much room for scientific studies or critical thought; the Renaissance influenced Spain only in its more innocuous aspects. A Spaniard like Juan de Valdes, some of whose writings have been compared with those of Erasmus, was not truly representative of Spanish culture. Inevitably affected by European contacts, more especially by Spanish interests in Italy,

Spanish cultural life was nevertheless more steeped in medieval ideas than that of most other European countries. Thus it was in the realms of Canon Law and scholastic theology to which European scholars as a whole were paying less and less attention that Spanish scholarship excelled. Even its literature and drama owed much to medieval tradition while its art and architecture were intrinsically Catholic and religious. It was this ' genius for religion ', a phrase bound to cause acute disagreement, which overshadowed *el siglo de oro* of Spanish culture.

Roughly speaking this cultural development covered the period 1550 to 1650 and owed its existence to three things, the comparative well-being of the Spanish Church, for which Ximenez' reforms must bear much of the credit; the increasing wealth of Spain which enabled Spaniards to patronise art and learning; and the zest, enthusiasm and vitality of a proud people which were so soon to disappear. University after university was founded; some soon had a European reputation. The number of scholars grew at an ever-increasing rate, and the men who occupied the professorial chairs were often thinkers of considerable power. Salamanca, which had sixty or more professors, had nearly seven thousand students in 1584. Francisco Vitoria, a theologian of eminence, was also one of the founders of the science of international law. Paez de Castro, Zurita, Morales and Mariana were historians—but to list names which can mean little to the ordinary reader can serve no useful purpose. It is enough to state that in certain restricted fields Spanish scholarship was equal to any in Europe.

A significant advance was made in popular literature. The religious devotion of the Spaniard and his battles against the Moors had given rise to a large number of Christian romances which told with mounting monotony how gallant knights were ever on the alert to rescue fair ladies in distress. The chivalric romance, originally inspired by the medieval *Amadis de Gaul*, had in fact become sentimental and insipid. Yet in its own way this type of story formed the precursor of the new ' picaresque ' novel, a healthy reaction to the erotic sentimentality of the late medieval romance, and of the greatest of all chivalric stories, Cervantes' *Don Quixote*. The author, Miguel de Cervantes y Saavedra (1547–1616) who died on the same day of the same year as Shakespeare, was a man of varied and venturesome experience. He had studied under the humanist Hoyos, had attended Cardinal Acquaviva as a chamberlain before adopting the profession of a soldier; he served on board the galley *Marquesa* at the battle of Lepanto, but later had the misfortune to be captured by Algerian pirates who mistook him for a man of rank and fortune. After five years in captivity he returned to Spain, served as a collector of provisions for the Armada, suffered imprisonment and lived in great poverty. Seven years before he died he joined the brotherhood of the *Esclavos del Santisimo Sacramento.* The first part of his great work, *Don Quixote*, was published at Madrid in 1605. It is the story of a Spanish gentleman, who was so affected by reading chivalric romances that he determined to be a knight errant himself; taking an old hack, Rosinante, as his steed, and a country-girl, Dulcinea de Toboso, as his fair lady he sets out with his rustic but lovable squire, Sancho Panza, in search of adventure. Although it was intended as a satire on the out-moded but still popular chivalric romances, it became in fact the richest and best-written of the *libros de cabellaria.* Its good humour, its pithy sayings, and its depiction of character, that of *el ingenioso hidalgo* Don Quixote above all, counterbalance the disjointed nature of the plot and have assured it a permanent place in the world's literature. The novel is tinged here and there with anti-clericalism but this owed nothing to the author's humanist education. It is the broad common-sense of the religious man who can laugh at religious things because of his profound faith in the fundamentals on which they are based; only a humourless Inquisitor could find anything to criticise in *Don Quixote.*[1]

There was indeed much that was competent, if little else that was really outstanding, in Spanish literature of the period. Cervantes' *Novelas ejemplares*, inferior to *Don Quixote* but notable for their broad humour, represented the ' picaresque ' type of novel, the stories based on the humorous and exciting adventures of an attractive ' rogue ', which was exceptionally popular with Spaniards of his time. Spanish poetry of the period has little modern appeal. Luis de Leon, an Augustinian friar hauled up before the Spanish Inquisition in 1572 on account of his Jewish blood and lack of respect for the Vulgate,[2] wrote lyrical poems of moving beauty and intense sensibility, but the stilted and affected verse of the more popular Luis de Gongora has little intrinsic merit.

It was perhaps in dramatic writing that the Spanish literary movement reached its climax, although no permanent theatre was built at Madrid until 1579. The revival of the Spanish drama, owing

---

[1] And did so. See p. 198 n.

[2] He was charged with heresy on the grounds that he had made a new translation of the *Song of Songs* which deprived it of its supernatural meaning. After a trial lasting five years he was acquitted and recommenced his lectures to his students at Salamanca University with the phrase ' Dicebamus hesterna die '.

much to Lope de Rueda of Seville, gave a wonderful opportunity
to Lope de Vega to exercise his exceptional talents. He was a poet
and playwright of unique fertility. His friend, Montalban, asserted
that he was the author of 1800 full-length dramas, 400 *autos* and
a number of shorter pieces, of which 450 dramas and some of the
lesser works have survived; this was in addition to many poems,
one of which *La hermosura de Angelica* was written on board a
ship of the Armada which he had joined to save himself from the
clutches of the Spanish police. He wrote far too quickly to
create convincing plots, but his characters were well-drawn and
his dialogue is natural and witty. Two of his contemporaries,
Tirso de Molina and Calderon de la Barca, were also playwrights of
distinction.

The Spanish theatre, like the Spanish novel, was an essentially
national institution; but Spanish painting was less of an indigenous
product. This was in part a result of the artistic taste of the
Hapsburg kings—Titian, the Venetian, was the favourite painter
of both Charles V and his son, Philip II—and in part an effect of
Spain's Mediterranean empire. Since Philip ruled over Naples, a
notable artistic centre, as well as Spain, Spanish painting was
naturally affected by Italian example; thus the Spanish painter,
Ribera, lived at Naples and was much influenced by the style of the
Neapolitan, Caravaggio.

The most original of the Spanish painters of the period, El
Greco, was a Cretan by birth. Originally a pupil of Titian, he
lived from 1577 at Toledo where he developed an authentic style of
his own. The way in which he combined light and shade, the
peculiar elongation of his figures, the spiritual depth of his painting,
were very striking and, in King Philip's view, disagreeably un-
conventional. El Greco had indeed no mean idea of his own merits;
writing to the council of Santo Tome, which was disputing the payment for his famous picture *The Burial of Count Orgaz*, he added
to the final receipt the words: ' As surely as the rate of payment is
below the value of my sublime work, so surely will my name go down
to posterity . . . as one of the greatest geniuses of Spanish painting.'

His younger contemporary, Diego Velasquez de Silva, was a
more formal painter but no less brilliant. Indeed his colouring and
his ability to convey an atmosphere would have made him one of
the world's foremost artists, even if he had not been an unsurpassed
painter of portraits. He was as skilled as Da Vinci in depicting the
physically abnormal as paintings of the court dwarfs show. He is
perhaps best known for his realistic portraits of members of the
Spanish royal family, of the tired, unemotional face of Philip IV,

of the Infant Don Balthasar Carlos on his spirited pony and of the Infanta Margaret Teresa dressed in rose silk brocade stiff with pearls.

Although Velasquez was not himself primarily a religious painter, religion played a prominent part in the life, learning, literature and art of Spain's 'golden century'. The emotional and intellectual fibre of the contemporary Spaniard was well-suited to religious zeal; in the splendid ritual of the Mass, in his devotion to saints, in penitence and pilgrimage rather than in moral theology and discussion about religious ideas the Spaniard found a faith which gave colour and meaning to his ordinary life and a key to eternity. It is hardly an accident that many of the interiors of the Gothic cathedrals and churches of Spain, of Saint Maria del Pina at Barcelona, of the cathedrals at Gerona and Tarragona among others, were designed to allow the congregations to fasten their attention on the altar. No nation paid so much reverence to its saints. St. Teresa of Avila, a business-like mystic if ever there was one, mixed freely with the highest society and opened her conversation with King Philip II with the words: ' Sire you are thinking, " I see before me this gad-about woman ",' a description bestowed upon her by an unkindly papal nuncio. But the author of *The Interior Castle* and *The Way of Perfection*, the founder of no less than seventeen convents, was a woman of serene and profound vision. Nor was she by any means a lone figure in Spanish religious life. Her contemporary, Friar Juan de la Cruz, St. John of the Cross, was a poet who strove to pierce the obscure materialism of life to catch a glimpse of the divine vision :

> Forth unobserved, I went
> In dark and security,
> By the secret ladder, in disguise,
> In secret, seen of none,
> Oh night more lovely than the dawn !
> Lost to all things and myself,
> And, amid the lilies forgotten,
> Threw all my cares away.[1]

Spanish religion, superstitious and narrow as it often was, was as much a part of Spanish life and history as the orange groves of Andalusia and the fishing fleets of Barcelona.

The deterioration in religious thought and experience was therefore a clear indication of Spain's decline in every other field of activity. During the late sixteenth and early seventeenth century the scholastic theology taught at the Spanish universities remained

---

[1] Quoted in V. Sackville-West, *The Eagle and the Dove* (1943). The complete works of St. Teresa and of St. John of the Cross have been edited with great skill by Allison Peers.

comparatively virile. But there was a marked fall in quality, coinciding with a decline in the standard of scholarship and a reduction in the number of university students in the last half of the seventeenth century. Religious art lost its grace and strength and became mawkish or merely theatrical; even the paintings of Murillo lack the idealism that had marked, for instance, the religious pictures of his elder contemporary Zurbaran. Sanctity itself became more and more a matter of trifling miracles and saccharine piety. Superstition and orthodoxy combined to stifle spiritual and intellectual advance, thus symbolising the whole of Spanish life as the reign of Philip IV closed, a golden age now sadly transmuted into base metal.

CHAPTER XXI

THE EASTERN QUESTION

1. *The Ottoman Empire*

LYBYER'S generalisation ' war was the external purpose, government the internal purpose, of one institution, composed of one body of men '[1] truly indicates the character of the Turkish people and explains their successful advance in the sixteenth and early seventeenth centuries. The Ottoman empire, wholly without parallel in Europe, was a military despotism carried by a series of able Sultans from Asia Minor to Constantinople, and thence to the gates of Vienna. But the Turks were not barbarians. In some sense they were the conscious heirs of the Byzantine empire. Sultan Mohammed II took the additional title of Kaisar-i-Rum (i.e. Roman emperor) on seizing Constantinople in 1453. Even the ceremonial of his court was modelled on that of the tenth-century Byzantine emperor, Constantine Porphyrogenitus.

The Ottoman state consisted of two authorities, the Ottoman ruling institution or government and the Moslem institution or church. Both were founded on Mohammedan Sacred Law, the *Sheri*, which formed the basis for the written decrees or *kanuns* of the Sultan himself, the *adet* or established customs and the *urf* or sovereign will of the Sultan. The ruling institution consisted of the Sultan, the chief officers of his government headed by the Grand Vizier, and a standing army which included the famed Janissaries. The Moslem institution comprised the teachers, the theologians and the jurists; it was in the main concerned with the interpretation of the Sacred Law. The influence of the *muftis* on the development of the Ottoman state cannot be discounted for they ' embodied and fortified that conservatism and changelessness which are the basis of the faith of Islam '. It would be roughly correct to describe these two institutions as the temporal and spiritual aspects of Ottoman government.

The Sultan was the head of both institutions; his will was in theory only limited by the *Sheri* and the recognised customs of the state. By becoming ' Protector of the Holy Cities ' Sultan Selim I

---

[1] A. H. Lybyer, *The Government of the Ottoman Empire under Suleiman the Magnificent*, 91.

in effect became the spiritual as well as the temporal head of Islam.[1] The Sultan was therefore a complete autocrat. Islamic law provided that the soil of a conquered territory became his personal property. Each member of the ruling institution from the Grand Vizier downwards was his *kul* or personal slave. The women of the harem, like his sons, were completely subservient to the imperial will. A *kanun* of Mohammed II had even declared that the son who reached the throne was entitled to execute his brothers,[2] justified by the theologians by a verse in the Koran which declared that 'revolution is worse than executions'. Yet although personal slavery meant absolute dependence on his sovereign whim, his slaves enjoyed valuable privileges; thus they could receive the Sultan's *kullar* or exemption from taxation carrying certain judicial privileges with it. The Sultan embodied supreme spiritual, military and political authority in his own person.

The Janissaries formed the most remarkable and a unique aspect of the ruling institution. They were originally Christian-born children, enrolled as the Sultan's slaves between the ages of ten and twenty, so that they might become the core of the Turkish army. They were recruited as a result of capture, purchase or tribute (*devshurmeh*), the latter appearing the most normal method. Every four years a group of officials was sent to the region from which the tribute was to be exacted in order to select the best possible candidates. While many parents disliked the system as it meant a renunciation of the Christian religion, others welcomed it as throwing open the highest possible offices to their boys. There were even cases of Moslem parents persuading Christians to take their sons in order that they too might be eligible to become the Sultan's helots. Although the Janissaries were never allowed to forget that they were his personal slaves, the more able did in time rise to the highest positions in the Ottoman empire. Suleiman's Grand Vizier, Ibrahaim, provides an illustration of this point.

[1] It is usually asserted that Sultan Selim took the title of Caliph from the last of the Abbasids, but it is to be noted that although some of his predecessors had occasionally used the title, neither Selim I nor his son, Suleiman, made use of it. The first known diplomatic document describing the Sultan as Caliph is the Treaty of Kuchuk-Kainardji (1774). Mecca and Medina were the 'Holy Places'.

[2] Since there was no law safeguarding the succession of the eldest male until 1617, the probable death of the Sultan was often the occasion for plotting; rebellions in the father's lifetime were frequent. The most ambitious tried to be stationed as near as possible to the seat of government in order to be the more able to seize power when his father died. Sultan Murad III had his five brothers strangled. Mohammed III had nineteen brothers, all of whom were executed, to assure his own safety.

A Christian Greek by birth, he was captured by pirates, was eventually enrolled as a Janissary, became grand falconer, chief of the corps of pages, *beyleybey* of Rumelia and in 1523 Grand Vizier. He was evidently a cultured man, acquainted with four languages (Turkish, Persian, Greek and Italian) and a performer on the viol. After the slaves had been selected, they were divided into two classes. Those who showed intellectual promise received a thorough training as a result of which they rose to occupy high administrative office. The less-mentally agile were given a training that was mainly physical and became the Janissaries or infantry. In either case promotion depended on merit and ability. Ogier Ghiselin de Busbecq, the Imperial representative at Constantinople from time to time between 1555 and 1565, incidentally a classical scholar and botanist who introduced the horse-chestnut, the lilac and tulip into western Europe, and a shrewd observer bears witness to this : ' In making his appointments ', he wrote, ' the Sultan pays no regard to any pretensions on the score of wealth or rank, nor does he take into consideration recommendations or popularity ; he considers each case on its own merits, and examines carefully into the character, ability and disposition of the man whose promotion is in question. . . . Each man in Turkey carries in his hand his ancestry and his position in life, which he may make or mar as he will.' Another foreigner, the Venetian *bailo*, Marcantonio Barbaro, commented a few years later : ' It is a fact truly worthy of much consideration that the riches, the forces, the government, and in short the whole state of the Ottoman Empire is founded upon and placed in the hands of persons all born in the faith of Christ ; who by different methods are made slaves and transferred into the Mohammedan sect.' ' Thus the Turkish state took young men whose ancestors had borne the Christian name for centuries, and made them rulers in the greatest of Mohammedan states, and soldiers and generals in invincible armies whose chief joy was to beat down the Cross and elevate the Crescent.' [1]

The ruling institution formed then an exceptionally efficient instrument in warfare, for government was subordinate to the needs of the army. It is possible that the military skill of the Ottoman empire has been over-emphasised, but all contemporaries recognised the discipline, courage and force of the Turkish armies. Although the ruling institution was primarily a military machine, it was not necessarily a tyranny. The provincial administration

[1] A. H. Lybyer, *The Government of the Ottoman Empire under Suleiman the Magnificent*, 45, to which I am deeply indebted for much of the information in this section.

was allowed a good deal of freedom.[1]   It is probable that the Ottoman empire was neither more oppressive, given its less advanced culture, nor more intolerant than similar European states.

But this complex government machine contained within itself the seeds of its own decay.   Providing the core of the government was sound, all was likely to be well, but a rotting core could, and did, infect the whole institution.   The Sultan was invested with such autocratic authority that he was likely either to distrust his ministers or to be their tool.   Even the best of the Sultans, Suleiman, was not immune from this weakness.   He allowed his beautiful Russian wife Roxelana to divide him from his capable if boastful Grand Vizier, Ibrahaim, whose death he ordered.   When to suspicion were added degeneracy and incapacity the dangers inherent in absolute power were clearly apparent.   Selim I and Suleiman I were able and vigorous rulers.   Selim II, nicknamed the Drunkard, was incapable and indeed only saved from disaster by his very competent Grand Vizier, Mohammed Sokoli.   Of his successors only Murad IV (1623-40) showed real ability ;   several were dethroned and one murdered.   They became the prey of the women of the harem, of scheming generals and ministers and of low-born favourites.

A Grand Vizier [2] might save the state from these evils but if his powers were great, so were the dangers of his position.   Centre of all the jealousies harboured by an eastern court, he could fall from power as quickly as he could rise.   Of some two hundred viziers who acted as chief minister during the history of the empire, some twenty were executed and many more disgraced.   Of Suleiman's own viziers four out of the nine died a natural death, two were deposed and executed and three deprived of their offices.   Nevertheless a competent Grand Vizier could hold the empire together in an emergency, especially if he was a commander-in-chief of the army ;   later Sultans preferred a sybaritic existence at Constantinople to the ardours of camp-life and so lost contact with the heart of their government.

The army, especially the Janissaries, formed the third part of the ruling institution.   While they too in time decayed, they remained a vigorous body in the period under discussion.   But

[1] Moslem Law even protected Christian subjects of the Sultan from forcible conversion so long as they paid the *Kharaj* or land-tax imposed on all non-Moslems.

[2] Of forty-eight Grand Viziers who held office between 1453 and 1623 only five were Turks.   Of the remaining forty-three, of whose racial origin anything is known, all were renegades and Christians by birth, including six Greeks, eleven Albanians and Serbs, one Italian, one Armenian and one Georgian.

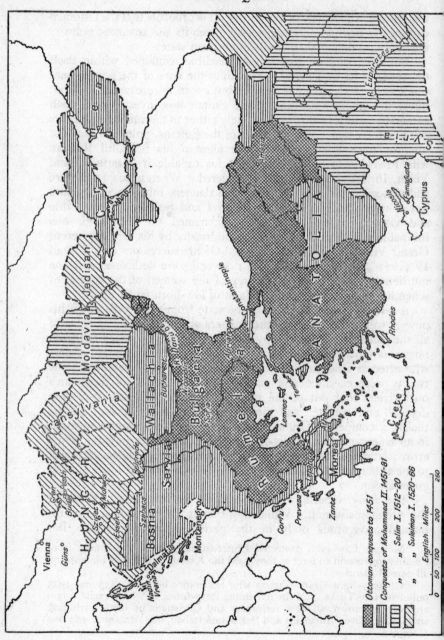

R. Euphrates

S y r i a

Cyprus

Famagosta

Nicosia

A N A T O L I A

Rhodes

Crete

Constantinople

Adrianople

Moldavia

Jedisan

Transylvania

Wallachia

Bucharest

R. Danube

R U M E L I A

Bulgaria

Sofia

Servia

Belgrade

Szabacs

Bosnia

Montenegro

Morea

Prevesa

Corfu

Zante

Dalmatia

Vienna

Güns

Raab

Gran

Buda

Pesth

Szeged

Mohacs

Essek

Vienna

H U N G A R Y

Lemnos

Tenedos

Ottoman conquests to 1451

Conquests of Mohammed II. 1451-81

    „   Selim I. 1512-20

    „   Suleiman I. 1520-66

English Miles

0 50 100 200 250

clearly the Janissaries were, like the Praetorian Guard of Imperial Rome, capable of settling a disputed succession to the sultanate and of dethroning and appointing Sultans themselves. Even Sultan Suleiman was faced with a Janissary revolt in 1525 which he had to suppress by a mixture of severity and the distribution of bribes. A strong Sultan or a capable Grand Vizier could usually control the Janissaries but masterless they might dominate the empire they were supposed to serve.

Apart from these major weaknesses, there were others which doomed the Ottoman empire, like that of Spain, to a slow decline. It lacked an efficient civil service, a full treasury (though Sultan Suleiman was much better served in this respect than Charles V or Philip II) and the cultural and economic development necessary for the maintenance of a great empire. Furthermore since the army was the government, the vagaries of war affected the country's future more than did anything else. War with the Hapsburgs or the Venetians might necessitate peace with the Persians, a people with whom the Turks were in repeated conflict. Moreover the Turkish army was essentially a summer fighting-force. If the Turkish cavalry, itself useless at capturing fortresses, was retained in service in the winter, the horses died or their owners deserted. The Sultan had often to return to Constantinople at a critical moment in a campaign in the west because of events in distant parts of his empire. The army was the focal-point of the state, but it was impossible to build a progressive and efficient modern empire round it.

2. *Turkey and Europe*

The course of events can only be understood within the general context of European history. Turkish policy was always more founded on expediency than on far-sighted diplomacy. Turkish aggression was usually a response to external pressure or foreign alliances. Thus prolonged war was often astonishingly indecisive. Four themes governed Turkish policy, the hostility of the Persians; the alliance with France; trade and war with Venice; and the opposition to the Hapsburgs in eastern Europe and the Mediterranean. These themes were often closely interrelated. So 'the sacrilegious union of the Lily and the Crescent' confronted a Hapsburg who found willing helpers in the senators of the Venetian republic and the Shiites of Persia.[1] During the sixteenth century

[1] That the Persians were Shiites (a sect of Islam separated from their opponents by a bitter controversy concerned with the succession to the early Caliphate) and the Turks were Sunnis made the struggle more bitter.

Persia had undergone a renaissance in power and culture under Shah Ismail, the first of the Safavid dynasty, and his successor, Abbas the Great (*c.* 1557-1628). The declining hold of religious sanctions was thus confirmed by the strange spectacle of the Sunnite Turk relying on French Catholic help against the Catholic Hapsburg Emperor in the unusual company of the Shiite Shah of Persia.

The French alliance with Turkey arose out of expediency but long remained one of the constant factors in the complex story of eastern Europe. Francis I would indeed have allied with the devil if the latter would have fought against Charles V, and would have deserted him with equal facility if it had suited his interests. As it was he found the Ottoman Sultan a reliable substitute who could be depended on to harass the Hapsburg army in Hungary and the Hapsburg fleet in the Mediterranean. It was in the winter of 1534-35 that Francis sent his country's first resident representative, Jean de la Fôret, to Constantinople. As a result a treaty, full of substantial privileges for France, was signed in 1536. The French were empowered to buy and sell throughout the Turkish empire on the same terms as the natives. The Turks recognised that the French merchants should be under the jurisdiction of French law administered by resident French consuls. The French were allowed to worship freely in Ottoman territory and were even given the right to mount guard over the Holy Places of Palestine. Perhaps this commercial and military accord reached its peak in 1543 when the Turks were allowed to hold Toulon.

There is a little more to be said in respect of the two other themes. The opening of the western seaboard had already reduced the economic and political significance of Venice but the Republic still ruled over a considerable territory, including the mainland along the Dalmatian coast and a number of islands in the Adriatic and Aegean Seas. The Turkish armies made repeated onslaughts on Venetian territory while pirates pillaged the city's galleys; but Venetian policy was never consistent. War between the two powers was by no means continuous nor were the Venetians willing to sacrifice their valuable trade to support a Crusade. Although Venice was still strong enough to hold the Turk in check, it could do little by itself to defeat him.

This may help to explain the close connection which existed between the Venetian and Hapsburg policy. The hostility of the Hapsburg to the aggressive moves of the anti-Christian Turk was indeed far more natural than Hapsburg-Valois rivalry. The fear that the crescent might yet replace the cross on St. Stephen's Cathedral, Vienna, never wholly disappeared. Spanish communications were cut and her possessions in the Mediterranean were pillaged by Turkish corsairs. The Counter-Reformation Popes were eager to reintroduce the idea of a Crusade, but what enthusiasm there was was more secular than religious. Only a fanatic like Pope Pius V could apply the words ' There was a man sent from God whose name was John ' to the courageous but self-centred Don John of Austria.

The period opened with unusual peace in eastern Europe. The mild and studious son of the conqueror of Constantinople, Sultan Bayezid II, who was no lover of war, was too involved in struggles with the rising Persian state and the Mamelukes of Egypt to pay much attention to events in the west. His three sons disputed the succession to his throne before his death. The ablest and the least pleasant, Selim I, won the support of the Janissaries and forced his father to abdicate in his favour. Then, with a thoroughness typical of his repellent nature, he poisoned his father and murdered his two brothers and eight nephews. Having consolidated his throne with the blood of his nearest, but not dearest, relations, he turned to other and equally rewarding projects.

Although Selim hardly intervened in European affairs during his short reign of eight years (1512-20), he was responsible for once more initiating a forward policy. Turning against the Persians he defeated them decisively at Chaldiran in 1514 and so brought northern Mesopotamia under Ottoman rule. On the grounds that the Mameluke rulers of Egypt had been allied with his enemies the Persians, the Sultan made war on them, adding Syria, Egypt and the overlordship of Arabia to his empire. The acquisition of Egypt was itself of momentous importance, being in the opinion of one modern historian of greater significance than the conquest of Constantinople itself. Apart from producing corn, rice and dates, Egypt was so placed between the Mediterranean and the Indian Ocean that the Turk could henceforth play a great part in the spice trade and in the commerce in African gold. Sultan Selim was about to launch an attack on the island of Rhodes, held by the militant crusading order of the Knights Hospitallers, when he died of plague (September 21st, 1520).

His successor, Suleiman, justly called the ' Magnificent ' by non-Turks and the ' Lawgiver ' by his subjects, was the ablest as well as one of the most attractive of the Sultans. ' He is tall, but wiry ', wrote a Venetian commentator on the first month of his accession, ' and of a delicate complexion. His neck is a little too long, his face thin, and his nose aquiline. . . . He has a shadow of a moustache and a small beard ; nevertheless he has a pleasant mien, though his skin tends to pallor. He is said to be a wise Lord, fond of study, and all men hope for good from his rule.'[1] More cultured and far-sighted than most of his line, an efficient administrator and a fine general, he gave his subjects security and a semblance of efficiency while he advanced the borders of his empire to their furthest possible limits. As soon as he succeeded his father he realised that the two chinks in Turkish armour were the fortress-city of Belgrade and the heavily-fortified island of Rhodes; the first endangered the security of his northern frontiers and the second threatened the communications between Cairo and Constantinople. Szabacs and Belgrade fell in the summer of 1521, thus opening the rich Hungarian plains to his invading armies. A year later the Knights Hospitallers under their gallant Grand Master, Villiers de L'Isle Adam, surrendered Rhodes after a siege lasting one hundred and forty-five days, as a result of which, as Pope Adrian VI commented, ' the passages to Hungary, Sicily and Italy lie open to him '.[2]

An open clash with the Hapsburgs was the obvious sequel, though the suggestion which Francis I of France, now a prisoner of Charles V in Spain, put forward that the Sultan might like to attack Hungary, may have prompted Suleiman to make a direct attack. The conditions favoured a Turkish invasion, for whereas the western powers were, as usual, much divided, the eastern world was under the control of an autocrat whose every word was law. The Turkish armies crossed the river Danube in 1526 and on August 28th imposed a decisive defeat on the army of King Louis II of Hungary and Bohemia who was himself drowned fleeing from the field on which the flower of his nobility lay slain. He was, it has been said, ' born too soon, married too soon, king too soon, and dead too soon '. ' With all these murderous swords stretched out to lay hold on the garment of life ', wrote Kemal Pasha Zadeh with typical oriental hyperbole, ' the plain seemed like a fiend with a thousand arms; with all these pointed lances, eager to catch the bird of life in the midst of slaughter, the battlefield resembled a dragon with a thousand heads.' Suleiman might have advanced further had not the season been already far advanced and had not trouble in the eastern half of his empire called him back. As it was, the battle of Mohacs

---

[1] Quoted in R. B. Merriman's, *Suleiman the Magnificent*, 33. The Imperial ambassador, Busbecq, noted that towards the end of his reign when his health was evidently declining he used rouge ' his notion being that foreign powers will fear him more if they think that he is strong and well.'

[2] The Knights Hospitallers went first to Crete but were given the right to rule Malta and Gozo by the Emperor Charles V in 1530; here they remained until the time of Napoleon.

was one of the decisive battles of the world. It opened the way to the west as well as gave him Buda and Pesth.

Three years later the Turkish host again crossed the Danube, made contact with John Zapolya, the *vaivode* of Transylvania (who claimed the Hungarian throne against Ferdinand,[1] Charles V's brother), re-occupied Buda and appeared before the gates of Vienna (September, 1529). For twenty-four days the Viennese watched the Turks levelling the houses outside their city-walls and preparing siege-mines and then the crescent wavered and the Turkish levies again marched east. ' If the King of Spain ', the Sultan wrote, ' is of a high and mighty spirit let him encounter me in the field, and that which God shall decree will then take place.' But the extremely long lines of communication, the approach of winter and the unwillingness of the Turkish army to encamp so far away from their own homes prevailed upon Suleiman to raise the siege. It was a severe blow to his prestige about which, like so many oriental potentates, he was unduly sensitive.

There were three other major expeditions in the next thirty years. In 1532 the Turkish advance was held by the courageous resistance of the fortress of Güns near the Hungarian border under Niklas Jurisic. Nine years later (1541) Suleiman invaded Hungary and once more occupied Buda, so acquiring the greater part of Hungary and Transylvania. In 1547 the Emperor's brother and King of Hungary, Ferdinand, admitted Turkish suzerainty over the small strip of Hungarian territory which he still retained by agreeing to pay an annual tribute of 30,000 ducats. The war was resumed in 1551 but neither side showed much vigour. It was on the last of these expeditions, as his army was encamped outside the fortified Hungarian outpost at Sziget that the great Sultan died (September 5th, 1566).

Warfare on the northern frontiers of the empire formed only one aspect of Turkish attack against the Hapsburgs. Suleiman's able lieutenant, Khaireddin Barbarossa, a Greek by birth, ravaged the coasts of Italy and Spain and defeated Spanish galleys. In 1534 he seized Tunis from the Mohammedan who ruled it with the intention of making it a stronghold of Islamic power and a jumping-off ground for an attack on Sicily. The Emperor perceived his danger and won his greatest victory by forcing the town's surrender in 1535. But in some ways it was a Pyrrhic triumph. Instead of garrisoning Tunis, it was handed over to a Mohammedan puppet-ruler ; recaptured by the Spaniards in 1573 it passed once more into

---

[1] Louis II, King of Hungary, killed at Mohacs in 1526 was childless. Ferdinand had married his sister Anne.

Turkish hands in 1574. Nor were Barbarossa's outrages at an end. In 1538 he defeated the combined fleets of Spain, Venice and the Papacy at the battle of Prevesa, assisted by a gale under cover of which the Christians retreated towards Corfu. Three years later the Emperor Charles V met with a bitter repulse at the hands of the elements and Barbarossa's subordinate, Hassan Aga, when he failed to capture Algiers. He had hoped to repeat his success before Tunis but it was already too late in the year when he started on his venture. Driving rain made the powder too damp to use and so permitted the defenders to make a sortie. This was turned back but not before panic had begun to spread among the Imperial soldiery, made the worse when dawn showed that the rough seas had beached no less than one hundred and forty ships. Charles decided to retreat; his expedition had cost him one hundred and fifty ships and twelve thousand men. The Turks were thus able to defeat their adversaries and to take new territory under their control; the net cost to the Venetians of their defeat amounted in land to Malvaria, Napoli di Romana, Vrana and Nadin along the Dalmatian coast and a number of islands in the Aegean in addition to a war indemnity of some 300,000 ducats.

When Suleiman died in 1566 he was the master of a great empire stretching from the borders of Persia, Mesopotamia and Arabia, with an armed spearhead still pointed at the heart of Hapsburg power and with a fleet able to dominate the Mediterranean; but he lacked the one thing necessary for ensuring the permanence of his power, a son worthy to govern such vast domains. This was in part his own fault for his wife, Roxelana, in an attempt to secure the throne for her incompetent son, Selim, had persuaded the Sultan to agree to the deaths of his favourite minister and son. Meanwhile the Turkish empire fast approached the crisis of its existence. The Grand Vizier hoped to consolidate Turkish power in the Mediterranean by conquering Cyprus which was still controlled by Venice. He was deceived into believing that the Venetian fleet had been destroyed in the great fire which had broken out at the Arsenal at Venice in September, 1569, but the Venetians were still more misled by the hopes they placed on foreign help. A Turkish army invaded Cyprus on July 1st, 1570; the fortified cities of Nicosia and Famagusta were put to the fire and the sword. Meanwhile the fear of Turkish aggression had at last brought the Mediterranean powers together in some sort of unity, with the result that a Holy League was formed between Spain, Venice and other Italian states under the lead of Pope Pius V. A great fleet sailed under the command of Philip's half-brother, Don John of Austria, and practically annihilated the Turkish fleet of Ali Pasha in the narrowest part of the Gulf of Corinth, not far from Lepanto, on October 7th, 1571.[1] ' Only by a miracle ', wrote Marco Colonna, ' and the great goodness of God was it possible for us to fight such a battle, and it is just as great a miracle that the prevailing greed and covetousness have not flung us upon one another, in a second battle.' Such words were to prove prophetic. If the prospect of defeat had united the allies, a great victory was bound to divide them. Taking advantage of these divisions Mohammed Sokoli restored the Turkish navy and by skilful bargaining obtained so satisfactory a peace with Venice that Lepanto might almost have been a Turkish victory. Venice ceded Cyprus, increased the tribute she paid to the Turk for Zante and paid a further 300,000 ducats as a war indemnity.

Yet Lepanto was the true signpost to the decline of Turkish power—even though the road was to be long. It doomed Turkish maritime supremacy in the Mediterranean and heralded a general slow decay, which the history of the first half of the seventeenth century, with its feeble Sultans and prevailing inefficiency, revealed to the world. There was indeed some sort of a political and military revival under the Grand Viziers of the Kiuprili family but the defeat which the Turkish fleet suffered at the hands of the Venetian admiral Mocenigo in 1656 indicates the extent of the decline; the Venetians, themselves a decaying force in world politics, captured Lemnos and Tenedos, and the horrified Moslems glimpsed Venetian sails from the walls of Constantinople itself. The moment passed and was indeed redeemed by Turkish triumphs, but the lesson was not lost on the world.

The struggle with the Hapsburgs continued in a desultory fashion; the truce concluded between Sultan Selim II and the Emperor Maximilian II in 1569 did not actually end until 1593. It was followed by thirteen years of intermittent warfare, which was brought to a close by the Treaty of Sitvatorok in 1606. By this the Sultan agreed to give up his suzerainty over Transylvania and the annual tribute of 30,000 ducats which he had been exacting since 1547 from the Hapsburgs for a part of Hungary. But the period of peace which followed was really another indication of growing Turkish weakness. If the Turks had wished to maintain the forward march of the sixteenth-century Sultans, they should have availed themselves of the splendid opportunities for trouble-making in central Europe afforded them by the outbreak of the Thirty Years' War. A Turkish army on the eastern frontiers of the Empire, possibly in league with the Protestant prince of Transylvania,

[1] On Lepanto, see Braudel, *La Méditerranée*, 923-42.

Bethlen-Gabor, would have been at least disconcerting and even disastrous for the Imperialists ; but the Ottoman remained strangely quiet. As the period of history closes, the appointment of Mohammed Kiuprili as Grand Vizier with absolute powers in 1656 betokened a renewal of the aggressive policy of earlier Sultans ; but the phase was in the main a temporary one. A great empire had arisen, reached its maximum of power under Suleiman the Magnificent and had passed into a slow but steady decline. By 1660 the Ottoman Empire had ceased to imperil, if not to assail, western Christendom.

CHAPTER XXII

EPILOGUE

BY the middle of the seventeenth century a Europe had emerged, many of the ideas, manners and customs of which would have astonished a man of 1450. At the same time it is essential to emphasise that history is always a continuous stream, if varying in the speed of its flow; the civilisation of the sixteenth and seventeenth centuries had grown out of the medieval past. Indeed, many things that seemed to typify the medieval world continued to survive long after 1660. Men and women were as superstitious as their forebears had been. When, for instance, Christopher Schorer climbed Mount Pilatus in Switzerland in 1649, he tells us that he was horrified to see a snake-like object with bat-like wings fly from a cavern on the mountain-side, throwing out sparks as it flew away. Even educated people continued to believe implicitly in dragons who flew through the air, and in goblins who played tricks by turning milk sour; this was only one aspect of a widespread demonology, culminating in satanism and witchcraft. Witches, usually ugly old women, confessed their evil deeds under torture applied by their credulous captors; no less than three hundred and six people were executed for witchcraft on estates belonging to the Abbey of St. Maximin near Trier between 1587 and 1593, and a single French judge, Nicholas Rémy, declared that he had sentenced as many as seven hundred people to death between 1576 and 1591. Manuals of witchcraft, such as Bodin's *Démonomanie* had a wide sale; a highly intelligent man like King James I of England never doubted that witches had a real existence. Such was the more sombre side of the contemporary mind which the sceptical writings of men like Montaigne and Johann Weyer could do little to controvert. Even in the twentieth century such superstitions survive in remote districts of Europe.

It is hardly surprising that what might be called the educated medieval mind continued to exert almost as marked an influence over the thought as well as the manners of the new age. The stranglehold of Aristotelianism, in its way a singularly impressive and coherent logical system, over the European universities remained exceptionally strong. Padua, described by an Englishman in 1670 as ' the Imperial University for Physic of all others in the world ' and graced by the studies of Vesalius and Harvey, was for long a fortress of

Aristotelian ideas. Harvey published his book *De Motu Cordium*, describing the circulation of the blood, in 1628 but it was not until twenty years later that a French Professor, Lazarius Riverius, taught his ideas at the famed medical University of Montpellier, only to be dismissed for his action. In the sixteenth century the French scholar Pierre de la Ramée had done much to discredit the writings of the great Greek philosopher, and the falsity of the Aristotelian view of the universe had been confirmed by Galileo; but as late as 1669 a professorial chair at the Sorbonne was given to an Aristotelian who opposed the teaching of the philosopher Descartes. In our own days we have learned to evaluate medieval scholastic thought more sympathetically than did the advanced minds of sixteenth and seventeenth-century humanists, but in its latter days Aristotelianism kept up a powerful rear-guard action.

The world of the Renaissance, the Reformation and the Counter-Reformation was indeed a synthesis of the medieval past and what had either grown out of it or had been grafted on to it. Scholastic thought continued to dominate Catholic theology in spite of Cartesianism. Contemporary scientific ideas continued to be a strange mixture of medieval legend and mathematical reasoning; the highly-intelligent astronomer, Johann Kepler, making significant observations of the planet, Mars, was also persuaded to cast the horoscope of Wallenstein. In politics the continued existence of the Divine Right of Kings, a theory which had grown out of medieval ideas of kingship, showed how deeply monarchy was embedded in the medieval tradition. On the other side, the increasingly fashionable notion of a Social Contract between king and people, permitting the latter to curb the power of the former, had some affinity with the medieval theory of a king's obligation to his people. The medieval Estates, representing the Church, the nobility and the *bourgeoisie*, continued to exist in most countries, even though diminished in strength; the English Parliament alone grew in power and importance. A Europe that was still mainly rural would not have appeared outwardly so different to Chaucer had he travelled to Italy in the mid-seventeenth century.

But harping on the European indebtedness to the past cannot lessen the immense significance of the changes that had occurred between 1450 and 1660. Christendom was no longer united. Even to a man familiar with the Great Schism the spectacle of the rule of the sects would have seemed horrifying. The necessity for finding a *modus vivendi* which would enable Catholic and Calvinist to live side by side was gradually forcing into view the strangely unpopular notion of toleration. There were indeed only a few scholars who believed that some form of reconciliation between the conflicting sects was both possible and desirable ; in 1565 one Jacopo Aconzio published a book to show that religious disunity was a work of the Devil and that a simple credal statement should be prepared as a basis on which all could unite. But the majority of men were too passionately convinced of the rightness of their own beliefs to think along these lines.

The early seventeenth century was still a profoundly religious age ; the disputes between Anglicans and Puritans in England, for instance, cannot be understood properly apart from the religious framework inside which they originated. The writing of History was still largely moulded by religious beliefs. Thus the *Magdeburg Centuries*, compiled between 1559 and 1574 by Matthias Flacius, was history written from a Protestant point of view just as the *Annales Ecclesiastici* of Cardinal Baronius was essentially Catholic. The Bible, now translated into all European languages, continued to be widely read. Sceptics and atheists were still rare ; Thomas Hobbes' rumoured atheism horrified men far more than the subject matter of his book, the *Leviathan*.

But while religious belief continued to dominate men's minds and influence their lives, there were signs that religion as a force, embracing all men's activities, was losing its hold. The fanaticism of the Calvinist and the Jesuit could not entirely counteract the secular notion of life held and taught by some of the Renaissance humanists. The scepticism of a Montaigne was not a unique phenomenon ; increasing knowledge of the laws of nature brought a certain but as yet timid questioning of the miraculous. Even Shakespeare can make Lafeu say in *All's Well That Ends Well* : 'They say miracles are past ; and we have our philosophical persons to make modern and familiar, things supernatural and causeless. Hence is it that we make trifles of terrors ; ensconcing ourselves into seeming knowledge, when we should submit ourselves to an unknown fear.' But criticism either of religion or of the Church was still unusual. The greatest minds of the century, Descartes, Pascal, Spinoza and Sir Isaac Newton, were implicitly religious, and, apart from Spinoza, convinced of the truth of the Christian Revelation. Religion was no spent force but other and stronger loyalties were springing into existence, and new ideas were attracting the attention once given to religion.

The evidence of the period under consideration should have disclosed by now that nothing was more important than the emergence of the sovereign territorial state. The two great international institutions, the Holy Roman Empire, and the Papacy were in decline while the sovereign state mounted to its zenith. G. N. Clark [1] has made the shrewd comment that ' France is the first clear example in European history of a national state which over-shadowed the whole politics of Europe without passing from the national form to an international form like that of the Spanish or even the Austrian power.' By 1660 Europe was about to witness Louis XIV's bid for hegemony. The revival of Roman Law with its reiterated ' What pleases the King has the force of law ' had done much to reinforce the absolute authority of the contemporary monarch. Griffenfeld's *Kongelov* (King's Law), published in 1666, was so complete a justification of the autocratic authority of the King of Denmark as to be a landmark in the development of monarchy; it is hardly surprising that Louis XIV esteemed the author one of the greatest of European ministers. In England Thomas Hobbes' *Leviathan*, published in 1651, showed how it was possible to justify the absolute authority of the Crown without accepting certain fundamental theological assumptions. It was a sign of the times that the King's position in the Church, Catholic or Protestant, was practically unquestioned. In every European state the clergy had become the most vehement supporters of the monarchical régime. Thus the sovereign territorial state, unrestrained by the authority of the Pope or of the Emperor or by the moral sanctions of theology, was to be the political unit of the future.

The new state was more particularly concerned with the pursuit of power, whether expressed in terms of culture, capital, territory or even prestige. Whereas Aristotle had insisted that man's final object should be the cultivation of the good life, the society of seventeenth-century Europe was most concerned with the advancement of its own interests. This did not mean that there were no idealists who sought the good of all men rather than those of a particular section or that kings and nobles were necessarily lacking in a sense of responsibility. But it does mean that power on a major scale counted with European kings more than it had done four centuries earlier. The King's power had not gone unchallenged, either by the feudal Church or the feudal nobility, but in practice the King had emerged victorious, except possibly in England and Holland. ' It lay perhaps in the dialectic of history itself that in the long conflicts between Protestant and Catholic the secular state should rise to independence and should secure an arbitral position over what now seemed to be mere religious parties within it.' [2] Already master of the Church, the King either defeated the nobles or drew them into

[1] G. N. Clark, *The Seventeenth Century*, 163.
[2] H. Butterfield, *The Origins of Modern Science*, 167.

his entourage while the peasantry and the workers became the instruments of his policy. The middle class, members of which became increasingly important as government officials, traders or as members of professional bodies like the lawyers, doctors and schoolmasters, was generally eager to assist in the ' substitution of a simpler and more unified government for the complexities of feudalism '. It was doubly necessary that the King should possess the loyal support of the commercial classes for he depended to a greater extent than ever before upon outside financial help. His obligations and his expenses had increased in proportion to his power. This dependence forced him into the hands of the bankers, and the bankers in their turn into the hands of the Crown. ' The whole success of the monarchies ', G. N. Clark has written, ' sprang from their being rich, just as their fall at the end of the old régime began with bankruptcy.' Thus monarchy in the seventeenth century was founded upon the support of the nobility and the financial assets of the middle class, and the labour, economic and military, of the peasantry.

Whatever their sense of responsibility towards God and his subjects, the kings of the period aspired to power, usually at the cost of a rival. It is sometimes said that the period witnessed the end of the religious wars and the beginning of the wars of trade; it would be better to say that power was the object of both kinds of wars, but power differently defined. By the end of the age commercial motives were certainly more important in causing war than they had been at the end of the Middle Ages. War was more usual than peace in the sixteenth and seventeenth century. It has been reckoned that there were only four years between 1450 and 1660 in which there was no organised fighting in Europe, 1548, 1549, 1550 and 1610.

There were profound changes in the nature of warfare which reflected the immense significance of European rivalries. Although armies still consisted largely of mercenaries, engaged for the campaigning season and paid off at the end of it, they were increasing in size and efficiency. Gunpowder, employed in battle as early as the third decade of the fourteenth century, came into increasing use for artillery and infantry. This meant that supplies of saltpetre and the manufacture of firearms both played a more important part in a country's economy. It is surprising that more attention was not paid to the developments of large-scale armaments industries; the evidence suggests that even in France small units of production were still the rule in the seventeenth century. A more scientific interest was displayed in the technology of weapons, leading to the publication of scientific treatises on projectiles, ballistics and fortification; the mathematician, Simon Stevin of Bruges, who had an expert knowledge of fortification, persuaded the University of Leyden to include fortification in its curriculum and advised the Stadholder Maurice of Nassau. Niccolo Tartaglia, whose *Quesiti et inventioni* was published many years earlier, in 1538, was another mathematician who boasted that he had never fired a gun and held that 'the eye of the mind sees more deeply into general things than does the eye of the body into particulars'. War and science were already in habitual and sinister alliance.[1]

The foundations of war and of power-politics were primarily economic. Both were more expensive than they had ever been before. No state was ever harnessed to the needs of policy as in the twentieth century, but contemporary economists and statesmen were concerned with making their state rich in order that it might be militarily strong. The economic thought and practices of medieval Europe had been particularist, thus leaving a mass of tolls, customs and other factors which impeded the trading facilities of a modern state. The sovereigns of the sixteenth and seventeenth centuries did what they could to unify their states in an economic sense, as far as possible regulating and restricting enterprise and commerce with the object of enriching the state, so that in the last degree they might be rich enough to fight a successful war. The possession of treasure, not in the sense of potential trade but actual monetary wealth or bullion, was necessary to the conduct of a successful war. Contemporary economists, such as the Italian Serra, the Frenchman Montchrétien and the Englishman Thomas Mun, argued that the richest state was that which had the greatest amount of gold and silver within its borders, which in Mun's words, exported 'more to strangers yearly than we consume of theirs in values'. Nor was it questioned that such revenue was ultimately to be used for the defence of the state, then as now an ambiguous term.

Moreover the very fact that the Europe of the seventeenth century was a much richer place than it had been two centuries earlier helped to bring about the creation of the modern state. The vast expansion of Europe abroad freed raw materials as well as gold and silver for European markets, and served to stimulate enterprise and industry; inter-continental trade expanded at an ever increasing rate, thus leading to the expansion of a finance market in some ways resembling that of modern capitalistic society.

[1] The interrelationship between war, science and industrial progress in this period is discussed in J. U. Nef's *War and Human Progress* (1950), 1-144.

Furthermore the break-down in religious authority made it more possible to evade the teaching which had prohibited the taking of usury or engaging in business transactions the moral value of which was dubious. Salmasius first put forward modern views on the taking of interest in 1638-40.

The development of this rich, belligerent Europe had occurred as the frontiers of men's minds and of the outside world widened. Man's fundamental experiences remained the same. He was emotionally no different from what he had been in the past, but his environment was slowly changing. The baronial castle had given way in some western lands to the unfortified château. The upper classes travelled more and in greater ease and security. There were many new amenities, represented by carpets, glass windows, proper chimneys and water-closets; by forks, corks to stop bottles, ice creams and pins. There were a surprisingly large number of inventions to bear witness to the fertile enterprise of the age: the printing press, the blast furnace, the furnace for separating silver from argentiferous copper ore by the use of lead, horse and water-driven engines for draining mines, railed ways for waggons carrying coal, the stocking-knitting frame, coke for drying malt, firehoses, the speaking trumpet, the telescope, the barometer, the pendulum-clock, the making of ruby glass, the thermometer, and the microscope all date from the sixteenth and mainly from the seventeenth centuries. European life was in many ways still extraordinarily primitive, usually bereft of the elements of sanitation and only superficially graced by good manners. If crimes were frequent, evoked by unrestrained passion and greed, punishment was severe and often brutal. Yet it is possible that life was a little less ' nasty, brutish and short ' than it had been two hundred years earlier. A book of etiquette written about the middle of the fifteenth century which insisted that a guest should refrain from wiping his nose on the tablecloth or picking his teeth with his knife would have been less necessary in 1600, if by no means even then indispensable. The increase in luxury, the introduction of new commodities and the improvement in manners helped to create a new social class which in its upper and middle levels would have had relatively little in common with its counterparts of the Wars of the Roses and the Hundred Years' War.

The actual area of the Earth's surface known by 1660 was immensely greater than it had been two hundred years earlier. Nothing reveals this better than the making of maps which showed, if only broadly, how Europe's frontiers were widened to include great tracts of land, much of it still unexplored but some already open to trade and conquest.[1] The mathematician Gerhard Kremer (usually known as Mercator) and his friend the Flemish merchant Abraham Ortelius helped to free geography from its age-old domination by the Roman map-maker Ptolemy. Lucan Wagenaer of Enkhuisen began to prepare accurate nautical charts. The Jesuit Athanasius Kircher for the first time marked the currents of the sea on a chart in 1605. These were indispensable aids to navigation in foreign seas. Nothing was indeed more important in European history than the expansion of Europe which reached its climax in the Victorian age. It did much to determine the politics of the future and enriched the countries who took part in the struggle for trade and territory. Moreover it vastly increased the number of goods available for consumption and altered the taste of men and women. It is difficult to gauge precisely its intellectual effects. The knowledge that Europe was only one unit among many, and that Christianity was only one among many religions may have tended to diminish religious passion. But greatly interested as contemporary men were in the discoveries, it was long before they realised their full implications.

The geographical discoveries coincided with a broadening of man's intellectual interests. In part they served to evoke them ; new plants and new races formed new subjects of study for the botanist and physiologist. In part they represented the result of the desire for knowledge originally initiated by the Renaissance. The Renaissance had been less of an innovation than a culmination of the process by which the thought of antiquity was restored ; by 1660 much that it had brought into being had either disappeared or come to an end. But the adventurous element in Renaissance life and thought was now in the process of bringing about what a historian has called ' one of the great episodes in human experience ', the Scientific Revolution of the seventeenth century.[2]

The Scientific Revolution was important because it was in the course of time to impose a new view of the universe upon the thinking world. Copernicus, Brahe, Kepler and their fellow-scientists

---

[1] G. N. Clark mentions that ' a frontier was ceasing to be an area and tending to become a line ' (p. 143) but that ' he has not been able to discover a case of a frontier fixed literally on the map until the year 1718 '. (*The Seventeenth Century*, 144.) The word ' frontier ' is therefore used advisedly in the broadest possible sense.

[2] H. Butterfield, *The Origins of Modern Science*, 163. He adds : ' The new factor immediately began to elbow at the other ones, pushing them out of their places—and, indeed, began immediately to seek control of the rest . . . since the rise of Christianity, there is no landmark in history that is worthy to be compared with this.' (p. 174).

had prepared the way for this by loosening the fabric of accepted Aristotelian ideas; but it was their successors in the next century, Galileo, Descartes, Francis Bacon, Boyle and Isaac Newton, a consideration of whose work falls outside the scope of this book, who ensured the triumph of the new view.

Thus while the sixteenth and seventeenth centuries saw changes of the greatest significance taking place in every field of human activity, the modern age was only in process of formation. The period is indeed primarily important because it made possible the movements of the next century and a half, thus emphasising what is so profoundly true, that no period of world history is in any way detached from the earlier or later period unless it be a forgotten civilisation; and that western civilisation is still very far from being.

RELIGION AND THE RISE OF CAPITALISM

How far Protestantism affected and even caused capitalistic enterprise[1] has given rise to acute discussion and controversy among scholars. The German sociologist, Max Weber, asserted in his important *The Protestant Ethic and the Spirit of Capitalism* (1904-05 : translated 1926) that the Protestant view of calling or vocation (*die Beruf*) by way of allowing practices banned by Catholic teaching and so stimulating the 'capitalist spirit' encouraged capitalistic enterprise, for each man felt it his duty to God to apply all his talents to the particular activity or work to which he felt 'called'. These arguments have been disputed and modified by successive writers. Amintore Fanfani, like G. O'Brien in his *An Essay on the Economic Effects of the Reformation* (1923), vindicated the Roman Catholic position, basing his reply on a considered study of Thomist philosophy. He concluded : 'Thus Protestantism appeared as the religious sanction of the free efforts of man to attain wealth. . . . Protestantism only marked a further stage in the emancipation of human action from supernatural limits.' (*Catholicism, Protestantism and Capitalism*, Trans. 1935). Contrariwise H. M. Robertson in his *Aspects of the Rise of Economic Individualism* (1933) held that Catholicism was as formative an influence in producing capitalism as Protestantism, and found the main explanation for contemporary capitalism (i.e. of the sixteenth century) in the rise of the national state and the effects of the geographical discoveries. His general argument was a welcome reply to those who had assumed that Calvinism was naturally sympathetic towards capitalistic enterprise ; he showed that the 'economic zeal' of Calvinist countries owed little to religion and much to their geographical location. He writes, not wholly justly, that 'The Spaniards and Portuguese were content to exploit, without developing, the large areas which they had appropriated. But the French, the English and the Dutch had their enthusiasm roused' (p. 187). It is his conclusion that 'The

[1] Much of the argument in the discussion has turned on differing definitions of capitalism. I have used capitalism to mean both the emergence of a spirit favourable to large-scale business enterprise, and more particularly as representing a society based on a money economy in which the employers own and control the means of production for the purpose of private profit.

development of Protestant thought on usury was certainly no more significant than the development of Catholic thought on rent charges and threefold contracts, and on implicit contracts of which the legitimacy was secured by good intentions. The attempts at strict regulation of the economic life made by the Calvinist Churches were definite hindrances to capitalistic development and the spread of capitalistic ideas which formed a strong contrast to the comfortable and accommodating religion of the Jesuits ' (p. 160). But he based his study of the Jesuits on too many unscholarly witnesses like their redoubtable opponent the Bishop of Angelopolis, and his attempt to link them with the expansion of capitalistic enterprise was convincingly rebuffed by Fr. Brodrick, S.J., in his *The Economic Morals of the Jesuits* (1934).

The most distinguished popular product of this literary controversy remains R. H. Tawney's *Religion and the Rise of Capitalism*, first published in 1926. Tawney adopted a modified version of Weber's view, holding that there was no necessary connection between the development of capitalism and Protestant teaching, but stressing that later Protestant teaching was particularly sympathetic towards the kind of economic initiative represented in a capitalistic society. ' If ', he writes ' it is true that the Reformation released forces which were to act as a solvent of the traditional attitude of religious thought to social and economic issues, it did so without design, and against the intention of most reformers. In reality, however sensational the innovations in economic practice which accompanied the expansion of financial capitalism in the sixteenth century, the development of doctrine on the subject of economic ethics was continuous, and the more closely it is examined, the less foundation does there seem to be for the view that the stream plunged into vacancy over the precipice of the religious revolution. To think of the abdication of religion from its theoretical primacy over economic activity and social institutions as synchronizing with the revolt from Rome, is to antedate a movement which was not finally accomplished for another century and a half, and which owed as much to changes in economic and political organisation, as it did to developments in the sphere of religious thought ' (p. 84-85). He concludes that among the numerous forces which had gone to form ' a new type of economic character ' and ' a new system of economic organisation ', ' some not inconsiderable part may reasonably be ascribed to the emphasis on the life of business enterprise as the appropriate field for Christian endeavour, and on the qualities needed for success in it, which were characteristic of Puritanism. These qualities, and the admiration of them, remained, when the religious reference, and

the restraints which it imposed, had weakened or disappeared '
(p. 273).

The mass of facts and theories seem to point to certain definite
conclusions :

(1) The late medieval age was certainly proto-capitalistic, in the
sense that many of the characteristics of later capitalism could be
found in its more developed societies, especially in the Italian and
Netherlands clothing cities. What was new in the sixteenth century
was the scale of such capitalistic enterprise, and the appearance of
a wealthy *bourgeoisie* which took an increasingly important part as
agents and collaborators of national monarchs.

(2) The medieval Church, following the teaching of Aristotle
and the Fathers that *pecunia non parit pecuniam*, condemned usury
and regarded the trader with suspicion, but there had always been
ways and means of evading the canons, especially if risk was involved in the enterprise.[1] The teaching of later scholastics, including Gabriel Biel and Archbishop Antonino of Florence, was less
stern, but no less condemnatory of unjust business activity.

(3) The Reformers' teaching on the subject was conservative
and Catholic. In a famous letter written to Claude de Sachins
Calvin agreed that it was impossible to judge usury and interest
by reference to Biblical texts which referred to conditions differing
from those existing in the sixteenth century, but his approval of
interest was so qualified that his position in the controversy was
conservative rather than radical. Later Protestant theologians were
almost as dogmatic as the Roman Catholic writers in their condemnation or qualified approval of business and business activities.

(4) Attempts to prove that Catholic moral theology, especially
that of the Jesuits, favoured the capitalistic spirit have failed for
lack of evidence.

(5) Yet it is undeniable (a) that there was a great increase in
capitalistic enterprise, affecting both Catholics (e.g. German business
houses) as well as Protestants, (b) that this activity was more notice-
able in Protestant than in Catholic countries. It is probable that
this was a historical and economic accident, arising in part out of
the geographical discoveries.

(6) It is thus apparent that the Reformation did not cause, or
even encourage, except incidentally, the development of capitalism ;
Protestants and Catholics remained very suspicious of unethical
business enterprise, such as capitalism undoubtedly stimulated.

[1] See p. 17.

(7) Nevertheless Protestantism (even more than Catholicism) may have done much, even in its early days, to stimulate efficiency and success in business, e.g. (*a*) the Calvinist doctrine of election could be interpreted to mean that the successful business man was one of the Elect and that conversely the poor man might be one of the Damned, (*b*) the emphasis which the Calvinist placed on work, thrift, sobriety, etc., tended to create the good workmen and good business men.

(8) By the eighteenth century popular Protestant theology had come round to the view that capitalistic enterprise was often linked with God's prevailing grace, whereas the sacramental side of Catholic theory still tended to insist that all work was an instrument in God's hands. It has always been the fate of the Church to accommodate itself to the prevailing economic and political order. Catholicism had adapted itself to Feudalism. Catholicism and Protestantism both came to terms with the rising power of capitalism. It should be remembered that capitalism did not emerge as a dominant force until the nineteenth century. By that time religious sanctions had so weakened that the Church's approval was remembered after its significant moral qualifications had been largely forgotten.

APPENDIX 2

LIST OF CONTEMPORARY RULERS

1. *The Papacy*

Nicholas V (Thomas of Sarzana)	. .	1447-55
Calixtus III (Alfonso Borgia) .	. .	1455-58
Pius II (Aeneas Piccolomini) .	. .	1458-64
Paul II (Pietro Barbo) .	. .	1464-71
Sixtus IV (Francesco della Rovere)	.	1471-84
Innocent VIII (Giambattista Cibo) .	.	1484-92
Alexander VI (Rodrigo Borgia)	.	1492-1503
Pius III (Francesco Todeschini)	.	1503 (Sept.-Oct.)
Julius II (Giulio della Rovere)	.	1503-13
Leo X (Giovanni de' Medici)	.	1513-21
Adrian VI (Adrian of Utrecht)	.	1522-23
Clement VII (Giulio de' Medici) .	.	1523-34
Paul III (Alessandro Farnese)	.	1534-49
Julius III (Giovanni del Monte)	.	1550-55
Marcellus II (Marcello Cervini)	.	1555
Paul IV (Pietro Caraffa)	. .	1556-59
Pius IV (Gian-Angelo de' Medici) .	.	1559-65
Pius V (Michele Ghislieri)	. .	1565-72
Gregory XIII (Ugo Buoncompagno)	.	1572-85
Sixtus V (Felix Peretti) . . .	. .	1585-90
Urban VII (Giambattista Castagna)	.	1590
Gregory XIV (Niccolo Sfondrato) .	.	1590-91
Innocent IX (Gian-Antonio Fachinetto)	.	1591
Clement VIII (Ippolito Aldobrandini)	.	1592-1605
Leo XI (Alessandro de' Medici)	.	1605
Paul V (Camillo Borghese)	. .	1605-21
Gregory XV (Alessandro Ludovisi)	.	1621-23
Urban VIII (Maffeo Barberini)	.	1623-44
Innocent X (Giambattista Pamfili) .	.	1644-55
Alexander VII (Fabio Chigi)	. .	1655-67

2. *The Holy Roman Empire. House of Hapsburg*

Frederick III	. . . . .	1440-93
Maximilian I	. . . . .	1493-1519
Charles V	.	1519-56 (d. 1558)

Ferdinand I	1556-64
Maximilian II	1564-76
Rudolf II	1576-1612
Matthias	1612-19
Ferdinand II	1619-37
Ferdinand III	1637-57
Leopold I	1657-1705

3. *France.* *The House of Valois*

Charles VII	1422-61
Louis XI	1461-83
Charles VIII	1483-98
Louis XII	1498-1515
Francis I	1515-47
Henry II	1547-59
Francis II	1559-60
Charles IX.	1560-74
Henry III	1574-89

The House of Bourbon

Henry IV	1589-1610
Louis XIII	1610-43
Louis XIV	1643-1715

4. *Spain.* *The Catholic Kings*

Isabella of Castile . . .	1474-1504
Ferdinand of Aragon . . .	1479-1516

The House of Hapsburg

(Joanna of Castile . . .	1504-55)
(Philip I	1504-06)
Charles I (V)	1516-58
Philip II	1558-98
Philip III	1598-1621
Philip IV	1621-65
Charles II	1665-1700

5. *Portugal.* *The House of Avis*

John I	1383-1433
Duarte	1433-38
Alfonso V	1438-81

John II	 1481-95
Manuel I	 1495-1521
John III	 1521-57
Sebastian	 1557-78
Henry	 1578-80

The Spanish Kings

Philip I (II)	 1580-98
Philip II (III)	 1598-1621
Philip III (IV)	 1621-40

The House of Braganza

John IV	 1640-56

6. Sweden. The House of Vasa

Gustavus I	 1523-60
Eric XIV	. . . 1560-68 (dep., d. 1577)
John III	 1568-92
Sigismund	. . 1592-1604 (dep., d. 1632)
Charles IX	 1604-11
Gustavus II Adolphus	. . . 1611-32
Christina	. . 1632-54 (abd., d. 1689)
Charles X Gustavus	. . . 1654-60

7. Denmark and Norway. The House of Oldenburg

Christian II	. . 1513-23 (dep., d. 1559)
Frederick I	 1523-33
Christian III	 1533-59
Frederick II	 1559-88
Christian IV	 1588-1648
Frederick III	 1648-70

8. The United Provinces. The House of Orange

William I	. . . murdered 1584
Maurice	 1584-1625
Frederick Henry	 1625-47
William II	 1647-50

9. Turkey

Mohammed II	 1451-81
Bayezid II	 1481-1512

Selim I	1512-20
Suleiman I	1520-66
Selim II	1566-74
Murad III	1574-95
Mohammed III	1595-1603
Ahmad I	1603-1617
Mustafa I	1617-18 (dep.)
Osman II	1618-22
Mustafa I (restored)	1622-23
Murad IV	1623-40

10. *England. The House of Tudor*

Henry VII	1485-1509
Henry VIII	1509-47
Edward VI	1547-53
Mary	1553-58
Elizabeth	1558-1603

The House of Stuart

James I	1603-25
Charles I	1625-49

The Commonwealth . . .	1649-60

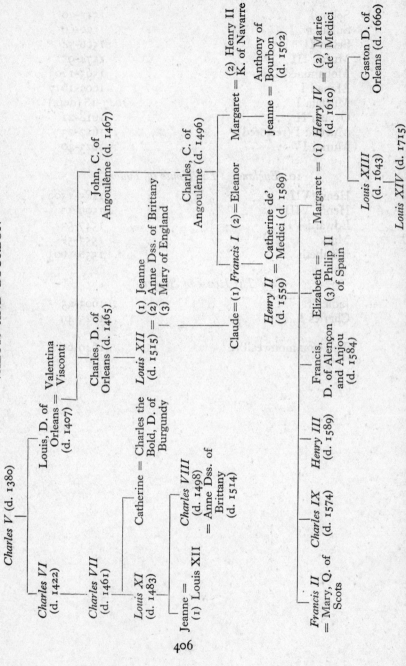

VALOIS AND BOURBON

THE HOUSE OF BOURBON (CONDÉ)

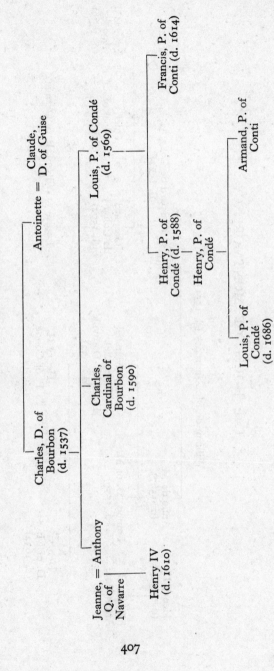

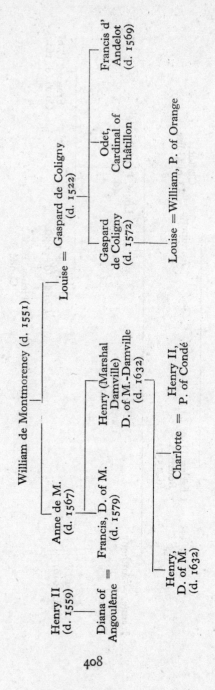

THE HOUSE OF MONTMORENCY

THE HOUSE OF GUISE

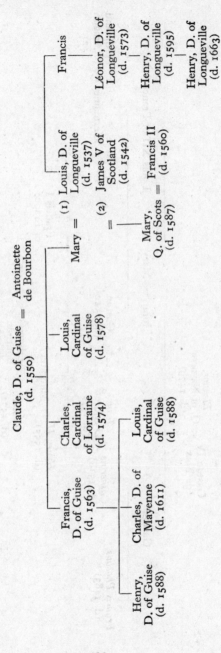

Claude, D. of Guise (d. 1550) = Antoinette de Bourbon

- Francis, D. of Guise (d. 1563)
  - Henry, D. of Guise (d. 1588)
  - Charles, D. of Mayenne (d. 1611)
  - Louis, Cardinal of Guise (d. 1588)
- Charles, Cardinal of Lorraine (d. 1574)
- Louis, Cardinal of Guise (d. 1578)
- Mary
  = (1) Louis, D. of Longueville (d. 1537)
    - Francis
    - Léonor, D. of Longueville (d. 1573)
      - Henry, D. of Longueville (d. 1595)
        - Henry, D. of Longueville (d. 1663)
  = (2) James V of Scotland (d. 1542)
    - Mary, Q. of Scots (d. 1587) = Francis II (d. 1560)

NAVARRE

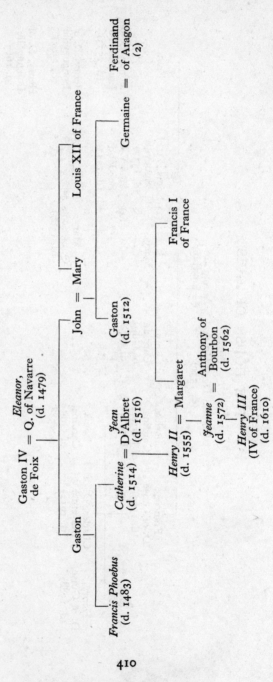

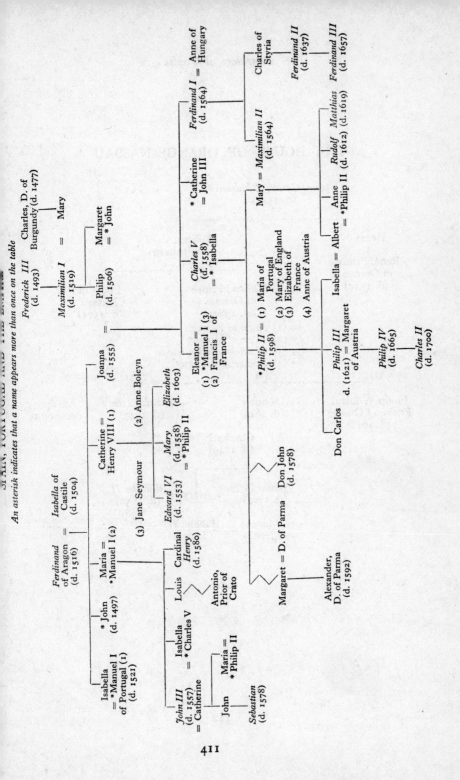

SPAIN, PORTUGAL AND THE EMPIRE

An asterisk indicates that a name appears more than once on the table

THE HOUSE OF ORANGE–NASSAU

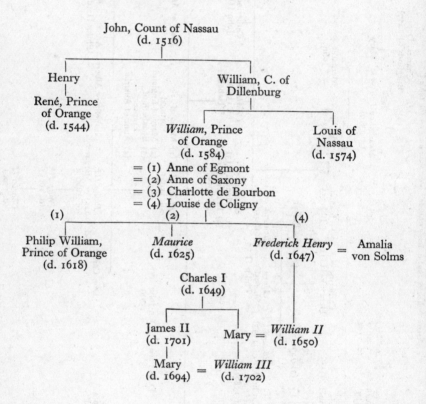

John, Count of Nassau
(d. 1516)

Henry

René, Prince
of Orange
(d. 1544)

William, C. of
Dillenburg

William, Prince
of Orange
(d. 1584)
= (1) Anne of Egmont
= (2) Anne of Saxony
= (3) Charlotte de Bourbon
= (4) Louise de Coligny

Louis of
Nassau
(d. 1574)

(1)

Philip William,
Prince of Orange
(d. 1618)

(2)

Maurice
(d. 1625)

(4)

Frederick Henry = Amalia
(d. 1647)   von Solms

Charles I
(d. 1649)

James II
(d. 1701)

Mary = *William II*
(d. 1650)

Mary   = *William III*
(d. 1694)   (d. 1702)

SWEDEN

THE HOUSE OF VASA

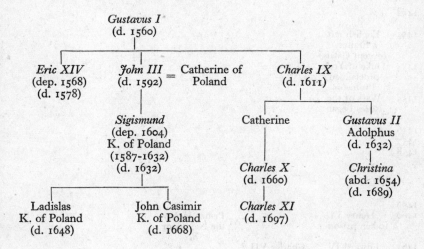

JÜLICH–CLEVES

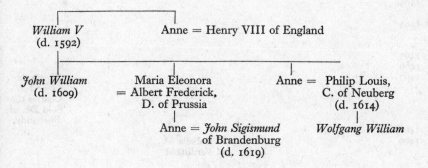

	1 ENGLAND	2 FRANCE	3 SPAIN AND PORTUGAL	4 THE EMPIRE	5 NETHERLANDS
1450	Jack Cade's Insurrection				
1451					
1452					
1453	English left France (except Calais)				
1454	Duke of York proclaimed Protector				
1455	Wars of the Roses began				
1456					
1457					
1458					
1459					
1460	Henry VI taken prisoner		Prince Henry the Navigator d.		
1461	Edward IV Kg.	Charles VII d. Louis XI Kg.			
1462					
1463					
1464					
1465					
1466					
1467					Philip the Good d. Charles the Bold Dk. of Burgundy.
1468					
1469			Isabella m. Ferdinand		
1470	Lancastrian rising Edward IV in Flanders				

6 ITALY	7 SWITZERLAND	8 N. EUROPE	9 OUTSIDE EUROPE	10 CULTURE	
Francesco Sforza Lord of Milan					1450
			Mohammed II Sultan		1451
				Leonardo da Vinci born	1452
			Fall of Constantinople		1453
					1454
Nicholas V d. Calixtus III Pope				Fra Angelico d. Reuchlin born	1455
					1456
					1457
Pius II Pope Ferrante Kg. of Naples (until 1494)				Lorenzo Valla d.	1458
					1459
					1460
Bull Execrabilis pub.				Villon's Le Grand Testament	1461
		Ivan III Gd. Dk. of Muscovy			1462
			Turks took Trebizond		1463
Cosimo de' Medici d. Paul II Pope				Nicholas of Cusa d.	1464
					1465
				Donatello d.	1466
				Erasmus born	1467
					1468
Lorenzo de' Medici in Florence				Machiavelli born	1469
				Fra Lippo Lippi d.	
				Printing-press at Paris	1470

	1 ENGLAND	2 FRANCE	3 SPAIN AND PORTUGAL	4 THE EMPIRE	5 NETHERLANDS
1471	Yorkist victory at Tewkesbury				
1472					
1473					
1474			Isabella Qn. of Castille		
1475	English invaded France	Tr. Pecquigny			
1476			Cortes of Madrigal		
1477				Maximilian *m.* Mary of Burgundy	Charles the Bold *k.*
1478			Inquisition in Castile		
1479			Ferdinand Kg. of Aragon Tr. of Alcaçovas		B. Guinegâte
1480			Cortes of Toledo		
1481			Alfonso V of Portugal *d.* John II Kg.		
1482					Mary of Burgundy *d.* Tr. Arras Maximilian Regent
1483	Edward V murd. Richard III Kg.	Charles VIII Kg.	Inquisition in Aragon	Luther born	
1484				Berthold Elector of Mainz	
1485	B. Bosworth Henry VII Kg.			Diet of Frankfort	
1486	Simnel's re- bellion			Frederick Elector of Saxony	
1487					
1488				Swabian League est'd.	
1489					
1490					

416

6	7	8	9	10	
ITALY	SWITZERLAND	N. EUROPE	OUTSIDE EUROPE	CULTURE	
Sixtus IV Pope				Dürer born	1471
				Card. Bessarion *d.*	1472
				Alberti *d.*	1473
				Ariosto born	1474
				Michelangelo born	1475
	B. Grandson B. Morat				1476
				Titian born Caxton printing at Westminster	1477
					1478
Ludovico 'Il Moro' Regent of Milan					1479
Lorenzo's visit to Naples					1480
			Mohammed II *d.*	Sistine chapel frescoes begun	1481
			Portuguese at Elmina	Luca della Robbia *d.*	1482
				Raphael born Politian prof. at Florence	1483
Innocent VIII Pope	Zwingli born				1484
				Agricola *d.*	1485
			Dias circum-navigated the Cape		1486
					1487
				Verrocchio *d.*	1488
					1489
				Aldine Press est'd at Venice	1490

	1	2	3	4	5
	ENGLAND	FRANCE	SPAIN AND PORTUGAL	THE EMPIRE	NETHERLANDS
1491		Charles VIII *m.* Anne of Brittany	Loyola born		
1492	Warbeck in Ireland	Tr. Etaples	Fall of Granada Expulsion of Jews		
1493		Tr. Senlis Tr. Barcelona		Maximilian I Emp.	
1494		Charles VIII in Italy			
1495			Manuel I Kg. Portugal	Diet of Worms	
1496	Magnus Intercursus		Joanna *m.* Archduke Philip		
1497	Warbeck exec'd		John *m.* Archduchess Margaret		
1498		Louis XII Kg.	Torquemada *d.*		
1499		Expedn. to Italy	Revolt in Granada	Tr. Basle	
1500		Tr. Granada with Spain		Diet of Augsburg	Charles V born
1501					
1502					
1503					
1504		1st Tr. Blois	Isabella *d.*	Arbp. Berthold *d.*	
1505		2nd Tr. Blois		Luther joined Augustinians	
1506			Philip I *d.* Columbus *d.* Ferdinand *m.* Germaine de Foix		Charles Dk. Burgundy
1507					Margaret Regent
1508				Luther went to Wittenberg	
1509	Henry VIII Kg.	Calvin born	Catherine *m.* Henry VIII		
1510				Diet of Augsburg	

6	7	8	9	10	
ITALY	SWITZERLAND	N. EUROPE	OUTSIDE EUROPE	CULTURE	
Savonarola Prior of San Marco				Froben printer at Basle Caxton d.	1491
Lorenzo de' Medici d. Alexander VI Pope			Columbus discovered America	Reuchlin studied Hebrew	1492
			Papal bull *Inter Caetera*		1493
Fr. expdn. to Italy			Tr. Tordesillas	Politian d. Brandt's *Narrenschiff*	1494
Charles in Naples B. Fornovo				da Vinci began *The Last Supper*	1495
			Cabot's voyage to Newfoundland and Labrador		1496
				Holbein born	1497
Savonarola exec'd			Vasco da Gama sailed to India	Erasmus at Oxford	1498
Fr. occupied Milan	Tr. Basle		Alonso de Ojeda at Venezuela	Alcala Univ. founded Ficino d.	1499
B. Novara			Cabral discovered Brazil		1500
					1501
				Wittenberg Univ. founded	1502
B. Garigliano Julius II Pope					1503
				Sannazaro's *Arcadia*	1504
		Basil III Russian ruler		Latin trans. *Euclid*	1505
	Zwingli at Glarus			Bramante designed St. Peter's	1506
Caesar Borgia d.					1507
League of Cambrai					1508
B. Agnadello	End of French alliance		B. Diu	*The Praise of Folly*	1509
	Julius II allied with the Swiss	Russians annexed Pskov	Albuquerque capt'd Goa	Reuchlin-Pfefferkorn controversy began	1510

1	2	3	4	5
ENGLAND	FRANCE	SPAIN AND PORTUGAL	THE EMPIRE	NETHERLANDS

	1	2	3	4	5
1511				Luther visited Rome	
1512			S. Navarre became Spanish		
1513	B. Flodden	B. Guinegâte			
1514	Wolsey Arbp. of York	Louis XII *m.* Mary Tudor			
1515		Francis I Kg. Italian expdn.	St. Teresa born		
1516		Concordat of Bologna	Ferdinand *d.* Charles I (V) Kg.		
1517			Charles in Spain Ximenez *d.*	Luther's 95 Theses	
1518					
1519				Charles V Emp.	
1520	Field of Cloth of Gold		Revolt of *Comuneros*	Luther excomm'd	
1521	Henry VIII made Defender of the Faith		B. Villalar Manuel of Portugal *d.*	Diet of Worms	
1522			Charles V in Spain	Knights' War	
1523				Von Sickingen *d.* Diet of Nuremberg	
1524		Francis crossed Alps into Italy		Peasants' War	

6	7	8	9	10	
ITALY	SWITZERLAND	N. EUROPE	OUTSIDE EUROPE	CULTURE	
Holy League formed	Schinner created a Cardinal		Albuquerque capt'd Malacca	Botticelli *d.* Erasmus at Cambridge	1511
B. Ravenna Machiavelli exiled			Amerigo Vespucci *d.* Selim I Sultan		1512
B. Novara Leo X Pope		Christian II Kg. of Denmark, Norway and Sweden	Balboa reached Pacific	Machiavelli's *The Prince* written	1513
			Turks defeated Persians at Chaldiran	Hutten's *Epistolae Obscurorum Virorum*	1514
B. Marignano			Albuquerque *d.*		1515
Tr. Noyon	Zwingli at Einsiedeln Perpetual Peace of Fribourg		de Solis at Rio de la Plata	Ariosto's *Orlando Furioso* More's *Utopia* Erasmus' Greek Testament	1516
Oratory of Divine Love est'd			Sultan Selim occupied Egypt		1517
	Zwingli at Zürich			Tintoretto born	1518
	Zwingli denounced Indulgences			da Vinci *d.*	1519
		Stockholm Blood Bath	Straits of Magellan passed	Raphael *d.*	1520
			Fall of Belgrade		1521
Adrian VI Pope B. Bicocca			Fall of Rhodes Conquest of Mexico completed	German N.T. Reuchlin *d.*	1522
Clement VII Pope	1st public disputation in Zürich	Christian II fled from Denmark Gustavus Vasa Swedish Kg.		von Hutten *d.*	1523
Theatines est'd	Diet of Lucerne Catholic League est'd		Vasco da Gama *d.*	Ronsard born	1524

1	2	3	4	5
ENGLAND	FRANCE	SPAIN AND PORTUGAL	THE EMPIRE	NETHERLANDS
1525			B. Franken-hausen Luther married	
1526			Diet of Speyer B. Mohacs Ferdinand Kg. Bohemia and Hungary	
1527	Alliance of Henry VIII and Francis I	Philip II born		
1528				
1529	Fall of Wolsey	Berquin burnt at Paris		Diet of Speyer Turks besieged Vienna
1530				Diet and Confession of Augsburg
1531	Henry VIII Hd. of English Ch.			League of Schmalkalden est'd	Mary of Hungary Regent
1532				Religious Peace of Nuremberg	
1533	Henry VIII m. Anne Boleyn	Henry II m. Catherine de' Medici Calvin left France			William of Orange born
1534		Loyola founded Jesuits	St. Teresa entered Carmelites		
1535	Act of Supremacy		Expedition to Tunis	Anabaptist Rising at Münster	
1536	Anne Boleyn exec'd Dissolution of smaller monasteries	Treaty with Turks			
1537	Jane Seymour *d.*				
1538				Catholic League of Nuremberg	
1539	Remaining monasteries suppressed				Revolt of Ghent
1540	Henry VIII m. Anne of Cleves			Reopening of War with Turks	Reduction of Ghent

6 ITALY	7 SWITZERLAND	8 N. EUROPE	9 OUTSIDE EUROPE	10 CULTURE	
B. Pavia			Babur conquered India	Pomponazzi *d.*	1525
Tr. Madrid League of Cognac		Reformation in Denmark		Tyndale's N.T.	1526
Sack of Rome Machiavelli *d.*		Diet of Västerås			1527
	Berne adopted Reformation			Dürer *d.* Veronese born	1528
Tr. Barcelona Tr. Cambrai	Civil war 1st Tr. Kappel	Confession of Örebro	Tr. of Saragossa Mendoza Viceroy New Spain	Vischer *d.*	1529
Imperial Coronation at Bologna			Babur *d.*		1530
	B. Kappel : Zwingli *k.*	Christian II attacked Norway			1531
	Farel arrived in Geneva	Christian II defeated	Conquest of Peru		1532
		Ivan III Russian ruler	War between Turks and Persia	Ariosto *d.*	1533
Paul III Pope			Cartier sailed up R. St. Lawrence	German O.T.	1534
	Reformation in Geneva			Coverdale's Bible First part of *Gargantua and Pantagruel.*	1535
War between Francis I and Ch. V	1st Helvetic Confession Calvin in Geneva	Swedes def'd Lübeck		*Institutes of Christian Religion* Erasmus *d.*	1536
					1537
Truce of Nice	Calvin expelled from Geneva				1538
					1539
Pope approved Jesuits					1540

	1	2	3	4	5
	ENGLAND	FRANCE	SPAIN AND PORTUGAL	THE EMPIRE	NETHERLANDS
1541			Expedition to Algiers	Religious Colloquy of Ratisbon	
1542	Catherine Howard exec'd		' New Laws ' (Spanish America)		
1543		Turks held Toulon	Philip *m.* Maria of Portugal		
1544				Diet of Speyer	
1545					
1546				Luther *d.* Diet of Ratisbon Schmalkaldic War	
1547	Edward VI Kg.	Henry II Kg. Chambre Ardente est'd	Cortes *d.*	B. Mühlberg	
1548				Interim of Augsburg	
1549	1st Prayer Book Fall of Somerset	War with England			
1550					
1551					
1552	2nd Prayer Book	Tr. Chambord Fr. invaded Lorraine		Tr. Passau	
1553	Mary Qn.			Maurice of Saxony *k.* at Sievershausen	
1554	Mary *m.* Philip		Philip *m.* Mary of England		
1555				Religious Peace of Augsburg	Charles V abd. at Brussels
1556	Cranmer burnt	Truce Vaucelles	Philip II Kg.	Ferdinand I Emp.	
1557		B. St. Quentin Credit crisis at Lyons	Repudiation of debts John III of Portugal *d.*		

6 ITALY	7 SWITZERLAND	8 N. EUROPE	9 OUTSIDE EUROPE	10 CULTURE	
	Calvin returned to Geneva		Pizarro *k.* Xavier at Goa		1541
War between Francis I. and Ch. V Inquisition at Rome					1542
				Copernicus' *De Revolutionibus* Vesalius' *De Fabrica*	1543
Tr. Crépy			Viceroy of New Castile app.	Clement Marot *d.*	1544
Council of Trent opened		Calvinism spread in Poland	Silver mines at Potosi opened	Cardan's *Ars Magna*	1545
			B. Anaquito (Peru)	Vitoria *d.*	1546
Council moved to Bologna		Ivan IV proclaimed Czar of Russia		Cervantes born Cardinal Bembo *d.*	1547
				Spiritual Exercises	1548
Council suspended	*Consensus Tigurinus*				1549
Julius III Pope					1550
Council reopened at Trent					1551
Council suspended		Russians took Kazan	Xavier *d.*		1552
	Servetus exec'd	Chancellor visited Moscow		Rabelais *d.* Montaigne born	1553
				Ronsard acclaimed ' prince of poets '	1554
Paul IV Pope			Tr. Amasia (Turks and Persians)		1555
					1556
					1557

O*

1	2	3	4	5
ENGLAND	FRANCE	SPAIN AND PORTUGAL	THE EMPIRE	NETHERLANDS
1558 Elizabeth Qn.	Capture of Calais	Charles V *d.*		
1559 Acts of Supremacy and Uniformity	Tr. Câteau-Cambrésis Francis II Kg.			
1560	Tumult of Amboise Charles IX Kg.	Repudiation of debts Philip II *m.* Elizabeth of Valois	Melanchthon *d.*	
1561	Colloquy of Poissy Edict of January			
1562 English occupied Havre	1st Religious War		Peace of Prague (with Turks)	League of nobles against Granvelle
1563 Thirty-nine Articles	Peace of Amboise	Escurial begun		
1564		B. Los Gelves	Maximilian II Emp.	Granvelle left Netherlands
1565	Conference of Bayonne			Inquisition in Netherlands
1566		Edict against Moors	Suleiman of Turkey *d.*	The ' Compromise'
1567	2nd Religious War		Philip of Hesse *d.*	Rebellion Alva arrived
1568 Mary Qn. of Scots in England	Peace of Longjumeau 3rd Religious War	Don Carlos *d.* Moorish rebellion		*Ex.* of Egmont and Horn Flight of Orange
1569 Catholic rising	B. Jarnac B. Moncontour			
1570 Papal bull *v.* Elizabeth	Peace of St. Germain	Philip II *m.* Anne of Austria		
1571 Ridolfi Plot		B. Lepanto		
1572 Tr. Blois (with France)	Massacre of St. Bartholomew 4th Religious War			Sea-beggars seized Brill
1573	Peace of La Rochelle	Spaniards held Tunis		Alva recalled Requesens Gov.
1574	5th Religious War Henry III Kg.	Tunis re-capt'd by Turks		Relief of Leyden

426

6	7	8	9	10
ITALY	SWITZERLAND	N. EUROPE	OUTSIDE EUROPE	CULTURE
				1558
Index pub. Pius IV Pope		Christian III *d.* Frd. II Kg. (Denmark)		1559
Carlo Borremeo Arbp. of Milan		Gustavus I *d.* Eric XIV Kg. (Sweden)	Francis Bacon born	1560
		Esthonia annexed to Sweden Tausen *d.*		1561
Council reopened at Trent			Lope de Vega born	1562
Close of Council				1563
Creed of Pius IV pub.	Calvin *d.*		Shakespeare born Galileo born	1564
Pius V Pope Relief of Malta (from Turks)		Jesuits in Poland	Michelangelo *d.*	1565
	2nd Helvetic Confession		Suleiman *d.* Selim II Sultan	1566
				1567
		Eric dep. John III Kg. (Sweden)		Campanella born	1568
		Union of Lublin		1569
Venice at war with Turks	Carlo Borremeo in Switzerland			1570
B. Lepanto Gregory XIII Pope			Drake attacked Nombre de Dios	Kepler born Camoes' *Lusiad* Ramus *d.*	1571 1572
Peace with Turkey (cession of Cyprus)		Anjou elected Polish Kg.		Ben Jonson born	1573
				Tasso's *Jerusalem*	1574

	1 ENGLAND	2 FRANCE	3 SPAIN AND PORTUGAL	4 THE EMPIRE	5 NETHERLANDS
1575			Repudiation of debts		
1576		Peace of Monsieur Catholic League est'd		Rudolf II Emp.	Spanish Fury in Antwerp Pacification of Ghent Don John Gov.
1577		6th Religious War Peace of Bergerac			'Perpetual Edict' Don John seized Namur
1578			Sebastian of Portugal *k. d*		B. Gembloux Parma Gov.
1579			Perez dismissed		Tr. of Arras Union of Utrecht
1580		7th Religious War Peace of Fleix	Kg. Henry *d.* Philip Kg. of Portugal		
1581					'Apology' of William of Orange
1582					
1583	Throckmorton's plot		St. Teresa *d.*	Wallenstein born	French Fury in Antwerp
1584	Mendoza expelled from London	Dk. of Anjou *d.*	Escurial completed		William murdered
1585		Tr. of Joinville War of Three Henries		Counterreformation in Würzburg	Leicester's expdn. Antwerp fell
1586	Babington plot		Card. Granvelle *d.*		Leicester Gov.-Gen. returned to England
1587	Mary Qn. of Scots *ex.*		Drake at Cadiz		
1588	Spanish Armada destroyed	Guise mur'd	Sp. Armada sailed		Maurice Capt.-Gen.
1589		Catherine de' Medici *d.* Henry IV Kg. B. Arques.	English attacked Lisbon		
1590		B. Ivry.			Maurice capt'd Breda
1591			Philip II def'd oppn. in Aragon		Maurice capt'd Zutphen, etc.

6	7	8	9	10
ITALY	SWITZERLAND	N. EUROPE	OUTSIDE EUROPE	CULTURE

		Red Book of John III			1575
				Blackfriars Theatre built Titian d. Brahe given Hveen island	1576
			Drake's voyage round the world (to 1580)	Rubens born	1577
					1578
				Theatre at Madrid	1579
				Essays of Montaigne pub.	1580
					1581
					1582
				Grotius born	1583
Carlo Borromeo d.		Ivan the Terrible d.			1584
Sixtus V Pope				Ronsard d.	1585
				Sir Philip Sidney d.	1586
		Sigismund Polish Kg.			1587
		Christian IV Danish Kg.		Vatican Library built	1588
				Veronese d. Ribera born	1589
Gregory XIV Pope					1590
Philip Neri d. Innocent IX Pope					1591

	1	2	3	4	5
	ENGLAND	FRANCE	SPAIN AND PORTUGAL	THE EMPIRE	NETHERLANDS
1592					Parma *d.* Archdk. Ernest Gov.
1593		Henry IV heard mass at St. Denis		War with Turks	
1594	Hooker's *Ecclesiastical Polity*	Henry IV entered Paris			
1595		Henry IV absolved			
1596	Anglo-French alliance with United Provinces	Assembly of Notables	Eng. expdn. to Cadiz Repudiation of debts		Archdk. Albert Gov.
1597		Amiens recaptured			B. Turnhout
1598		Peace of Vervins Edict of Nantes	Philip II *d.* Philip III Kg.		
1599	Oliver Cromwell born				
1600	East India Co. est'd.				B. Nieuport
1601	Poor Law				
1602		Biron exec'd			Dutch East India Co. est'd Arminius prof. at Leyden
1603	James I Kg.				
1604	Hampton Court Conf.	Paulette introduced	Peace with England		
1605	Gunpowder Plot				
1606				Donauwörth incident Tr. Sitvatorok (with Turks)	
1607			Repudiation of debts		
1608				Union of Evangelical Estates	

430

6 ITALY	7 SWITZERLAND	8 N. EUROPE	9 OUTSIDE EUROPE	10 CULTURE	
Clement VIII Pope		Sigismund Kg. of Sweden		Montaigne *d.*	1592
				Francis de Sales ordained Marlowe *d.*	1593
				Tintoretto *d.*	1594
			Hineraria of Linschoten pub.	Tasso *d.*	1595
				Descartes born	1596
				Peter Canisius *d.*	1597
		War between Sigismund and Dk. Charles		Mariana's *De Rege* Edmund Spenser *d.*	1598
		Sigismund deposed by Swedes		Velasquez born Campanella imprisoned	1599
Fr. invaded Savoy				Calderon born	1600
Tr. Lyons				Brahe *d.*	1601
				Francis de Sales Bp. of Geneva	1602
		Charles IX Kg. of Sweden			1603
					1604
Paul V Pope		Time of Troubles in Russia	Dutch took Amboina	Cervantes' *Don Quixote*	1605
			Janszoon discovered New Guinea	Rembrandt born	1606
			Virginia est'd		1607
			French at Quebec		1608

431

	1	2	3	4	5
	ENGLAND	FRANCE	SPAIN AND PORTUGAL	THE EMPIRE	NETHERLANDS
1609			*Moriscoes* expelled	Catholic Union Jülich-Cleves crisis Bohemian *Letter of Majesty*	Bank of Amsterdam est'd. Twelve Years' Truce with Spain Arminius *d.*
1610		Henry IV murdered Alliance with German Protestants Louis XIII Kg. Marie de' Medici Regent			Remonstrance drawn up
1611					
1612		Louis XIII *m.* Anne of Austria		Matthias Emp.	
1613	Elizabeth *m.* Fdk. V Elector Palatine				
1614		States-General met		Tr. Xanten	
1615		Richelieu minister			
1616		Huguenot rising			
1617		Concini murdered Luynes chief min.		Ferdinand Kg. of Bohemia	
1618				Defenestration of Prague Outbreak of 30 Yrs.' War	Synod of Dort
1619				Fdk. V Kg. of Bohemia Ferdinand II Emp.	Oldenbarne-veldt exec'd
1620				B. White Hill	
1621		Luynes *d.*	Philip IV Kg.	Catholic reaction in Bohemia	War with Spain re-newed

6 ITALY	7 SWITZERLAND	8 N. EUROPE	9 OUTSIDE EUROPE	10 CULTURE	
					1609
					1610
		War : Denmark v. Sweden Gustavus II Adolphus Kg.	Coen Gov. Dutch E. Indies		1611
					1612
		Tr. Knäred Romanoff dynasty in Russia est'd			1613
					1614
				Galileo before Inquisition	1615
				Cervantes d. Shakespeare d.	1616
		Tr. Stolbova *Riksdagordining*			1617
				Murillo born	1618
				Grotius imprisoned	1619
			Mayflower pilgrims in New England	Grotius escaped	1620
Gregory XV Pope			Dutch W. India Co. est'd		1621

1	2	3	4	5
ENGLAND	FRANCE	SPAIN AND PORTUGAL	THE EMPIRE	NETHERLANDS
1622	Richelieu a Cardinal		B. Wimpfen B. Höchst	
1623 Sp. marr. treaty broken off			Electorate conferred on Maximilian of Bavaria B. Stadtlohn B. Freisoythe	
1624	Richelieu chief min.			
1625 Charles I Kg.		War with England	Christian IV of Denmark entered war	Fdk. Henry Stadholder
1626	Chalais' plot Tr. Monzon with Spain		B. Lütter Mansfeld *d.*	
1627 Buckingham's expedn. to Ré	Siege of La Rochelle	Repudiation of debts	New Bohemian Constitution	
1628 Petition of Right	Fall of La Rochelle		Wallenstein Dk. Mecklenburg Siege of Stralsund	
1629 Charles I dissolved 3rd Parliament	Tr. Alais		Edict of Restitution Peace of Lübeck	Capt. of Bois-le-duc.
1630	Day of Dupes		Gustavus Adolphus landed Wallenstein dismissed Diet of Ratisbon	
1631	Tr. of Barwälde (with Sweden)		Magdeburg destroyed B. Breitenfeld	
1632	Montmorency exec'd		Wallenstein recalled B. Lützen	
1633 Laud Arbp.	Fr. occupied Lorraine		League of Heilbronn	
1634 Ship-money levied			Wallenstein murdered B. Nördlingen	
1635	Tr. Compiègne (with Sweden) War declared against Spain		Tr. Prague	French alliance

6	7	8	9	10	
ITALY	SWITZERLAND	N. EUROPE	OUTSIDE EUROPE	CULTURE	
				Francis de Sales *d.*	1622
Urban VIII Pope				Velasquez settled at Madrid	1623
	Fr. occupied Valtelline		Massacre of Amboina		1624
				El Greco *d.* Grotius' *De jure belli et pacis*	1625
	Tr. Monzon			Bacon *d.* St. Peter's completed	1626
					1627
Mantuan War of Succession began			B. Matanzas Bay	Harvey's *De Motu Cordium*	1628
					1629
Fr. occupied Savoy		Sweden entered 30 Yrs.' War		Kepler *d.*	1630
Tr. Cherasco				Rembrandt settled at Amsterdam	1631
		Christina Qn. of Sweden		Vermeer born	1632
				Spinoza born	1633
		Ars Regeringsform	Dutch capt'd Curaçao	Voetius prof. Utrecht	1634
	Fr. occupied Valtelline			Lope de Vega *d.*	1635

	1 ENGLAND	2 FRANCE	3 SPAIN AND PORTUGAL	4 THE EMPIRE	5 NETHERLANDS
1636					Tulip mania
1637	Hampden's Case			Ferdinand III Emp.	Fdk. Henry captd Breda
1638	Scottish National Covenant	Fr. Joseph *d.* Louis (XIV) born		Siege of Breisach	
1639	1st Bishops' War		B. of the Downs	Bernard of Saxe-Weimar *d.*	
1640	2nd Bishops' War Long Parliament		Revolt of Portugal Revolt of Catalonia	Fdk. Wm. Elector of Brandenburg	
1641	Strafford exec'd Grand Remonstrance				Alliance with Portugal
1642	Civil War began	Cinq-Mars Plot Richelieu *d.*		B. Breitenfeld	
1643	Solemn League and Covenant	Louis XIV Kg., Anne of Austria Regent	Fall of Olivarez B. Rocroi		
1644	B. Marston Moor				Sas van Gent captured
1645	B. Naseby			Peace congresses opened	Hulst captured
1646	Fall of Oxford				
1647		Repudiation of debts			William II Stadholder
1648	2nd Civil War	Outbreak of 1st Fronde	B. Lens Peace of Münster (with Dutch)	Tr. Westphalia	Spain recognised Dutch independence
1649	Charles I exec'd	Tr. Rueil			
1650	B. Dunbar	Condé arrested Princes' Fronde			William II *d.*
1651	B. Worcester Navigation Act	Mazarin left France			
1652	War with Dutch	Mazarin re- turned but again left			War with England

6 ITALY	7 SWITZERLAND	8 N. EUROPE	9 OUTSIDE EUROPE	10 CULTURE	
			van Diemen Governor Dutch East Indies		1636
	Fr. left Valtelline			Descartes *Discourse on Method*	1637
					1638
Peace of Milan				Campanella *d.*	1639
			Dutch in Ceylon	Rubens *d.*	1640
			Dutch capt'd Malacca		1641
			Tasman's voyage	Galileo *d.* Rembrandt's *The Night Watch*	1642
		Swedes invaded Denmark			1643
Innocent X Pope					1644
		Tr. Brömsebro			1645
					1646
Masaniello headed revolt in Naples					1647
Pope condemned Tr. Westphalia	Swiss independence recognised	Christian IV *d.*			1648
					1649
				Descartes *d.*	1650
					1651
			Jan van Riebeck at Cape of Good Hope		1652

	1	2	3	4	5
	ENGLAND	FRANCE	SPAIN AND PORTUGAL	THE EMPIRE	NETHERLANDS
1653	Cromwell Protector	Mazarin returned			Jan de Witt Pensionary
1654		End of Fronde			Peace with England
1655	Jamaica capt'd	Commercial treaty with England			
1656	England and France in alliance against Spain				
1657	Humble Petition and Advice			Leopold I Emp.	
1658	Cromwell *d.*	Dunkirk capt'd			
1659		Tr. Pyrenees			
1660	Restoration of Charles II	Vincent de Paul *d.* Louise XIV *m.* Maria Teresa			

6	7	8	9	10	
ITALY	SWITZERLAND	N. EUROPE	OUTSIDE EUROPE	CULTURE	
					1653
		Christina abd. Charles X Kg.	Dutch expelled from Brazil		1654
Alexander VII Pope		Ch. X in- vaded Poland			1655
		Swedes in- vaded Denmark		Ribera d.	1656
					1657
		Tr. Roskilde Reopening of war	Dutch controlled Ceylon		1658
					1659
		Tr. Copenhagen Tr. Oliva		Velasquez d.	1660

BIBLIOGRAPHY

This bibliography can pretend to be no more than a list of books selected for further reading. No attempt has been made to be fully comprehensive or to include more than a minimum of foreign works. Many of the books mentioned below contain full bibliographies.

I. GENERAL HISTORIES

Abbott, W. C.. *The Expansion of Europe*, 1925.

Allen, J. W., *A History of Political Thought in the Sixteenth Century*, 1928.

Acton, Lord, *Lectures on Modern History*, ed. J. N. Figgis and R. V. Laurence, 1906.

Bowle, J., *Western Political Thought*, 1947.

Braudel, F., *La Méditerranée et le Monde méditerranéen à l'époque de Philippe II*, 1949.

Cambridge Modern History, Vols. I-IV, 1902-06.

Clark, G. N., *The Seventeenth Century*, 1929.

Ehrenberg, R., *Capital and Finance in the Age of the Renaissance*, trans., H. M. Lucas, 1928.

Figgis, J. N., *From Gerson to Grotius*, 1923.

Fisher, H. A. L., *History of Europe*, 1935.

Grant, A. J., *A History of Europe, 1494-1610*, fourth edn., 1948.

Heaton, H., *Economic History of Europe*, 1936.

Hauser, H., *La Prépondérance Espagnole, 1559-1660*, 1933.

Hauser, H. and Renaudet, A., *Les débuts de l'âge moderne*, 1946.

Heckscher, E., *Mercantilism*, trans., 1935.

Lavisse et Rambaud, *Histoire Générale*, Vols. IV and V.

Merriman, R. B., *Six Contemporaneous Revolutions*, 1938 (i.e. troubles in mid-seventeenth century in Catalonia, Portugal, Naples, France, England and the Netherlands).

Ogg, D., *Europe in the Seventeenth Century*, edn., 1943.

Oman, Sir Charles, *A History of the Art of War in the Sixteenth Century*, 1937.

Parry, J. H., *Europe and a Wider World, 1415-1715*, 1949.

Reddaway, W. F., *A History of Europe, 1610-1715*, 1948.

Renard, G. and Weullersee, G., *Life and Work in Modern Europe, Fifteenth to Eighteenth Centuries*, Eng. trans., 1926.

Sée H. and Rebillon A., *Le 16ᵉ siècle*, 1934.

Smith, Preserved, *A History of Modern Culture*, Vol. I (1543-1687), 1930.
Wakeman, H. O., *The Ascendancy of France, 1598-1715.*

II. THE RENAISSANCE

(a) Italy

Armstrong, E., *Lorenzo the Magnificent*, 1896.
Brown, Horatio, *Venice : a Historical Sketch*, 1893.
Burckhardt, J., *The Civilisation of the Renaissance*, trans. S. G. C. Middlemore, 1937.
Butterfield, H., *The Statecraft of Machiavelli*, 1940.
Ferguson, W. K., *The Renaissance in Historical Thought*, 1948.
Martin, A. von, *The Sociology of the Renaissance*, trans. W. L. Luetkens, 1944.
Schevill, F., *History of Florence*, 1939.
Sichel, E., *The Renaissance*, 1914.
Symonds, J. A., *The Renaissance in Italy*, 7 vols., 1875-86.
Trevelyan, J. P., *A Short History of the Italian People*, 1929.
Villari, P., *The Life and Times of Machiavelli*, 2 vols., 1892.
Villari, P., *The Life and Times of Savonarola*, 1897.
Whitfield, J. H., *Machiavelli*, 1947.
Woodward, W. H., *Cesare Borgia*, 1913.
Young, G. F., *The Medici*, 1911.

(b) Erasmus

Allen, P. S., *The Age of Erasmus*, 1914.
Allen, P. S., *Erasmus : Lectures and Wayfaring Sketches*, 1934.
Froude, J. A., ' Life and Letters of Erasmus ' ; ' Times of Erasmus and Luther ' in *Short Studies in Great Subjects*, 1894.
Huizinga, J., *Erasmus*, trans. F. Hopman, 1924.
Phillips, M. M., *Erasmus and the Northern Renaissance*, 1949.
Smith, Preserved, *Erasmus*, 1923.

(c) The Scientific Revolution

Armitage, A., *Copernicus the Founder of Modern Astronomy*, 1938.
Butterfield, H., *The Origins of Modern Science, 1300-1800*, 1949.
Dampier, Sir W. C., *A History of Science*, third edn., 1942.
Dreyer, J. L. E., *History of the planetary systems from Thales to Kepler*, 1906.
Gade, J. A., *The Life and Times of Tycho Brahe*, 1948.

Sarton, G. A. L., *The History of Science and the New Humanism*, 1937.
Singer, C. J., *The Evolution of Anatomy*, 1925.
Singer, C. J., *A Short History of Medicine*, 1928.
Taylor, F. Sherwood, *A Short History of Science*, 1939.
Wolf, A., *A History of Science*, 1935.

III. RELIGIOUS HISTORY

(a) General

Beard, C., *The Reformation of the Sixteenth Century*, 1883.
Brandi, K., *Die deutsche Reformation und Gegenreformation*, 1927-30.
Creighton, Mandell, *A History of the Papacy during the period of the Reformation*, 6 vols., 1897.
Cristiani, L., *L'Église à l'Époque du Concile de Trente*, 1948.
Imbart de la Tour, P., *Les Origines de la Réforme*, 3 vols., 1905-14.
Kidd, B. J., *Documents illustrative of the Continental Reformation*.
Lindsay, T. M., *History of the Reformation*, 2 vols., 1906.
Lucas, H. S., *The Renaissance and the Reformation*, 1934.
Mackinnon J., *The Origins of the Reformation*, 1939.
Pastor, L., *The Lives of the Popes*, 1891 *sqq.*
Pullan, Leighton, *Religion since the Reformation*, 1923.
Ranke, L. von, *History of the Popes*, 3 vols., 1841.
Sykes, N., *The Crisis of the Reformation*, 1938.

(b) Luther and Lutheranism

Bainton, R., *Here I Stand ; Luther*, 1949.
Belfort Bax, E., *The Rise and Fall of the Anabaptists*, 1903.
Boehmer, H., *Luther*, trans. E. Potter, 1930.
Dunkley, E. H., *The Reformation in Denmark*, 1948.
Funck-Brentano, F., *Martin Luther*, trans. E. P. Buckley, 1936.
Holborn, H., *Ulrich von Hutten and the German Reformation*, trans. R. H. Bainton, 1937.
Holl, K., *Gesammelte Aufsatze zur Kirchengeschichte, I. Luther*, 6th edn., 1932.
Mackinnon, J., *Luther and the Reformation*, 4 vols., 1925-30.
Macmillan, J. D., *Protestantism in Germany*, 1917.
Pascal, R., *The Social Basis of the German Reformation*, 1933.

Ranke, L. von, *History of the Reformation in Germany*, trans. S. Austin, 1905.
Rupp, E. G., *Luther's Progress to the Diet of Worms*, 1951.
Smith, Preserved, *The Life and Letters of Martin Luther*, 1911.

(c) Calvin and the Swiss Reformation

Bonjour, E., Offler, H. S. and Potter, G. R., *A Short History of Switzerland*, 1952.
Doumergue, E., *Jean Calvin*, 7 vols., 1899-1927.
Farner, Oscar, *Zwingli (1506-20)*, 2 vols.
Hunt, R. N. C., *Calvin*, 1933.
Hunter, Mitchell, *The Teaching of Calvin*, 1920.
Imbart de la Tour, *Calvin et L'Institution Chrétienne*, 1935.
Jackson, S. M., *Huldreich Zwingli*, 1903.
Mackinnon, J., *Calvin and the Reformation*, 1936.
Oechsli, W., *Switzerland since 1499*, trans. E. and C. Eden, 1922.
Torrance, T. F., *Calvin's Doctrine of Man*, 194.
Warfield, B. B., *Calvin and Calvinism*, 1931.

(d) The Counter-Reformation [1]

Bremond, H., *A Literary History of Religious Thought in France*, 1928 *sqq.*
Brodrick, J., *The Origins of the Jesuits*, 1940.
Brodrick, J., *The Progress of the Jesuits, 1556-79*, 1946.
Brodrick, J., *St. Peter Canisius*, 1935.
Evennett, H. O., *The Cardinal of Lorraine and the Council of Trent*, 1930.
Kidd, B. J., *The Counter-Reformation, 1550-1600*, 1933.
Sedgwick, H. D., *St. Ignatius Loyola*, 1923.
Van Dyke, Paul, *St. Ignatius Loyola*, 1926.

IV. SPAIN

Altamira y Crevea, R., *A History of Spanish Civilisation*, trans. P. Volker, 1930.
Altamira y Crevea, R., *A History of Spain*, trans. M. Lee, 1950.
Altamira y Crevea R., *Historia de España y de la civilización española*, Vols. II and III, 4th edn., 1935.
Bell, A. F. G., *Luis de Leon*, 1925.
Bertrand L. and Petrie, Sir C., *History of Spain*, 1934.
Bratli, C. J. B., *Philippe II, roi d'Espagne*, 1912.

[1] For *Inquisition* see under Spain.

Chapman, C. E., *History of Spain*, 1918.

Davies, R. Trevor, *The Golden Century of Spain*, 1937.

Entwistle, W. J., *Cervantes*, 1940.

Hamilton, Earl J., *American Treasure and the Price Revolution in Spain*, 1934.

Haring, C. H., *The Spanish Empire in America*, 1947.

Haring, C. H., *Trade and Navigation between Spain and the Indies in the time of the Hapsburgs*, 1918.

Hume, M. A. S., *The Court of Philip IV*, edn., 1927.

Hume, M. A. S., *Philip II*, 1897.

Hume, M. A. S., *Spain : its Greatness and Decay (1479-1788)*, 1898.

Kelly, J. Fitzmaurice, *A New History of Spanish Literature*, 1926.

Kirkpatrick, F. A., *The Spanish Conquistadores*, 1934.

Klein, J., *The Mesta*, 1920.

Lea, H. C., *History of the Inquisition of Spain*, 4 vols., 1922.

Lea, H. C., *The Moriscos of Spain*, 1901.

Madariaga, S. de, *Don Quixote*, 1933.

Madariaga, S. de, *The Rise of the Spanish American Empire*, 1947.

Mariéjol, J. H., *The Master of the Armada. The Life and Reign of Philip II*, trans. W. B. Wells, 1933.

Merriman, R. B., *The Spanish Empire*, Vols. II-IV, 1934.

Merton, R., *Cardinal Ximenes*, 1934.

Morison, S. E., *Christopher Columbus*, 1942.

Newton, A. P., *European Nations in the West Indies, 1493-1688*, 1933.

Parry, J. H., *The Audiencia of New Galicia in the Sixteenth Century*, 1948.

Parry, J. H., *The Spanish Theory of Empire in the Sixteenth Century*, 1940.

Peers, E. Allison, *Spanish Mysticism*, 1924.

Peers, E. Allison, *Studies of the Spanish Mystics*, 4 vols., 1927-35.

Prescott, W. H., *History of the Reign of Ferdinand and Isabella*, rev. edn., 1892.

Prescott, W. H., *History of the Conquest of Mexico*, rev. edn., 1901.

Prescott, W. H., *History of the Conquest of Peru*, rev. edn., 1902.

Prescott, W. H., *Philip II*, rev. edn., 1902.

Rutter, F., *El Greco*, 1930.

Scott, J. B., *The Spanish Origin of International Law*, 1926.

Seaver, H. L., *The Great Revolt in Castile*, 1928.

Slocombe, G., *Don John of Austria*, 1935.

Trend, J. B., *The Civilisation of Spain*, 1944.

Turberville, A. S., *The Spanish Inquisition*, 1932.

Walsh, W., *Isabella of Spain*, 1932.

444

V. PORTUGAL

Beazley, C. R., *Prince Henry the Navigator*, 1904.
Legrand, T., *Histoire du Portugal*, 1928.
Livermore, H. V., *A History of Portugal*, 1947.
Prestage, E., *The Portuguese Pioneers*, 1933.
Whiteway, R. S., *The Rise of Portuguese power in India, 1497-1550*, 1899.

VI. FRANCE

Armstrong, E., *The French Wars of Religion*, 1892.
Bailly, A., *The Cardinal Dictator*, 1936.
Baird, H. M., *History of the Rise of the Huguenots*, 1879.
Baird, H. M., *The Huguenots and Henry of Navarre*, 1887.
Bloch, M., *Les caractères originaux de l'histoire rurale Française*, 1931.
Bridge, J. S. C., *A History of France from the death of Louis XI* (to 1515), 5 vols., 1936.
Boulenger, J., *The Seventeenth Century*, trans., 1920.
Burckhardt, C., *Richelieu* (to 1624), trans., 1940.
Dedieu, J., *Le Rôle politique des Protestants Français*, 1921.
Delaborde, H. F., *L'expédition de Charles VIII en Italie*, 1888.
Dix, E. A., *Champlain, the Founder of New France*, 1903.
Doolin, P. R., *The Fronde*, 1935.
England, S. L., *The Massacre of St. Bartholomew*, 1938.
Fagniez, G., *Le Père Joseph et Richelieu*, 1894.
Federn, C., *Mazarin*, 1934.
Glasson, E., *Le Parlement de Paris, son rôle politique*, 1901.
Grant, A. J., *The Huguenots*, 1934.
Grant, A. J., *The French Monarchy*, 1910.
Hanotaux, G., *Richelieu*, 3 vols., 1893-1933.
Hauser, H., *La naissance du protestantisme*, 1940.
Huxley, A., *Grey Eminence*, 1941.
Lavisse, *Histoire de France*, Vols. V (1) and V (2) (Henri Lemonnier), Vol. VI (J. H. Mariéjol).
Mariéjol, J. H., *Catherine de Médicis*, 2nd edn., 1920.
Neale, J. E., *The Age of Catherine de Medici*, 1943.
Nef, J. U., *Industry and Government in France and England, 1540-1640*, 1940.
Pagès, G., *Naissance du Grand Siècle : La France de Henri IV à Louis XIV, 1598-1661*, 1948.
Reinhard, M., *Henri iv*, 1943.

Roeder, R., *Catherine de Medici and the Lost Revolution*, 1937.
Romain, C., *Louis XIII*, 1934.
Romier L., *La conjuration d'Amboise*, 2nd edn., 1923.
Romier, L., *Les origines politiques des guerres de religion*, 2 vols., 1913-14.
Romier, L., *Le Royaume de Catherine de Médicis*, 2 vols., 1925.
Romier, L., *Catholiques et Huguenots à la Cour de Charles IX*, 1924.
Sedgwick, H. D., *The House of Guise*, 1938.
Sée, H., *L'Évolution commerciale et industrielle de la France sous l'ancien régime*, 1925.
Thompson, J. W., *The Wars of Religion in France, 1559-1576*, 1909.
Vaissiere, P. de, *Henri IV*, 1928.
Van Dyke P., *Catherine de Médicis*, 2 vols., 1923.
Whitehead, A. W., *Gaspar de Coligny*, 1904.
Wedgwood, C. V., *Richelieu and the French Monarchy*, 1949.

VII. THE UNITED PROVINCES

Blok, P. J., *History of the Peoples of the Netherlands*, trans., 1900.
Edmundson, G., *History of Holland*, 1922.
Geyl, P., *The Revolt of the Netherlands (1559-1609)*, 1932.
Geyl, P., *The Netherlands Divided (1609-1648)*, 1936.
Harrison, F., *William the Silent*, 1897.
Kervyn de Lettenhove, *Les Huguenots et les Gueux* (1560-85), 6 vols., 1883-5.
Motley, H. L., *The Rise of the Dutch Republic*, 1855.
Motley, J. L., *The United Netherlands*, 1860, 1867.
Pirenne, H., *Histoire de Belgique*, Vols. III and IV.
Putnam, R., *William the Silent*, 2 vols., 1895.
Vlekke, B. H. M., *Evolution of the Dutch Nation*, 1945.
Wedgwood, C. V., *William the Silent*, 1944.

VIII. THE EMPIRE

Armstrong, E., *The Emperor Charles V*, 2 vols., 2nd edn., 1910.
Belfort Bax, E., *The Peasants War in Germany*, 1899.
Brandi, K., *Charles V*, trans., C. V. Wedgwood, 1939.
Bryce, Lord, *The Holy Roman Empire*, edn., 1904.
Coxe, W., *History of the House of Austria*, 3rd edn., 1847.
Janssen, J., *History of the German Peoples since the end of the Middle Ages*, i-xvi, trans. A. M. Christie, 1896-1910.
McElwee, W. L., *Charles V*, 1936.
Pagès, G., *La Guerre de Trente Ans.*, 1939.

Ranke, L. von, *Ferdinand I and Maximilian II of Austria*, trans. Lady D. Gordon.
Watson, F., *Soldier under Saturn. Wallenstein*, 1938.
Wedgwood, C. V., *The Thirty Years' War*, 1938.

VIII. SCANDINAVIA

Ahnlund, N., *Gustaf Adolf*, trans. M. Roberts, 1940.
Bain, R. Nisbet, *Christina of Sweden*, 1890.
Bain, R. Nisbet, *Scandinavia*, 1905.
Fletcher, C. R. L., *Gustavus Adolphus*, 1900.
Hallendorf, C. and Schück, A., *History of Sweden*, trans. L. Yapp, 1929.
Toyne, S. M., *The Scandinavians in History*, 1948.
Watson, P. B., *The Swedish Revolution under Gustavus Vasa*, 1889.

IX. THE OTTOMAN EMPIRE

Downey, Fairfax, *The Grand Turk. Suleyman the Magnificent*, 1929.
Eversley, Lord and Chirol, Sir Valentine, *The Turkish Empire*, 1934.
Freeman, E. A., *The Ottoman Power in Europe*, 1877.
Hubbard, G. E., *The Day of the Crescent*, 1920.
Lane Poole, S., *Turkey*, 1886.
Lybyer, A. H., *The Government of the Ottoman Empire under Suleiman the Magnificent*, 1913.
Marriott, Sir J. W., *The Eastern Question*, edn. 1947.
Merriman, R. B., *Suleiman the Magnificent*, 1944.
Penzer, N. M., *The Harem*, 1936.

X. CONTEMPORARY WORKS

Ariosto, *Works*.
Calvin, Jean, *The Institutes of the Christian Religion*, trans. H. Beveridge, edn. 1949.
Castiglione, *The Courtier*.
Cellini, Benvenuto, *Autobiography*.
Cervantes, *Don Quixote*.
Erasmus, *Letters*, ed. P. S. Allen.
Erasmus, *The Education of a Christian Prince*, ed. L. K. Born, 1936.
Erasmus, *The Praise of Folly*, ed. H. M. Allen, 1913.
Erasmus, *The Whole Familiar Colloquies of Erasmus*, ed. N. Bailey, 1887.
The Fugger News Letters, ed. V. Klarvill, Eng. trans., 1924.

Grimmelshauser, H. J. C. von, *Simplicissimus the Vagabond*, trans. A. T. S. Goodrick, 1924.

Grotius, H., *De Jure Belli ac Pacis*, trans. F. Kelsey, ed. J. B. Scott, 1925.

Grotius, H., *The Freedom of the Seas*, ed. J. B. Scott, 1916.

Loyola, St. Ignatius, *The Spiritual Exercises*, ed. W. H. Longridge.

Luther, M., *Correspondence*, ed. Preserved Smith, 2 vols., 1913.

Luther, M., *Primary Works*, trans. and ed. H. Wace and C. A. Bucheim.

Machiavelli, *The Prince*.

Montaigne, *Essays*.

Rabelais, *Gargantua and Pantagruel*.

Richelieu, Cardinal de, *Le Testament Politique*.

Vindiciae contra Tyrannos, trans. and ed. H. J. Laski, 1924.

INDEX

The Index contains names and places mentioned in the text. The dates are the dates of birth and death. Figures in italics indicate the page of the map containing the place mentioned.

Index

451

Index

462